Asia

Saudi Arabia

India

SEASONAL MONSOON WINDS

SEASONAL MONSOON WINDS

SEASONAL MONSOONS

SEASONAL MONSOON WINDS

S.E. TRADES

S.E. TRADES

ROARING FORTIES

ING FORTIES

Pathfinders

FELIPE FERNÁNDEZ-ARMESTO

Pathfinders

A GLOBAL HISTORY OF EXPLORATION

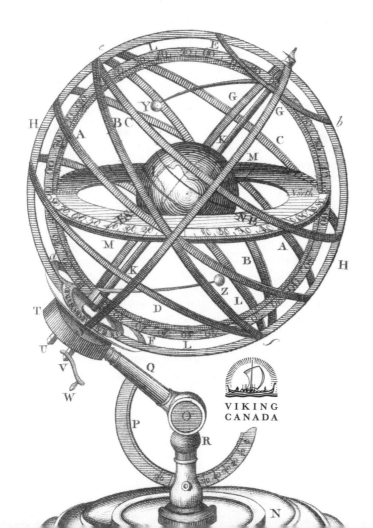

VIKING
CANADA

VIKING CANADA

Published by the Penguin Group

Penguin Group (Canada), 90 Eglinton Avenue East, Suite 700, Toronto, Ontario, Canada M4P 2Y3
(a division of Pearson Canada Inc.)

Penguin Group (USA) Inc., 375 Hudson Street, New York, New York 10014, U.S.A.
Penguin Books Ltd, 80 Strand, London WC2R 0RL, England
Penguin Ireland, 25 St Stephen's Green, Dublin 2, Ireland (a division of Penguin Books Ltd)
Penguin Group (Australia), 250 Camberwell Road, Camberwell, Victoria 3124, Australia
(a division of Pearson Australia Group Pty Ltd)
Penguin Books India Pvt Ltd, 11 Community Centre, Panchsheel Park, New Delhi – 110 017, India
Penguin Group (NZ), cnr Airborne and Rosedale Roads, Albany, Auckland 1310, New Zealand
(a division of Pearson New Zealand Ltd)
Penguin Books (South Africa) (Pty) Ltd, 24 Sturdee Avenue, Rosebank, Johannesburg 2196, South Africa

Penguin Books Ltd, Registered Offices: 80 Strand, London WC2R 0RL, England

Published in Canada by Penguin Group (Canada), a division of Pearson Canada Inc., 2006
Published in the United States by W.W. Norton & Company, New York, 2006
Published in Great Britain by Oxford University Press Inc., Oxford, 2006

1 2 3 4 5 6 7 8 9 10   (RRD)

Copyright © Felipe Fernández-Armesto, 2006

Typeset by RefineCatch Limited, Bungay, Suffolk

Manufactured in the U.S.A.

ISBN-10: 0-670-06497-1
ISBN-13: 978-0-670-06497-7

Library and Archives Canada Cataloguing in Publication data available upon request
British Library Cataloguing in Publication data available
American Library of Congress Cataloging in Publication data available

Visit the Penguin Group (Canada) website at **www.penguin.ca**

Special and corporate bulk purchase rates available; please see
www.penguin.ca/corporatesales or call 1-800-810-3104, ext. 477 or 474

To Rafael del Pino

So give me those two powers of love and longing
That numb gods' thoughts and every human notion,
For I must reach the ends of springing, thronging
Earth, and cross the god-begetting Ocean.
Homer, Iliad 14

sociedad
geográfica
española

FUNDACIÓN
RAFAEL
DEL PINO

First, my son, observe that in this world we travel through likenesses and enigmas since the spirit of truth is not of this world nor can it be seized through it. We are carried off towards the unknown, but only metaphorically . . .

Nicholas of Cusa, letter to Nicolaus Albergati

Preface

This book is about encounters—encounters between cultures—and the outreach of ambitions, imaginations, efforts, and innovations that made them possible. The book, too, is the result of a meeting of minds. The ambition to write something like it has been rattling inside my head for at least a decade and a half—ever since I began work on *The Times Atlas of World Exploration*. But I never really expected to have the chance or to be able to devise a practicable approach to the vast and unwieldy subject until the dinner table conversation of my friends Carlos Martínez de Campos, President of the Sociedad Geográfica Española, and Virgilio Oñate, President of the Fundación Geográfica Española, impelled me to it and helped me begin to see the way forward.

The decisive influence has been that of Rafael del Pino y Moreno, engineer, businessman, and outstanding philanthropist. At the time of our meeting, he had completed a journey in the wake of great maritime explorers in a yacht he had designed himself. 'I hope,' he said, 'to see you write a global history of exploration before I die.' There was a touch of morbid humor in this irresistible proposal, for he was then a robust and vital octogenarian of delightful sprightliness. But while I was at work on the early stages of the book, a terrible accident befell him, which induced almost total paralysis, and made the project a heartfelt and urgent endeavour for me. Don Rafael bore his affliction with exemplary fortitude. I am indebted to him for the stimulus to write it, as well as for the interest and input of ideas with which he nourished and sustained it. My debt to the Foundation which bears his name, for a research grant, and for a further munificent grant toward the cost of maps and illustrations, is almost equally profound: without that generous help, I could not have set aside time for the work. Throughout, Amadeo Petitbò, Director of the Fundación del Pino, has been endlessly helpful, understanding, and supportive. As I wrote, he and Virgilio Oñate took great pains to read the text and help me reflect on it and improve it.

I am also grateful to the readers of Oxford University Press for helpful and insightful comments, and to my editors, Luciana O'Flaherty of Oxford University Press, Steve Forman of Norton, and Mauricio Bach of Destino, for their skill and forbearance. My colleagues in the History and Geography Departments and the Arts Research Centre at Queen Mary, University of London, where most of the book was written, provided—with the help of the College's exceptionally enlightened leadership and management—the best environment imaginable in which to teach and learn. I finished the book in the History Department at Tufts University, where I have been lucky to find a generous welcome and inexhaustible collegiality. Over a longer period, I learned most of what I know about exploration from my fellow members of the Hakluyt Society and my collaborators in *The Times Atlas of World Exploration*. Of course, patches of ignorance and errors of fact must mar the book: those, at least, are all my own.

F.F.A.

Contents

Illustrations

Plates

Maps

The original maps in this book were drawn by David Atkinson of Hand Made Maps (*www.handmademaps.com*)

1 Stretching

The First Trail Finders from Gathering Cultures to Great Empires

So many gods, so many creeds,
So many paths that wind and wind . . .

Ella Wheeler Wilcox, 'The World's Need'

HISTORY has two big stories to tell. The first is the very long story of how human cultures diverged—how they parted and developed differences, in ignorance or contempt of one another. The second is the main subject of this book: a relatively short and recent story of convergence—of how human groups got back in touch, exchanged culture, copied each other's lives, and became more like each other again.

The first story occupies most of history, extending over about 150,000 years, roughly from the emergence of *Homo sapiens* almost to the present day: the record of how human cultures formed, became mutually differentiated, drew apart, and grew more disparate and dissimilar, until we got to where we are: in a world teeming with difference, in which pluralism is, paradoxically, the one great shared value we dare not forgo. Imagine a cosmic observer, contemplating humankind from immensely remote space and time, seeing us with the kind of objectivity that we—who are enmeshed in our own history—are unable to attain. Imagine asking her—for, perhaps on the basis of my own experience of home life, I see omniscience and omnipresence as female qualities—how she would characterize the history of our species on our planet. Imagine her answer. It would be brief: such puny creatures as we are, in such a tiny patch of the universe, would hardly be worth much comment. The cosmic observer would surely say that our history was, above all, experience of increasing diversity.

The second story, which matters so much to us but which, I suspect, the cosmic observer might hardly notice, has overlapped with the first for perhaps the last 10,000 years or so. Gradually, it has become the predominant story, as cultural exchange has speeded up and extended its range, until, today, the way global culture seems to get more and more homogeneous—even more uniform—has become, to us, the most conspicuous theme of human experience all over the world.[1]

Both stories, I contend, are stories of exploration. But we know too little about the first for it to get more than a few pages' coverage in what follows. Societies would never have grown apart without the pathfinders who led them along divergent routes into contrasting environments and separate homelands. They would never have resumed mutual relations, and changed each other, without later generations of explorers, who found the routes of contact, commerce, conflict, and contagion that rejoined them. Explorers were the engineers of history's infrastructures, the builders of the causeways of culture, forgers of links, spinners of webs.

Convergence generated a lot of surviving evidence; the era of divergence has left almost none. Convergence is the story we think of as ours: it is what we need to explain to ourselves in order to understand the world we live in and plan its future. That is the justification for devoting a book to explaining how it happened. But, first, it is worth looking back briefly at the work of the pathfinders who led human communities apart from one another, because that work, too, was a triumph of exploration. By sketching it into the background, we can see the achievement of later explorers in more vivid relief, and understand how important it was in the making of the world we live in now.

Divergence' Begins

The big question for historians is 'Why does history happen?' You can see the point of the question if you compare humans with other social and cultural animals. Human societies change much faster than those of other species. The process of change, which we call history, is so slight and slow for most species, or so unvaried or so repetitive, that a history of, say, a school of whales or a colony of ants is almost unthinkable. It is just about possible to write the history of a tribe of chimpanzees. Jane Goodall chronicled the crises and conflicts of leadership among chimpanzees she observed in the wild, and her narrative is not unlike an account of the politics of some simple human groups—the history of a gang, say, or an ill-regulated chieftaincy. Another pioneering primatologist, Frans de Waal, has exposed the structures of chimp power politics and likened the principles of chimpanzee politics to those of Machiavelli, as rivals for leadership conspire for support, wage campaigns of subversion, and conduct coups.[2]

Still, as far as we know at the present stage of research, even chimpanzee societies, which, among those of non-human creatures, most resemble our own, have none of the dazzling volatility of human culture. Among chimps, and other nonhuman social animals, political changes happen within predictable parameters. The leaders change, the alliances form, split, and form again, but the patterns are always the same. Nor do chimpanzee groups differ nearly as much from one another in other kinds of culture as humans do. Nor do those of other cultural species.

Nonetheless, chimpanzees and many other animals certainly have culture: they develop new practices, techniques, and strategies for coping with their environments, especially for gathering and distributing food. They teach and learn those strategies and pass them down from generation to generation. In some ways and in some rare instances, it even makes sense to speak of chimpanzees ritualizing food distribution: hunting chimps, for instance, distribute the food they gain in fairly fixed patterns, roughly determined by the hierarchy of the tribe and the sexual strategies of the leading hunters. Once they have acquired cultural innovations, cultural animals transmit them by tradition. In consequence, cultural divergence begins. Separated groups grow unlike each other. In the forests of Gabon, for instance, some chimpanzee groups fish for termites with sticks; others crack nuts with stones they use as hammers and anvils. In the East African plains, some baboon societies practice serial monogamy, while others are organized in harems by polygamous males. In Borneo and Sumatra, orangutans play different games. In the best-documented case, which developed under the eyes of primatologists in Japan, a macaque monkey genius called Ima discovered how to wash sweet potatoes, and taught the practice to her tribe. That was in 1950. Ever since, the monkeys have continued the practice, which has remained unique to their colony.[3]

Against this background, it is not surprising that human cultures, too, change and, therefore, diverge. After all, humans are primates and we should expect our history to evince primate characteristics. What we want to know, however, is why human societies diverge so much, and why they change so fast.

In the effort to understand these questions, the best point to start from is our most recent common ancestor: the woman—or, rather, the strand of DNA—that paleoanthropologists know as the 'mitochondrial Eve,' about 150,000 years ago.[4] In Eve's day, we can reasonably suppose, the few thousand humans who inhabited East Africa shared the same culture: the same economy, the same technology, the same food, and, presumably, if such things existed at so early a date, the same sort of religion and language. Slowly and fitfully at first, unknown, unnameable explorers began to steer communities out of the homeland of the mitochondrial Eve into new environments, where they changed to adapt. They lost touch with each other and started to develop increasing differences in relative isolation.[5]

The first great problems of the history of exploration are therefore: How did people spread over the world? How was it possible? Who led them and why? How did they change along the way?

These are really big, really perplexing problems, which no comparisons can help us solve. Other species remain much more resolutely committed to the environments to which they are best adapted. When they migrate, they do so seasonally, in search of environmental stability. When they disperse, they stick to contiguous areas and often revert to their former habitat at the end of whatever crisis moved them. Foxes are almost as widely dispersed as human beings, but there are far wider genetic variations among different species of foxes, from one habitat to another, than are measurable between groups of humans. Some help in understanding how and why people migrated may be offered by other cases of species which have crossed environments: a well-studied recent case is that of the mountain gorillas of Rwanda, who seem to have moved into their present high, relatively cold habitat as refugees from the competitive environment of the tropical forest lowlands. At the cost of depleted foraging, which has perhaps contributed to make these exclusively vegetarian creatures smaller and weaker than other gorillas, they have forged a viable way of life. But this is a case of very limited relocation in an environment adjacent to the gorillas' former habitat. It cannot be a model for explaining the long reach of the first human colonizers.

Even human populations rarely, if ever, seek new environments willingly or adjust to them easily. In recent well-documented cases over the last half-millennium or so, the most successful colonizations have tended to lead to environments similar to those of the migrants' place of departure. Generally, when migrants move, they try to re-create the feel of home in their adopted country. Colonists founded New England, New France, New Zealand, New South Wales, and other lightly modified versions of home. They created New Spain and, when they were acclimatized there, moved on to New Mexico. They clung to culture like a comforter and packed in their baggage as much of their physical environment as they could. They took familiar animals and familiar crops with them: this usually meant finding new areas similar to those they had left.

In the great era of European colonization of many unfamiliar parts of the world in the nineteenth and twentieth centuries, Europeans stayed in and transformed 'New Europes'—areas with climates like those of their home-lands, in temperate North and South America, South Africa, and Australia. Toward the end of the period, they abandoned most of the tropical environ-ments they had come to inhabit as essentially temporary elites, administering, defending, developing, or exploiting imperial territories. These are still the prevailing habits of migrant communities. Chinese settlers today turn parts of central Asia into what looks, smells, and sounds like China; they do much the same to Chinatowns in the West. All our current anxiety about the chances of sustaining the success of multiculturalism arises from this fact: when humans move to a new environment, they do not normally reject their old one.

The African Eve's homeland was no Eden; but it suited our ancestress and her offspring. Here they could make up for the deficiencies with which they had evolved. They were poor climbers; but in mixed grassland and woodland they could compensate by standing erect and looking afar. They could wield fire to manage the grazing of the animals they hunted. They could find materials for weapons and tools, especially the fire-hardened staves or spears they used to kill game, and the sharp stones they struck to butcher the carcasses. By comparison with competitor species, humans have inferior senses of sight, smell, and hearing, slow movements, unthreatening teeth and nails, poor digestions, and weak bodies that confine us to the ground. We have—at least, those of us who are good physical specimens of our species have—just two big physical advantages: first, our capacity to sustain energy over long chases, while sweating profusely to keep cool; secondly, our dexterity with missiles—accurate throwing-arms and well coordinated eye–arm movements—to ward off rival predators.

For all these reasons, we might expect that *Homo sapiens* would stick to the savanna. But their migrations relocated them in challengingly different environments: deep forests and swamplands, where their accustomed tech-niques were of limited use; cold climates, to which they were less well suited; deserts and seas, which demanded technologies previously undeveloped. In all these new environments, unfamiliar diseases can be presumed to have bred; yet migrants continued to penetrate and cross them, led by history's first explorers. We are still struggling to understand how it happened.

It had happened before—or something very like it had. Somewhere around a million and a half years ago, hominids we call *Homo erectus* began to leave East Africa and seem to have spread over most of what are now Africa and Eurasia. This was a slower and patchier civilization than our own species has achieved. It took at least 300,000 years and probably more like half a million, whereas *Homo sapiens* got further—equalling the furthest limits of *erectus* in Asia and Africa, penetrating much more of Europe, and even reaching Australia in no more than a third of the time and perhaps, by the most favorable calculations, in as little as a tenth.[6] In some ways, the spread of *erectus* foreshadowed that of *sapiens*: it covered much of the same ground. Somehow, too, as in the case of *sapiens*, the travelers managed to cross open sea, for there are *erectus* fossils in parts of Indonesia separated from the Asian land mass at the time of the colonization. *Erectus* may even have had a corps of dedicated—it is tempting to say 'professional'—explorers at the helm. Clive Gamble has argued that in hominid societies young males would be sent out to forage, partly to keep them away from their elders' female companions and partly because of their relative mobility. This specialization would lead to others: first, scouting for routes of seasonal migrations, and then longer-range investigations of remoter foraging opportunities.[7] But there is a danger in pressing too far the possible analogies between the cases of *Homo erectus* and *Homo sapiens*. *Erectus* stayed immobilized in Africa for something like half a million years before the outreach began—two or three times as long as the entire span of the existence (so far) of *Homo sapiens* as a species. A similar spread was achieved by migrant groups of a species apparently ancestral to modern humans, usually known as *Homo helmei*, perhaps about 250,000 years ago; but subsequent severe glaciation wiped out all *Homo helmei*'s extra-African colonies, and those that remained in Africa soon disappeared, displaced or destroyed, perhaps, by our own ancestors.

The outline of where and when *Homo sapiens* traveled during our ancestors' peopling of the earth can be reconstructed—even though the archeological evidence is very patchy and, in the present state of analysis, often seems contradictory—by measuring present populations' differences in blood type, DNA, and, to some extent, language.[8] Crudely speaking, the greater the differences, the longer the ancestors of the people concerned are likely to have been out of touch with the rest of humankind; therefore, the earlier their migrations to their present destination.

These are hard sums to do with confidence or accuracy. Isolation rarely lasts long. Over most of Eurasia and Africa, where population movements have been extremely volatile in recorded history, mixtures have been subject to frequent restirring. For languages, there are no agreed ways of measuring the differences, and subjective judgment may distort findings based on such elusive evidence. Still, for what it is worth, the best-informed scheme currently available puts Eve's progeny in the Middle East by about 100,000 years ago. But the colony failed and was reestablished perhaps about 20,000 to 30,000 years later. All extra-African humans are descended from this single migrant group, whose descendants radiated across the world with surprising rapidity. They seem to have reached the neighborhood of Penang in Malaysia by 74,000 years ago, when a volcanic eruption covered one of their settlements in ash. The earliest agreed archeological evidence of *Homo sapiens* in China is at least 67,000 years old (although some digs have yielded puzzlingly earlier dates for remains which seem uncannily to resemble those of *sapiens*).

Settlement seems to have proceeded, at first, along the coasts of Africa and Asia, probably by sea, by beach clinging and island hopping. It may seem surprising that nautical technology had been developed at so early a date: but the first colonizers of Australia, perhaps 60,000 years ago, must have used it, since at that time what are now Australia and New Guinea were already separated from Asia. In a way, the odd thing about the people of Australia is not that they should have arrived so early, but that they should subsequently have remained isolated for so long. Narrow or monsoonal seas, easily traversable, separated them from Java and New Guinea. There was certainly trade with New Guinea over many centuries before the arrival of new waves of explorers from further afield in modern times. Though there is no evidence for it, it seems incredible that there was no contact with Java. The fact that the first inhabitants of Australia arrived by sea may be challenging in itself—but it makes the paucity of the subsequent history of navigation there all the more mysterious.[9] According to a theory held in contempt by most paleoanthropologists, *Homo sapiens* evolved from an 'aquatic ape'[10]—which, if true, might explain our vocation for the sea. But the arguments are at best very tenuous, and based entirely on imperfect resemblances between humans and aquatic mammals.

Once settlements were established in new lands, migrants struck out inland. The likelihood that we shall be able to reconstruct the route finders' work seems remote; but two assumptions are fair: they followed game and stuck close to water. Presumably, therefore, they started by exploring the drainage areas of the rivers that empty into the Indian Ocean; but once beyond those limits, how did they proceed? Perhaps they traveled from the upper Indus and Yellow River, in the shadows of the mountains of central Asia, along what later became known as the Silk Roads; or, more probably, from the headwaters of the Amur across the Siberian steppe, north of the Gobi desert: here, the region of Lake Baikal and the valleys of some of Siberia's major rivers are dotted with sites over 30,000 years old.[11]

Europe received *Homo sapiens* only about 40,000 years or so ago: there and thereabouts our ancestors met and outlasted—perhaps exterminated—Neanderthals. The colonists of Europe did not travel out of Africa by a separate, direct route of their own: they too were among descendants of the same migrants who began the peopling of Asia. They traveled from the headwaters of the Tigris and Euphrates, probably around the coastal edge of the Anatolian plateau, and along the northern Mediterranean littoral or up the Danube valley.

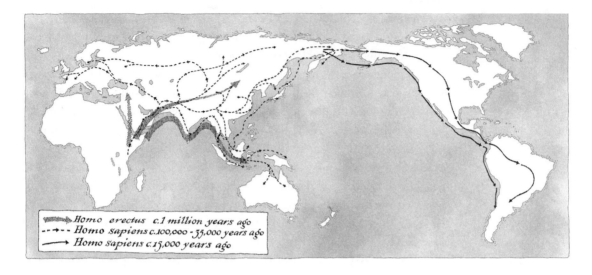

Homo erectus c.1 million years ago
Homo sapiens c.100,000 - 35,000 years ago
Homo sapiens c.15,000 years ago

Genetic evidence suggests a further route, opened up perhaps 10,000 years later, from the Russian steppe and across the north European plain.[12] Northern Asia and America—isolated at the critical time by impenetrable screens of cold climate—were probably colonized much later; the chronology is fiercely disputed; as we shall see, there is still no generally accepted archeological evidence in the New World for settlement prior to about 15,000 years ago. Again, however, the genetic evidence seems unequivocal: the migrants who settled America were also, ultimately, descendants of the same group of migrants from Africa. Of the currently inhabited world, only Polynesia then remained unpeopled: that required the development of high-seas navigation, which was not available until about 3,000 or 4,000 years ago.

If correct, this scheme of the expansion of *Homo sapiens* implies astonishing population growth. We have no idea—beyond guesswork—of the actual numbers who engaged in the migrations, but we can postulate a figure in millions by the end of the process. The children of Eve multiplied so much that they could spread over most of the habitable Old World in less than 100,000 years. But was population growth the cause of the migrations or one of the effects?

Everyone at the time seems to have foraged to survive. Foragers usually limit their families: they either have strict regulations on who can mate with whom, in order to diminish the numbers of breeding couples; or they practice forms of population control. Their main contraceptive resource is protracted lactation: mothers who are breast-feeding their babies are relatively infertile. Large numbers of children are unsuited to the foraging life, because mothers cannot easily carry more than a couple of infants around with them in the course of a

The explorations of Homo sapiens and Homo erectus

nomadic life.[13] Foraging communities therefore have stable populations. The population growth that peopled the earth seems to shatter the normal patterns. The search for an explanation has to embrace two related features of the people of the time: multiplication and mobility.

One possible contribution to an explanation invokes cooking with fire. This had huge potential for improving people's nutrition and increasing their numbers, because it boosted the digestibility and palatability of food. For creatures like us—who have short guts, weak jaws, blunt teeth, and only one stomach each, and who are therefore very limited in the energy sources we can masticate and digest—anything that increased the range of available foods was a major evolutionary advantage. But we simply do not know when fire-fuelled cooking first happened. The incontrovertible evidence dates back about 150,000 years, coinciding neatly with the beginnings of the population explosion; but it is highly likely that traces of fires that burned in caves half a million years ago were deliberately kindled by hominids with cooking in mind. Zhoukhoudian, in China, furnishes a highly persuasive example. Here the Jesuit savant Pierre Teilhard de Chardin, one of the fathers of modern ecology, excavated the evidence in 1930. A hero of modern archeology, the Abbé Breuil, instantly identified it as the remains of a hearth. 'It's impossible,' said the Jesuit, 'it comes from Zhoukhoudian.' 'I don't care where it comes from,' the Abbé replied. 'It was made by a human and that human knew the use of fire.'[14] More recently, one of the world's leading paleoanthropologists, Richard Wrangham, has argued that cooking with fire started more than 2 million years ago: the argument, however, is based not on direct evidence but on inferences from the evolving shape of hominid teeth, which, it is said, got smaller and blunter at that period in presumed response to food modified by flames.[15] No proof survives of domesticated fire at such an early date.[16] The same uncertainty applies to the chronology of other technologies which might have improved diet by facilitating the hunt: producing fire-hardened spears (the earliest examples known are only 150,000 years or so old), or making corrals and arranging stones to form lanes along which to drive prey.

If humans were not empowered to migrate by new techniques, perhaps they were driven to do so by new stresses. Depleted food stocks or ecological disasters might explain the necessity, but no evidence supports speculations along these lines. Deficiencies and disasters seem incompatible with rising population. In every other case we know of, in all species, population falls when food sources shrink.

There is, however, another possible source of stress: warfare. Among the horsemen of the Apocalypse war is the odd man out: plague, famine, and natural catastrophe tend to inhibit human action, whereas war spurs and drives us to innovate. But when did wars start? It is one of the most fascinating problems of history. According to a respectable liberal tradition, war is 'natural' to humans. The commander of British forces in the Second World War, Field Marshal Montgomery, used to refer people who asked for his justification of war to Maeterlinck's *The Life of the Ant*. A distinguished series of twentieth-century anthropologists were of the same mind, arguing, by analogy with other animals, that humans had aggressive and violent instincts implanted by evolution.[17] Romantic primitivists demurred: human nature was essentially peaceful, until corrupted by competition. Margaret Mead, the great liberal anthropologist of the 1920s and 1930s, insisted that war was 'an invention, not a biological necessity.'[18] At first, the evidence seemed equivocal. We still know of no archeological proof of large-scale warfare before the world's earliest known full-scale battle was fought at Jebel Sahaba, near the modern Egyptian–Sudanese frontier, about 11,000 years ago, in a context when agriculture was in its infancy.[19] The slaughter was of unmitigated ferocity, intended not just to winnow and kill but to butcher and exterminate. Many victims were stabbed over and again. This, moreover, was total war, waged not against the enemy's warriors alone, but against women and children. One female body bore twenty-two stab wounds. The strategy of massacre is found today among peoples who practice rudimentary agriculture as well as those supposedly representative of 'modernity' and 'civilization.' These facts make it tempting to speculate that the earliest warfare was between settled communities contending to control resources. At least, wars seem to have taken on a new intensity or to have been waged in a more systematic way once people settled down to tend stands of crops.

It seems, however, that organized intercommunal warfare must have started much earlier. Jane Goodall first reported warfare among chimpanzee communities in the forests of Gabon in the 1970s. The chimps fought with special savagery to eliminate 'splinter groups' who secede from their societies of origin. This may be a clue to the process that set human migration going: conflicts may have forced or urged early human splinter groups to migrate to safety. If correct, this suggestion would imply further problems: What stresses caused warfare 100,000 years ago? Rising population again? Or increasing competition for supposedly diminishing food stocks? Or do we have to revert to assertions about the ubiquity of 'animal' aggression?[20]

It took so long to people the earth that the process must surely have had multiple causes, in different combinations, in different places, at different times. Some migrations were surely *sui generis*: 'one-off' events, unaffected, uneffected, by routine causes. Because we now like to think of pioneers as revolutionaries and frontiersmen as innovators, we probably underestimate the force of conservatism in inducing some communities to move. Recent, documented migrations include those of persecuted religious and ideological minorities—from Amish in the Appalachians to Nazis in the Chaco—who risked transfer to a new environment to preserve an old way of life. I like to imagine the first 'boat people' who colonized Australia as the 'dropouts' of 50,000 years ago, opting out of worlds of change in order to settle a new continent, where they could maintain a traditional way of life. In general, if people moved into new environments, they must have been drawn, not driven. It was not a shortage of resources in their old homes that made them move, but an abundance of new resources elsewhere induced and seduced them. Underlying, and perhaps causing, the new opportunities were inescapable environmental changes: new trends in global climate.

The 'Ice' Man Cometh

The peopling of the world spanned the most convulsive period of climatic change *Homo sapiens* experienced prior to our own times. We should not say that climate change 'caused' the great migrations; but it was an inescapable influence. Cooling and warming phases of the planet are regular occurrences. One or the other is always going on. Every 100,000 years or so the earth's orbit undergoes a distortion, which tugs the northern hemisphere away from the sun. At more frequent, rather irregular cycles, the earth tilts and wobbles on its axis. When these phenomena coincide, temperatures change dramatically. Ice ages set in. A great cooling began about 150,000 years ago: roughly coinciding with the beginnings of the great world-girdling migrations, as if humans did not just welcome the cold, but actively sought it.

Then, about 20,000 years ago, the cooling ended. The world began to emerge from the Ice Age. We think of global warming as a current problem: and indeed it is. But the peculiarly intensive global warming we experience today is only the most dramatic phase of a warming that has been going on ever since.

Cold climates actually suited the humans of the time. The human frame is feeble and, by comparison with most of our ancestors' predators and competitors, ill adapted for survival. Because—to recapitulate—we are slow, weak, blunt in tooth and short in claw, with fastidious digestive systems. Most of our evolutionary advantages are mental: physically, we are a disadvantaged species—the cripples of nature. There are, however, two important ways in which human physiques score high marks in the evolutionary stakes in times of major climatic change.

First, we have frames well adapted to a variety of climates. Apart from the microorganisms that infest our bodies and accompany us wherever we go, and foxes, which are found in just about every type of habitat, we have the most environmentally adaptable bodies in creation. In principle, this made it possible for humans to explore routes of migration across and between climatic zones even during periods of intense and rapid climate change.

Our second big advantage is one already well developed and much exploited in our ancestors' savanna homelands: our relative prowess in throwing missiles. Other primates also throw objects, but they rarely hit anything. Human hand–eye coordination enabled our ancestors to develop missiles as a means of killing competitor species too fast to catch or too big or powerful to overcome at close quarters. Missile use was not, it must be said, the favorite killing method of Ice Age hunters. The easiest and most productive strategy was to drive herds of big quadrupeds over cliffs, where, to this day, the bones of hecatombs of victims too numerous to eat remain as evidence of the hunters' deadly profligacy. But where no cliff was to hand, the best alternative method was to use a river, lake, or mire to trap the animals in: at that point, dexterity with a spear would come in handy. In any event, missiles were always useful for defense, or to drive off scavengers from the scene of a kill.

In combination, these two features—climatically adaptable bodies and handiness with missiles—drew human communities toward the edge of the ice. Cold was not just a tolerable environment: it was actually congenial for missile-equipped hunters who could exploit large animals for food. The bigger the animal, the bigger the reward: it takes relatively less energy to drive a mammoth over a cliff than to stalk smaller, more agile prey; and you get a bigger food bonus back. On the whole, moreover, the colder the climate, the bigger the animals' stocks of fat. And fat—though unfairly despised by today's dietitians—has, for most of history, been the most prized human food, because it confers intensely impacted energy.

Life was good close to the ice edge, and when the ice retreated, people followed it. The far north of Scandinavia had already been repopulated more than 11,000 years ago. Even apparently marginal uplands were colonized by about 7,000 BC. Forests followed the receding ice cap northward. Birch, with its appetite for cold, became widespread by about 11,000 years ago. Oak was about as widely distributed 7,000 years ago as it is today.[21] For unadapted peoples, forests are a tougher environment than tundra: the flight northward of hunters of reindeer explains the alacrity with which areas exposed by deglaciation were settled.

Meanwhile, behind the climatic frontier, environments diversified and species multiplied. The departure of the ice left some of the best-equipped environments for humans: temperate climates, fertile soils, navigable rivers, ore-rich mountains. The opportunities can be read in the well-worked middens of southern France of 10,000 to 20,000 years ago, with their increasing numbers of bones of deer and pig, auroch and elk; or in the settlements of gatherers that grew up a little later in the fertile crescent, and in parts of California and Japan, where forests of nuts and acorns or stands of edible grasses were abundant enough to sustain life. As habitats diversified, migrants headed off in every direction. Cultural divergence became more acute in consequence, as culture adapted to environment.

Even so, the migrations that peopled the Americas seem hard to account for. The long-accepted version is that toward the end of the Ice Age, while the seabed was still exposed across what is now the Bering Strait, a race of hunters crossed from Asia and spread rapidly over the hemisphere. Though American archeology is still really only in its infancy, the evidence now makes that myth untenable. There are so many sites, scattered from the Yukon to Uruguay and from near the Bering Strait to the edge of the Beagle Channel, over so long a period, in so many different stratigraphic contexts, with such a vast range of cultural diversity, that one conclusion is inescapable: colonists came at different times, bringing different cultures with them. Some of them came, no doubt, across the land bridge from Asia; others could well have come by sea.

No generally accepted evidence dates any inhabited site in the hemisphere to earlier than about 15,000 years ago; and, puzzlingly, some of the earliest known sites are in what are now the eastern United States, between the Ohio and Savannah Rivers.[22] By about 12,500 years ago, a community of hunters lived at Monte Verde, in Chile, in a 20-foot-long dwelling of wood covered with hides. They butchered mastodons and brought salt from the coast and herbs from the mountains, from over a radius of 40 miles. Half-chewed lumps of seaweed still show the image of their dental bites. A boy's footprints survive in the clay lining of a pit.[23] If these people got to the southern cone of the Americas as a result of migrations from Beringia, it would be wonderful to know the story of how it happened: colonization across so many climatic zones, adapting to so many unfamiliar environments along the way, is rare.

If we synthesize the evidence and arguments, we come up with a plausible scheme of explanation of the peopling of the world. It started in a time of intense global cooling, when some human groups abandoned the savanna for a shorebound, partly maritime way of life, close to the abundant food sources of lagoons and rock pools. They discovered the food sources of cold steppes, tundras, and the ice edge. When cooling peaked, and the ice cap began to creep northward, some of them followed it. Migrating groups, it seems, were doubly dynamic: not just mobile but also subject to social change—fissile and violent, but also with collaborative, constructive ways of organizing their lives. Surviving evidence hardly illuminates these, but we can make some informed guesses. Crises and opportunities stimulate changes in leadership. Leaders of secessions head toward new lands. Pathfinding was probably one of the functions of new kinds of chief whom climate change elevated to prominence.

Cultural divergence continued even when migration stopped. In some ways, it intensified when people settled down in fixed communities, for, until then, a lot of culture was shared even among the most widely dispersed groups: all had foraging economies and, consequently, similar diets and food practices, similar technologies, and, so far as we know from the evidence of cognitive archeology, similar spiritual lives, probably based on shamanism and the cults of divine, fertile females. We think worldwide uniformities of culture are a new phenomenon of our era of globalization. Nothing could be more wrong: the great age of global culture—the most 'globalized' era in history—was in the Stone Age. When that age ended, diversification accelerated. When some peoples began to abandon foraging and take up farming, and to forget nomadism in favor of urban life, there arose the sharpest differences of culture ever experienced by any species.

The Beginnings of Convergence

So the cosmic observer—if I read her mind correctly—would be right. Divergence has dominated most of the human past. Yet that is not how most people see history, and it is certainly not how historians write it. Overwhelmingly, we are more interested in the history of convergence than of divergence. We live in convergent times—abnormal times by the standards of most of history—because we are globalizers. Our societies are overlapping and interdependent, exchanging influences with great zeal and speed. Our global economy and information web spread comparable kinds of culture all over the world.

This is more than just a story of 'Westernization', or the worldwide triumph of consumerism, individualism, capitalism, and democracy, or the appeal of American 'soft power', or the global cogency of big business, or 'McDonaldization' or 'Coca-colonialism'—although all those phenomena are immensely important in making everywhere familiar to everyone and overlaying our plural world with a topdressing of common culture. The signs of convergence mark the world even more deeply. The last remaining forager cultures are disappearing. A few religions of universal appeal divide the allegiances of most of the world's people between them, and 'interfaith' dialogue makes them more like each other. Languages are dying, dialects disappearing. English and, perhaps, a few other major 'second languages' have become global lingua francas. Environmental change means that, increasingly, the same or very similar major food species are grown in every part of the world and eaten everywhere.

The current state of the world in these respects—the intense, worldwide nature of cultural exchange—has a broad background, remote origins, and a long prehistory. Convergence is almost as old a phenomenon as divergence, since we can be fairly confident that as soon as societies became separated they began to reach out toward one another, and to make contact with neighboring communities; as soon as they developed cultural differences, they became specialists in peculiar techniques, which then became marketable to others. As soon as they adapted to new environments, they became, potentially, purveyors of unfamiliar products to people in other climes.

Convergence is intense today (though it would be rash to assume that divergence is over, or that divergence and convergence cannot go on simultaneously at different levels and in different ways). For perhaps the last 500 years—a scrap of time too insignificant, so far, for the cosmic observer to bother much with—convergence has been conspicuous. Exploration laced the world together with routes of contact. Migration, trade, and cultural exchange followed on a massive scale. So we know far more about convergence than about divergence. In the last half-millennium or so—the period in which, because of the pace of global demographics, most human beings have lived—it has been most people's experience. Because of the interest people have taken in the origins and background of cultural convergence, we can begin to trace it back, deep into the past.

To reconstruct the beginnings of the story, imagination needs to fill in the gaps left by the evidence. Route finding between cultures became an important and perhaps, to some extent, a specialized activity, when people needed to make contact with neighbors in different habitats in order to obtain products unavailable in their own heartlands. The earliest long-range trades were in luxuries: it would not make sense for people to settle where necessities were unavailable. Magical objects—red ochre and fire—were probably the first items of commerce. In some cultures, fire is too sacred to kindle locally: it has to be obtained from afar and carried, unextinguished, to wherever it is required. Even materialistic modern societies retain echoes of this ancient prejudice, tending Olympic torches and 'eternal' flames consecrated to war dead. In historic times, some aboriginal Australian communities insisted on getting fire from neighboring tribes, not because they were incapable of striking a light but because their customs forbade such sacrilege. Ochre was a very widespread, if not universal, source of magic, hallowed as a grave-offering in burials 40,000 years old—including some of the oldest burials in which grave goods are found. Some offerings were placed hundreds of miles from the source at which they were mined and are therefore likely to have been obtained by some of the world's earliest trade. Unguents and aromatics and items of personal adornment followed.

It is not, on reflection, surprising that luxuries predominated in early trade. The American anthropologist Mary W. Helms, has united a fascinating array of evidence about the way people appreciate the exotic.[24] Such esteem seems to be an example of that rare thing: a universal feature of human cultures. Objects gain value with the distance they traverse. According to the same research, people, as well as objects, attract esteem by virtue of being well traveled (though they can also, in some cultural contexts, acquire negative connotations as sources of menace and bafflement). Although we cannot know the identities of the earliest explorers who laid down the routes of cultural convergence, we can be pretty sure that some of them, at least, would have been revered: sanctified by distance, made marvelous by the possession of exotic products.

With the rise of the earliest known farming towns, which grew up between about 9,000 and 11,000 years ago, in Anatolia and the Mediterranean Levant, hard evidence begins to accumulate of efforts to create and maintain routes of communication between widely separated communities. Traces of these explorers' tasks can be found at Çatalhüyük, the most spectacular of these towns. It stood on an alluvial plain, along one of the mouths of the river Çarşamba, where it flowed into a lake which has now disappeared. Nourished by wheat and pulses, the people filled a 32-acre honeycomb of mud-brick dwellings, linked not by streets as we understand them but by walkways across flat roofs. Çatalhüyük throve on communications with other settlements. A wall painting survives there of what may be another, similar urban settlement, linked, presumably, by ties of trade or allegiance. Trade goods came to Çatalhüyük from the Red Sea and the Taurus Mountains. A mountain is clearly depicted in a wall painting at the site: this should, perhaps, be considered the earliest known record of an explorer's report.[25]

Even earlier sites, smaller than Çatalhüyük but reminiscent of it, communicated with the relatively distant Jordan valley, where more settlements were concentrated: villages like Çayönü, inhabited by builders of skull piles, who performed sacrifices on polished stone slabs. By exchanging craft products for primary materials, the inhabitants became rich by the standards of the time, with treasures of fine blades and mirrors, made from obsidian, and products of the copper-smelting technology which they gradually developed.

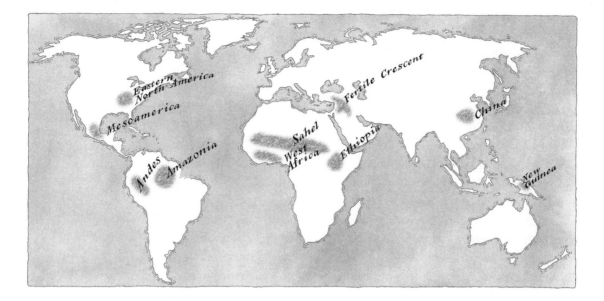

The rise of the earliest farming regions, BC 7000–BC 9000

Patterns discernible in what we now think of as the Eurasian Near East recurred wherever towns developed. Four and a half thousand years ago, for instance, large farmers' settlements grew up on alluvial plains in coastal Peru, especially in the Supe valley, where over thirty sites are located. They were trading emporia, uniting the products of different ecosystems, exchanging vivid marine shells, mountain foods, and featherwork from the forests east of the Andes.[26] Again, underlying the evidence of exchange, pathfinders can be presumed to have been at work. Food and basic building and clothing materials only entered the world of long-range commerce when large populations began to gather in particular places. In part, this was because sedentary farming peoples generated surplus food to exchange for the rarities of their neighbors; in part, because settlements sometimes outgrew locally available necessities, especially salt. Finally, urbanization led to specialization. Craftsmen congregated where markets were to hand—not necessarily where their primary materials were produced.

Explorers were vectors: they carried culture with them. Farming and sedentary life were themselves transferable forms of culture, spread by human contact.[27] Farming settlements existed in eastern Greece in the seventh millennium BC, but western and northern Europe received farming when the landscape opened up and the broad-leaved forest receded, between 5,000 and 6,000 years ago. Into this increasingly favourable environment, it seems likely (though the evidence is slight and subject to reinterpretation) that explorers—

whether as invaders or peaceful colonists or simply trading sojourners—infiltrated from the southeast. They brought with them their farmers' tool kits and their Indo-European speech—languages of the family from which most of Europe's present languages descend.

Similar migrations probably spread farming to parts of central Asia south of the steppeland. The farming which developed in alluvial environments in Anatolia and the Jordan valley colonized or converted every part of the region where it was viable: inhabitants of some sites in the Zagros region, at altitudes above 600 meters, replaced their wild grains with cultivates 8,000 or 9,000 years ago. Southern Turkmenistan had a moister climate generally than now in the period from the seventh to the fourth millennium before the Christian era, but it was already a land of dispersed oases, which, by about 6,000 years ago, were laced with comprehensive irrigation works suggestively similar to others, older, from further west. In the Indian subcontinent there was no intermediate phase between foraging and farming, no period when foragers led settled lives; so the sudden emergence of well-built villages in the same period was probably the result of influence from outside. The path of the route finders from southwest Asia can be traced via Mehrgarh in Baluchistan, where mud-brick impressions of domestic barley and wheat and the bones of domestic goats attest to a system of agriculture by about 9,000 years ago.[28]

In much of North America, cultural exchange was slow: barriers of climate and hostile topography held it up.[29] But of course human pathfinders must still have spearheaded it. The transmission of agriculture was marked by the spread of maize northward from its birthplace in Oaxaca in central Mexico—but this was a slow, millennia-long process, which demanded the repeated redevelopment of new varieties of maize, each adapted to a series of contrasting environments, as the crop crossed climate zones on its northward route; meanwhile, some North American peoples began to farm indigenous crops with edible seeds or roots, such as Jerusalem artichokes, sunflowers, and sumpweeds. In South America, too, it is possible to trace a route of influence along which the idea of agriculture spread from or across the high Andes, through the upper Amazon basin.

In trying to account for the beginnings of agriculture in Africa, it is hard to believe that the emergence of a plant food complex in the Egyptian Sahara is unconnected with that in the Nile valley about 9,000 years ago, or that wheat cultivation in the Nile valley was independent of earlier developments of a similar kind on the other side of the isthmus of Suez. If so, human agents, picking a way across the wastes, must have contributed to the process. The spread of agriculture southward from West Africa, between about four and a half and two and a half millennia ago, probably happened in the context of the migration, traceable from archeological and linguistic evidence, of Bantu-speaking people from their homeland in what are now western Cameroon and Nigeria southward along the Atlantic coasts, and eastward across the edge of the expanding Sahara to the Nile valley, where they turned south again.

The origin of the agriculture of the Pacific Islands is the subject of an unresolved debate. In particular, we do not know how or when the sweet potato—which, together with the pig, is the basis of the food production systems of most of the region—got there. The most widely respected account available so far represents the region's agriculture as the product of diffusion from New Guinea, undergoing many adaptations as it spread slowly across the ocean with seaborne migrants.

The Enigma of Early Maps

Before people recorded routes on maps, we have to infer the extent of route finding from the range of trade and the spread of culture. Of course, people did have maps, even in neolithic times. In the rock art of Africa topographical features are commonly depicted and animals, people, and dwellings are arrayed in relation to them. Lines and dots show the routes shamans take in trances, leading captive creatures to the camp, or traveling to the spirit world. Maps of rivers and mountain ranges, apparently intended as guides to the location of hunting grounds, are scattered across the North American southwest. Other examples have been persuasively interpreted as star maps or representations of celestial events. Village and town plans and maps of burial grounds or sacred sites can be found in some of the world's most traditional cultures.

The irresistible inference is that early maps were probably not route-recording devices. A clue to the earliest form of mapping is the kind most widely diffused among the world's cultures today. If cosmic diagrams—representations of the divine order of the universe—count as maps, they are preponderant in this category. The Dogon of central Africa, for instance, depict the universe as an antlike creature, whose placenta-like head represents heaven and whose legs symbolize earth.[30] In parts of the Congo and Angola, a four-part cosmogram—cross- or diamond-shaped, with sunlike finials—appears on many funerary and devotional objects.[31] In central Asia and China, petroglyphs dating back to as early as the third millennium BC have been plausibly interpreted as containing cosmographical symbols.

After cosmic diagrams, world representations in schematic form are the next most widely diffused kind of map. The oldest surviving attempt to depict the world as a whole was painted, perhaps about 7,000 or 8,000 years ago, on a cave wall at Jaora in Madhya Pradesh. Around an empty central disc, complex patterns—key-shapes, zigzags, lozenges, diamonds, and paddle-like forms—are arrayed in broadly vertical bands, like the skins of scaly beasts laid out to dry.[32] Aquatic plants and fish appear along one edge, ducklike aquatic birds on two more. Birds in flights approach the design from outside it.

It is possible, of course, that route finders shared records of their discoveries in the form of highly perishable maps, scratched in dust or composed of sticks, seeds, and pebbles. Maps that native informants drew in sand, or scraped together out of straws or sticks and pebbles, occur in many early European accounts of travel in Africa and the Americas: indeed, almost nowhere could Europeans have found their way around those continents without this kind of local help. But, for people who knew the routes already, such methods of recording and transferring their knowledge would surely be exceptional measures to help the uninitiated. The obvious way to record routes was to remember them in one's head, perhaps with the help of landmarks and sky marks, chants or verses, rituals and gestures. To this day, the initiation rites of the Luba of the Congo require the candidate to learn the locations of chiefly centers, shrines, and rivers with the aid of maps chalked on a wall.[33] Caroline Island navigators in the eighteenth and nineteenth centuries knew star maps by heart in a form of verse they recited by chanting: they called it 'breadfruit-picking.'

Alternatively, route finders could mark the record of their discoveries directly on the landscape with signs, like the thread Ariadne dangled through the labyrinth. As far as we know, few, if any, such signs have survived, though one can speculate about the purposes of otherwise unexplained cairns and petroglyphs. But the use of route markers is well attested in later evidence from societies that had literacy practices akin to those of preliterate and subliterate peoples. The Incas, as far as we know, had no maps as we normally understand them, but they seem to have relied for route finding on patterns formed by conspicuous mountain top shrines, and lines laid along ridges where armies

The Gold Disk from Moordorf, found near Aurich, West Germany. The central continent is surrounded by concentric rings: the first, an ocean; the second, another continent (with mountains); the third, another ocean with islands (represented as triangles)

and pilgrims passed. European visitors among the Iroquois noticed how trees were marked with carvings along the routes of trade, warfare, or the hunt. Sedentary societies had, perhaps, less need to record hunters' routes—though hunting remained, as far as we know, as a supplementary food-obtaining strategy or an elite activity in all of them. Other kinds of topographical record were useful. One of the earliest surviving paintings from an agrarian settlement is the town plan at Çatalhüyük. From the point of view of the history of exploration, however, maps remained marginal devices.

Communication Between Civilizations

So far, our story of reconvergent route finding has involved relatively short-haul journeys such as linked the early farming settlements of the Near East, and long-range but slow and incremental transmissions of culture such as spread farming into new areas from the few, scattered centers where agriculture developed independently. The big story—of how sundered civilizations got in contact with one another—is still to come. That story begins with the tentative outward reach of the four great civilizations of Eurasia and Africa in the second millennium BC: in the valleys of the Nile, the Tigris and Euphrates, the Indus, and the Yellow River. It continues in earnest with the contacts established across Eurasia, linking China, India, the Near East, and the Mediterranean in the first millennium BC. (Subsequent efforts, which brought civilizations of sub-Saharan Africa and the Americas into the loop, belong in later chapters.)

The cities of the Indus in the early second millennium BC throve on long-range contacts. Their outposts were clearly sited with trade in mind—to attract or guard ships and caravans from afar. At Shortughal, in what is now northern Afghanistan, lapis lazuli and copper could be traded. In the same region, at the caravan emporium of Mundigak, behind formidable walls with square bastions, the wreck of a great citadel lunges over the landscape, baring rows of deep, round pilasters at its flank—grimly eroded now, but still enormous—like the ribs of a squat beast, staring across the plain to watch over the routes of trade. The layout of the river valley cities was reproduced in a contrasting environment on the Gulf of Cambay, at the port of Lothal. From here, some of the world's longest-frequented sea routes linked the civilization with that of Mesopotamia, via ill-documented island kingdoms off the Arabian coast.

The pioneers who opened those routes of trade are unknowable, because the Indus people have left no readable records and those of Mesopotamia recorded only local routes and the arrival of tribute, from as far afield as the Taurus and the mountains of Iran. From China, only legends survive to recall the internal

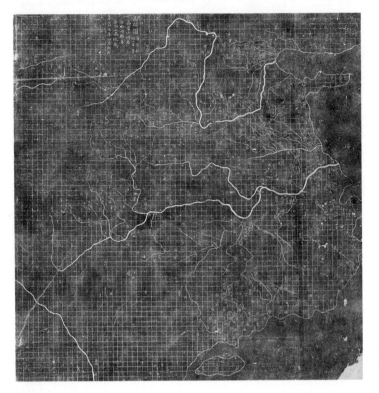

The Yu ji tu (Map of the Tracks of Yu the Great), rubbing from the carved stone dated AD 1136. It shows the grid used by the Chinese cartographer, on which the rivers and coastline are drawn stunningly accurately

explorations of the second millennium BC, which meshed the Yellow River basin into a state crisscrossed by roads and canals, and gradually extended the frontier southward to encompass the Yangtze. Legends of Yu the Great personify the process, representing him as a heroic engineer–emperor, a sculptor of landscape in the tradition of storytelling about giants. 'The Tracks of Yu the Great' was a name later given to maps of China: an example under that name exists from the year 1136.

By contrast, relatively copious records of exploration survive from ancient Egypt. Here we meet the first flesh-and-blood explorers and explorers' patrons, whom we know by name and whose adventures we can share. Egypt from the third millennium BC was a long, thin kingdom, united by the Nile. Internal communications were simple. The river route for royal progresses led between 'mooring-places of the pharaoh.' The flanking deserts confined the territorial ambitions of Egyptian kings, but to extend the empire southward along the Nile was one of their most constant objectives. Egyptians' attention was drawn southward by the abundant ivory and mercenaries that Nubia supplied, and the riverborne trade that made gold in Egypt 'as plentiful as the sand of the sea.'

Egyptian exploration of the potential zone of imperial expansion in central Africa had begun around the middle of the third millennium BC,

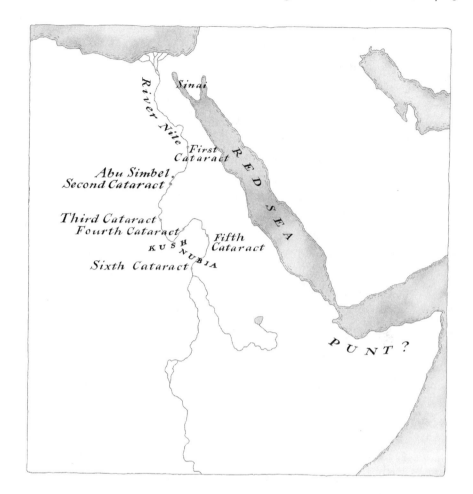

Egyptian exploration southward

when Harkhuf, whom we can fairly call a specialized explorer, made three expeditions. He brought back 'incense, ebony, scented oil, tusks, arms, and all fine produce.' The boy pharaoh Pepi was fascinated by Harkhuf's captive pygmy, 'who dances divine dances from the land of the spirits.' Writing to the leader of the expedition, the pharaoh commanded the utmost care in guarding him: 'inspect him ten times a night. For my Majesty wishes to see this pygmy more than all the products of Sinai and Punt.'

Contact and commerce led to the formation of a Nubian state in imitation of Egypt, beyond the second cataract. From about 2000 BC, Egypt tried to influence or control it, sometimes by erecting fortifications, sometimes by invasion, sometimes by pushing its own frontier southward to beyond the third cataract. Pharaonic inscriptions piled curses on the Nubians as they became more powerful and more intractable. Eventually, around 1500 BC, Tutmose I launched a campaign beyond the fourth cataract, breaking the state then known as Kush and making Nubia a colonial territory. Egypt studded the land with forts and temples. The last temple, to Rameses II, at Abu Simbel, was the most crushingly monumental edifice Egyptians had built for 2,000 years. It has remained a symbol of power ever since. For Egypt to abandon Nubia in the late second millennium BC, after so much effort and after the investment of so much emotion, the need for retrenchment must have been severe.[34] At the time, gyrations and incursions of migrants and invaders convulsed the eastern Mediterranean world, in what historians sometimes call 'the crisis of the Bronze Age.'

In the same period, Egypt was engaged in the exploration of new commercial routes along the Red Sea. The most vivid evidence was painted around the middle of the second millennium BC over half a wall of the funerary temple of Queen Hatshepsut, the redoubtable female pharaoh. The scene depicts a shipborne expedition to the remotest land in the world the Egyptians knew, rich in incense and ivory, panthers and monkeys, turtles and giraffes, gold, ebony, and antimony. We do not know where the land of Punt was, but as the artist depicted it, it was recognizably African, with a tropical or semitropical climate. Somalia is the most likely candidate. Hatshepsut planned a garden of incense sacred to the god Amun-Re, and the purpose of her expedition was to buy the trees. An underlying purpose is obvious: the struggle to legitimate her rule in a state where female pharaohs were a highly irregular aberration. Like a true pharaoh, she was supposedly conceived by the love of the god Amun-Re, penetrating her mother's body, 'with the flood of divine fragrance, and all his odours were those of the land of Punt.'

The route involved a long voyage down the Red Sea. Any Red Sea voyage under sail tends to be long and hazardous because of the torturous sailing conditions. The spice trees were relatively low-bulk, high-value goods, but the Egyptians had to send five ships to get them, because they had to pay for them with vast amounts of the foodstuffs that Egypt's sophisticated agriculture produced in abundance. Punt possessed 'all marvels,' the Egyptian text records, whereas Egypt in return offered 'all good things.' The gold of Punt was measured out with bull-shaped weights, and the live incense trees were potted and carried aboard the Egyptian vessels. The Egyptians paid for them with 'bread, beer, wine, meat, fruits.'

Unless the Egyptian text is embellished—as it well may be—the people of Punt were astonished at the explorers' arrival. 'How have you reached this land unknown to the men of Egypt?' they are made to ask, with hands uplifted in surprise. 'Have you descended hither by the paths of the sky or,' they added, as if it were equally improbable, 'have you sailed the sea?'[35] Columbus claimed that the islanders who greeted him at the end of his first transatlantic crossing used similar words and a similar gesture. The claim that seaborne explorers' hosts supposed their visitors to be heavenborne is, indeed, such a widespread topos as to be barely believable.

As well as probing the Red Sea and the upper Nile, Egyptian explorers developed a mesh of routes in the eastern Mediterranean, linking Crete and—at least—cities on the Levantine mainland. Beyond the reach of Egyptian navigation, islands of the Mediterranean had housed maritime cultures for millennia, but it is impossible to be precise about the range of the routes their seamen mastered. In the fourth millennium BC, Malta had the world's oldest monumental stone buildings; other western Mediterranean islands had, 1,000 years later, elites who built vast chambered tombs. In the late third millennium, the Cyclades Islands housed courts that have left luxurious bits of material culture: elegant sculptures of harpists, jeweled mirrors, baths. Crete in the second millennium was dotted with trading cities and palace storehouses: trade with Egypt is apparent in some of the exotica depicted in surviving wall paintings. Cities in southern Greece grew up shortly afterwards, sustaining a lively trade in Baltic amber, which, presumably, reached them by way of a series of intermediate traders. Some of their edifices have remarkable resemblances to tombs already thousands of years old in northwest Europe—in Britain and Brittany. It seems unlikely that any explorer actually traversed or rounded the whole of Europe from Greece to Britain or Scandinavia as early as the second millennium BC, but traders had clearly traced a series of routes across the continent.

From the Mediterranean to the Atlantic

Late in the second millennium BC, all the great civilizations of Eurasia experienced extinction, displacement, or transformation. Those of Crete, southern Greece, and Anatolia collapsed. The eastern Mediterranean entered a 'dark age' without written records until the eighth century BC. The cities of the Indus turned to dust; when the centers of civilization in the region reemerged in the following millennium, they were far distant from the former heartland, in the Ganges valley and what is now Sri Lanka. China was conquered by an intrusive dynasty from the fringes of the culture area of the Yellow River, and, by the seventh century BC, had dissolved into what Chinese historians ever since have called the 'warring states.' Egypt, meanwhile, barely survived invasions and migrations that destroyed the cities of the Levant in about the thirteenth century BC.

Yet a remarkable Egyptian traveler's account, fairly reliably dated to the year 1075 BC, conveys a sense of the new world which reemerged from the chaos of the time. 'Guided,' he says, 'only by the light of the stars,' Wenamun, an Egyptian ambassador, crossed 'the Great Syrian Sea' on his way to the city-state of Byblos, on the shore of what is now Lebanon. His mission: to procure timber for the Egyptian fleet from the forested mountains that lined that coast.

On arrival Wenamun rented quarters and set up an altar to Amun, the god who supplied pharaohs with oracles. At first, King Zeker-Baal refused to see him, preferring, he claimed, to reserve his forests for his own purposes. He kept Wenamun waiting for weeks. When he sent a sudden summons at dead of night, it was presumably a negotiating ploy. Wenamun's report, however, represented it as a dramatic change of heart induced by prophetic utterances. 'I found him,' says Wenamun, 'squatting in his high chamber, and when he turned his back against the window, the waves of the Great Syrian Sea were breaking against the rear of his head.' Word for word, the ambassador recorded the dialogue that followed—doctored, no doubt, but still highly revealing. There were posturings on both sides.

'I have come,' Wenamun began, 'after the timber contract for the great and august ship of Amun, king of gods.' He appealed to the precedents of Zeker-Baal's father and grandfather, who had sent timber to Egypt, but the king resented the implication that timber was due as tribute.

'They did so by way of trade,' he replied. 'When you pay me I shall do it.' After some bickering over the price, the negotiators exchanged defiance. 'I call loudly to the Lebanon which makes the heavens open,' claimed Zeker-Baal, 'and the wood is delivered to the sea.'

'Wrong!' retorted Wenamun. 'There is no ship which does not belong to Amun. His also is the sea. And his is the Lebanon of which you say, "It is mine." Do his bidding and you will have life and health.'

It was impressive rhetoric. In practice, however, the Egyptians had to pay Zeker-Baal's price: four 'jars' of gold and five of silver, unspecified amounts of linen, 500 ox hides, 500 ropes, twenty sacks of lentils, twenty baskets of fish. 'And the ruler was pleased and he supplied 300 men and 300 oxen. And they felled the timber, and they spent the winter at it and hauled it to the sea.'[36]

The document is arresting not only for its vividness and drama, which excel fiction, and the capture of real dialogue, but also for the picture it conveys of urban recovery on the Levantine coast of what came to be called Phoenicia and the survival or resumption of ancient trade routes. Cities like Byblos, and others which, from the eighth century onward, began to grow up in Greece, became nurseries of heroic explorers. They had no alternative: the Levantine cities had limited hinterlands, forcing their citizens to accumulate wealth as traders. 'Greece and poverty,' meanwhile, as a poet complained, were 'sisters.'[37] Most Greek cities relied on manufactures—principally olive oil and ceramics—for wealth, and needed to find suitable markets. From both regions, where surplus population could not be accommodated because of local economic constraints, colonies spilled across the sea.

Phoenician traders were active in southwest Spain in the first half of the first millennium BC. According to a Greek tradition, the Phoenician colony of Gadir, now Cadiz, was established before the beginning of the millennium, though the real date is likely to have been no earlier than the ninth century BC.[38] Greek colonies on Spain's east coast followed by the seventh century of the same era. The incoming Orientals found a ready-made market in a silver-rich civilization. Herodotus gives, in different places, rival versions of the discovery of Tartessos, on the Atlantic shore of lower Andalusia:

> A ship from Samos, whose captain was Coleos, was sailing for Egypt but . . . they were blown by the east wind beyond the Pillars of Hercules and by divine providence reached Tartessos. This market was at that time still unexploited. Therefore when they returned to their own country the men of Samos made more profit from their wares than any other Greeks we know of save Sostratos of Aegina—for there is none to compare with him.

Herodotus' other version is even richer in historical context and circumstantial detail:

> The Phocaeans were the earliest of the Greeks to make long sea-voyages. It was they who discovered the Adriatic Sea and the Tyrrhenian and Iberia and Tartessos, not sailing in round freight ships but in 50-oared vessels. When they came to Tartessos, they made friends with the king of the Tartessians, who was called Arganthonios. He ruled Tartessos for eighty years and lived for 120 years. The Phocaeans so won this man's friendship that he first entreated them to leave Ionia and settle in his country where they would; and when he could not persuade them and heard from them how the power of the Persians was increasing, he gave them money to build a wall around their city. Without stint he gave it.[39]

In other words, Phocaean relations with Tartessos were well established by the mid-sixth century BC—roughly a generation after the settlement of the first Greek colonies in Catalonia. Tartessian subsidies were aired, perhaps, as a legendary explanation of the strength of the famous wall that withstood the siege by Cyrus the Great in 546 BC. The king's eagerness to attract a Greek colony to his shores hints at a desire to play off Phoenician monopolists or to strengthen his defenses against a Phoenician or inland threat. Or it may signify a desire to acquire ships and entrepreneurs to take advantage of widening circles of commerce.

Tartessos, which faced the Atlantic, was a way station to remoter markets and sources of wealth. The trade routes of the Phoenician and Greek trailblazers led north from the pillars of Hercules to the metal-rich British Isles. Their colonies were staging posts in the making of a new economy—helping goods, people, and ideas to cross or get around the sharply divisive watershed that separates Mediterranean from Atlantic Europe. In the fourth century BC, the Greek colony in what is now Marseilles had plausible accounts of routes to Shetland and the Elbe. Parts of the Indian Ocean, too, were already seaways of long-range commerce.

Late in that century BC, a traveler who was not, apparently, a merchant, but a disinterested scientific enquirer, made a well-attested voyage from Marseilles, apparently with the aim of exploring the markets of northern Europe. Probably, rather than circumnavigating Iberia, Pytheas took the direct, overland route from his home city to the Atlantic, sailing up the Aude and down the Garonne and Gironde. Though his account of his voyage survives only in fragments copied by later hands, some of the discoveries he reports are easily identifiable. He found Brittany—a huge salient with many promontories projecting into the Atlantic. He visited the tin-producing region now called Cornwall and made observations—not necessarily at first hand—on the amber trade of Scandinavia. He reported that Britain was surrounded by numerous islands, naming the Orkneys, the Hebrides, Anglesey, the Isles of Man and Wight, and other groups perhaps identifiable as the Shetlands and the Scillies: it looks as if he sailed northward, between Britain and Ireland, in search of the northernmost accessible land. Pytheas described Britain as roughly triangular in shape and made an attempt at calculating its dimensions. He marveled at the tides. Along his route, he made observations with a gnomon to determine his latitude. He described the relationship of the Pole Star and the Guard Stars.

How far did Pytheas go? He called his northernmost stopping point 'Thule.' The evidence closest to his own words is quoted in a text of the mid-first century AD: he says, among the observations recorded by him in *On the Ocean*, 'The barbarians pointed out to us on several occasions the place where the sun lies down. For it happens that around these places the night is very short: two hours in some, three in others, so that after the setting, although only a short time has elapsed, the sun straightaway rises again.' At least he got far enough north to register this sort of detail from local knowledge.[40]

Beyond the Strait of Gibraltar it was possible to head south, into the African Atlantic, as well as north, in pursuit of trade in gold, which, according to Herodotus, was practiced on the Saharan coast by 'dumb trade,' in which traffickers left their wares on the beach, retired, and returned to collect gold left in payment by the natives.

Herodotus records a Phoenician voyage, commissioned by an Egyptian pharaoh around the turn of the sixth and seventh centuries BC, into the Indian Ocean from the Red Sea.

> When autumn came they went ashore wherever they might happen to be and, having sown a tract of land with corn, waited until the grain was fit to cut. Having reaped it, they again set sail; and thus it came to pass that two whole years went by, and it was not until the third year that they doubled the Pillars of Hercules and made good their voyage home. On their return they declared—I for my part do not believe them but others may—that in sailing around Libya they had the sun on their right hand. In this way the extent of Libya was first discovered.[41]

Probably toward the end of the fifth century, a Carthaginian adventurer left an inscription recording an exceptionally ambitious voyage along the African coast. The inscription survives only in a much-copied and, consequently, much-garbled version. But the outline of a plausible story emerges. After founding a series of trading settlements along the coast, Hanno reached a country of elephants, then another of crocodiles and hippopotamuses. In a land where lava streams from a volcanic mountain met the sea, he hunted beasts 'with shaggy bodies, whom our interpreters called gorillas.' If any of these details are reliable, the explorers must have got as far as Sierra Leone and perhaps saw Mount Cameroon.

At about the same time, fragmentary sources, which ancient geographers and poets culled from sailing directions, credit another Carthaginian, Himilco, with explorations deep into the Atlantic. Among fantastic and incredible elements—monsters and mid-ocean shallows—descriptions of great masses of seaweed and windless latitudes evoke the Sargasso Sea and the Doldrums. Himilco's voyage may have been fictional, but Carthaginian knowledge of the mid-Atlantic seems to have been based on real experience.[42]

Exploration fed cosmography. Greek geographers gradually built up a picture of the world. The first Greek world map we know of was a diplomatic device, displayed in Miletus around 500 BC in an attempt to persuade Greek states to take up arms against Persia. It showed a world dominated by a vast Europe, towering over diminutive Asia and Africa. Speculative maps proliferated, to judge from Herodotus' scorn for 'maps of the world drawn without any reason to guide them.' But the enterprise proved irresistible, for both strategic and scientific reasons. In the fourth century BC, Alexander the Great's vision of world conquest demanded a notion of the world as a whole. Savants scoured sailing directions and the accounts of travelers such as Pytheas. Egyptian and Mesopotamian geographical and cartographical work, now lost to us, nourished their efforts. A surviving Babylonian map, carved on stone, of the mid-first millennium BC, shows the possibilities: it depicts the Euphrates and names Babylon, Assyria, and Armenia. In about 200 BC Eratosthenes, the librarian of Alexandria, produced his astonishingly accurate estimate of the size of the world by using the shadow cast by a gnomon at points presumed to be on the same meridian to measure the distance subtended by a degree of latitude on the surface of the earth. He also estimated, roughly correctly, that the known world occupied only a third of the surface of the globe. In the second century BC, Ptolemy proposed the construction of a map of the world by means of a grid of lines of latitude and longitude. The suggestion was premature, since longitude could only be very roughly estimated, at best. But it stimulated numerous attempts.[43]

Strenuous speculation filled the gaps in knowledge. Herodotus treated central Asia as a kind of dreamland from which travelers might return only as ghosts. Strabo, striving to reconstruct Homer's world picture in the first century BC, derided fellow geographers who worried about the far Atlantic, where, perhaps, a series of unknown worlds awaited discovery. 'It is not necessary,' he affirmed, 'for geographers to bother about places outside our inhabited world.'[44] The puzzle of what lay beyond the Sahara, and, in particular, the question of where the Nile rose, proved of obsessive interest to Greek geographers. Ptolemy thought the Indian Ocean might be landlocked. Augustus' minister Maecenas—at least, in the flattering speculations of his client, the poet Horace—was always worrying about what the Chinese were up to.[45]

The Silk Roads

It is not likely that Maecenas was really much concerned with the doings of the Chinese, but trans-Eurasian trade routes were certainly developing fast at the time, bringing Rome and China at least into mutual knowledge, albeit not direct touch. The trade of Eurasia exposed disparities of wealth that helped to shape the history of the next two millennia. Already in the first century CE, the Roman geographer Pliny worried about it: the Roman world produced little that its trading partners wanted. The silks of the overland road across Eurasia, the spices and aromatics of Arabia and the Indian Ocean, were items of universal demand. The only way for people in Europe to pay for them was in cash. Nowadays, we should call this an adverse balance of trade. The problems of financing it—and ultimately of overcoming and reversing it—became a major theme of the history of the West and, in the long run, of the world.

Sea routes were more important for global history than land routes: they carried more goods, faster, more economically, in greater amounts. Nevertheless, in the early stages of the development of trans-Eurasian communications, most long-range trade was small-scale, in goods of high value and limited bulk. It relied on 'emporium trading'—onward-transmission through a series of markets and middlemen—rather than expeditions across entire oceans and continents. In the axial age, the routes that linked Eurasia by land were at least as important, in the history of cultural contacts, as those by sea.

It was already, by Pliny's day, a trade of great antiquity. From around the middle of the first millennium BC, scattered examples of Chinese silks appeared across Europe, in Athens, Budapest, and a series of south German and Rhineland burials. By the end of the millennium, a route of diffusion of Chinese manufactures became traceable, from the southern Caspian to the northern Black Sea, and into what were then gold-rich kingdoms in the southwest stretches of the Eurasian steppe. Meanwhile, starting from Greece, Alexander's armies had used the Persian royal roads to cross what are now Turkey and Iran, conquer Egypt and Mesopotamia, reach the Persian Gulf, and, at the extremities of their eastward march, touch the Pamir Mountains and cross the Indus. Merchants could also have used these routes.

The first written evidence of this presumed commerce occurs in the report of Zhang Qian, a Chinese ambassador who set out for Bactria—one of the Greek-ruled kingdoms established in central Asia in Alexander's wake—in 139 BC. His main missions were, first, to recruit allies against the aggression of steppeland imperialists who raided China's northern borders, and, secondly, to obtain horses for the Chinese army from the best breeders, deep in central Asia. His mission was one of the great adventures of history. Captured en route, he remained a hostage with the steppelanders for ten years, before escaping to continue his task, crossing the Pamir Mountains and the river Oxus, and returning, without encountering any potential allies, via Tibet. He was captured again, escaped again, and got home, with a steppeland wife in tow, after an absence of twelve years. From a commercial point of view, his reports were highly favorable. The kingdoms beyond the Pamir had 'cities, houses and mansions as in China.' In Ferghana the horses 'sweat blood and come from the stock of the heavenly horses.' He saw Chinese cloth in Bactria. 'When he asked how they obtained these things, the people told him their merchants bought them in India, which is a country several hundred li south-east.' From the time of his mission, 'specimens of strange things began to arrive' in China 'from every direction.'[46]

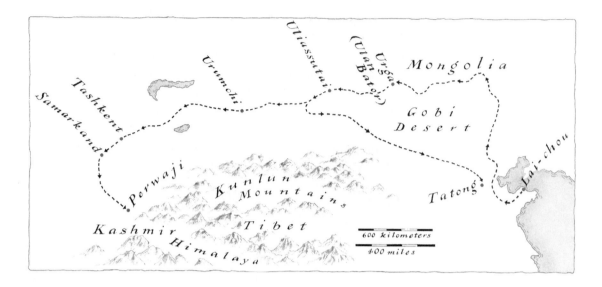

In 111 BC a Chinese garrison founded the outpost of Dunhuang—the name means 'blazing beacon'—beyond the western limits of the empire, on the edge of a region of desert and mountains. Here, according to a poem inscribed in one of the caves where travelers sheltered, was 'the throat of Asia,' where 'the roads to the western ocean' converged like veins in the neck. We now call them the 'Silk Roads.' They skirted the Taklamakan Desert, under the mountains which line it to north and south. It was a terrible journey, haunted, in Chinese accounts, by screaming demon drummers—personifications of ferocious winds. But the desert was so demanding that it deterred even bandits, and the mountains offered some protection from the predatory nomads who lived beyond them. The Taklamakan took thirty days to cross—clinging to the edges, where water drains from the surrounding mountains. Further west, to get to the markets of central Asia, or to reach India, some of the world's most formidable mountains had to be climbed.

A few years after the founding of Dunhuang, a Chinese army, reputedly of 60,000 men, traveled this road to secure the mountain passes at the western end and to force the horse-breeders of Ferghana to trade. A painted cave shows the general, Wudi, kneeling before the 'golden men' that Chinese forces seized. (The painter made them buddhas, perhaps fancifully.)[47] In 102 BC, the Chinese invaded Ferghana, diverted a river, and obtained 30,000 horses in tribute. Meanwhile, caravans from China reached Persia, and Chinese trade goods became common in the Mediterranean Levant.

In AD 79 China did send an envoy, Kan Ying, to Rome, but he turned back at

Route of the Chinese ambassador Zhang Qian

the Black Sea, deterred by warnings from local enemies of Rome, who did not want the mission to succeed. They said to him, 'If the ambassador is willing to forget his family and home, he can embark.' From what data he was able to glean, Kan sent home a favorable report on the Romans: 'the people have an air comparable to those of China. . . . They trade with India and Persia by sea.' That was as close as the Roman and Chinese empires ever came to direct mutual dealings.[48]

Explorers of the Monsoon

Kan Ying was right to assert that merchants from the Roman world traded with the Indian Ocean by sea. Alexander's campaigns introduced Greeks to the allure of Arabian emporiums and access to India—goals previously monopolized by Persian merchants. Toward the end of the sixth century BC, Darius I, an emperor enthusiastic for exploration, ruled Persia. He ordered reconnaissance of the seas from Suez to the Indus. This venture probably extended the range of navigation in the region, since the Red Sea, with its concealed rocks and dangerous currents, was notoriously hard to navigate. Among the consequences were penal colonies on islands of the Persian Gulf. A canal built from Suez to the Nile indicates there must have been existing traffic for it to serve, and the result was to increase it further.

Before Alexander the Great died in 323 BC, he sent naval expeditions to give Greeks first-hand experience of the Red Sea route to the Indian Ocean, and reconnoiter the way from the Persian Gulf to the mouth of the Indus. Thereafter, Greeks began to compile their own sailing directions, maps, and information for the shores of what they called the Erythraean Sea—the Arabian Sea, in modern terms, together with the Red Sea and the Persian Gulf. Data on the exploration of the Red Sea were gathered by Agatharchides of Cnidos, a Greek colony in what is now southern Turkey, probably in the mid-second century BC: fragments survive of other texts recording expeditions from Greek colonies in Egypt, in search of trade in elephants and aromatics, or in pursuit of military and naval exploits. Pliny thought he knew the length of a voyage from Aden to India. The ports of western India and of almost the whole length of the East African coast were enumerated in *The Periplus of the Erythraean Sea*, a Greek guide for Indian Ocean merchants, probably of the mid-first century AD.[49]

Arabia was, in effect, a fulcrum of long-range commerce, linking the maritime worlds of the Mediterranean Sea and Indian Ocean, as well as a source of trade aromatics used in incense and cosmetics, especially frankincense, myrrh, and an Arabian cinnamon substitute called cassia. Important ports for long-range trade lined Arabia's shores. At Gerrha, for instance, prob-ably near modern Al Jubayl, merchants unloaded Indian manufactures. Nearby, Thaj also served as a good place to warehouse imports, protected by walls of dressed stone more than a mile and a half in circumference and 15 feet thick. From Ma'in, in southern Arabia, a merchant supplied Egyptian temples with incense in the third century BC: we know this because he died in Egypt and his sarcophagus is engraved with the story of his life.

Omani trading cities had a glowing reputation among Roman and Greek writers in the two centuries around the birth of Christ. Yemen was a land so rich in spices that men were said to 'burn cassia and cinnamon for their everyday needs.' The author of a text of the second century AD, referring to the principal trading peoples of Arabia, believed that 'No nation seems to be wealthier than the Sabaeans and Gerrhaeans, who are the agents for everything that falls under the name of transport from Asia and Europe. It is they who have made Syria rich in gold and have provided profitable trade and thousands of other things to the enterprise of people in the Mediterranean Levant.' Arabia's location and busy port cities explain the deathbed wish of Alexander the Great, the would-be world conqueror, to conquer Arabia.[50]

Routes developed in the Arabian Sea contributed to a far more widespread series of links, which joined almost all the coasts of maritime Asia and extended to much of the coast of East Africa. The world maps drawn by Indian geographers of the period provide clues to the explorations involved. The maps look, it must be said, like the product of stay-at-home minds. The well-known world picture of post-Vedic times, the 'Four-Continent World', is of a world centered on the Himalaya. Four 'island continents' radiate from a mountainous core, the Meru, or Sineru, surrounded by seven concentric circles of rock. The biggest, to the south, is the Jambudvipa, where most of India is located. To the east lies Bhadravati, which is probably intended to include Nepal and part of northern Bihar. The northern continent, Uttarakuru, seems to correspond to central Asia. The fourth, Ketumala, stretched west. From the second century BC, this picture gradually gave way to a 'Seven-Continent World', apparently even further removed from reality. Each continent now appeared surrounded by a different sea, respectively of brine, sugarcane juice, wine, ghee, curds, milk, and water. This was essentially Buddhist geography. That of Jain writers was even more fanciful, representing the cosmos as a series of truncated pyramids.

However, one should not suppose, on the basis of their formal, sacred cosmography, that Indians of the time were ignorant of the world. That would be like inferring that Londoners thought that the Underground map was an accurate representation of the course of the Tube lines. Real observations from explorers' reports are detectable under the metaphors of the maps. The world is grouped around the great Himalaya Mountains, including the triangular, petal-like form of India, with Sri Lanka falling from it like a dewdrop. Of the separate seas, some are imaginary or little known, but others represent real routes to frequented destinations and commercial centers. The sea of milk, for instance, corresponds roughly to what we now call the Arabian Sea, and the sun worship attributed to the people of the milk-lapped continent of Saka resembles the religion of Zoroastrians in Persia, with their rites of welcome of dawn. Kusa, in its sea of butter, suggests Ethiopia.

Indians had plenty of direct experience of those seas. Stories of Indian seafaring from late in the first millennium BC, perhaps the third or second century, appear in the Jatakas, collected tales of Buddhahood, guides to how to become enlightened. Here, piloting a ship 'by knowledge of the stars' is a godlike gift. The Buddha himself pilots his ship by the stars, 'knowing the course of the celestial luminaries,' acquainted with the parts of a ship and all the signs a navigator must observe, including the 'fish, the colour of the water, the gleanings of the seabed, the birds, the rocks'. So 'being skilled in the art of taking a ship out and bringing her home, he exercised the profession of one who conducts merchants by sea to their destination.' The Buddha saves sailors from cannibalistic goblin seductresses in Sri Lanka. He improvises an unsinkable vessel for a pious explorer. A merchant from the city of Benares, following the advice of an enlightened sage, buys a ship on credit and sells the cargo at a profit of 200,000 gold pieces. Manimekhala, a guardian deity, saves shipwreck victims who have combined commerce with pilgrimage 'or are endowed with virtue or worship their parents.'[51] These are legends, but the surviving tales contain so many practical details that they only make sense against a background of real navigation. Similar legends appear in Persian sources, like the story of Jamshid, the hero who is both king and shipbuilder and who crosses oceans 'from region to region with great speed.'

The reason for the long seafaring, sea-daring tradition of the Indian Ocean lies in the regularity of the monsoonal wind system. Above the equator, northeasterlies prevail in winter. But when winter ends, the direction of the winds is reversed. For most of the rest of the year, the winds blow steadily from the south and west, sucked toward the Asian land mass as air warms and rises over the continent. By timing voyages to take advantage of the predictable changes in the direction of the wind, navigators could set sail, confident of a fair wind out and a fair wind home.

It is a fact not often appreciated that, overwhelmingly, the history of maritime exploration has been made into the wind. When I edited *The Times Atlas of World Exploration*, I realized with astonishment that most would-be

Carved ship from a Jataka depicted on a wall at the temple of Borobudur, Java

discoverers have preferred to sail against the elements—actually avoiding a following wind—presumably because it was at least as important to get home as to get to anywhere new. This was how the Phoenicians and Greeks opened the Mediterranean to long-range commerce and colonization, for in that sea the prevailing winds are westerly. As we shall see, the same strategy enabled South Sea Island navigators of this period to explore and colonize islands of the Pacific, sailing always into the prevailing southeasterlies.

The monsoonal wind system in the Indian Ocean liberated navigators from such constraints. One must try to imagine what it would have been like, feeling the wind, year after year, alternately in one's face and at one's back. Gradually, would-be seafarers realized how the changes of wind made outward ventures viable: they knew the wind would change, and so could risk an outward voyage without fearing that they might be cut off from the chance of returning home. The Indian Ocean has many hazards. It is racked by storms, especially in the Arabian Sea, the Bay of Bengal, and the deadly belt of habitually bad weather that stretches across the ocean below about 10° south of the equator. The tales of Sinbad are full of shipwrecks. But the predictability of a homeward wind made this the world's most benign environment for long-range voyaging. In contrast, the fixed-wind systems of the Atlantic and Pacific were almost impossible to cross with ancient technology; we know of no round trips across them.

Even compared with other navigable seas, the reliability of the monsoon season offered other advantages. No reliable sources record the length of voyages in this period, but, to judge from later statistics, a trans-Mediterranean journey from east to west, against the wind, would take fifty to seventy days. With the monsoon, a ship could cross the entire Erythraean Sea, between India and a port on the Persian Gulf or near the Red Sea, in three or four weeks in either direction.

Despite the growing importance of maps in documenting the world known to scholars in the major Eurasian civilizations, new routes were rarely, if ever, mapped. Cultures that made maps used them for other purposes: Greeks for diplomacy, Indians for religion, Chinese for war and administration. The *Guanzi*, a Chinese treatise on generalship of the third century BC, rates mastery of maps among the highest qualifications for generalship: 'All military commanders must first examine and come to know maps. They must know thoroughly the location of winding mountain passes, streams that may inundate their chariots, famous mountains, passable valleys, arterial rivers, highlands and hills, the places where grasses, trees and rushes grow; the distances of roads, the size of city and suburban walls, famous cities and deserted ones, and barren and cultivated lands' and above all 'the ways in and out' of the lands their armies traverse.[52] A soldier's tomb, probably of 239 BC, in Tianshui, Gansu province, contains what are obviously military maps of the region, with transit routes of armies stretching between settlements and across rivers. Fragments of administrators' maps survive from about the same period in China, and many texts confirm their importance and place in official records of the state. But the form of the world as a whole was an indifferent matter for early Chinese mapmakers; except for diagrams of the cosmos, in which the earth usually appears as a rectangular shape at the center of a spherical or egg-shaped universe, no representations of the whole world survive from Han times. Long-range route finding between remote cultures and distant markets was a practical art of merchants and sailors, of no relevance or esteem to the scholarly, heiratic, and administrative elites that were responsible for map-making. Merchants seem simply to have remembered their routes. Seamen, at most, recorded them in the form of sailing directions.

The Limits of Convergence

The world began shrinking in the second half of the first millennium BC in three main ways. Land trade routes opened communications across Eurasia. Sea travel joined the Mediterranean to Europe's Atlantic shore. Development of monsoon-driven communications began to spread a network of communications around maritime Asia and much of East Africa. Additionally—though this is mainly a story for the next chapter—the beginnings of regular contacts across the Sahara can be dimly detected, between the Mediterranean littoral and emerging civilizations in West Africa. Much of the infrastructure of global history was therefore already laid. Exchanges of ideas and techniques across Eurasia were now possible, and had formative effects on the civilizations that lined the region. But the ties that joined them were still few and fragile. And most of the world—the Americas, the Pacific, Australia, and much of Africa and boreal Asia—remained outside the web. The story of the rest of this book is of how route finders strengthened the existing links and filled in the abiding gaps.

2 Reaching

Exploring the Oceans to About a Thousand Years Ago

So what remains? The ocean that lies dark
Around, and blessed islands. Come, embark.

Horace, Epode 16. 41–2

We are the Pilgrims, master; we shall go
    Always a little further: it may be
Beyond that last blue mountain barred with snow,
    Across that angry or that glimmering sea.

James Elroy Flecker, *The Golden Journey to Samarkand*

WE live in a water world. Water fills over 90 per cent of the biosphere and occupies over three-quarters of the surface of the earth. To put every part of the world in touch with every other part of it, route finding by sea was essential. Along navigable coasts, it was easy. Within relatively small, enclosed or almost enclosed seas it required only a little intrepidity; in monsoonal wind systems, long-range, ocean-crossing voyages became normal at prodigiously early dates.

Big oceans, however, where fixed-wind systems are dominant, cover most of the world. These environments were much harder to cross. Explorers had to crack—like codes—the patterns of their winds and currents, before navigators could establish permanent routes of communication back and forth between opposite shores. For world-changing cultural exchange to unfold, it was essential to develop routes of cultural significance: routes, that is, capable of carrying vital influences between peoples productive in life-changing ideas and techniques.

For most of history, most such peoples lived in a narrow, densely populated band of the world, stretching across Eurasia from Japan, China, and Korea, through south and southwest Asia, to the Mediterranean basin and Europe and, in the New World, in Mesoamerica and the northern and central Andes. Routes that put these regions of Eurasia and the Americas in touch with one another had to cross the widest stretches of the Atlantic and Pacific. They had to await the development of appropriate technology and the emergence, in fifteenth- and sixteenth-century Spain, of explorers with the right kind of culture and spirit—and Spain's unique role in this respect demands to be explained in later chapters. The Arctic, where ice impedes any sort of navigation, had to wait even longer to become an arena of exchange. It is still only beginning to play a full part in global communications, because it is only fully traversable by air or submarine transport.

Nevertheless, in the period around 1,000 years ago, which is the subject of this chapter, explorers took the first steps toward the long-range exploration of transatlantic routes, of causeways far into the high Pacific, and of Arctic avenues of communication. The penetration of the Pacific was the work of native pilots of the South Seas, especially Polynesians. The Arctic navigators were natives of the north Pacific, who worked their way around the north coast of America, colonizing as they went, as far as Greenland. The crossing of the Atlantic was the work of Norse seamen, who, starting from Scandinavia, reached Iceland and Greenland by stages and touched America.

Their stories, which occupy the next few pages, include the story of the last great episode of global divergence. To retrieve those stories from a period from which few written sources survive, we can use the resources of archeology and anthropology, orally transmitted traditions, and the work modern explorers have done in an effort to reconstruct ancient predecessors' routes. While some of the world's sundered peoples reestablished contact, divergence continued, across the last unsettled frontiers of the habitable world, in the Pacific. Here, Polynesian navigations opened up the last habitable parts of the planet and established—beyond reach of regular contact with the outside world, or, in the case of some settlements, any contact at all—some of the most isolated and peculiar cultures in the world. By contrast, the odysseys of the Arctic and Atlantic explorers constitute a phase of remarkable convergence: they met in Greenland. Finally, after telling their stories, we can turn to the Indian Ocean to see how monsoonal routes continued to develop and grow, while the first long-range explorations of the fixed-wind systems were taking place.

The Last Divergence: Polynesian Exploration of the Pacific

The migrations that took humans to Australia, perhaps 50,000 years ago, also took them to New Guinea, the Bismarck Archipelago, and the Solomon Islands. Beyond the Solomons, however, the ocean was largely uninhabited. Much of it seems still to have been without people, for unambiguous evidence of human settlement at the time is extremely rare. Thousands of years elapsed before people from a seafaring culture began to explore the region. They launched their long exploration only in the second millennium BC and for a long time their progress was still tentative and slow.

Where and how did that seafaring culture come into being? The story of the formation of the people who first mastered the Pacific begins—as far as we can tell in the present state of knowledge—in the mid-fourth millennium BC, with ambitious, outward-looking societies in islands off southeast Asia. At about that time, a huge volcanic explosion—one of the biggest human beings have ever witnessed—coated the region in ash. Above the ash layer lie traces of settlements larger than before; tools—especially fishhooks—are superior; traded obsidian blades are common; domestic animals—dogs, chickens, and pigs—are numerous; pottery is abundant. Eventually, from around the middle of the second millennium BC, distinctive round pots appear in the record, intricately patterned by pressing tooth-shaped stamps into the clay. By about that date, people who practiced this culture—Lapita, as archeologists call it—occupied much of the offshore world of southeast Asia, from Taiwan, across the Philippines, to Sulawesi, Halmahera, the Bismarck Archipelago, and surrounding islands. This suggests exploration by island hopping, perhaps from a homeland in Taiwan.

After a hiatus of 200 or 300 years, the pattern resumed toward the end of the millennium, with navigators seeking lands further afield. They skirted New Guinea without establishing settlements—which perhaps suggests that they were deliberately seeking small islands, preferably with few or no inhabitants. In other words, these voyages were—or became—colonial ventures rather than trading missions. By about 1,000 BC the voyagers had spread their way of life across the Solomon Islands to the Reef Islands, Tikopia, Vanuatu, the Loyalty Islands, New Caledonia, and even as far away as Fiji, Samoa, and Tonga. These were extraordinary journeys, ranging over many hundreds of miles of open sea at a time: unprecedented in the earlier island-hopping phase of Lapita expansion, and unparalleled elsewhere in the world at the time.

If you plot the affected islands on a map, the underlying rationale becomes obvious. All these journeys were made directly into the wind, in a part of the Pacific where the southeast trades blow reliably throughout the year. The navigators set their prows against the wind, which tells us something about their nautical technology, for their vessels must have been rigged with maneuverable, triangular sails to cope with the conditions. Occasional reversals of the prevailing wind—which are inevitable in any wind system, however regular—would help them along, without carrying them out of range of return. They then sailed until they found something worth exploiting or ran short of provisions—in which case, they were assured of a rapid return. This is the sort of practice which, surprisingly perhaps, explains one of the great paradoxes of the history of maritime exploration. One might expect great voyages to be made with the wind, and sometimes they are. Normally, however, as we have seen and shall see again repeatedly in the course of this book, except in monsoonal seas, explorers head into the wind, because it is as important for them to find their way home as to discover something new.

Once all the discovered islands were populated, it was possible to maintain contact between them, and to exchange trade items: indeed, goods, especially of obsidian, were traded over the entire 4,500-kilometer stretch of lands occupied by the Lapita culture. So people became habituated to long-range navigation with a following wind. It is understandable, therefore, that they tried varying their course a little to explore the seas north and south of the main trade wind corridor. To the south, there was nothing within an accessible distance. To the north, however, lay the islands of Micronesia.

To judge from the currently available archeological evidence, Micronesia was probably first colonized about 2,000 years ago, not from the relatively nearby Asian mainland but from the southeast, from bases in the Solomon Islands and New Hebrides, or perhaps even from Fiji and Samoa. In its new environment, the culture the newcomers brought changed—relatively suddenly and at vastly different rates on different islands—in a way that awaits explanation. The most precocious island was Pohnpei, at the Carolines' eastern end: closest, in other words, to the place of origin of the settlers and furthest away from southeast Asia, with relatively limited opportunities to experience the modifications of culture that exchanges with alien societies can bring. Pohnpei, moreover, is small—probably incapable of supporting more than 30,000 people—but it was a center of startlingly ambitious activity toward the year AD 1000. Large-scale labor was mobilized to carve out artificial islets with increasingly monumental ceremonial centers for tombs and rites, including turtle sacrifices and the nurture of sacred eels. On nearby Kosrae Island a similar history began soon after. Within a couple of hundred years, cities were arising around paved streets within high walls of massive construction—observed with 'total bewilderment' by a French expedition that came on the city of Lelu by accident in 1824.

What happened in Pohnpei could be treated as a model for the way cultures developed in the Pacific: the further exploration took the colonies from their place of origin, the more freely and widely their cultures diverged.

Beyond Micronesia, in the South Pacific, and beyond the reach of the Lapita people, lay one of the world's most daunting frontiers: an ocean too big to traverse with the technology of the time, where the winds blow almost unremittingly from the southeast, and where vast distances separate exploitable islands. The conquest of this environment was the work mainly of the second half of the first millennium AD. The people who accomplished it were those we now call Polynesians.

Polynesians are easily defined as speakers of closely related languages; it is harder to find a common cultural profile for them in other respects. It is possible, however, using archeological and linguistic evidence, to piece together the way of life they led during the early centuries of their dispersal through the Pacific. They grew taro and yams, supplemented with coconut, breadfruit, and bananas; they kept chickens. They named 150 kinds of fish, and exploited them for tools—files made of sea urchin spines, fishhooks from oyster shells. They consumed kava, a fermented drink made from a plant whose roots have narcotic properties, to induce trances and celebrate rites.[1] Their notions of the sacred cannot be retrieved by archeology but can be inferred from language and later evidence. The world as they understood it was regulated by mana, a supernatural force believed to enliven all things and to make them what they are. The mana of a net, for instance, makes it catch fish; the mana of a herb makes it heal.

The Polynesians' was a frontier culture in origin. It grew up in the central Pacific, probably in the islands of Tonga and Samoa, beginning about 3,000–2,000 years ago, perhaps in the same way as the city-building culture of the Caroline Islands: as a modification of Lapita culture that occurred in consequence of the settlers' remoteness and relative isolation from the lands of their forebears. The chronology of Polynesian expansion is relentlessly debated and deeply uncertain. But the general trajectory of Polynesian civilization—outward and seaborne—is beyond doubt. These people were, from their first emergence in the archeological record, constant voyagers, venturing ever further into the paths of the southeast trade winds, which restricted the range of navigation but which at least promised explorers a good chance of getting home.

Toward the end of the first millennium BC and in widely separated spurts of exploring during the subsequent 1,000 years, there were clearly periods of 'takeoff', from which archeological finds multiply across the ocean, encompassing thousands of islands, as far as Easter Island. The chronology is inexact and intensely contested, because archeologists disagree among themselves about the value of some kinds of evidence. Where direct signifiers of human habitation are unavailable, for instance, what degree of importance should attach to environmental indicators, such as pollen evidence of loss of forest cover, or the presence of rats or snails, which are believed to have accompanied human migrants across the Pacific?[2] In the case of the islands of New Zealand—so large that the chances of finding evidence of the first human habitation are slight—scholars have traditionally relied on the generation counts of indigenous genealogical lore to reckon the date of the first arrivals: this yields solutions between about AD 800 and 1300. The nearest thing to a consensus arises among interpreters of other data—mainly evidence of environmental modification and feats of statistical prestidigitation, including attempts to back-project the date of the first arrivals from later native demographic statistics. These methods, for what they are worth, suggest that the first settlers arrived in about AD 1000.

Why was the period of the Polynesians' confinement so long-lasting in their islands of origin? And why did they break out so suddenly, relatively speaking, to cover so much of the ocean? In the present state of knowledge, which future digs will surely improve, the best attempt at a synthesis of the evidence might be to say that their explorations preceded their colonizations, and that at intervals from the late first millennium BC onward, they must have needed more space, perhaps because of demographic stresses, or maybe because a changing social or religious or legal dynamic drove outcasts and exiles to seek freedom or escape.

Presumably, they built up their picture of the Pacific beyond the wind corridor by edging out, little by little, into regions where the wind pattern was unknown, but from which they could reasonably hope to beat their way back to the trade winds if they got desperate. From the Polynesian heartland, it is obvious that the Cook Islands, Society Islands, Tahiti, and the Tuamotu Islands, as far as Mangareva, all lie on the familiar trajectory, right in the path of vessels heading directly into the wind. The Marquesas, to the north, and the Austral Islands and Rapa, to the south, are a few points off the wind, but are within the range one might suppose to be accessible by adventurous, but not reckless, crews.

Easter Island is a long way further out into the ocean, but lies on a continuation of the straight path from the heartland through the intervening archipelagos. According to the latest data, it must have been settled not later than about AD 400. There is no doubt about the direction the migrants came from. Thor Heyerdahl's canard can be dismissed—the claim that Easter Island was not, in origin or essence, a Polynesian foundation at all but was reached and influenced by native South American navigators in balsa wood rafts. Heyerdahl demonstrated that a voyage from Peru was possible in such craft as the Inca had, and wrote a fine yarn about how he did it; but there is a big gap between possibility and reality.[3] The culture of the island is too saturated in features of obvious Polynesian origin for the thesis to be worth considering. Pukapuka and Phoenix lie well to the north but might have been discovered on returning voyages from the outer discoveries toward the heartland: they are in the path of the trade winds and, indeed, were common landmarks for European shipping in the Pacific in modern times.

In further phases of expansion, Polynesians colonized northward as far as Hawai'i, by about AD 500, ultimately settling New Zealand and the Chatham Islands, perhaps about 1,000 years ago. These islands are different from the long, intermittent series that stretch into the wind from the Polynesian heartland. Not only are they a long way off the pathways of the trade winds: they actually lie in what, from the point of view of Polynesian seamen, were navigational black holes, where the wind did not lead. New Zealand is easily reached if you approach from the west, with the Roaring Forties, but not from the north, where the Polynesians came from. Hawai'i is so inaccessible that even the European explorers who determinedly scoured the Pacific in the early modern era missed it for over a quarter of a millennium.

To colonize so many islands, many of which seemed dauntingly far apart, was such a surprising achievement that scholars who investigated it long assumed that it must have happened by accident. Historians formerly refused to believe that the ancient Polynesians could have crossed thousands of miles of open sea except by 'drifting' haphazardly as a result of being blown to new lands by freak winds. But those were false assumptions. Computer simulations yield no examples of islands beyond central Polynesia discoverable by aimless drifting. You simply cannot get to Hawai'i, say, or New Zealand that way.

Long-range navigation is part of the logic of life on small islands—a characteristic way of maximizing resources, extending economic opportunities, diversifying the ecosystem. It was the achievement of people inspired by a culture of adventure. That culture was recorded in their many epics about heroic voyages. It was demonstrated by their rites—the cannibal feast, for instance, in honour of a Tongan navigator's homecoming from Fiji, witnessed by an English mariner in 1810. These sea peoples also practiced sea exile, rather as the Vikings did, and, according to their own legends, made long maritime pilgrimages to attend distant rituals. The 'experimental archeologist' Ben Finney attempted reconstructions of voyages from Tahiti to Hawai'i and from Raratonga to Easter Island in the 1970s. He proved they could be done in typical sail-powered canoes of the migration era: of course, he knew where he was going, whereas the first discoverers did not, but his efforts showed that conventional assumptions were false.

We can get some idea of what the Polynesian navigators' world was like, and how they devised and maintained their high-seas technology, by turning to anthropologists' accounts of more recent South Sea island seafaring. Typically, the night before starting work on a new vessel, a canoe builder would lodge his axe in a sacred enclosure to the accompaniment of ritual chants. After a feast of fatted pig, dedicated to the gods, he rose before dawn the following day to cut and assemble the wood, watching all the time for omens. For a long-range voyage, he would build an outrigger or double hull, rigged with claw-shaped sails to keep the mast and rigging light. A paddle at the stern would steer the vessel; or else a 'dagger board' might do the job—a wooden slab, plunged into the sea near the bow, to turn into the wind, or if the helmsman wanted to swing downwind, maneuvered at the stern. For food the sailors took dried fruit and fish, coconuts, and a cooked paste made of breadfruit, kumara, and other vegetable matter. Stowage was limited and long hunger must have been endured on the longest voyages. Water—not much of it—could be carried in gourds, the hollows of bamboo or seaweed skins. A small crew sufficed: two steersmen, a sail man, a bailer, and a spare hand so that workers could take a rest. Most important of all was the navigator, whose years of training enabled him to find his way, without instruments or a fixed star, in the vastness of the Pacific.[4]

Means almost unimaginable to today's sailors kept vessels on course. Polynesian navigators literally felt their way. 'Stop staring at the sail and steer by the feel of the wind on your cheeks' was a traditional navigator's advice, recorded as recently as the 1970s. Some navigators used to lie down on the outrigger to 'feel' the swell at night. According to a European observer, 'the most sensitive balance was a man's testicles.' They could correct for a few degrees' variation in the wind by checking against the long-range swells generated by the trade winds. Although currents cannot be felt, navigators built up prodigious knowledge of them. Caroline Islanders interviewed in modern times knew the currents over an area nearly 2,000 miles broad. Above all, they judged their latitude by the sun and monitored their exact course by the stars. The Caroline Island navigators learned to judge their bearings by observing sixteen groups of guiding stars, whose movements they remembered by means of rhythmic chants. A surviving example likens navigation to 'breadfruit picking', star by star. They could associate stars with particular destinations accurately enough, according to a Spanish visitor of 1774, to find the harbor of their choice at night, where they cast their rough anchors of coral and stone. The Tahitian navigator Tupaia, whom Captain Cook admired, knew of islands in almost all the major archipelagos of the South Pacific. Charts made of reeds mapped the lie of islands and the strength and direction of the swells. Some of these maps, made in the Marshall Islands during the last few hundred years, survive in Western museums.[5]

Traditional stories hint at the range of the voyages and the prowess of the navigators. The most heroic tale is perhaps that of Hui te Rangiora, whose journey from Raratonga in the mid-eighth century took him through bare white rocks that towered above monstrous seas to a place of uninterrupted ice. Some myths ascribe the discovery of New Zealand to the godlike Maui, who baited the giant stingray with his own blood; a less shadowy figure is the indisputably human Kupe, who claimed to be guided from Raratonga, perhaps in the mid-tenth century, by a vision of the supreme god Io. Maybe, however, he just followed the migration of the long-tailed cuckoo. His sailing directions were: 'Let the course be to the right hand of the setting sun, moon or Venus in the second month of the year.'[6]

By about the year 1000, the Polynesians may have got close to the limits of navigation accessible to them with the technology at their disposal. Their dispersal left isolated communities in the remotest places they touched: the Hawai'ian Islands, New Zealand, Easter Island, and the Chatham Islands. For centuries to come the inhabitants of those outposts of humankind had no contact with the rest of the world. Hawai'i lay adrift of the wind; its discovery had been a one-off event, unrepeatable, except by accident, until revolutionary technology brought new kinds of ships to the Pacific in the eighteenth century. Easter Island, New Zealand, and the Chathams were simply too remote to keep in touch with the Polynesian heartlands. They lapsed into utter loneliness, out of reach of the rest of humankind. Even Pitcairn and Henderson Islands, which lie only a few days' sail from Mangareva, became so completely isolated that, when war disrupted their trade with Mangareva about 500 years ago, their inhabitants abandoned them. If Easter Island had remained in touch with other Polynesian societies, it would surely have acquired dogs and pigs: but the island's only livestock were chickens, presumably because that was all the first colonists were able to transport alive. Nor would Easter Island have developed so much distinctive culture had it not been left alone: it was the only Polynesian island to develop writing, and its famous stone statues, though similar to those of the rest of Polynesia, have a style of their own. New Zealand's cultures diverged enormously from those of the rest of Polynesia. The languages are still just about mutually intelligible, but aesthetics, ritual life, and chiefly institutions showed surprisingly little overlap by the time ethnographers began to compare them in the nineteenth century. Hawai'i was more like the rest of the Polynesian world, but had distinctive, peculiarly intensive agriculture and relatively large chiefdoms that eventually coalesced into an archipelago-wide empire. The Chatham Islanders, by contrast, gave up agriculture—the basis of life in every other Polynesian society.

If Polynesian navigation could not keep up contacts within the island world, it was obviously incapable of getting any further. Polynesians were the most intrepid and inventive of premodern seafarers. On the open sea, they created networks embracing routes thousands of miles long that dwarfed anything of the sort that any other society could attain at the time outside monsoonal waters. The islanders' outreach completed the peopling of the world. But it never quite got across the Pacific. Nor could it establish sustainable two-way routes embracing the whole of their area of settlement. Those achievements had to await the more powerful technology of a later age.

The Great Convergence: The Arctic and the Atlantic

Almost at the very moment when the Polynesian effort climaxed, similar heroic feats of exploration revealed new routes in two other oceans that seemed, in their way, equally intractable to the technology of the time: the Atlantic and the Arctic. Even more amazingly, their efforts met.

About 1,000 years ago, a relatively warm spell disturbed established ways of life in Arctic North America. Migrants spread along the southern edge of the Arctic Ocean, following, from west to east, the line of what we now think of as the Northwest Passage. Today we call those migrants the Thule Inuit. Modern scholars chose the name Thule after an archeological site in Greenland, but it seems deeply appropriate: Ultima Thule was the limit of the classical imagination, the land at the end of the West. As we saw, it was Pytheas' ultimate objective in his forays on the ocean.[7]

The Thule people were at home on the sea. They were whale hunters, who made long open-sea journeys in frail craft, towing home the whales they killed. They inflated seal or walrus bladders to make floats on which to mount their harpoons. The bladders were so buoyant that they helped to keep wounded whales from diving to safety. The Nakaciuq, or Bladder Festival, still celebrated annually in southwestern Alaska at about the same time as Christmas, perpetuates some of the rites the Thule celebrated when they prepared the bladders or discarded them after use. The bladders are believed to contain the souls of the creatures they belonged to in life, whom the natives honor as partners in the hunt. After a series of feasts, dances, masquerades, and ritual fumigations, the used bladders are ceremoniously reconsigned to the deep.[8]

The Thule feat seems astonishing. Western technology could never find a way through the North American Arctic ice pack until 1904, when Roald Amundsen managed it with a prodigious modern ice cutter. But this was one of many cases in which technology we think of as 'primitive' was well suited to the environment for which it was devised. The Thule had two types of craft: slim kayaks, piloted by individual hunters on short journeys, and substantial vessels called umiaks for long voyages. The umiak is an impressive craft. In the 1970s, the explorer John Bockstoce acquired one that was some forty years old and close in construction to traditional types. He repaired it with traditional materials: five walrus hides stretched over wooden ribs, lashed with sealskin rope. The thick hides were hard to sew, with needles drawn halfway through to make watertight seams. The result was a vessel capable of holding eight or nine passengers with their baggage, a tent, two stoves, a motor, barrels of 110 gallons' capacity, two large seals, a dozen duck, and a brace of geese.[9]

The Eskimos who taught Bockstoce how to sail his umiak called him Old Blubber because of his willingness to eat anything at need. His determination was as robust as his appetite. By undertaking a reconstruction of the Thule navigation around America, he showed how it was managed. His effort fits the known facts. Though Bockstoce made auxiliary use of an outboard motor, he could see how the early ice navigators coped. With boats that drew only a couple of feet of water, they could hug the shore, and work inside the grounded pack ice, eluding the floes that later clogged the big European ships that tried to explore the Northwest Passage. Their craft were light and easy to lift out of the jaws of closing floes. The crew could come ashore to make camp whenever they liked and use an upturned umiak for shelter. So, bit by bit, they worked their way around America and reached Greenland, probably in the twelfth century.[10]

Meanwhile, Norse colonists had arrived in the same region by means as different as possible by the standards of boreal navigation at the time. While the Thule crossed the Arctic by hugging the coast, the Norse had to make vast open-sea crossings to penetrate and traverse the Atlantic. They built big wooden ships, held together with iron nails and propelled by sails. Bards in Iceland remembered—or claimed to remember—how they did it. According to the bards, all the colonizations of the Norse were heroic products of stormy seas and stormier societies. They ascribed the first sighting of Greenland to a freak wind that drove Gunnbjorn Ulf-Krakason unwontedly far west in the early tenth century. According to the same group of Icelandic traditional

John Bockstoce's expedition with the umiak, poling through the ice and shallows, Russell Inlet, northern Canada, July 1978

stories, Eirik the Red began the colonization of the same island when he was expelled from Iceland for murderous feuding in 982. The New World was supposedly first sighted by a venturer who was trying to follow his father to Greenland and overshot his mark.

In reality, nothing was more natural than that Norse navigation should span the Atlantic. A series of currents and winds curl under the Arctic circle, linking Norway to Newfoundland. The last stage of the crossing, from Greenland to Newfoundland, is a short haul, current-assisted. On the return voyage to Iceland, however, with the prevailing westerlies, long-range navigators had to take the risk of long stretches on the open sea.

The true heroism of the Norse navigators was not of the kind the bards ascribed to them, but simply their willingness to follow the winds and currents: to cross the monster-filled seas depicted in the arts of the time. Again, the peculiar feature of these voyages, compared with most episodes of seaborne exploration, was the fact that they did not limit themselves to voyages made into the wind. The Norse in the Atlantic soared above such inhibitions. As far as we know they found havens and crossed open sea without charts and almost without technical aids. The compass had not yet reached Europe from its region of origin in the Indian Ocean. The only device available was the so-called sun compass—a piece of wood with a pointer sticking out of it. If the navigator was lucky enough to encounter cloudless skies, he could compare

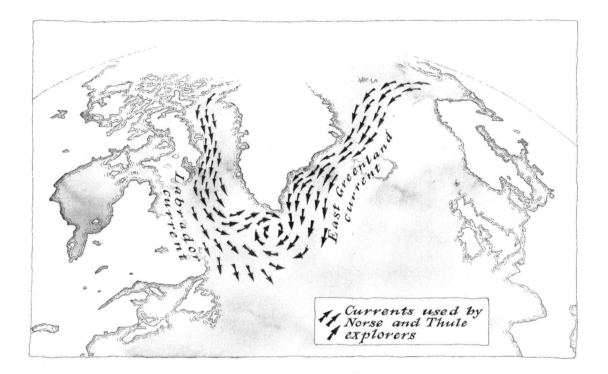

The great convergence, c.AD 1000

the shadow thrown by the pointer at noon on successive days. That would confirm whether he was maintaining his latitude.

To sailors dependent on the compass or electronic pinpointing devices, it seems miraculous that the Norse ever got anywhere with such rudimentary technology. But advanced technology corrupts seamen's powers of observation, in which Norse pilots were deeply practiced. Even without recourse to the sun compass they could make rough judgments of their latitude, relative to a familiar place, by scanning the height of the sun or the Pole Star with the naked eye. When it was cloudy or foggy, of course, all they could do was steer by guesswork until the sky cleared. When they approached land, they read the cloudscape or followed the flight of homing birds, like the legendary discoverers of Iceland in the ninth century, who carried ravens which they released at intervals. Like the Polynesians, and some modern Atlantic fishermen, the settlers who followed Leif Eiriksson to Newfoundland in the early eleventh century may also have used familiar swells to guide them.

Their ships were not the slinky serpent-vessels used by Viking raiders, nor the 'gold-mouthed, splendid beasts of the mast' prized by Norse poets. They were broad, deep craft. Archeologists unearthed a fine example at Skuldelev in 1962. Keel and ribs were of oak. The overlapping planks of the outer shell were of pine, fastened with snugly expanding pegs of lindenwood. Other fixings were by iron rivets, made, perhaps, by the solemn, bearded smith who works with bellows, hammer, and tongs in a twelfth-century carving at Hylestad. Caulkers stuffed the gaps between the planks with animal hair skeins soaked in pine pitch. The central mast had a square sail of coarse woolen cloth, useful mainly with a following wind. When furled, the sail rested on great T-shaped crutches. On some ships there was a small extra sail for maneuverability. For these were sailing ships, not oar-powered. There were just a few oar holes fore and aft for working inshore. Rudderless, the ships steered by means of a pole dangled over the starboard side toward the stern. Lacking a full upper deck for drainage, they required almost constant bailing with wooden buckets. Stores—salt provender, sour milk, beer—lay in open hold amidships, in skins and casks which could not be kept dry. No cooking could be done on board, but the excavated ships all had huge cauldrons for use ashore—a hint of the longings with which sea voyages were endured. As to 'your enquiry what people go to seek in Greenland and why they fare thither through such great perils,' the answer, according to a Norwegian book of 1240, 'is in man's threefold nature. One motive is fame, another curiosity, and a third is lust for gain.' Norse penetration of the Atlantic was part of a long outpouring of settlers from Scandinavia. Between the eighth and twelfth centuries colonists spread as far as the Black Sea and the Caspian—along the valleys of the Volga and Don—across much of the British Isles, into Normandy and, from there, to the Mediterranean, establishing kingdoms and principalities in Ireland, England, Sicily, Novgorod, Kiev, and Antioch.

As far as Iceland, the Atlantic story was, in part, one of island hopping across seas already pioneered by Irish monks, who had colonized the Faeroes in the early eighth century. As one of them reported, 'two days' and nights' sailing with full sails and an undropping fair wind' brought them to where, around the summer solstice, nights were so bright that 'whatever task a man wishes to

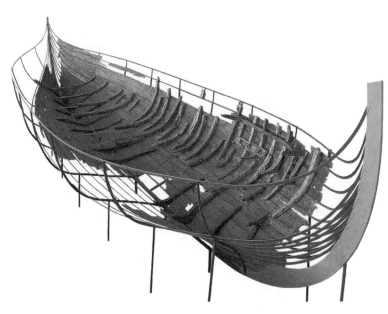

The Skuldelev 1 Viking ship after restoration

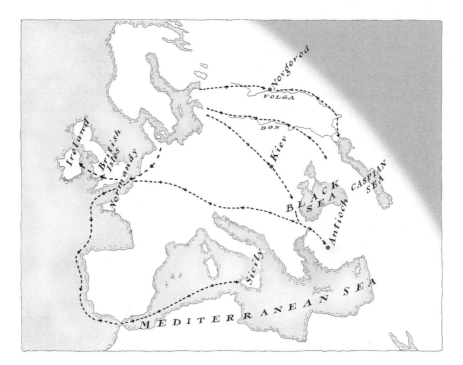

*Norse penetration of
Europe*

perform, even to picking lice out of his shirt, he can manage it precisely as if in broad daylight.' From there 'one day's sailing to the north they found the frozen sea.'[11]

Irish monks went to impressive extremes in self-imposed penitential wanderings or in search of deserts in which to imitate the isolation of John the Baptist and the tempted Christ. They used vessels constructed along the lines of traditional Irish fishermen's curraghs, made with materials characteristic of a pastoral society: ox hide stretched over light frames and waterproofed with fat and butter, rigged with ox hide strips. They hoisted only a single square sail, for they travelled in a spirit of penitential exile, and consciously entrusted themselves to God. Like Abraham, they were bound not for a target destination of their own choosing, but for 'a land that I shall show thee.' 'Is not God the pilot of our little craft?' are the words with which, in a text of the tenth century, an abbot reproaches his crew when they row for shore with excessive zeal. 'Lay off,' the abbot continues, 'since He directs us whither He wills.'[12] Because they were willing to abandon themselves to wind and current, the monks were inherently more likely to go further and find more than more purposeful navigators.

Of course, they were also more likely to come to grief or get stranded without hope of return. It seems amazing that their craft could endure the high seas of the North Atlantic, but the indefatigable explorer Tim Severin tried a reconstruction in the 1980s and reached Newfoundland from Ireland without mishap.[13] It seems possible, at least, that some of the early turf dwellings that archeology has revealed on Greenland and even on Newfoundland were the work of Irish hermits. Construction methods and materials were common to both the Norse and Irish traditions.

The *Navigatio Sancti Brandani Abbatis*, a hagiographical work which survives in scores of versions from the tenth century onward, and which probably goes back to a sixth-century prototype, purports to tell the story of the sea wanderings of a group of monks in search of the earthly paradise, or 'promised land of the saints.' It is evidently a fable. It mixes Irish traditions of the land of the fairies with commonplaces from Christian ascetic literature. Brendan meets Judas in his place of torment; he lands on a whale, which he mistakes for an island; he encounters pillars of fire, cloud, and ice; he expels demons, escapes monsters, converses with fallen angels in the form of birds, and ascends by penitential stages to the state of grace in which the earthly paradise is revealed to him. Some of the details reveal the imagination of the writer: an island of sheep fatter than oxen suggests a monkish fantasy of mardi gras. But, at the same time, the *Navigatio* describes the sea in terms that reveal the influence of real accounts, related from direct experience. The discovery of an island inhabited by a solitary hermit was an episode such as might really have happened on the rovings of Irish monks. The text includes a passable description of an iceberg. At the close of the work, the mysterious, rather angelic guide who joins Brendan on his journey alludes explicitly to an explorer's agenda and entrusts Brendan with proofs of his discoveries, while also striking a mystical note.

> He then said to St Brendan: 'This is the land you have sought for so long; but you could not find it at first, because God wished to show you His divers secrets in the vast ocean. Return therefore to the land of your birth, taking with you as much of the fruits of the land and of its gems as your boat can carry; for the days of your pilgrimage are drawing near, when you shall rest among your ancestors. After many years, in truth, this land will be displayed to those who come after you, when persecution shall befall Christians. The great river you see here divides this island. As it appears to you now, teeming with ripe fruits, so does it ever remain, undarkened by night, for its light is Christ.'
> . . . Then indeed St Brendan accepted fruits of the land, and all kinds of precious stones, and having received the blessing of this young man and of the guide, embarked with his brethren and began to sail back through the midst of darkness.[14]

Brendan directly inspired later voyages from Europe into the Atlantic. 'St Brendan's Isle' appeared on many charts and atlases of the fourteenth and fifteenth centuries. Bristolian navigators, to whose activities we shall return in the next chapter, actively sought it in the 1480s. Columbus alluded to the legend on his own last transatlantic voyage.[15] Atlantic cloudscapes, which often give a false impression of land at hand, reinforced the myth. In the sixteenth century, a chronicle of the conquest of the island appeared. Although St Brendan's Isle did not exist, the navigations of Irish anchorites really happened. Whether or not they crossed the Atlantic, they certainly got as far as Iceland, and in the 790s they began to establish monasteries there.

The Norse followed the Irish, at first with malign intent. The monks on the Faeroes seem to have been exterminated in the early ninth century, leaving, according to an Irish report, isles full of sheep. The Norse replaced them. What happened next would be predictable to any student of the history of colonization. Each frontier generates colonists for the next. By the 860s settlers from Norway and the Faroes were sharing Iceland with the monks and, relatively quickly, displacing them. Irish priority seems acknowledged in one of the early Norse names for Iceland, 'the Isle of Irishmen'; but Norse tradition, asserting priority, claims that the name was bestowed in token of escaped Irish slaves whom the colonists massacred. By 930, 400 Norse families—according to the earliest surviving accounts—had divided the island between them, bringing many more Irish slaves with them. Iceland, indeed, was more or less a Norse–Irish condominium: there were so many Irish mixed, mainly as slaves and concubines, among the settlers.

The discovery of Iceland is told in many mutually contradictory sagas, but that of Greenland is the subject of a single tradition, which is, therefore, perhaps, somewhat more likely to be reliable. Eirik the Red was a man of wrath, expelled from Norway for manslaughter and then from Iceland for the same offense. He therefore set out to find the land Gunnbjorn Ulf-Krakason had sighted when storm-driven westward some years before. He spent the three years of his banishment exploring the coast and planning the colonization. Back in Iceland he gathered twenty-five ships' full of settlers, of which fourteen arrived in Greenland to lay the foundations of a colony that endured for some four and a half centuries.

For island-hopping navigators, Newfoundland is easy to reach from Greenland: a short hop, sped by a favorable current. In the sagas, the story of the first crossing is riven with inconsistencies, but can be synthesized, for what it is worth. In 987 a visiting Norwegian, Bjarni Herjólfsson, attempted to sail from Greenland by a route unknown to any of his crew, got lost, and sighted a previously unknown land. After an interval of fifteen years, Leif Eiriksson, son of Eirik the Red, followed up Bjarni's find and sailed down a long coast, to parts of which he gave the names of Helluland, Markland, and Vinland. The saga's description of the last is compatible in every way with northern Newfoundland. A colonizing mission followed under Thorfinn Karlsefni, a trader inspired by Leif's story, but ran afoul of the hideous natives, whom the Norse called the Skraelingar. The settlement had to be abandoned, at an unknown date early in the eleventh century.

Did the Norse get any further? When I was a visiting professor at the University of Minnesota I found it amusing that the local football team was called the Vikings. But I soon found that to many citizens of the state, it was no joke. In the nineteenth century, the state of Minnesota was heavily settled by Scandinavians. To this day, some communities eat lutefisk for Thanksgiving. Pride in a supposed Norse heritage is, for many denizens, validation of a proud identity. Claims that runic inscriptions dotted around the state prove the presence of the Norse in Minnesota are legion on web sites and in other venues where the like-minded gather to confirm each other's prejudices. The presumption is that the Norse pursued their navigation from Greenland upriver along the St Lawrence, eluding the rapids and waterfalls by porterage, and then sailed across the Great Lakes. Even more embarrassing elaborations of the same tradition have them pursuing their way along the fledgling Mississippi deep into the American interior. Meanwhile, other legends have them striving beyond Newfoundland, along the Atlantic coast, to New England and even further south. The Vinland Map—a treasure of Yale University Library and, purportedly, a medieval record of Norse knowledge of the world—shows Vinland punctuated by two great inlets, which have been read variously as allusions to the St Lawrence and just about every other substantial body of water from the Hudson via the Chesapeake to the Caribbean.

There is no evidence for any of these speculations. The alleged runes of Minnesota are manifest forgeries. So, probably—albeit less manifestly so—is the Vinland Map, not only or principally because scientific tests cast doubt on the antiquity of its ink, but chiefly because it resembles in style and drafts-manship no other map of its presumed era: it just does not look convincing to anyone who knows the context. The 'experts' who validated it when it first came to light—suspiciously enough, in a commercial transaction with no convincing provenance—were, like so many experts in similar circum-stances, misled by momentary intoxication, then locked into self-interested partisanship.

This does not mean that the true history of the Norse navigations and colonizations is historically insignificant. When they started, the colonies in Iceland and Greenland were the only oceanic destinations for trade from any part of Europe. They retained that status until the development of the Canaries and the Azores in the fourteenth and fifteenth centuries. The Norse experience, moreover, demonstrated facts of enormous significance for the future of the world. To come from behind was no disadvantage in the medieval space race, and a place on the margins of civilization was a good spot from which to start. For the success of commercial and imperial initiatives, motivation was more important than technical prowess. Poverty could be a source of compulsion, wealth of complacency. When global exploration was eventually launched from European bases, it was again peripheral and poor communities, in Spain, Portugal, and the Netherlands that led the way. In every case, an appropriate social system and scale of values counted for more than the ample means available to Asian powers.

The *Indian* *Ocean:* *Extending* *and* *Developing* *the* *Monsoonal* *Routes*

As we have seen, the Indian Ocean was already an arena of long-range exchange in antiquity. There was plenty of scope, however, for explorers to enhance and extend the traditional routes. As wealth accumulated around the ocean, commercial voyages multiplied. The evidence is mainly archeological: trade goods from either end of the Indian Ocean world turning up at the other; but such documents as survive corroborate the picture. Much of the long-distance trade originated in India. Indian merchants, already familiar with the Persian Gulf and the Red Sea, extended activities eastward. A story of the fifth century AD seems to belong to a tradition of geographical curiosity unparalleled elsewhere at the time. The story is of a ship blown to a mountain called Srikunja. 'Hearing the account as related by the ship's captain, the prince Manohara noted down on a wooden board the details of the particular sea, direction and place. With this information the prince ordered a ship manned by an experienced captain and went in search of the spot. Borne by a favourable wind, he reached his desired destination.'[16] What did Manohara's wooden board show? If it was a nautical chart, it was, by several centuries, the world's earliest reference. More likely, these were sailing directions of a kind well known at the time in other cultures and generally preferred by seamen.

Southeast Asia, where Indian and Chinese commerce met, became a cradle of heroic navigation. Sumatran states were sending embassies to China in the mid-fifth century[17] though the link was never very secure. The wrecks of Sumatran ships as old as from the seventh century, lash-lugged without nails, have been found on the Chinese coast. The last embassy recorded from Srivijaya, the best-documented Sumatran state of the time, reached China in 742.

By then, the most ambitious seafarers seem to have been concentrated on the neighboring island of Java. In 767 Chinese forces drove Javanese invaders from the Gulf of Tonkin. In 774 Javanese ravaged the south coast of Annam. Cham inscriptions from what is now southern Vietnam shudder over 'men born in foreign lands, living on a diet even more horrible than human corpses, frightening, very black and thin, and dangerous as death, who came in boats.' More inscriptions, from 778 onward, record invasions by 'armies of Java who landed in boats.' A tenth-century Arabic compilation of merchants' tales of the Indian Ocean records a Javanese expedition to Cambodia to replace a truculent king with a compliant vassal. It is not unusual for great trading and imperial peoples to start as pirates. The Vikings were doing much the same thing at much the same time. Later, the Venetians, Genoese, English, and Dutch would be among the founding peoples of seafaring and commercial empires who started as pirates. Borobudur, the great temple built in southwest Java by kings of the Sailendra dynasty in the late eighth and early ninth centuries, is decorated with reliefs of celebrated voyagers. One of the most famous reliefs depicts the voyage of Hiru to his promised land. This faithful minister of the legendary monk–king Rudrayana earned the goodwill of heaven by intervening with the king's wicked son and successor, who proposed, among other iniquities, to bury his father's spiritual counselor alive. Miraculously advised to flee in advance of a sandstorm that would smother the court, Hiru was carried to a happy shore, lined with granaries, peacocks, varied trees, and hospitable inhabitants. In the Borobudur relief, he arrives on a ship equipped with outriggers, with teeming decks, and with raked sails, billowing on two main masts and a bowsprit. The artist had seen such scenes. He knew what every detail of a ship looked like and how it worked. The parallel with the St Brendan story is irresistible. Here, too, the keynotes are fantasy and piety, but here, too, evidence abounds of genuinely increasing knowledge of the sea and of the worlds and possibilities beyond it.

The same sculptor carved another scene nearby, which is even more expressive of the values of a maritime people. It depicts a shipwreck: the crew hauling down the sails, the passengers piling into a tender fitted with its own mast. The episode comes from the story of the virtuous merchant Maitrakanyaka. He was the son of a merchant from Benares who died at sea. His mother sought to protect him from the same fate by pious lies. He tried in turn all the callings his mother claimed his father had followed, making fortunes at each trade and giving them in alms. To get rid of him, business rivals told him the truth.

Taking a brusque leave of his mother, he explored the high seas, encountering lovely asparas wherever he went, until finally he was lashed to a wheel of torture in penalty for his cruelty to his mother. He would be released, his captors told him, only when a successor appeared to relieve him after 66,000 years. But Maitrakanyaka said he would rather endure eternal punishment than allow a fellow creature to endure the same pain—whereupon he was promptly released into Buddhahood. This story surely captures something of the reality of Javanese life at the time: religion allied to commerce, and commerce stimulating exploration.[18]

At a disputed date, not later than the tenth century, an extraordinary episode took Austronesian settlers right across the Indian Ocean from Indonesia to Madagascar and nearby coastal parts of the African mainland. This was a momentous event in the history of the ocean because it represents, for the first time as far as we know, a voyage or voyages outside the range of the monsoonal system. The Waqwaq, as they are usually called, may have used the monsoons for part of their journey, but at some point, in order to reach Madagascar, they must have risked going south beyond the reach of the monsoon, across the path of the prevailing southeast winds, presumably using them to make their westing, but still steering well to the south of the path of the wind. Alternatively, they may have set off from somewhere in the Indonesian archipelago and, skirting the monsoonal zone to the south, used the southeast trade winds to get across the ocean. If so, this was a remarkable achievement, because it was made with a following wind—something formerly ventured, as far as we know, only in monsoonal seas, where the explorers could be sure of eventually finding a homebound wind. But why the migrants undertook such a long and risky journey, with no hope of return, remains a mystery. Descendants of these Waqwaq navigators still inhabit Madagascar, which still speaks a language of obvious Austronesian origins.

As far as we know from surviving examples, the geographical knowledge accumulated as a result of the development of Indian Ocean routes was still not getting registered on maps. There was evidently a disjuncture between practical navigators' real knowledge of the world and the sacred images that continued to dominate the way the learned imagined the planet and represented the globe. Apart from a text an Indian geographer wrote in imitation of Chinese world-descriptions in about AD 900, there was nothing in India that resembled the academic geography of Islam, Christendom, and China. Chinese world maps only began to show the Indian Ocean in any detail in the thirteenth century. Java was to have something of a golden age of nautical chart making in the late fifteenth and early sixteenth centuries—but we only know about it from Portuguese reports and it may indeed have started in response to

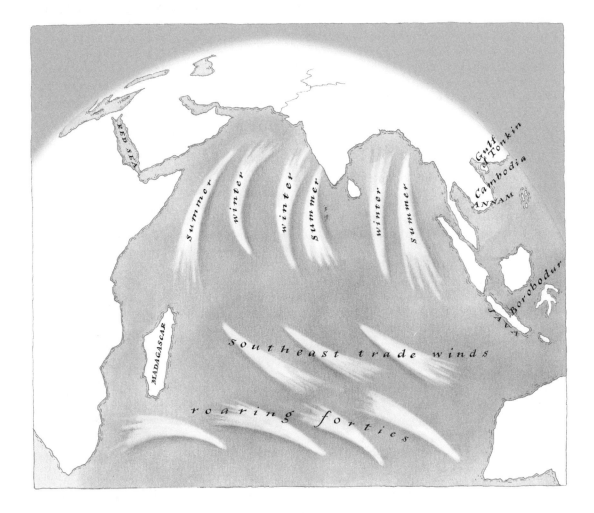

European demand: locals and initiates from within the Indian Ocean world did not need charts: they knew their way around.

The Indian Ocean showing monsoonal systems

Islam made an enormous difference, for three reasons. First, the scope of the Arab conquests of the seventh and eighth centuries united a great swathe of territory, facilitating every kind of exchange and enhancing the opportunities for trade. Secondly, Muslim geographers had access to the learning of classical Greek and Roman antiquity, and to that of Persia and India. Finally, as Islam spread, so did pilgrim traffic to Mecca. The opportunities to find new routes and make money out of them had never been so abundant.

Some geography was informed by real experience. The ninth-century geographer al-Ya'qubi, for instance, was an indefatigable traveler, whose itineraries of Islam and neighboring lands, including those of the Byzantine empire, are not simply compiled from earlier works but owe something, at least, to his own input. Early in the following century, al-Maʿsudi supplemented his academic works with an account, now lost, of journeys he made in person, ranging from the Mediterranean to the Caspian Sea. Some of his speculations now seem comically ill informed. He thought, for instance, that a northern passage around Asia's Arctic shore must link the Pacific to the Black Sea. But real evidence inspired this theory: Arab ship's timbers the writer had seen washed up on a Cretan shore. Later in the tenth century the Syrian al-Muqaddasi emerged as the leading geographer of the Muslim world. His survey proceeded in detail from Syria to Khurasan, listing in order great cities, provincial capitals, towns, and villages.[19]

Meanwhile, the initiative in Indian Ocean navigation passed to Muslim merchants, both Arab and Persian. Within 100 years or so of Muhammad's death, Muslim ships were frequent callers at ports in India, especially at Daybul, near the mouth of the Indus, and on the Malabar coast, where the great pepper emporiums were concentrated. In the ninth century, the Muslim trading network came to include China. Stories of Sulayman the merchant, purportedly from the middle of that century, include references to China. Arabic sailing directions of that time include data for destinations as distant as Korea.[20] When rebels sacked Canton in 878, thousands of Muslims were said to be among the victims. Al-Maʿsudi heard of Arab, Persian, and Chinese trade meeting in the Malay Peninsula. He reported Muslim merchant communities, thousands strong, settled on the west coast of India.

Buzurg ibn Shahriyar, who was the son of a Persian sea captain and therefore well informed of the sea lore of his day, compiled some of the best stories of Indian Ocean navigation. The most remarkable concerns Abhara, the renowned seafarer of the age, who, starting from his homeland in the Persian Gulf, and went to China and back seven times in an era when to survive two such voyages was unusual. On one occasion, an Arab merchant ship bound for China spotted him afloat alone in a small boat in the Gulf of Tonkin. Guessing that his ship had come to grief in that storm-tossed, rock-strewn sea, the crew invited him aboard. Abhara refused. They asked again. He refused again. They besought him to save himself in their company. He refused, except on the condition that they made him their captain, obeyed him instantly and unquestioningly, and agreed to recompense him with the unprecedented salary of 1,000 dinars. 'Your situation,' he warned them, without explaining why, 'is worse than mine.' They were thrown into consternation, but reasoned among themselves that it would be worth a great price to have advantage of the presence of the greatest seaman of the age in such a dangerous sea, and that if Abhara felt able to demand such exigent terms, he must know something to their advantage. So they submitted and took him aboard. He immediately ordered the ships to be stripped of all but the barest essentials of rigging and anchors, and insisted that all but the most valuable cargo should be thrown overboard. True to their bargain, but seething inwardly, the crew obeyed. No sooner had they carried out Abhara's orders than the telltale sign of a typhoon appeared: a cloud 'no bigger than a man's hand.' Thanks to Abhara's precautions, they survived the storm, reached China, and returned with a handsome profit. The story so far is not implausible. But now comes a Munchausen touch—an exaggeration that smacks of fantasy. On the way home, as they passed through the Gulf of Tonkin, Abhara steered them to the very rocks on which their discarded anchors washed up.[21]

Although it is impossible to reconstruct the stages by which new routes emerged within monsoonal seas, some of the stages and some of the context are apparent. The volume of direct traffic between the Arabian Sea and China was substantial in the eighth century: there were, already by that time, large Muslim merchant communities in China's major ports. Increasingly that direct traffic went straight across the ocean via the Maldives, instead of sticking to the slow, coastal cabotage routes between established emporia.[22]

Abhara and his contemporaries took, typically, seventy days to cross the breadth of the ocean from the Persian Gulf to Palembang in Sumatra; the journey could be shortened by departure earlier in the season, but this was rarely advisable for trading missions. It was handier for diplomats and pilgrims because it imposed a longer turnaround time for the voyage; merchants would be left for longer in their host ports, waiting for the wind to turn. Once in Sumatra, another forty days would suffice to get to China.

Gradually, the ocean became a sort of Muslim Lake: at least, the region within the range of the monsoons as far east as Indonesia became bound by Muslim-ruled and often Muslim-populated coasts, and dominated by Muslim shipping. In the fourteenth century, the greatest travel writer of his day—of all time, some say—traveled around the region. Ibn Battuta found Islam deficient in some of the places he visited. He was shocked by the bare breasts of the women in Mogadishu and the loose morals he found in the Maldives, where his knowledge of the shariah made him sought after as a judge. But everywhere as far as Java he found coreligionists to welcome him.

About 100 years later, the consummate pilot Ahmad ibn Majid synthesized centuries of oral and written traditions about these seas. The earliest sailing directions he cited were of the early twelfth century, and incorporated data from texts a century older. But most of the information was garnered in recent times by professionals, of whom his own father and grandfather, who were pilots before him, were paramount. Tirelessly self-congratulatory, ibn Majid ascribed a good deal of exploration to himself. In the Red Sea, he verified

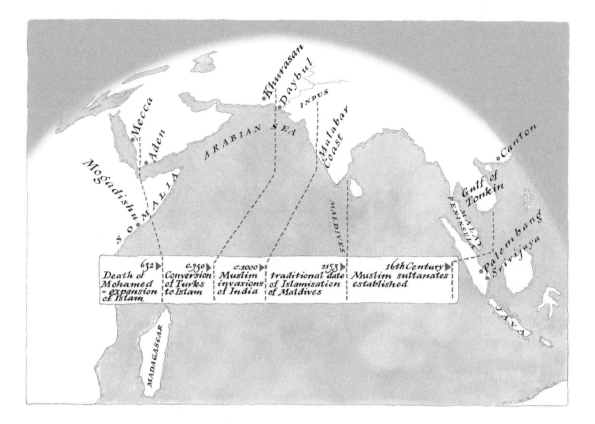

632 ▶
Death of
Mohamed
- expansion
of Islam

c.950 ▶
Conversion
of Turks
to Islam

c.1000 ▶
Muslim
invasions
of India

1153 ▶
traditional date
of Islamisation
of Maldives

16th Century ▶
Muslim sultanates
established

Islam in the Indian Ocean

conflicting pilots' accounts of recommended routes in person. He was justly proud of 'my unique knowledge' of the Red Sea,[23] where his account of the African coast was entirely drawn from personal observation. His reputation grew to the point where sailors from Aden regarded him as a saint and offered him prayers for their safety when they launched their boats.[24]

To understand why the Indian Ocean was so prolific and so precocious in nurturing navigation, by comparison with other big seas, the best route for our enquiry to take is—paradoxically, perhaps—via Japan. At their utmost extremity, monsoonal routes reached Japan. *The Tale of the Hollow Tree*, a tenth-century Japanese text, tells of a freak journey borne by the wind all the way to Persia. Probably, however, the writer's knowledge of Persia was compiled via intermediate Chinese sources. Really, Japan's home seas were themselves so formidable to navigation that sailors rarely strayed beyond them, except, infrequently, to Korea, China, and Ryukyu. A document of 936 vividly evokes what Japan's home waters were like. In diary form, it tells the story of a journey by sea from Tosa, in Kochi prefecture, southern Shikoku—at the time, the remotest province of the empire—to the Bay of Osaka. On the map the distance seems short but in its day this was an immense journey—a crossing from a far frontier, a link between the capital and a distant island outpost. The author is identified as the wife of a returning governor. 'Diaries are things written by men, I am told,' she says. 'Nevertheless, I am writing one, to see what a woman can do.' Scholars routinely challenge the author's self-description on the grounds that the work cannot really be by a woman. Some of the humor—there is an episode where the wind gets up the lady's skirt—is said to be indecorous in a woman's work; male prejudice tends to assign the text, which is wonderfully well written, to male authorship. Nevertheless, women were among the most distinguished writers of Japan a couple of generations later, and the Tosa diary has the ring of truth. The excitement of being caught up in a fine piece of writing can blind a reader to the difference between factual narration and literary artifice, but even the embellishments in this work convincingly reflect genuine experience, though one may suspect that not all the incidents can have happened quite as they are recounted.

Although the route was familiar to the voyagers, the text captures something of the spirit in which Japanese sailors, over a period of many centuries, gradually groped their way around their own shores, building up their picture of the outlines of Japan. The pages of the diary are full of the fear of the sea. At the journey's beginning, amid farewells 'that lasted all day and into the night,' the travelers prayed 'for a calm and peaceful crossing' and performed rites of propitiation of the sea gods, tossing charms and rich gifts into the water. After seven days' sailing, adverse winds delayed them at Ominato, where they waited for nine days, composing poems and yearning decorously for the capital. On the next leg, they rowed ominously out of the comforting sight of the shore, 'further and further out to sea. At every stroke, the watchers slip into the distance.' As fear mounts and the mountains and sea grow dark, the pilot and boatmen sing to rouse their spirits. At Muroto, bad weather brings another five days' delay. When at last they set out with 'oars piercing the moon', a sudden dark cloud alarms the pilot. 'It will blow. I'm turning back.' A dramatic double reversal of mood follows: a day dawns brightly and 'the master anxiously scans the seas. Pirates? Terror! . . . All of us have grown white-haired. Tell us, Lord of the Islands, which is whiter: the surf on the rocks or the snow on our heads?'

The pirates are eluded by a variety of techniques: prayers are intoned 'to gods and buddhas.' More paper charms are cast overboard in the direction of the danger, while 'as the offerings drift' the prayer goes up: 'Vouchsafe the vessel speed.' Finally the crew resort to rowing by night—an expedient so dangerous that only a much greater danger can have driven them to it. They skim the dreaded whirlpool of Awa, off Naruto, with more prayers. A few days into the third month of the journey, a persistent wind frustrates them.

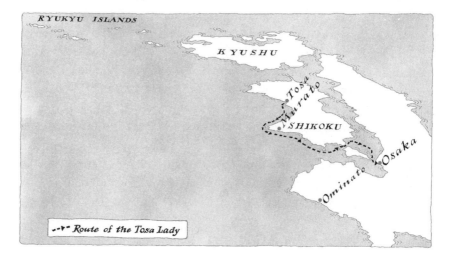

RYUKYU ISLANDS

KYUSHU

Tosa
Mwrato

SHIKOKU

Osaka

Ominato

--▸- *Route of the Tosa Lady*

Japan, showing the Tosa lady's route

'There is something on board the god of Sumiyoshi wants,' the pilot mutters darkly. They try paper charms without success. Finally, the master sacrifices his precious mirror to the waves, and the journey resumes. They reach Osaka the following day. 'There are many things which we cannot forget and which give us pain,' concludes the writer, 'but I cannot write them all down.'

The journal form makes it possible to be precise about the length of the voyage. It began on the twenty-second day of the twelfth moon and ended on the sixth day of the third moon of the new year. For a journey which cannot greatly have exceeded 400 miles, the expedition therefore appears to have spent sixty-nine days at sea or in intermediate harbors waiting for a favorable wind. There are all sorts of reasons why this may have been an exceptionally slow journey. The dignity of the travellers, perhaps, demanded a safe and stately pace. Reluctance to travel at night may have been greater, in this company, than normal. The presumably large galley may have been compelled to keep inshore, so as to have ready access to supplies and fresh water, at the sacrifice of open-sea short cuts. But even if taken as a maximum duration, sixty-nine days seems dauntingly long. Alternatively, the diarist may have stretched the timescale for dramatic effect, to distribute incidents effectively throughout the narrative. Even so, the order of magnitude must have been reasonable, or the work would have lost realistic impact.[25]

The Tosa diary shows the difficulties of navigation in Japan's home seas and, by contrast, points up the advantages of the Indian Ocean. In consequence of those advantages, some of the great world-changing exchanges of history took place across and around the Indian Ocean during the period of the development of its internal routes: transmissions of Hinduism, Buddhism, and Islam to

southeast Asia; the shipping of pilgrims—those agents of cultural exchange—
to Mecca; the transformation of the ocean, in what we think of as the late
Middle Ages, into an Islamic lake; the seaborne trade of east Asia with Africa
and the Middle East, and, in part, the westward transfer of Chinese technology.
The amount of traffic the Indian Ocean carried was incomparably higher than
that of other early maritime highway systems, such as the Mediterranean, the
Baltic, the Caribbean, the Bight of Benin, and the coastal waters of Atlantic
Europe and Pacific Japan. Before we turn to the stories of how the Atlantic and
Pacific came to surpass it, we have to catch up with what was happening
meanwhile worldwide, as far as we know, in landward exploration.

3 Stirring

Landward Explorations in Late Antiquity and the Middle Ages

'O where are you going?' said reader to rider,
'That valley is fatal when furnaces burn,
Yonder's the midden whose odours will madden,
That gap is the grave where the tall return.'

              W. H. Auden, 'O Where Are You Going?'

Away! For we are ready to a man!
Our camels sniff the evening and are glad.
Lead on, O master of the Caravan:
Lead on the merchant princes of Baghdad.

    ·   ·   ·

We travel not for trafficking alone:
By hotter winds our fiery hearts are fanned.
For lust of knowing what should not be known
We make the Golden Journey to Samarkand

James Elroy Flecker, *The Golden Journey to Samarkand*

TOWARD the turn of the last millennium—in, say, the three centuries or so before the year 1000—the oceanic routes of the Norse, Thule, and Polynesians were the big new achievements in exploration. But there are important, if less conspicuous, stories to be told about land routes in the same period. Just as the existing routes within the Indian Ocean were developed and extended, with little trace in the records but enormous effects in the world, so were the land routes by which dispersed cultures were connected. At the same time, especially in parts of Eurasia, exploration multiplied the internal routes that meshed particular states and civilizations together, connecting and extending their frontiers, bringing formerly isolated communities into their networks of command and exchange.

These are processes hard to reconstruct with the sources available to us. New or developing routes from this period tend to be documented, in surviving materials, relatively late in the day, by people who made use of them when they were already well established—merchants, pilgrims, mapmakers, missionaries, diplomats, bureaucrats, warriors, wandering scholars, and curious travelers—rather than by explorers who pioneered or improved them. Sometimes, geographers—numerous in Islam from the ninth century onward, and not unknown in Christendom, India, and China—questioned route finders and recorded their results, in a sort of dialogue of reader and rider. With the help of such records as we have, we can sketch the development of some new routes, or, at least, of routes previously undocumented, beginning in Asia, before turning to trans-Eurasian, African, and American routes. The picture cannot be complete, and it covers the planet only patchily, but it does disclose some of the emerging long-range highways of the world, which later became threads in a global network of routes: the 'roads' that radiated from China and connected the ends of Eurasia; the great arteries of commerce and cultural exchange in Africa across the Sahara and along East Africa's Rift Valley; the routes along which key crops and customs spread outward in the Americas from 'cradles' of civilization in Mesoamerica and the northern and central Andes. As with earlier forms of cultural exchange, trade is an inescapable part of the story: it strew the routes explorers pioneered with the only evidence we have of their efforts.

Extending the Silk Roads

In what Westerners call the Middle Ages, caravans bound from China to India seem almost always to have followed a tortuously long route, pursuing the Silk Roads deep into central Asia, before turning south and east again to enter India across the Hindu Kush. This laborious approach could, in theory, have been shortened by a route via Tibet, where, after all, many caravans were bound as their final destination; but the dearth of passes out of that country to the south perhaps explains the relative neglect of that route. Alternatively, the obvious, straight, short approach to India led southwest, across Szechuan and Yunnan. This Southern Silk Road, as scholars now call it, was, however, extremely slow to develop.[1]

Szechuan was hardly part of China until the eleventh century. It was, to Chinese observers, a 'country of streams and grottoes'—a name which sounds romantic in English but which filled Confucians with abhorrence. Ou-yang Hsiu, a bureaucrat who was unusually susceptible to the romance of the frontier, described it:

> Purple bamboo and blue forests rise to shroud the sun.
> Green shrubs and red oranges glow out of autumn's face
> Like make-up. The paths are steep everywhere. Men bend under heavy loads.
> Living beside rivers, the natives are strong swimmers.
> New Year's fish and salt markets throb at morning.
> Drums and flutes at unauthorised shrines play all holiday long.
> Under heavy rains, cliffs cascade into the river.[2]

This was China's Wild West, a colonial frontier awaiting exploitation and sinification. The tribal chief who ruled the forests of bamboo and fir had a magical or demonic reputation, comparable to that of the British demons who, in Anglo-Saxon imaginations, haunted the East Anglian fens. The Chinese classified the tribes as 'raw' or 'cooked' according to their levels of imputed savagery. A chief known as the Demon Master led the wildest—the Black Bone Yi. In 1014 the most successful of a series of campaigns reduced the tribes to something like docility. Meanwhile, administrative reforms divided the province into 'routes,' along which the government distributed land in gigantic parcels: this was a rare case of the promotion of aristocratic-led settlement by the Chinese state, at variance with the mandarins' usual preference for centralization and bureaucratic control. Settlers from China began to modify the landscape: the effect on the empire was as transforming, in its way, as the colonization of Sinkiang and Tibet has been for the China of our own day. For Szechuan, the outcome was even more dramatic. The 'forbidden hills' became denuded of forests. In 1036 the Demon Master became an official of the state. Salt mines were the 'springs of avarice' that inspired the Song state to appropriate the province; tea and mulberry plantations were secondary economic attractions.[3]

Szechuan remained a frontier region for half a millennium. Beyond lay Yunnan, a land of silver, enticing but even harder to explore. The tropical climate was hostile. There was no nerve center of authority for the Chinese to seize or control, no security for settlers. Chinese armies scythed through the region in the late thirteenth century, and the tribespeople gradually became habituated to paying tribute to China and thinking of themselves as subjects of the empire; but it took centuries more for the region to be integrated. Beyond Yunnan, Burma was always an obstacle on the southern route to India: an intractable land, of which China never succeeded in conquering more than the edges, and through which caravans could normally travel only by purchasing security at prohibitive prices.

Because of these problems, the Southern Silk Road remained under-frequented—a route mainly in potential—between China and India throughout the Middle Ages. It was impassable when the Buddhist explorer Fa Hsien set out from Ch'ang-an in AD 399. His was the first—or the first recorded—of a great series of journeys to India by Chinese monks, impelled by piety to visit Buddhist shrines, inspired by scholarship to seek pure texts of Buddhist scriptures. The Chinese monks who made such pilgrimages presumably followed routes pioneered by Buddhist missionaries from India, of whom we know little in detail, but who were active in China from the time of the arrival of the monk Kumarajiva, translator of Buddhist scriptures into Chinese, in the late fourth or early fifth century.

By then a network of monasteries was beginning to mark the route, housing travelers and attracting benefactions. The cave paintings of Dunhuang depict the life of the roads, the piety of the merchants, and even, in some cases, the faces and families they left behind. They reveal the monastery as a great crossroads of the world, where the cultures of Eurasia met—the place where, according to Chinese sayings, 'nomads and Chinese communicate,' at the 'throat of Asia,' where the roads 'to the western ocean' converged 'like veins in the neck.' The holes in the cliff face were places of repose for travelers across thousands of miles, linking China, India, central Asia, and what we call the Near East. The roads that converged there fed into other systems of communications, which reached Japan and Europe and crossed the Indian Ocean to southeast Asia, maritime Arabia, and East Africa.[4]

The road to Dunhuang lay across the Gobi, between military way stations at irregular intervals, where guests could sleep in goatskins and procure fresh horses. Between them, camel dung marked the route and provided the only fuel in an almost brushless waste. 'Show me camel dung,' said one of Owen Lattimore's companions on his Gobi crossing in 1926, when the traditional disciplines and dangers of the road were still largely unchanged, 'and I will go anywhere.'[5] Beyond the Edsin Gol, four days' forced march led across the most desolate stretch. Here Lattimore saw camels' corpses strewn almost end to end, rotting but in the freshest cases still displaying blood boils and blistered pads.

Fa Hsien crossed the Gobi under the shadow of the Kunlun Mountains, but found the road inhibiting, menaced by marauders. The caravan he traveled with therefore plunged deep into the Takla Makan desert for safety—but paid a heavy price in misery, enduring what the monk called 'unparalleled

Eighth-century bandits holding up merchants on the Silk Road. Desert routes offered the best—but not inviolable—security

sufferings' in 'the desert of evil demons and hot winds.'[6] On the edge of the Takla Makan, caravans paused for a week's refreshment and stocked up with a month's provisions. The normal rule was: the bigger the caravan, the safer. But not many more than fifty men at a time, with their beasts, could hope to survive on the modest water sources they might expect to find over the next thirty days: an occasional salt marsh, an unreliable river, as it shifted course among the dunes, or froze over in the cold of a desert night. The worst danger was getting lost, 'lured from the path by demon-spirits,'

> and even by daylight men hear these spirit voices and often you fancy you are listening to the strains of many instruments, especially drums, and the clash of arms. For this reason bands of travellers make a point of keeping very close together. Before they go to sleep they set up a sign pointing in the direction in which they have to travel. And round the necks of all the beasts they fasten little bells, so that by listening to the sound they may prevent them straying off the path.[7]

A fourteenth-century painter imagined the demons as black, athletic, and ruthless, waving the dismembered limbs of horses. The Mongols recommended smearing your horse's neck with blood as a way of warding them off.

Sandstorms were, guides claimed, a demon's device for the disorientation of travelers. The sky would go suddenly dark. Dust veiled the air. The wind hurled up a rattle of pebbles and a clash of sizable rocks, which would collide in mid-air and dash down upon men and beasts.[8]

After the desert came the mountains. The Tianxan, the 'heavenly mountains' screen the Takla Makan to the north: 1,800 miles long, up to 300 miles wide, and rising to 24,000 feet. Few mountains are more formidable. Deep depressions make the region even odder: mentally disturbing as well as physically trying. Turfan, in the midst of the mountains, lies at more than 500 feet below sea level. When Owen Lattimore tried to cross these mountains in 1926, a 'ghoulish' wind forced him back, 'driving snow before it that rasped like sand,' while a thousand camels ground their teeth against the cold 'with a shrieking that goes through one's ears like a nail.'[9]

Faxian emerged at the great trading oasis of Khotan in eastern Turkestan. Already this was more than an emporium—a manufacturing center famed for rugs, silks, and jade work. Then, astride the way to India, more mountains had to be faced, 'where snow rests winter and summer and where dragons spit wind.' Faxian descended east of the Hindu Kush to Peshawar in what is now Pakistan. At last, at Jetavana monastery, he arrived at the first object of his journey and paused to reflect. He then descended the Ganges valley, turning aside frequently to make touristic side trips and visits to monasteries, before taking ship for home in the Bay of Bengal. He sailed via Sri Lanka, where he heard of demon traders who had once inhabited the island.

Faxian was genuinely a trailblazer. In the late seventh century the monk Yijing, who made his own pilgrimage to India in 671, recorded fifty-six subsequent journeys of broadly the same character by Buddhist monks in search of enlightenment. Many followed in Faxian's footsteps, along the Silk Roads. Others went via Tibet and Nepal.

The most detailed surviving account is of the journey of Xuanzang, who, in 629, began sixteen years of travel 'not for riches or for worldly profit or fame but only for the sake of religious truth.' He was an exile, an escapee from the political turbulence of his times, who, according to his disciples, foresaw the fall of the Sui dynasty in 618. Inspired from youth to 'spread the light of Buddhism,' he consciously followed the 'noble example' of Faxian 'for the guidance and profit of the people.' A dream of scaling Meru, the sacred mountain at the center of Buddhists' mental map of the world, impelled him on his path. His prospective guide warned him, 'The western routes are bad and dangerous. At times streams of drift sand obstruct, at others demons and burning winds. No one who encounters them can escape. Often big caravans

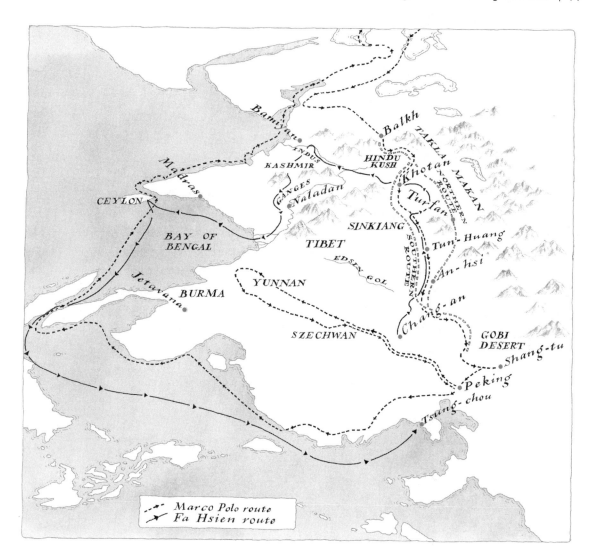

Silk Roads

lose themselves and perish.' Undeterred, the pilgrim set off and continued alone when his guide deserted him. The Gobi desert tortured him with problems of direction finding in a trackless environment:

> Alone and abandoned he traversed the sandy waste, with no means of finding his way except by following the heaps of bones and the piles of horse-dung. . . . In all four directions the expanse was boundless. No trace was there of man or horse and in the night the demons and goblins raised fire-lights to confound the stars. . . . Reciting passages from the Heart of Wisdom Sutra and praying to the Boddhisattva of Mercy, he came, as if by a miracle, on a grassy area and a pool of water.

Forced to ascend the Tianxan to avoid brigands, the pilgrim suffered from snow blindness but still managed to elude avalanches. He made a detour to Turfan, where the local khan warned him against trying to continue to India: 'I am afraid you will succumb to the heat,' he said. 'The people are like savages. It's not worth going all that way to see them.' Fortified, however, by the conviction that 'it is better to die in the attempt to go to the west than to live by returning to the east,' Xuanzang pressed on over the Tien Shan into an area where he felt at home among a plethora of Buddhist communities.

At Balkh there were 100 monasteries and over 3,300 monks. At Bamiyan, Xuanzang saw the famous Buddha '140 or 150 feet high, of a brilliant gold colour,' carved from the rock—the statue the Taliban blew up in 2002. Crossing the Hindu Kush into India, he spent two years in spiritual preparation in Kashmir before following the course of the Ganges from monastery to monastery. He spent the years from 633 to 637 at Nalanda in Bihar, making excursions by elephant to Buddhist holy sites, before following the east coast of the subcontinent as far as Madras. When his hosts heard he wanted to depart, 'India,' they said, 'is the place of Buddha's birth. What greater happiness can you have than spending the rest of your life visiting the holy sites? Moreover, China is a land of barbarians and so the Buddhas are never born there.' Xuanzang replied, 'Just because Buddha did not go to China does not mean that it is an insignificant kingdom.' Rather than return by ship, he crossed India, ascended the Indus, and retraced much of his own outward journey on his way home, bearing 150 particles of Buddha's flesh, six statues, and 657 volumes of sacred scriptures on twenty horses.[10]

The text of Xuanzang's journey recalls the accounts of journeys in the Jatakas or the *Navigatio Brandani*:[11] it hallows long-range travel, which becomes an analogue of the soul's journey toward perfection. The demands of piety, the edifying encounters with buddhas and teachers, the intrusions of miracles, and attestations of the power of prayer can make readers forget that this is the story of a real journey, and evidence of the development of one of the world's great highways of cultural exchange. Xuanzang behaved as a missionary as well as a pilgrim, and the text includes accounts of conversions to Buddhism, especially of Zoroastrians and, on one occasion, of a whole town of Hindus. The writer dwells on his hero's championship of the Mahayana tradition, his resistance to temptations, and the kings who try to turn him aside with offers of power. But he mixes mundane details with sacred topography: climate, whereabouts of mines, observations of elephants of unusual color.

The Mongol Effect

Subsequently, the biggest development in the history of the Silk Roads was not the multiplication of routes but the increase in security that accompanied the rise of the Mongol empire in the thirteenth century. The 'Pax Mongolica' united the great corridor of communications across Asia, from the frontiers of Europe to China, under a single authority. As Mongols themselves put it, the unity of the sky was echoed on earth. The first stage in the process was the unification of steppeland peoples into a single confederacy under Genghis Khan, between his elevation to supreme rule among the Mongols in 1206 and his death a little over twenty years later.

Changzhun, a Taoist sage, experienced the effect on the Silk Road when Genghis Khan summoned him to his presence in 1219. 'To cross a river,' the khan explained, 'we make boats and rudders. Likewise we invite sage men and choose assistants for keeping the empire in good order.' Changzhun professed himself 'ready at the first call of the Dragon Court.' At the age of 70, after 'long years in the caverns of the rocks' as a recluse, he began the arduous three-year journey from his home at Laizhou on China's coast, on what is now the Shandong peninsula, to meet the khan at the foot of the Hindu Kush.

An eyewitness described Changzhun: he sat with the rigidity of a corpse, stood with the swiftness of a tree, moved swift as lightning, and walked like a whirlwind.[12] His reputation for sanctity was such that, according to the disciple who has left us an account of the journey, even brigands withdrew when they heard his name. 'The Master,' an admirer who knew him wrote, was 'setting out to cover thousands of miles of most difficult country, through regions never mapped, across deserts unwatered by rain or dew.'

Early in March 1221, Changzhun's party left China, traveling north from Peking toward the Khingan Mountains, where 'China—its customs and climate—suddenly come to an end,' before heading west into Mongolia. In some ways, he was a fastidious traveler. He would not travel with recruits for the imperial harem or venture into a land without vegetables—by which he meant the steppe. But he crossed the Gobi, climbed 'mountains of huge cold,' and braved wildernesses where his escort followed the usual Mongol practice, daubing their horses' necks with blood as demon-repellent. Taoist monasteries eased his route.

Changzhun's disciple's account of the route shows the sensitivity to landscape that came easily to Taoists, whose reverence for nature made them excellent observers. He notes wild garlic and willows on the banks of the Kerulen, pine-clad mountains, the trail of wild onion and sweet-scented grasses that led along the Uliassutai River, and the aubergines of Samarkand, 'shaped like monstrous fingers and deep purple in color.' He reports tales of demons and goblins 'on which the master made no comment.' The party reached Samarkand in December 1221, finding, to their surprise, Chinese gardeners tending some of the best plots of land.

When Changzhun finally met the khan in May 1222, the anticlimax was painful. Despite all Genghis Khan's asseverations about his love of wisdom and need of learning, his first question to the sage was 'What medicine of immortality have you brought me?' and the nearest they got to a meeting of minds was in a discussion about the propriety of hunting—and they disagreed even on that. When he returned to China, Changzhun found a letter from the emperor, which perfectly expressed the ways in which Mongol power policed and promoted the use of the routes:

> Holy adept, between the spring and summer you performed no easy journey. I wish to know whether you were properly supplied with provisions and remounts. At Hsuan-te and the other places where you lately stayed, did the officials make satisfactory provision for your board and lodging? Have your appeals to the common people resulted in their coming over to you? I am always thinking of you and I hope you will not forget me.[13]

With added security came added range. As a result of the Mongol Peace, it became relatively easy to cross the whole of Eurasia from Europe to China. Merchants and missionaries took advantage and became common participants in the traffic of the Silk Roads. Marco Polo is the best witness of the abiding rigors of the route, as well as one of the most influential travel writers of all time. By his own account, he left his native Venice to travel the Silk Roads as a boy in 1271–4, in the company of his father and uncle, who were already experienced China hands. Seventeen years' service in the imperial court and provincial administration made no impact on China, but left Marco with impressions that dazzled Europe when he confided them on his return. According to the book in which they were recorded, he dictated his recollections to a fellow prisoner after capture in an incident of war at sea between Venice and Genoa. Like most travel writing, for which they became a model and pattern, Marco's pages were full of fantasy and sensationalism, but they also contain an enormous amount of evocative and broadly reliable description.

'They were hard put to it to complete the journey in three and a half years,' Marco Polo reported of his own party's experience of the Silk Road, 'because of snow and rain and flooded rivers and violent storms in the countries through which they had to pass, and because they could not ride so well in winter as in summer.'[14] Robbers, official extortions, and bureaucratic delays combined to slow caravans down. The authenticity of the travelogue ascribed to Marco has often been doubted, on the grounds that Chinese sources make no mention of him and because his observations of China seem capriciously selective. But Chinese sources normally slight contemptible barbarians. And we should beware of an argument *ex silentio*. The fact that Marco does not mention something does not mean that he never saw it or heard about it. Tea, for instance, may have seemed too commonplace to record for someone who had become used to the Chinese way of life; the Great Wall was probably, in his day, in a state of disrepair, and its importance would have been much diminished under the Mongol empire, which straddled it. In any case, these reflections miss the point: Marco Polo was a sort of male Scheherazade, whose job—to judge from the data he collected for his book—was to entertain the supreme khan with interesting titbits illustrative of the extent and diversity of his Chinese dominions.

At almost the same time as Marco Polo arrived in China from Europe, the traveler we know as the monk Rabban Bar Sauma set off on a comparable journey—unique, as far as we can now tell—in the opposite direction, westward from Peking. Bar Sauma was a subject of the Chinese emperor, and called himself a Tatar or Mongol. Like all his family, he was Christian and, more exactly, Nestorian—a believer, that is, in the doctrine that Christ's human and divine natures were divided between human and divine persons. It was not unusual at the time to be a Chinese Nestorian, especially among Chinese of central Asian origin. Indeed, in central Asia and China, Nestorianism throve in the late Middle Ages, when persecution and mainstream contempt had eliminated it in Europe. Nestorian monasteries, as well as Buddhist foundations, studded the Silk Roads. Chinese culture clearly influenced Bar Sauma's clan, as their communications with him include references to concern about their ancestors and the continuation of the family line. He had a personal history of spiritual restlessness, abjuring his marriage and defying his parents in order to espouse the monastic life, withdrawing for a time into solitude.

When Bar Sauma set out from China, probably in or around 1276, his motive was to make a pilgrimage to Jerusalem in company with a Turkish fellow monk named Markos: again, there were plenty of Nestorian Turks, although Christianity had never become a majority taste. Pilgrimage was clearly not a traditional form of piety practiced in their monastery, if we judge by Bar Sauma's account of the efforts their fellow monks made to dissuade them. But, driven by Markos's ambition to see the Holy Land, they persisted. Along the Silk Road, they could be sure of finding sympathetic Nestorian monasteries in which to lodge.[15]

They took the southern route, under the Kunlun Mountains, and took two months to reach Khotan from the Nestorian monastery at Ning-Hsia, where they prepared for the desert crossing. Early sources—though not Bar Sauma's own account or any official Chinese records—claim that the mission was encouraged and partly financed by Kublai Khan. This would be consistent with Kublai's general policy of showing favor to religious minorities.

By the time they reached Persia, they had been captured and then released by enemies, tortured by desert and mountain crossings, and lost all their belongings—whether to brigandage or disaster Bar Sauma's surviving account does not say. When they got to Persia, they met the patriarch of Nestorianism at Maragha in what is now Azerbaijan. At the time, it was a center of learning unsurpassed in the world. Its library contained 400,000 books. Its observatory, newly created, was a showpiece of astronomical technology and a meeting place of scholars: a way station for westward-bound Oriental wisdom.

The patriarch prophesied that Bar Sauma would complete his journey, then did his best to stop him by persuading the traveler to enter his service. On the patriarch's death, Bar Sauma's traveling companion was elected to succeed him. Eventually, in 1286, Bar Sauma was able to resume his travels—but not to Jerusalem, at least not at first. The ruler of Persia commissioned him to visit Christian courts in Europe in the hope of making an alliance against Egypt. The message he bore ran: 'the king of the Mongols, who is joined in the bond of friendship with the Catholicus'—that is, the Nestorian patriarch—'hath the desire to take Palestine, and the countries of Syria, and he demandeth from you help in order to take Jerusalem.'[16] Two Italian merchants returning from China accompanied him as interpreters.

Bar Sauma's probable route took him overland to Trebizond, where he embarked for Constantinople, arriving early in 1287. He contemplated the relics with piety and the huge churches with awe: he had never before been in a country where Christianity was the majority religion and that of the state. He saw Mount Etna erupt on 18 June and a battle between rival dynasts in Naples on 24 June on his way to Rome. 'Meanwhile Rabban Sauma and his companions sat upon the roof of the mission in which they lived, and they admired the way in which the Franks waged war, for they attacked none of the people except those who were actually combatants.'[17] When he arrived, a papal election was under way and no business could be completed. The cardinals seemed more interested in discussing Bar Sauma's profession of faith than in the proposed alliance. So he traveled on to Paris, where he admired the university, and Bordeaux, where he gave communion to the king of England. From the new pope, Nicholas V, he received the same sacrament on Palm Sunday 1288. Before returning to Persia, he affixed his seal, along with fellow clergy, to some indulgences at Veroli, with the inscription 'Barbazoma, Tartarus Orientalis.' He devoted his remaining years, until his death in 1294, mainly to building a church to house the relics he had acquired on his travels.

Bar Sauma did not succeed in forming an alliance. His journey showed how Eurasia at the time, though bridged by the roads the Mongols policed, was still divided by chasms of culture. He had to use Persian to try to communicate with his hosts in Christendom and it is evident that a lot of what he and they said to each other was lost in translation. He mistook diplomatic demurrals for substantive assent, and expressions of Christian fellowship for doctrinal agreement. Nevertheless, the fact that he completed the journey at the same time that Marco Polo and other Westerners were doing so in the opposite direction demonstrates the efficacy of the Mongol peace in making Eurasia traversable. Indeed, Bar Sauma's text—tattered and torn as it is—remains the most startling evidence of the mutual accessibility of the extremities of the land mass. It is hard to resist the conclusion that the revolutionary experiences of Western civilization at the time—the technical progress, the innovations in art, the readjustment of notions of reality through a new kind of science—were owed in part to influences exerted along the Silk Roads and steppeland routes.

After that, the Silk Road became routine: a 'road safe by day and night.' The *Libro dell pratticatura*, a guidebook of the 1340s, gave Italian merchants handy hints. 'You must let your beard grow and not shave.' At Tana, on the Sea of Azov, you should hire a good guide, regardless of expense. 'And if the merchant likes to take a woman with him from Tana, he can do so.' On departure from Tana, only twenty-five days' supplies of flour and salt fish were needed—'other things you will find in sufficiency, especially meat.' It was important to take a close relative with you; otherwise in the event of the merchant's death his property would be forfeit. The guide specified rates of exchange for each stop and suitable conveyances for each stage: ox cart or horse-drawn wagon to Astrakhan, depending on how fast you wanted to go and how much you wanted to pay; camel or mule train thereafter until you reached the river system of China. Silver, the guidebook advised, was the currency of the road but had to be exchanged for paper money with the Chinese authorities on arrival.[18]

Crossing the Steppeland

The most extraordinary thing about the Silk Roads is that they should have existed at all. Eurasia is united by the steppeland causeways that stretch almost across its length. There are few obstacles. Pasture is abundant. Water is available for most of the way. Anyone interested in traveling between Europe and Asia

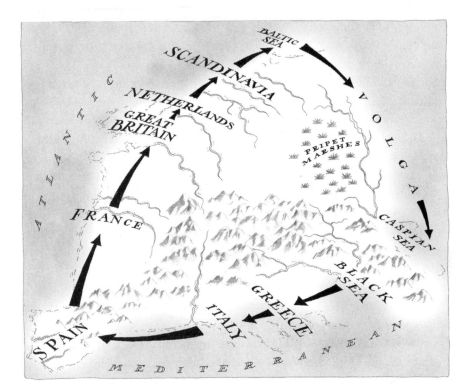

Schematic Europe

Europe is a rough triangle, bounded by three cause-ways of historic exchange: the Mediterranean, the Atlantic narrows, and the Volga. Breakwaters of mountains and marsh separate them. From one point of view, European history has been the story of the integration of these three zones, and the development of communications between them

would—other considerations being equal—find it far easier to take the steppe-land route than to endure deserts and climb mountains. Even for caravans bound for India, since the southern road was normally closed, and travelers from China were in any case condemned to cross much of Asia and approach India from the west, it would make sense to head north of the Tianxan: the journey would be even longer, but, in terms of topography, much easier.

For most of the past, however, the steppeland road was unavailable. The steppe was the abode of pastoralists, who saw commerce rather differently from their sedentary neighbors. As they lacked goods for exchange, they treated caravans as objects of loot or opportunities for tolls and ransoms. Usually, their domain was divided between hostile and warring groupings, in conditions unpropitious for travelers and, at best, likely to be expensive for merchants. The virtue of the Silk Roads arose precisely from the fact that they eluded the steppelanders. Deserts were relatively secure precisely because they were scantily populated. The Tianxan was tolerable to travelers precisely because it was hostile to the people of the plains and their horseborne raiding parties. Of course, even on the Silk Roads security was imperfect. Nomad raiders were a common hazard. Zhang Qian[19] was captured by war parties from China's steppeland adversaries, the Xiongnu, both on his outward and on his return journeys. But the difference between the Silk Roads and the steppes was obvious: it was the difference between acceptable risk and inevitable disaster.

In the thirteenth century all that changed. The Mongols burst out of their heartlands, screened from China by the Altai mountains. As a fourteenth-century bishop of Peking proudly boasted, 'before the days of the Mongols nobody believed that the earth was habitable beyond these mountains . . . but the Mongols crossed them, by God's permission, and with wonderful exertion. . . . And so did I.'[20] The empire of Genghis Khan brought peace to the steppeland and made it traversable. The envoy John of Piano Carpini left the first account of a journey over the steppeland under Mongol protection. Teams of Mongol horses took his self-confessedly portly bulk 3,000 miles across it in 106 days in 1246. He met the Mongols about three weeks' ride beyond Kiev and was entertained at a camp on the Volga, just south of Saratov. From there on he encountered Mongol way stations, on average, every 30 miles, as he skimmed the Caspian and Aral Seas to the north and followed the south bank of Lake Balkhash, until finally they crossed the Altai mountains and reached the supreme khan's court near Karakoram.

From a diplomatic point of view, the mission was disastrous. John returned horrified by the Mongols' arrogance, savagery, and willingness to bend the world to their dominion. 'Therefore,' he concluded, 'if Christians want to save themselves,' they should 'send men to fight against the Tatars before they begin to spread over the world.'[21] The Mongols were the most outlandish, conceptually challenging people European ethnography had ever encountered—the most disturbing discovery to appear before Western eyes, as the world known to Westerners dilated. They were not quite in the category of 'similitudines hominis' or monsters with which medieval cartography scattered the edges of Asia: dog-headed men, Sciapodes, and 'men whose heads do grow beneath their shoulders.' But they were hard to assimilate into the known categories—the panorama of humankind that biblical and classical authority spread before the learned. They were variously classified as a scourge of God, a punishment for sin, demons and beasts. According to sometimes conflicting accounts, they were bestial in their habits, barked like dogs, and had flat faces like monkeys. They ate raw flesh and drank blood: that at least was true, as steppelanders, who had no vegetables, needed to feed on fresh blood and organ meats to get the dose of amino acids that are essential to health.

They were even accused of cannibalism. It was a false charge. Chinese, Tibetan, Armenian, and Georgian sources also evince abomination of the Mongols but do not accuse them of this particular form of excess. Mongol laws do not forbid it—presumably because there was no need to.[22] The accusations are not the fruit of observing but of reading, thinking, and fearing. Cannibalism was one of the features of the savagery classical writers ascribed to northern barbarians. More significantly, it was part of a range of activities deemed by medieval received wisdom to be contrary to natural law. This was important, because those who offended against natural law were deprived of its protection and therefore were fitting objects of war and enslavement.

Nonetheless, Western courts persisted in trying to come to some sort of understanding with the Mongols. Envoys were exchanged. Missionaries followed, continuing to use the steppeland route— as well as the Silk Roads and, occasionally, the sea route across the Indian Ocean—to reach the Mongol heartland and even China. The most detailed observations of the steppe route were those of Friar William of Rubruck, who took his leave of the king of France in the spring of 1253, bound on a mission he saw as purely spiritual but which, from the king's point of view, had diplomatic and intelligence-gathering potential. William crossed the Black Sea and in May set off from Tana to cross the steppe aboard a wagon. 'After three days,' he recorded, 'we found the Mongols and I really felt as if I were entering another world.' By November, he had reached Kenkek, 'famished, thirsty, frozen and exhausted.' In December, he was high in the dreaded Altai Shan, where he chanted the creed 'among dreadful crags, to put the demons to flight.' At last, on Palm Sunday 1254, he entered the Mongol capital, Karakoram—a magnet, as William saw, for craftsmen from all over Eurasia, including a Parisian goldsmith and monks from all over Asia.[23]

William of Rubruck and his fellow friar taking their leave of Louis IX and (below) on their journey

Thanks to the development of trans-Eurasian routes, cultural influences from China had a dynamic effect on European thought and technology. Gunpowder arrived in Europe in the thirteenth century, the blast furnace in the fourteenth. The revival of empirical science in the West coincided with this period of open communications—which raises the suspicion that this, too, was a result of the pollination of Western thinking by Chinese, and particularly Taoist, traditions of observing nature. It is hard to imagine the great discovery of the beauties of nature in the West at the time—which we associate especially with St Francis of Assisi—without cross-fertilization with Chinese civilization, which already had a conspicuous record in the appreciation of landscape.

Internal Explorations: The Examples of Japan and Europe

Exploration, however, does not only happen outward: there are often inward crevices and gaps to fill, slack to take up. The case of Japan is one of the best documented in the period under review, because, at the same time as an imperially inspired program of surveying got under way to map the territory, the state was being bureaucratized along Chinese lines and archives were fairly well organized. The earliest survey was ordered in about 645; if, however, maps of that date were actually made, none has survived. The earliest Japanese maps still extant are eighth-century estate maps, which survive in large numbers and which demonstrate the precocity and accuracy of Japanese surveying at the time. Efforts of Buddhist missionaries supplemented those of the state. Gyogi (*c.*688–749), a missionary who traveled the length and breadth of the country, made maps as he went, building or inspiring the building of roads, bridges, and canals.[24]

The empire at the time occupied only central and southern Honshu, Kyushu, and Shikoku. Early maps show how slow the Japanese were even to explore their own islands. The northern part of Honshu appears sketchily and inaccurately. This was still beyond the reach of Japanese power—the domain of the native Ainu, who were only gradually forced back. Hokkaido was hardly known. To the south lay a 'land of demons' who ate shipwrecked sailors. The only sea routes that were thoroughly well known were those to Korea, China, and the Ryukyu Islands.

Japan's was not the only state or civilization of the time to promote internal exploration. In 971 a project for surveying imperial China began: by the early eleventh century it had grown to 1,566 chapters. Early in the twelfth century, one of the most famous maps of China was engraved on stone: the stunningly accurate Map of the Tracks of Yu the Great.[25] The Arab and Persian geographers encountered in the last chapter were engaged on a similar project of coordinating data on the dar al-Islam, as well as locating Islam in the context of world geography. But it was perhaps in Latin Christendom that the task of accumulating knowledge was most closely allied to internal exploration: this, after all, was a region still underdeveloped by comparison with China and Islam. Neighboring communities had more to learn of each other; routes of communication needed to be lengthened and meshed together.

From the eleventh to the early fourteenth centuries, while the horizons of Latin Christendom broadened, a process of internal expansion was also under

way. Population grew. New resources were exploited, while new technologies enhanced the productivity of old ones. New lands were cultivated, sometimes with new crops, or turned from wilderness to pasture. Forests fell. Bogs were drained. Settlement encroached on marginal soils and headed uphill. New kinds of economic activity became possible in growing towns. Church and state grasped communities formerly isolated by forest, marsh, or mountain—Europe's inner barbarians, whose evangelization, before this period, was sometimes sketchy and whose habitats were often blanks on the map.

A map of Japan in the tradition of the wandering surveyor, the monk Gyogi, dated 1305, showing provinces (listed in the text on p. 87) and routes. South is at the top

Human mobility accelerated and developed in range. Long-range travel was still a rare experience, confined to pilgrims and those, such as merchants, warriors, scholars, and churchmen, with some professional interest in it. But the numbers in those categories grew. New trade routes linked Atlantic and Mediterranean seaboards in a single economy. Naturally, western Europe has two economies—Mediterranean and northern—separated by a strait with widely different sailing conditions along the two seaboards and by a chain of breakwaters, which determines the flow of rivers and therefore the directions of exchange. For much of Europe's history, communication between these two zones was not easy. Limited access through the Toulouse gap, the Rhône corridor, and the Alpine passes kept restricted forms of commerce alive, even in periods when commercial navigation from sea to sea was abandoned. In the thirteenth century, Mediterranean craft, mainly from Genoa, Majorca, and Catalonia, resumed large-scale ventures along Atlantic coasts. German merchants unified the northern seas in a similar way, linking London and Bruges with Lübeck and Riga. Lübeck, founded in 1143, was the pioneer city of what became the Hanseatic League.

Traffic grew and people moved peacefully in increasing numbers—as migrants, merchants, pilgrims, and 'wandering scholars'—along new arteries of what would now be called the infrastructure of Europe: roads and bridges and newly reconnoitered routes. Latin Christendom emerged as a genuinely

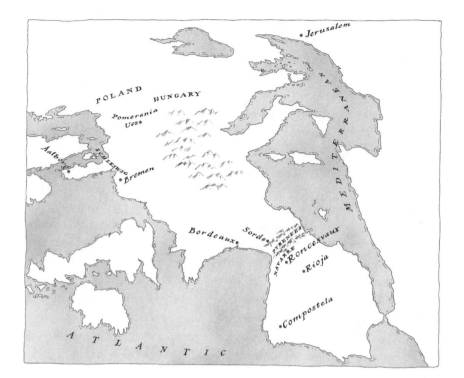

The spread of Latin Christendom

expanding world, as it stretched between increasingly remote horizons. In Christendom, too, pathfinders included pilgrims. Pilgrimage to Jerusalem increased enormously in the late tenth century, partly because of the pacification of the Magyars, which opened a safe land route across Hungary to the frontiers of the Bulgar and Byzantine empires, and partly because the growth of commerce in the eastern Mediterranean made the Holy Land increasingly accessible by sea. But in this direction Christian pilgrims cannot be said to have opened new routes. On the other hand, at about the same time, a new shrine near the western edge of Europe attracted a new sort of trailblazing. The pilgrimage to Compostela was, considered from one point of view, a war against the wilderness. It led to the northwest corner of Spain, the 'Finis Terrae', or end of the earth, one of 'the four corners' of the world—on maps, it really looked and still looks like a corner.

Hermits, stooping to smite the rocks, built roads and bridges for pilgrims' use as works of charity; 'and may their souls,' says the guidebook of the cleric who called himself Aimery Picaud, 'rest in everlasting peace.' Engineering came to the aid of environmental adaptation. Building roads and bridges was an urgent task of public utility, for which monarchs accepted some responsibility and for which, for example, Domingo de la Calzada, who built causeways and bridges for pilgrims to Compostela, was made a saint. Profiteers followed the pioneers. A universal obligation of hospitality rested on those who encountered pilgrims: 'whoever receives them,' according to the same writer, 'receives St James and God himself.' In practice, innkeepers were generally denounced as extortionate ('Judas lives in every one of them,' wrote the author of an exhortation to pilgrimage) or dishonest. Fortunately, however, the roads to Santiago were studded with the hospices of religious orders, whose only charge was alms at the pilgrims' discretion. In the Pyrenees, the Hospice of St Christine was warmly recommended by the guide writer but its main rival, that of Roland at Roncesvaux, issued particularly alluring publicity, promising attendance by 'comely and virtuous women,' who washed feet, combed beards, cut hair, and took 'more care besides than you can say.' These were the pools and shafts of civilization with which the medieval wilderness was lapped and pierced.

A twelfth-century guidebook lists all the hazards. Mosquitoes infest the marshy plain south of Bordeaux, where the pilgrim who strays from the road sinks up to his knees in mud. No food is to be had in this region, and he who would cross it must carry three days' supply. At Sorde, near the foot of the Pyrenees, pilgrims are ferried across the river on hollowed-out tree trunks, in peril of drowning. After a steep, 8-mile climb to a pass through the mountains, they meet extortionists who exact an illegal toll with whips. Spanish food should be avoided by the unaccustomed, 'and if anyone can eat their fish without feeling sick, then he must have a stronger constitution than most us.' By a salt stream on the far side of the mountains, Basque tanners live entirely on the profits of the hides of horses poisoned by the water. In Rioja, the natives pour poison into the streams to increase sales of their wine. Traveling companions, unavoidable on popular routes (the myth of the 'standard route' is a vulgar error), should be chosen with care, as a common ploy of robbers is to attach themselves to the unwary in pilgrim disguise. Wherever the roads pass through uninhabited tracts, professional beggars exploit the pilgrims' obligation to give alms, bloodying their limbs, simulating leprosy, and waving Jericho palms. The sensitive pilgrim—whom the guide writer assumes to be French—may find foreign habits disgusting, especially among the Navarrese. The mountains and forests house misplaced exotics, whose unnatural lusts—sodomy and bestiality—license pornography. When the guide writer describes the Basques, he clearly recognizes them as primitives, alluding to them in terms generally applied to peoples called 'barbarian' and classified by the science of the time as outside the pale of natural law and civilized life:

> Verily they dress filthily and eat and drink filthily . . . If you saw them eating you would think them like dogs and pigs. If you heard them speaking, you would be reminded of the howling of hounds . . . This is a barbarous race, unlike all others in customs and in essence, full of every malice, black in color, evil of visage . . . wild and sylvan . . . Basques even practice incestuous fornication—with cattle. A Basque is even said to fit a chastity belt to his own mare or mule, to prevent anyone else from getting at them.

A mule, declared the guide writer, was as good as a woman for the Basques' perverted purposes. The last sentence of the account is best left in the decent obscurity of a learned language: 'vulvae etiam mulieris atque mulae basia prebet libidinosa.'[26]

Thus neglected peoples were brought into the candle glow of scholarship. Yet alongside the self-indulgence of prejudice, some realistic images of marginal peoples and their societies emerged from genuine ethnographic 'fieldwork.' In the late twelfth century, for instance, the scholarly canon Giraldus Cambrensis, searching for his own Celtic roots in Wales and Ireland, wrote a remarkably sympathetic account of the native peoples of those lands, arguing that their pastoral way of life represented a stage in a universal pattern of human social development.

All over Europe, new settlement and new forms of exploitation converted previously uninhabited or sparsely inhabited environments. In mountain settings, Western civilization spread up slopes formerly unoccupied or abandoned to the domain of hostile highlanders, whom their lowland neighbors despised as barbarians. Meanwhile, other environments were transformed and ecologies disturbed, as the riverbankers of western Europe conquered the wild wood. This was more than an economic enterprise: it was a sacred undertaking—a kind of *reconquista*, reclaiming for God part of the terrain of paganism. The forest was stained with pagan sensuality and alive with sprites, demons, and 'wild men of the woods.' Trees hallowed by unenlightened generations fell to pious axe strokes.

Beyond the Frontiers of Christendom

To cleave paths east and north through the forest was a work of exploration—reconnoitering the routes of missionaries and armies. 'If you measure the distance direct from Schleswig to Aalborg,' reported one campaigner of the eleventh century, 'it is a matter of five to seven days' travel. That is the highway of the Caesar Otto,' who warred this way in 974, 'unto the farthermost sea at Wendila, which sea is to this day called the Ottisand for the king's victory.'[27]

To a historian in Bremen in the late eleventh century Sweden and Norway seemed 'another world . . . until now nearly unknown,' but Svein Estrithson, king of Denmark, who had plenty of experience of war on those fronts, was able to report 'that Norway can hardly be crossed in the course of a month, and Sweden is not easily traversed in two months. "I myself found this out," he said, "when a while ago I fought for twelve years in those regions under King James" ' in the late 1020s and 1030s.[28] A century later, when Bishop Otto of Bamberg set out to bring Christianity to Pomerania, his chaplain, Herbord, described the route:

> After passing the castle of Ucz, which lay on the borders of Poland, we entered the vast and bristling forest that divides Pomerania from Poland. But that way is as hard to follow as to describe: we should have been more likely to perish on it. For this wood had never previously been crossed by mortal men, except by the duke [of Poland] on a mission of plunder prior to the projected subjection of the whole of Pomerania. He sliced a path for himself and his army, marking and lopping trees. We held fast to the marks, but with great difficulty owing to the serpents and wild beasts of many kinds, and the importunities of the storks nesting in the branches of the trees, who vexed us with their screeching and flapping. At the same time the patches of marshy ground mired our carts and wagon, so that they had difficulty crossing the wood within six days and reaching the banks of the river which forms the boundary of Pomerania.[29]

Adam of Bremen in the late eleventh century was the witness or reporter of northward exploration and the geographer of the lands that eastward expansion was adding to the territory of Latin Christendom. It is worth dwelling on his work, because he was, for his day, a uniquely committed geographer with real contacts to explorers. He was the official chronicler of the 'deeds' of the bishops of Bremen, the gateway port into Germany for Scandinavian traffic. Adam served there as a canon of the cathedral, taking an impassioned interest in the progress of the conversion of the peoples to the north of the diocese, where missionaries were route finders. His book therefore became an account of the exploration of the Baltic, North Sea, and North Atlantic, enriched by the data he took down from the many merchants, seamen, and visiting Scandinavian clerics who thronged the port of Bremen.

Among his informants was Svein Estrithson himself, who, as a campaigner against Swedes and Slavs, was both paladin and pioneer. Adam also mentions supplicants who came to the bishop's court from Iceland, Greenland, and the Orkneys.[30] He reports a Baltic island where 'all the houses are full of pagan soothsayers, diviners and necromancers,' frequented by seekers after oracular

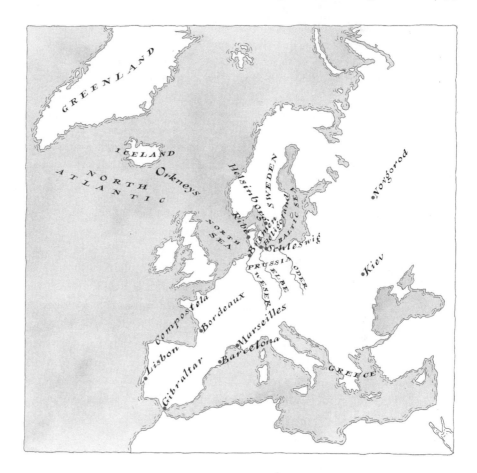

Places named by Adam of Bremen

responses 'from all parts of the world, especially by Spaniards and Greeks.' It is hard to imagine a more vivid expression of the way Europe was meshing together. Adam tells us that from Schleswig you can sail to nearby islands, Slavia, 'or even Greece'. He reports the existence of an overland route from Scandinavia to Greece, 'but the barbarous peoples who live between make this way difficult.' The Baltic 'extends a long way through the Scythian regions even to Greece.'[31]

Conscious exploration is a major theme of Adam's work. Describing the Baltic for instance, and referring to Einhard, the famous ninth-century chronicler of the deeds of Charlemagne, 'What Einhard says about the unexplored length of this gulf,' he observes,

> has lately been proved by the enterprise of the highly spirited men, Ganuz Wolf, a Danish leader, and Harald [Hardrada], the king of the Norwegians.

After exploring the compass of this sea with much toilsome travel and many dangers to their associates, they finally came back, broken and overcome by the redoubled blows of the pirates. But Danes affirm that many have often-times explored the length of this sea. With a favourable wind some have reached Ostrogard in Russia from Denmark in the course of a month. As to its breadth, he asserts that it is 'nowhere more than a hundred miles . . . and in many places much narrower . . . On leaving the bounds of Denmark, the sea stretches wide its arms, which come together a second time in the region of the Goths. The farther one goes, then, the farther do its coastlines spread apart.

In some manuscripts copious sailing directions are added, explaining, for instance, how long it takes to get from the Baltic to Compostela, Lisbon, Gibraltar, Barcelona, and Marseilles. Adam claims that Heligoland was dis-covered and colonized by a converted pirate and that 'all sailors hold the place in awe.' He recommends Helsingborg as the best route to Sweden. He is well informed about the weather and wildlife of the north lands, and describes the midnight sun without sensationalism. He always checks his data against classical authorities, identifying Iceland, for instance, with the Thule of Pytheas, and using Martianus Cappella's assertion of a frozen sea north of Thule to corroborate Svein Estrithson's report that beyond Vinland 'no habitable land is found in that ocean, but every place beyond it is full of impenetrable ice and intense darkness.'

Adam mentions voyages Harald Hardrada made to explore the ocean: the king turned back from 'the darksome bounds of a failing world.' A party of Frisians, Adam records,

> spread sail to the north for the purpose of ranging through the sea, because the inhabitants claimed that by a direct course toward the north from the mouth of the Weser River one meets with no land but only that sea called the Libersee. The partners pledged themselves under oath to look into this novel claim and, with a joyful call to the oarsmen, set out from the Frisian coast.

The account of their adventures with which they returned—a treasure island, giants, monsters—inspire no confidence that they genuinely pursued this purpose very far.[32]

Adam's ethnography is fantastical and mainly concerned with ascribing horrific barbarities to pagans—bloodthirstiness caused by addiction to idolatry, human sacrifices offered to dragons, a preference for murdering rather than enslaving wayfarers. Anthropophagi appear, as do Amazons impregnated by monsters 'who are not rare there.' Cynocephali 'are often seen in Russia as captives and they voice their words in barks.' 'In that territory live many other kinds of monsters whom mariners say they have often seen, although our people think it hardly credible.' This is more than the vestigial remains of folklore and ancient myth. Rather, it is the making of a new myth, of a 'civilizing mission' that justifies conquest by denigrating and demonizing the other. It is part of a program of the abjuration of alterity.

Yet Adam also pursued an uneasily compatible agenda of idealizing the other—in selected instances—in order to berate his fellow Westerners for their bad morals and deficient faith. Confusing—in pardonable ignorance—the Prussians, who lived just beyond the eastern edge of Christendom, with the Sami, or Lapps, who inhabited its northern extremities, he reports that Samland is

> inhabited by the Sembi, or Prussians, a most humane people, who go out to help those who are in peril at sea or who are attacked by pirates. Gold and silver they hold in very slight esteem. They have an abundance of strange furs, the odor of which has inoculated our world with the deadly poison of pride. But these furs they regard, indeed, as dung, to our shame, I believe, for we hanker after a martenskin robe as much as for supreme happiness. They exchange furs for woolen cloth. Many praiseworthy things could be said about these peoples with respect to their morals, if only they had the faith of Christ, whose missionaries they cruelly persecute.

Adam entertained high hopes of the conversion of the Swedes, who 'regard as nothing every means of vainglory; that is, gold, silver, stately chargers, beaver and marten pelts, which make us lose our minds admiring them. Only in their sexual relations with women they know no bounds.' He knew about Greenland and its inhabitants, whom he imagined as 'greenish in hue, from the salt water.'[33]

He also supplied detailed descriptions of the lands beyond the Elbe, which the Romans had never seen but which became familiar to Western warriors and missionaries from the eighth century onward. Adam's knowledge of 'Slavia,' as he called the land beyond the Oder, condensed explorers' reports—at least beyond Poland, knowledge of which he took for granted among his readers, in the vast domains still inhabited by pagans in his day. Tribal names dominate his account, with the names of shrines and cities, and laments about the benightedness of the Slavs' religion. Not until the fifteenth century, when Nicholas of Cusa collected data and recorded it in the form of astonishingly accurate maps, can this region be said to have been fully recorded.

Nicholas's effort was part of a project of his own, bending science to the service of theology. He came to 'believe that man can talk about what he does not know—God and nature—only by talking about what he does know—the world of his own experience and fabrication.'[34] He praised technology with the zeal of a *philosophe* designing plates for the *Encyclopédie*.

> For man alone discovers how to supplement weakness of light with a burning candle, so that he can see, how to aid deficient vision with lenses, and how to correct errors concerning vision with perspectival art. He makes raw food pleasing to the taste by cooking it, he drives out stench with fragrant fumes and he drives out cold with clothes and fire and homes. He helps himself to travel more swiftly with carts and boats, he aids himself in his own defence with weapons, and he helps his own memory with the invention of writing and the art of memory.[35]

Maps, in Nicholas's opinion, illustrate this peculiarly human power to fashion the world and, in a sense, to master it.

> When he has made a comprehensive description of the sensible world in his city, he collects it in a well ordered and proportionally measured map, so that he will not lose it. He turns more towards this map, dismisses the messengers, and transfers his internal view towards the Creator of the world. . . . He thinks Him to relate to the world in an anterior way, as he the cosmographer relates to the map, and from the relation of the map to the true world, the cosmographer speculates within himself like the Creator of the world, by contemplating in his mind the truth of an image, the signified in the sign.[36]

Of Russia, Adam of Bremen recorded nothing except the existence of cities at Novgorod and Kiev. This ignorance is surprising, for, while the Norse were exploring the Atlantic, Scandinavians also went east. The Rus—who were or at least included eastward-exploring Norsemen—made the Volga Europe's longest corridor of trade in the tenth century. How and when they got there is unknown. Headwaters that feed into the Volga are not far from the Baltic. Russian chronicle evidence of much later date makes the mid-ninth century the crucial period, alluding to wars between 'Varangians from beyond the sea' and native Slavs, culminating in 862 in the submission of the latter. Impelled by despair at the disorder among them, according to the Russian Primary Chronicle, the natives 'went overseas to the Varangian Russes' and said, 'Our land is great and rich but there is no order in it. Come to rule and reign over us.' If an event like this really happened, it must have been part of a longer story of penetration of the region by Scandinavian raiders, settlers, and merchants.

Ibn Fadlan, member of an embassy from Baghdad bound for the court of the Volga Bulgars in 922, devoted most of his report of his journey to the months spent among what he called the 'Russiya,' whom he described with revulsion for what seemed to him barbarisms of staggering savagery. When he witnessed a human sacrifice, the horror of it profoundly impressed him. The ceremony took place on a nobleman's pyre, built on a grounded river ship. The slave girl chosen for immolation with her master sang songs of farewell over her last beaker of liquor before ritual copulation with her executioners. An old woman called 'the Angel of Death' then wound a cord round her neck and handed the slack to men standing on either side. Warriors beat their shields to drown the victim's screams. When the cord tightened, the Angel of Death plunged a dagger repeatedly into the girl's breast. Bystanders then lit the pyre and fed it until pyre and ship were consumed to ashes. 'After this, on the spot where the ship had lain when they dragged it from the river, they built something that looked like a round mound. In the middle of it they wrote the name of the dead man and of the king of the Russiya. Then they went their way.'[37] Other sources make clear the basis of Rus activity: the fur trade. Sable and squirrel from the boreal forests were toted downriver to the Caspian and thence to Bokhara and Samarkand, in exchange for Arab silver, Persian glassware, and Chinese silks.

The extension of a network of Rus trading routes along the Volga and across the river's area of drainage marked the beginning of a new era in the history of cultural exchange in Eurasia. Europe resembles an approximate triangle. One side is the Mediterranean—the first great long-range route of exchange, which put all the peoples of Europe's southern shore in touch with one another at the time of the Greek and Phoenician explorations of the early first millennium BC. The southern tip of Spain is the vertex. From there, the Atlantic and North Sea coasts of Europe form the second side of the triangle. As we have seen, maritime communications linked this region, too, in remote antiquity. So, before the rise of the Roman empire, there were two European trading systems, two Europe-wide economies. But they were hard to integrate, divided by a watershed of mountains, from which rivers flowed in opposite directions. The available corridors, especially those along the Rhône and across and around the Alps, were much frequented, but the unification of the two zones into a single system really depended on an arduous task: the development of seaborne communications around the Strait of Gibraltar, where the current races, and across the Bay of Biscay, where storms lurk and thrash. Both the northern and southern sea routes terminated in culs-de-sac: the Baltic in the north and the Black Sea in the south.

But the Volga is Europe's third sea—a great waterway, navigable along virtually the whole of its length, broad and deep enough to carry as much traffic as its region can generate. It does not quite meet the other sides of the triangle: for most of history, a short but grueling portage overland linked the Volga to the Baltic. At its southern end it flows into a landlocked sea, the Caspian. To reach the Mediterranean, Volga valley traffic had to be diverted overland to the Don river system. So the Volga was harder to integrate into Europe's economy than the Mediterranean and the North Sea. Even to this day, the political and economic map of Europe shows how laggard the process has been. Russia, Belarus, Kazakhstan, and Ukraine, successor states of an empire that took shape in the Volga basin in the Middle Ages and the early modern period, remain outside the European Union. Among countries traditionally—albeit not universally—regarded as European, these are the only ones that are not already members or negotiating for admission. As I write, a political struggle is still echoing in Ukraine over whether the country should remain in Russia's economic orbit, or gravitate toward the rest of Europe.

Africa

Africa and the Americas are harder to explore than Eurasia. Africa is surrounded by lee shores that inhibit long-range navigation. Most of the interior is hard to traverse, riven by great deserts and malarial forests. Though some rivers cut deep into the continent, none except the Niger is navigable for much of its length. In most of the continent, the precipitate relief twists and pinches the rivers with cataracts and cuts waterfalls into their courses. There are no causeways across the continent comparable to the Silk Roads and steppelands of Eurasia. The Sahel is a belt of savannah that stretches from the Atlantic to the Nile valley; but no empire ever quite managed to unite it as the Mongols united the grasslands of Asia, and the civilizations of West Africa and Ethiopia seen never to have nourished each other with mutual contacts as did those of the extremities of Eurasia. The Americas present similar obstacles. Forest, mountain, ice, and desert barriers cleave the hemisphere. As far as we know, there was never any direct contact between the civilizations of Mesoamerica and those of the Andean region until Spanish conquistadores put them in mutual touch in the sixteenth century. Long-range navigation seems never to have been practiced beyond the Caribbean and the Gulf of Mexico until the same period.

   Still, it was possible for cultural transmissions, slowly or fitfully, to get around both land masses. Before the beginning of the Christian era, the languages and technology—farming and iron smelting—of West Africa spread through most of the continent south of the Sahara, perhaps by means of migrations, perhaps by the onward passage of influence. No permanent traffic kept those routes alive, but from about the fifth century onward, evidence of key trade routes gradually accumulates, especially along the Rift Valley in East Africa and across the Sahara. The former route is hardly documented, but its effects are obvious:

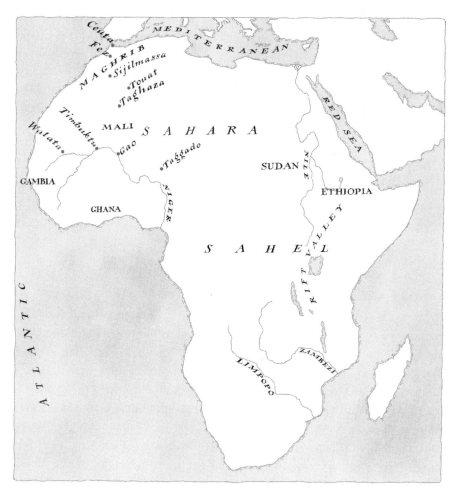

Trading places: the Maghrib and the Sahara in the middle ages

it helped to sustain successive empires in the highlands of Ethiopia, from where the emperors could dominate the traffic in civet, salt, ivory, and gold from the Zambezi and Limpopo valleys, and the plateau between them, as it headed north toward Ethiopia and the Red Sea.

The trans-Saharan routes, by contrast, inspired much literature, because of the fascination the gold they brought stirred in the Maghrib and the Mediterranean. In the mid-ninth century the Egyptian geographer Ibn 'Abd al-Hakam collected the earliest traditions about Arab exploration of the region. As the armies of conquest penetrated the Sahara in the 660s they asked at each place they overran, 'Does anyone live beyond you?' and kept going until positive answers petered out. An expedition to the 'land of the blacks' 'attained success the like of which has never been seen and got as much gold as [they] wanted.'[38]

A few years later, the work of al-Yaʾqubi includes circumstantial details—the names of kings and settlements—and relates the first reports by name of Ghana, the state that controlled most of the flow of gold. A source of the early tenth century records—for what it is worth—the first named Muslim visitor to the court of the 'king of the Sudan,' who found Muhammad bin ʾArafa to be 'handsome of face and handsome and awe-inspiring in appearance and deed.'[39] Before the opening up of sea routes around West Africa's bulge, there was no other way for Maghribi merchants to get their hands on the gold, except by trading salt for it across the desert.

Over the next 200 years, Maghribi geographers piled up knowledge of Ghana and its environs, and the oases that led there, and, above all, of its fabulous wealth; but they showed little interest in the logistics of the journey. The first detailed description of a Saharan crossing occurs in the work of Ibn Battuta, who made the journey in the mid-fourteenth century, when the Saharan gold trade was near its height. It took two months to get from Sijilmassa to Walata, on the frontier of the empire of Mali. There were no visible roads—'only sand blown about by the wind. You see mountains of sand in one place. Then you see how they have moved to another.' Guides therefore commanded high prices. Ibn Battuta's was hired for 1,000 mithqals of gold. The blind were said to make the best guides, for in the desert eyesight was delusive. Demons toyed with travelers, tricking them into losing their way.

After twenty-five days, the route led through Taghaza, the fly-blown salt-mining town that produced the one product the Malians would trade for gold. The houses of Taghaza were hollowed-out blocks of salt. The water was brackish but precious. The next stage of the journey was normally of ten waterless days—except for what might sometimes be sucked out of the stomachs of wild creatures that roamed the waste. The last well before Walata was nearly 500 kilometers from the town in a land 'haunted by demons,' where 'there is no visible road or track . . . nothing but sand blown hither and thither by the wind.' Yet Ibn Battuta found the desert 'luminous, radiant,' and character-building—until the caravanners entered an even hotter zone, a few days short of Walata. Here they had to march by night. On arrival, the writer, who came from a long line of intellectuals and sophisticates, found the people of sub-Saharan Africa disappointing. When he learned that their idea of lavish hospitality was a cup of curdled milk laced with a little honey, he decided that no good could be expected of them.

This was a common experience for visitors to Mali. Like every El Dorado, it was a land doomed to disappoint. Expectations were too high. Explorers from Latin Christendom felt the tug of those expectations. As early as the mid-thirteenth century promoters in Genoa were beginning to take an interest in trying to find the sources of African gold. In 1283 Ramon Llull, the Majorcan promoter of missions among Muslims, reported that a 'cardinal's messenger' had left Ceuta for Sijilmassa with the aim of finding the 'land of the Blacks.' In the 1320s, rumors of the ruler of Mali, which had replaced Ghana as the dominant empire of the Sahel, reached Europe: on a pilgrimage to Mecca, he had distributed so much gold to shrines en route that he had caused inflation in Egypt.[40] The Catalan Atlas, made in Majorca in the late 1370s or early 1380s, depicted him as 'the richest king' of the region—bearded and sceptered in European style. Mediated through Maghribi sources, Europeans' image of Mali gleamed spectacularly, with lavish mosques and palaces, myriad tributaries, arcane rituals at court. But by the time the first European explorers established a viable route to Mali—in the mid-fifteenth century, pushing up the Gambia from the sea, as we shall see in the next chapter—the empire was in decline, and its poverty and shabbiness disappointed onlookers and confirmed adverse prejudices about the blacks' capacities.

The return journey across the Sahara was even worse than the outward route. The oases turned white garments black. Dates were the only fresh provender, eked out with locusts caught before dawn. At the copper mines of Taggada, caravans had to load seventy days' provisions for the march to Sijilmassa. The snows of the Atlas mountains then tormented travelers on their way to Fez.

But the lure of gold kept drawing explorers from Europe to learn the route or find ways of improving it. In 1413 Anselme d'Isalguier was reported as returning to his native Toulouse from Gao on the Niger with three black eunuchs and a harem of negresses—though no one knew how he could have got so far. In 1447 Antonio Malfante set out to find the way across the desert on behalf of the Genoese state, but he only got as far as Touat before turning back. In 1470 Benedetto Dei, a Florentine merchant, claimed to have been to Timbuktu and to have observed there a lively trade in European textiles.

In view of the problems of the overland route to the sources of gold, it is surprising that it took so long for exploration to turn seaward. Despite the availability of abundant shipping and seasoned seafarers, Andalusis and Maghribis hardly showed any interest in the Middle Ages in exploring the African coast. According to al-Idrisi, adventurers from Lisbon 'embarked on the Sea of Darkness to see what was in it and where it ended,' but all he knew of their achievements was an obviously fictional, Sinbad-style tale. The only conscious explorer we know of by name who tried it was Ibn Fatima, whose claims were collected in a compilation made in Granada in about 1280. 'Ibn Fatima relates,' we are told, 'that he was once on a voyage on the Atlantic Ocean to Nul Lamta but his ship was blown off its course and got into a region of fog and shallows.' But since the adjoining coast housed Berber-speaking inhabitants, it does not sound as if this voyage got very far south, though Ibn Fatima also claimed to have made readings of latitude as far south as 1 degree short of the equator. An early fourteenth-century work, which collected numerous merchants' accounts of Mali and neighboring countries, includes an account of another adventitious landfall, by a commercial ship, where the inhabitants were 'a people of Sudan. When they saw that we were white they were amazed and made certain that we had coloured our bodies with whitewash.' But like much other information in the same source, this sounds like a conventional tale.[41]

So the Maghribis left it to the Europeans, whose navigations are described in the next chapter, to open the route to West Africa by sea. Why this timidity? Part of the inhibition may have arisen from legends of a 'Sea of Darkness,' patrolled by monsters and rimmed by boiling tropical waters. It is at least equally likely that Maghribis knew the gold came from far inland and supposed that a seaborne search would be unavailing.

Routes Within the Americas

Within the Americas, we do not know who reconnoitered the routes that emerged and developed in this period, nor even, in most cases, the exact course they followed. We can only infer their existence from the distribution of artifacts and the transmission of influence. Routes radiated from the two great centers of civilization in the Americas at the time: Mesoamerica and the northern and central Andes. But they never met. People in the two regions seem hardly to have known of each other's existence until Spanish conquistadores put them in mutual touch in the sixteenth century.

From the valley of Mexico, one set of routes led southward to the Maya lands and central America. Thanks to some fragmentary Maya inscriptions, the progress of one party of pioneers from the north can be followed. They arrived in Maya country in January, AD 378, soon after the beginning of the annual rainy season, in the moist, tropical lowlands of what is now eastern Guatemala. They came from Teotihuacan, 7,500 feet high in the mountain-ringed valley of central Mexico. The weather was unfamiliar: Teotihuacan had its rather scantier rainy season in summer. The travelers were not numerous or heavily armed, to judge from a picture an artist made of them, or others like them, as they completed their journey. Some of them looked and behaved like ambassadors, wearing the tasseled headdresses that signified ambassadorial rank, and carrying ceremonial vessels, carved or painted with mythic scenes and

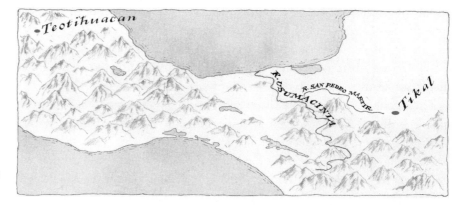

Country traversed by Siyaj K'ak

political messages, as diplomatic gifts. They crossed hundreds of miles of mountains and forests, or perhaps descended by sea along the coast. The leader of the group was known to the Maya as Siyaj K'ak: the name means 'fire-born'. Previously, historians called him Smoking Frog—a literal interpretation of his name glyph. Contemporaries in the Maya world added a nickname, 'the great man from the west.' But why had he come?

His destination was the city of Tikal, nearly 700 miles from his home, in the region now called the Petén, where the limestone temples and gaudily painted roof combs of the city rose above the dense forest. Tikal was one of the oldest and clearly the largest of the many city states among which the Maya world was divided. Its population at the time was perhaps over 30,000. But if Tikal was a great city by Maya standards, Teotihuacan dwarfed it, at probably more than three times its size. Teotihuacan, moreover, was no mere city state but the nerve center of an empire that covered the valley of Mexico and spilled into neighboring regions, now called Tlaxcala and Morelos. Teotihuacano influence and tribute gathering probed further still. Traders from central Mexico had penetrated deep into the Maya lands for many decades. Contacts with the jade-rich highland Maya, who lived in the mountainous regions to the south and west of Tikal, were multiplying.

Relations between Tikal and Teotihuacan were important for both cities, because of the complementary ecologies of their regions: the Maya supplied Mexico with products unavailable in the highlands, including the plumage of forest birds for ornament, rubber for the ball games favored by the elites of the region, cacao (which provided the elite with a mildly narcotic drink), jade for jewelry, and rare kinds of incense for rituals. But visitors like Siyaj K'ak and his Teotihuacanos were rare, or even, perhaps, unprecedented. As they approached, day by day, along the river now called after San Pedro Mártir, the communities they passed through recorded their passage without comment but presumably with apprehension, and passed on the news to neighbors down the line. What were the newcomers' intentions? Were they invaders or invitees? Conquerors or collaborators? Envoys or adventurers? Were they mercenaries, perhaps, or a marriage party? Had they come to arbitrate in existing disputes or to exploit them for purposes of their own?

The inscriptions that record the events are too fragmentary to answer these questions. But they tell a suggestive story. When Siyaj K'ak reached Tikal on 31 January, his arrival precipitated a revolution. On that very day, if the inscriptions can be taken literally, the life of the city's ruler, Chak Tok Ich'aak (or Great Jaguar Paw, as historians used to call him), came to an end. He 'entered the water,' as the Maya said, after a reign of eighteen years, ending the supremacy of a royal line that had supplied the city with thirteen previous kings. The monuments of his dynasty were shattered into fragments or defaced and buried: slabs of stone on which images of kings were carved, with commemorations of the wars they fought, captives they took, astronomical observations they recorded, and sacrifices they offered to the gods—sometimes of their own blood, sometimes of the lives of their captives.

To judge from the portraits left by his court sculptors, the new king, whom Siyaj K'ak placed on the throne, dressed in the style of his Teotihuacano patrons, wore adornments with images of central Mexican gods, and carried weapons of central Mexican design. His chocolate pots came from Teotihuacan or were copied from models made there. When he died early in the next century, he was buried with a carving of an underworld god, seated on a throne of human bones, holding a severed head.[42]

Siyaj K'ak installed new rulers not only in Tikal but also in several other, smaller cities in the region over the next few years. Imperfect inscriptions suggest that some, perhaps all, of the affected cities professed allegiance to a ruler whose name glyph shows an owl with a spear thrower: this is also a common image associated with war and power at Teotihuacan, suggesting that the supremacy of Teotihuacan, or at least of Teotihuacanos, was part of the new order. Moreover, a rash of new cities in the lowlands was founded from Tikal over the next few years, though they seem quickly, in most cases, to have asserted or exercised independence. It would exceed the evidence to speak of the birth of a new regional state, or the foundation of a new province of the empire of Teotihuacan. But at the least we can confidently assert that contacts across Mesoamerica were growing, that state formation was quickening and spreading, and that a complex political pattern was emerging: jealous Maya cities, competing and combining, with elites often drawn or sponsored from central Mexico.

The broader network of communications, of which the route traveled by

Siyaj K'ak was part, can only be tentatively recovered. Canoe-borne traffic around the Gulf of Mexico and the Caribbean was part of it: these were the routes Columbus saw in action and around them his native pilots guided him. By land, the Maya highlands in western Guatemala, as well as the lowlands approached by Siyaj K'ak, were accessible from central Mexico: Cortés made the journey to Honduras, with the aid of native guides and maps, in 1524. Other land routes reached north along the Mississippi valley from the Gulf of Mexico, or across the northern Mexican deserts and those of the North American southwest, via the desert emporium of Casas Grandes, where, in the late Middle Ages, there was a macaw feather processing plant, supplying chiefdoms to the north and south with plumage for ornamental headgear. Along these roads traveled the cultural influences that slowly spread features of Mesoamerican civilization deep into the north of the continent: monumental cities, ball courts, maize cultivation, and perhaps a common commercial language—a sort of pidgin Uto-Aztecan which seems to have been understood as far north as northern Texas and Arizona when Spanish explorers traversed these native trails in the sixteenth century.

In South America, the Andes were themselves a great axis of communication. Conquistadores in Peru in the sixteenth century could find guides capable of leading them all over the world of the high Andes from Tolima to the Bío-Bío. Yet this vast mental map was retained without, as far as we know, anything resembling a map. Andean geography may provide a clue to how this feat was achieved. Some vantage points yield views of up to 100 miles' extent in clear conditions. Pilgrimage routes were signposted straight between mountain-top shrines called huacas. The longest such route in use when the Spaniards arrived in the late 1520s led from Cuzco, the ceremonial center of the Inca state, over 185 miles to Tiahuanaco, through the 'house of the sun' at Vilcanota and the island of Titicaca—'island of the sun'—in a straight line. Regular devotions helped priests to memorize the grid of routes and sightlines.[43]

The rivers transmitted culture, too. One of the remarkable revelations of recent archeology has been of the continuities of culture that link environments as diverse as those of the high Andes, for example, and the rain-soaked lowlands of the Amazon. In the early 1540s, the first Spanish navigators of the Amazon found cities fed in part by aquaculture, hoisted on stilts at the riverside. The stone platforms Andean civilizations characteristically built seem echoed in the mounds of Majoaro, an island at the mouth of the Amazon.

The story of medieval exploration amounts to this: the new long-range routes of the Norse, the Thule, and the Polynesians led to dead ends, or left isolated communities at their extremities, and failed to open enduring communications. In the fourteenth century, environmental disasters checked the expansion of the great civilizations of Eurasia and North Africa: the beginnings of a 'little ice age' of diminished mean temperatures coincided with those of an 'age of plague,' which halted population growth in the fourteenth century and helped to restrain it for the following 300 years. Meanwhile, the Mongol empire crumbled. The descendants of Genghis Khan quarreled and went their separate ways. Mongol rulers were driven from China in 1368. The steppeland road across Eurasia again became unusable. The Silk Roads became hazardous once more. The new southern Silk Road from China to India remained intermittent at best. Route finders in Africa and the Americas never really conquered the constraints of geography. There were stirrings, strivings, in this period, but not much more than that. Still, the frustrations of the era fed the ambitions of the next. Internal exploration had been carried out thoroughly wherever it is documented—in Christendom, China, Islam, Japan, Java. In Europe, excited imaginations filled speculative maps with discoveries yet unmade. Gold traffickers, despairing of the Sahara, turned seaward. They were not alone. As we shall see in the next chapter, the late Middle Ages were a time of new maritime ventures in exploration as far afield as China, Russia, and—most persistently—Europe's Atlantic edge.

4 Springing

The Maritime Turn of the Late Middle Ages and the Penetration of the Atlantic

Shy traffickers, the dark Iberians come.

Matthew Arnold, 'The Scholar Gypsy'

PERHAPS because he was a usurper with a lot to prove, China's Yongle emperor was willing to pay almost any price for glory. From the time he seized the throne in 1402 until his death twenty-two years later, he waged almost incessant war on China's borders, especially on the Mongol and Annamese fronts. He scattered at least seventy-two missions to every accessible land beyond China's borders. He sent silver to the shogun in Japan (who already had plenty of silver), and statues of Buddha and gifts of gems and silks to Tibet and Nepal. He exchanged ill-tempered embassies with Muslim potentates in central Asia, and invested kings in Korea, Melaka, Borneo, Sulu, Sumatra, and Ceylon. These far-flung contacts probably cost more in gifts than they raised in what the Chinese called 'tribute': live okapi from Bengal, white elephants from Cambodia, horses and concubines from Korea, turtles and white monkeys from Siam, paintings from Afghanistan, sulfur and spears and samurai armor from Japan. But they were magnificent occasions of display, which gave Yongle prestige in his own court and perhaps some sense of security.[1]

The grandest and most expensive of the missions went by sea. Between 1405 and 1433 seven formidable flag-waving expeditions ranged the Indian Ocean under Admiral Zheng He. The scale of his efforts was massive. The first expedition was said to comprise sixty-two junks of the largest dimensions ever built, 225 support vessels, and 27,780 men. The vessels—to judge from a recently discovered rudder post—justified the awed terms of contemporary

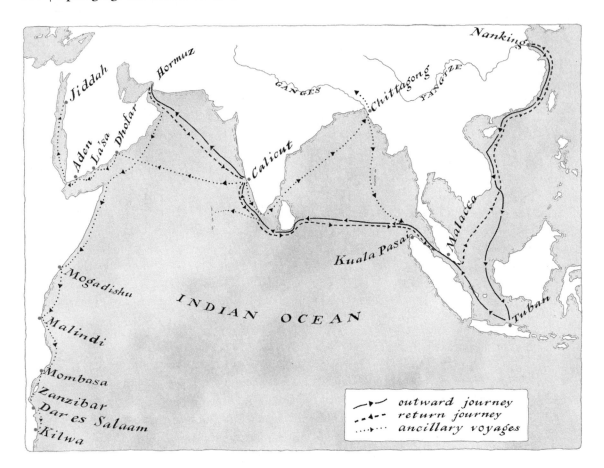

Routes of Zheng He

assessments, displacing, perhaps, over 3,000 tons: this was ten times the size of the largest ships afloat in Europe at the time. The voyages lasted, on average, two years each. They visited at least thirty-two countries around the rim of the ocean. The first three voyages, between 1405 and 1411, only went as far as the Malabar coast, the principal source of the world's pepper supply, with excursions along the coasts of Siam, Malaya, Java, Sumatra, and Ceylon. On the fourth voyage, from 1413 to 1415, ships visited the Maldives, Ormuz, and Jiddah, and collected envoys from nineteen countries.

Even more than the arrival of the ambassadors, it was the inclusion of a giraffe among the tribute Zheng He had gathered that caused a sensation when the fleet returned to China. No giraffe had ever been seen in China before. Zheng He acquired his in Bengal, where it had arrived as a curiosity for a princely collection as a result of trading links across the Indian Ocean with East Africa. Chinese instantly identified the creature as of divine provenance. According to an eyewitness it had 'the body of a deer and the tail of an ox and a fleshy boneless horn, with luminous spots like a red or purple mist. It walks in

Painting by Xendu of a giraffe with attendant, fifteenth century

stately fashion and in its every motion it observes a rhythm.' Carried away by confusion with the mythical qilin, or unicorn, the same observer declared, 'Its harmonious voice sounds like a bell or musical tube.'

The giraffe brought an assurance of divine benevolence. Xendu, the artist who made a surviving drawing from life, wrote accompanying verses describing the giraffe's reception at court:

> The ministers and the people all gathered to gaze at it and their joy knows no end. I, your servant, have heard that when a sage possesses the virtue of the utmost benevolence, so that he illuminates the darkest places, then a ch'i-lin appears. This shows that your Majesty's virtue equals that of heaven. Its merciful blessings have spread far and wide, so that its harmonious vapours have emanated a ch'i-lin, as an endless blessing to the state for myriad years.[2]

Accompanying the envoys home on a fifth voyage, which lasted from 1416 to 1419, Zheng He followed up the éclat of the giraffe's appearance. He collected a prodigious array of exotic beasts for the imperial menagerie: lions, leopards, camels, ostriches, zebras, rhinoceroses, antelopes, and giraffes, as well as a mysterious beast, the Touou-yu. Drawings made this last creature resemble a white tiger with black spots, while written accounts describe a 'righteous beast' who would not tread on growing grass, was strictly vegetarian, and appeared 'only under a prince of perfect benevolence and sincerity.' There were also many 'strange birds.' An inscription recorded, 'All of them craned their necks and looked on with pleasure, stamping their feet, scared and startled.' That was a description not of the birds but of the enraptured courtiers. Truly it seemed to Xendu, 'all the creatures that spell good fortune arrive.'[3]

In 1421 Zheng He's sixth voyage departed with the reconnaissance of the east coast of Africa as its main objective, visiting, among other destinations, Mogadishu, Mombasa, Malindi, Zanzibar, Dar es Salaam, and Kilwa. After an interval, probably caused by changes in the balance of court factions after the death of the Yongle emperor in 1424, the seventh voyage, from 1431 to 1433, was probably the furthest-penetrating. It sailed 12,618 miles in all, according to the best available estimate, and renewed contacts with the Arabian and African states Zheng He had already visited.[4]

Strictly speaking these were not route-finding voyages. As we have seen, the trade routes of the Indian Ocean, across maritime Asia and into East Africa, had been familiar to Chinese merchants for centuries. The early thirteenth-century Zhufanjie provided a practical handbook for commercial travelers in southeast Asia and India. There were certainly opportunities to increase commercial openings by backing initiatives with force. The trades of the region were highly lucrative, including spices, fragrant hardwoods, valuable medicinal drugs, and exotic animal products. The Chinese called Zheng He's ships 'treasure ships.' The motives,

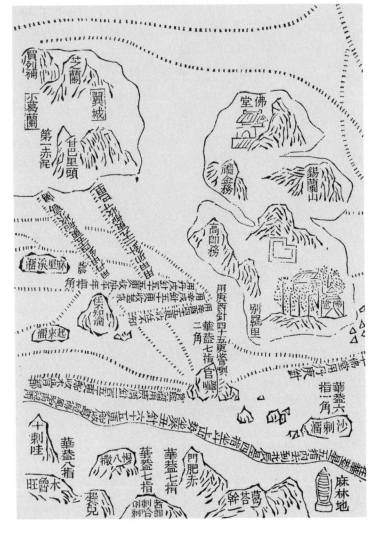

Official records of Zheng He's voyages to Africa were destroyed, but sailing directions in diagram form survived to be published in 1621. This example shows the Maldives and East Africa

however, transcended commerce. Zheng He was engaged on what would now be called flag-waving missions, impressing the ports he visited with Chinese power, and stimulating the awe of the emperor's home constituency with exotica which the Chinese classified as the tribute of remote peoples.[5] The official pretext for his commission—which few believed, then or now—was to search for a fugitive ex-emperor, who was supposed to be in hiding abroad. Strategic considerations were clearly involved. Zheng He intervened actively in the politics of some ports in southeast Asia that were important for China's trade and security. A potentially hostile empire had recently arisen in central Asia under the Turkic chief usually known in the West as Tamerlane: apprehension may have sent the Chinese sniffing for allies and intelligence around the edges of the new menace. Whatever the motives of the expeditions, part of the effect was to consolidate Chinese knowledge of the routes Zheng He took, and to compile practical maps and sailing directions for them.

The admiral was a Muslim eunuch of Mongol ancestry. Every feature of his background marked him as an outsider to the Confucian scholar elite that dominated Chinese political life. When the emperor appointed him to lead the first ocean-going task force in 1403, it was a triumph for four linked factions at court, whose interests clashed with Confucian values. First, there was the commercial lobby, which wanted to mobilize naval support for Chinese traders in the Indian Ocean. Alongside the merchants, an imperialist lobby wanted to renew the program of imperial aggression espoused by the previous dynasty but opposed by Confucians, who theorized that the empire should expand, if at all, by peacefully attracting 'barbarians' into its orbit. Then there was the always powerful Buddhist lobby, which wanted to keep state funds out of skeptical or anticlerical Confucian hands by diverting them to other projects, and which perhaps sensed opportunities for spreading the faith under the official aegis of imperial expansion.

The voyages did display China's potential as the launching bay of a seaborne empire: the capacity and productivity of her shipyards; her ability to mount expeditions of crushing strength and dispatch them over vast distances. Zheng He's encounters with opponents unequivocally demonstrated Chinese superiority. On the first expedition, he encountered a Chinese pirate chief who had set up a bandit state of his own in the sometime capital of Srivijaya in Sumatra. The pirates were slaughtered and their king sent to China for execution. On the third voyage, the Sinhalese king of Ceylon tried to lure Zheng He into a trap and seize the fleet. The Chinese dispersed his forces, captured his capital, deported him to China, and installed a pretender in his place. On the fourth expedition, a Sumatran chief who refused to cooperate in the exchange of gifts for tribute was overwhelmed, abducted, and eventually put to death. Of all Zheng He's acts of political intervention, perhaps the most significant, in terms of long-term consequences, was his attempt to set up a Chinese puppet kingdom to control the trade of the Strait of Melaka, the vital bottleneck in the normal route between China and India. He chose to elevate Paramesvara, a bandit chief who had been driven from his own kingdom and had established a stronghold in the swamps of what is now known as Melaka, on the Malayan coast. In 1409 Zheng He conferred the seal and robes of kingship upon him. Paramesvara traveled to China to pay tribute in person and established a client relationship with the emperor; Chinese patronage turned his modest stronghold into a great and rich emporium.

Zheng He's own perception of his role seems to have combined an imperial impulse with the peaceful inspiration of commerce and scholarship. A stela he erected in 1432 began in a jingoistic vein: 'In the unifying of the seas and continents the Ming Dynasty even goes beyond the Han and the Tang. . . . The countries beyond the horizon and from the ends of the earth have become subjects.' That was an exaggeration, but he added, more plausibly, in deference to traders and geographers, 'However far they may be, their distances and the routes may be calculated.'[6] An 'overall survey of the ocean's shores' was one of the fruits of the voyages. Copies of the charts survive thanks to the fact that they were reproduced in a printed work of 1621. Like European charts of the same period, they are diagrams of sailing directions rather than attempts at scale mapping. Tracks annotated with compass bearings show the routes between major ports, and represent in visual form the sailing directions Zheng He recorded, all of which have the form 'Follow such-and-such a bearing for such-and-such a number of watches.' Each port is marked with its latitude according to the elevation of the Pole Star above the horizon, which Zheng He verified by means of 'guiding starboards'—ebony strips of various breadths held at a fixed distance from the observer's face to fill the space exactly between the star and the horizon.

Mutual astonishment was the result of contacts on a previously unimagined scale. In the preface to his own book about the voyages, Ma Huan, an interpreter aboard Zheng He's fleet, recalled that as a young man, when he had contemplated the seasons, climates, landscapes, and people of distant lands, he had asked himself in great surprise, 'How can such dissimilarities exist in the world?'[7]

His own travels with the eunuch admiral convinced him that the reality was even stranger. The arrival of Chinese junks at Middle Eastern ports with cargoes of precious exotica caused a sensation. A chronicler at the Egyptian court described the excitement provoked by news of the arrival of the junks off Aden and of the Chinese fleet's intention to reach the nearest permitted anchorage to Mecca.

But the Chinese naval effort could not last. The reasons for its abandonment have been much debated. In many ways, it was to the credit of Chinese decision makers that they pulled back from involvement in costly adventures far from home: most powers that have undertaken such expeditions, and attempted to impose their rule on distant countries, have had cause to regret it. Confucian values, as we have seen, included giving priority to good government at home: 'barbarians' would submit to be ruled by China if and when they saw the benefits: attempting to bludgeon or coax them into submission was a waste of resources. By consolidating their landward empire, and refraining from seaborne imperialism, China's rulers ensured the longevity of their state: all the maritime empires founded in the world in the last 500 years have crumbled. China is still there.

Part, at least, of the context of the decision to abort Zheng He's missions is clear. The examination system and the gradual discontinuation of other forms of recruitment for public service had serious implications. China became increasingly governed by scholars, with their indifference toward expansion, and gentlemen, with their contempt for trade. In the 1420s and 1430s the balance of power at court shifted in the bureaucrats' favor, away from the Buddhists, eunuchs, Muslims, and merchants who had supported Zheng He. When the Hongxi emperor succeeded the Yongle emperor on the throne in 1424, one of his first acts was to cancel Zheng He's next voyage. He restored Confucian officeholders, whom his predecessor had dismissed, and curtailed the power of other factions. In 1429 the shipbuilding budget was cut almost to extinction. The scholar elite hated overseas adventures, and the factions that favored them, so much that they destroyed all Zheng He's records in an attempt to obliterate his memory. Moreover, China's land frontiers became insecure as Mongol power revived. China needed to turn away from the sea and toward the new threat.[8]

The consequences for the history of the world were profound. Chinese overseas expansion was confined to unofficial migration and, in large part, to clandestine trade, with little or no imperial encouragement or protection. This did not stifle Chinese colonization or commerce. On the contrary, China remained the world's most dynamic trading economy and its most prolific source of overseas settlers. From the fifteenth century onward, Chinese colonists in southeast Asia made vital contributions to the economies of every place they settled; their remittances home played a big part in the enrichment of China. The tonnage of shipping frequenting Chinese ports in the same period probably equaled or exceeded that of the rest of the world put together. But the state's hostility to maritime expansion, which—except in respect of islands close to China—never again abated for as long as the empire lasted, ensured that China never built up the sort of wide-ranging global empire that Atlantic seaboard nations acquired. An observer of the world in the fifteenth century would surely have forecast that the Chinese would precede all other peoples in the discovery of world-girdling, transoceanic routes, and the inauguration of far-flung seaborne imperialism. In fact, nothing of the sort materialized, and the field remained open for the far less promising explorers of Europe to open up the ways around the world.

Of course, the destiny of the world was not determined by a single decision made in China in 1433. China's renunciation of maritime imperialism belongs in a vast context of influences that help to explain the long-term advantages of Atlantic-side European peoples in the global 'space race.' These influences can be classified as partly environmental, partly economic. The limits of Zheng He's navigations are a clue to the environmental influences. Maritime Asia and coastal East Africa form a remarkably extensive monsoonal region, where long-range navigation relies, as we have seen, on the regular to-ing and fro-ing of the wind. In the fixed-wind environments beyond the region, navigators would find unfamiliar and uncongenial conditions; in the southern Indian Ocean, or, beyond southeast Asia, into the Pacific, they would be compelled to sail against the wind; or, in other directions, they would face the risk of sailing with a following wind and probably never getting home. Moreover, the Indian Ocean is hard to get out of. Below about 10 degrees south a belt of storms deters shipping. The route toward the Atlantic around southern Africa has to round lee shores in the region of what is now KwaZulu-Natal, which, in the sixteenth and seventeenth centuries, became a notorious graveyard for ships that ventured there. This was probably the location of the place called Ha-pu-erh on the maps generated by the Zheng He voyages, beyond which, according to the annotations, the ships did not proceed, owing to the ferocity of the storms. On its eastern flank, maritime Asia is hemmed by the typhoon-racked seas of Japan and the vastness of the Pacific.

To undertake voyages into such hostile seas, Indian Ocean navigators would need a big incentive. That is where economics came in. The Indian Ocean was an arena of such intense commercial activity, and so much wealth, that it would have been pointless for its indigenous peoples to look for markets or suppliers elsewhere. When merchants from northern or central Asia or Europe or the African interior reached the ocean, they came as supplicants, generally despised for their poverty, and found it hard to sell the products of their homelands. Generally, they could prosper only by becoming shippers or pedlars of existing trades.

Chinese disengagement from the wider world was not the result of any deficiency of technology or curiosity. It would have been perfectly possible for Chinese ships to visit Europe or the Americas, had they so wished. Indeed, Chinese explorers probably did get around the Cape of Good Hope, sailing from east to west, at intervals during the Middle Ages. A Chinese map of the thirteenth century depicts Africa in roughly its true shape. A Venetian mapmaker of the mid-fifteenth century reported a sighting of a Chinese or, perhaps, a Javanese junk off the southwest African coast.[9] But there was no point in pursuing such initiatives: they led to regions that produced nothing the Chinese wanted. Although the evidence that Chinese vessels ever crossed the Pacific to America is, at best, equivocal, it is perfectly possible that they may have done so. Again, however, it would have been folly to pursue such voyages or attempt systematic contacts across the ocean. No people lived there with whom the Chinese could possibly wish to do business.

To a lesser—but still sufficient—extent the same considerations applied to other maritime peoples of the Indian Ocean and east and southeast Asia. The Arabs, the Swahili merchant communities, Persians, Indians, Javanese and other island peoples of the region, and the Japanese all had plenty of commercial opportunities in their home ocean to keep them fully occupied. Indeed, their problem was, if anything, shortage of shipping in relation to the scale of demand for interregional trade. That was why, in the long run, they generally welcomed interlopers from Europe in the sixteenth century, who were truculent, demanding, barbaric, and often violent, but who added to the shipping stock of the ocean and, therefore, contributed to the general increase of wealth. Paradoxically, therefore, poverty favored Europeans, whom the paucity of economic opportunities at home compelled to explore for them elsewhere. The most spectacular explorations, moreover, departed from the edge of the edge—for Europe was the rim of Eurasia, and the rim of Europe, jutting into the ocean, was Iberia.

Why Iberia?

Madrid is as far from the sea as you can get in the Iberian peninsula; yet it is full of seafood restaurants and has the biggest fish market in Europe. The Castilian passion for the sea is a curious feature of the history and culture of a people whose heartlands are deep inland and who have been almost cut off from the coasts for formative periods of their pasts. Most of the Atlantic seaboard of the Iberian peninsula, with the mouths of the greatest rivers, the Tagus and the Duero, belongs to the Portuguese, who have maintained an independent state, often hostile to Castile, since the twelfth century. Speakers of Catalan or cognate languages occupy most of the Mediterranean coast: they were not fully incorporated into the Spanish state until long after Castile's worldwide seaborne empire was founded. The northern margins, which, behind their wall of mountains, look out over the Cantabrian Sea, have, for most of the last 1,000 years, belonged to the same political entity as Castile; yet the peoples who occupy most of their shore, along with most of the best harbors, are not Castilians, but Galicians and Basques—communities which contributed a disproportionate share of manpower to Spain's overseas enterprises. In the south, Castile's direct outlets to the Atlantic, via the river Guadalquivir, and to the Mediterranean, across the virtual wastelands of Murcia, were not acquired until the mid-thirteenth century. Before then, the economy of Castile relied on the laborious treks of mule trains to and fro across the mountains between the productive pastures of the northern plateau and the Cantabrian ports.

Astonishingly, from this unpromising starting point, late medieval Castile pursued a sort of collective maritime vocation with a zeal that produced, in the early modern period, the most extensive explorations and the most widespread empire the world had ever seen. The empire was also, incomparably, the greatest ever created with preindustrial technology. In the sixteenth and seventeenth centuries, the Atlantic and Pacific Oceans were Spanish 'lakes,' in which Spanish shipping controlled and virtually monopolized the best transatlantic routes. It is tempting to try to explain the apparent paradox psychologically—by analogy, say, with a former colleague of mine, whose interest in the sea was unaroused, he said, until he moved to Kansas.

Castile's sea-soaked ambitions in the late Middle Ages were part of a broader Iberian turn toward the sea. The Portuguese contribution to exploration, which also began in the fourteenth century and grew to prominence in the fifteenth, equaled or excelled that of Castile. In some ways, Portugal's seems a less surprising maritime career: the country has long coasts and little hinterland. But Portugal was ill-equipped in other respects.

'Portugal: not a small country' was a slogan of the Salazar years. Even the dictator, however, was willing to acknowledge that, before imperial expansion, Portugal was small. The contrast between the breadth of Portuguese imperialism and the modest dimensions of the home country is the most conspicuous mystery of Portuguese history and one of the most puzzling contrasts in the history of the world. The state of the statistics allows only very rough computations, but in the early sixteenth century Portugal's population was probably little more than half of England's and a quarter of Castile's, probably about a tenth of that of France and much smaller even than that of the Low Countries. Few other resources were available to make up for the lack of land and people. The salt pans of Setúbal were the only form of abundance conferred by nature. Poverty and famine were commonplace afflictions.[10]

The resource base seemed inadequate even for the maritime outlook which Portugal's position encouraged. Of her potential rivals in overseas empire seeking, only the Netherlands had less access to timber and iron for shipbuilding. Even the paucity at Portugal's command seemed vulnerable, with a long, awkward land frontier, unprotected by any easily defensible barrier and overlooked by a dauntingly powerful neighbor. The one advantage historians sometimes ascribe to Portugal—internal peace after the dynastic settlement of 1385, while much of the rest of western Europe was convulsed by fifteenth-century civil wars—was equivocal in its effects. Civil wars are often preludes to empire, because they create aggressive elites for whom employment must be found, and because they set off scrambles for resources which can lead far afield.

Whether we focus on Portugal or Castile, therefore, as a place from which to scatter global explorers and found great empires, Iberia invites the response of the yokel who, asked to direct a passing motorist, replied, 'If I was you, I wouldn't start from here.' Overseas dynamism is sometimes the result of over-flowing resources, superabundance of power, or spillage of surplus population. Iberia's belongs in a less privileged category. The seaward turn of Spain and Portugal resembled those of 'Third World' countries today, desperately drilling for offshore resources in initial reliance on foreign capital and savoir-faire, for Italian, especially Genoese, entrepreneurs and technicians played a major part in the seaward ventures of Spaniards and Portuguese in the fourteenth and fifteenth centuries.

Nothing can make the maritime careers of Spain and Portugal unsurprising; but the broader the framework of comparison, the easier they are to understand. Far-flung seaborne enterprise often starts from a home base which is poor or of limited exploitability, with restricted opportunities to landward. Marginal peoples, on or beyond the edges of great civilizations, are often tempted into colonial or commercial adventures. We have already met plenty of examples. The *locus classicus*, in every sense of the term, is that of ancient Greece—'the sister of poverty,' according to Hesiod, a skeleton land, in Plato's perceptions, where the bones of rock poked through the thin flesh of soil. The Greeks' great rivals in long-range colonization, the Phoenicians, started from a narrow coast. Southern Arabia, Gujarat, and Fukien have housed great ocean-going civilizations in similarly situated home bases.[11] Japan is not often thought of as home to long-range maritime imperialism; but she occupies a position comparable to Iberia's at the opposite extremity of Eurasia, and in key respects has experienced a comparable history; for the conditions of navigation in her home waters make the scale of Japanese empire building impressive, just within what we have come to think of as her own islands. Her two spells of wider-reaching seaborne imperialism are suggestive: in the late sixteenth century, she was foiled by the insufficiency of the available technology; in the twentieth, when steamships could break out of the restraining meshwork of the winds, she was defeated by insuperable odds.

In western Europe, too, until the late Middle Ages, the only long-distance, ocean-going initiatives we know of began in relatively poor and peripheral places: the seaborne pilgrimages of hermits from Ireland and the ventures of raiders, pirates, and colonists from Scandinavia. The seaborne empires of the medieval Mediterranean were founded from narrow rivieras, in the Genoese and Catalan cases; or from the unpromisingly salty, marshy islands of the Venetian lagoon. The explorers who, in their day, most successfully imitated and challenged those from Iberia came from the Netherlands, also a marginal and naturally disadvantaged place. France and England—places better equipped or more lavishly resourced, and apparently well positioned—were long dogged by ill success. In the race across early modern oceans, it helped to come from behind.

The leading roles of Spain and Portugal in world exploration, therefore, are only fully intelligible in the context of histories of outreach by other small, peripheral maritime communities. More particularly, they belong to an uniquely western European and maritime story. It is usual to speak loosely—and misleadingly—of 'European' seaborne imperialism in the early modern and modern periods. Virtually the only European seaborne empires, however, were founded, more locally, from western Europe's seaside rimland, where most of the explorers were bred. At first glance, it looks like an incoherent place. It stretches from the Arctic to the Mediterranean, across contrasting climates, ecozones, menus, churches, folklores, musical traditions, historical memories, ways of getting drunk. Languages become mutually unintelligible, with unshared roots in the last 4,000 years or so. Norwegians have a naturalized national dish called bacalau, after a Spanish or Portuguese prototype, and the recipe, at its best, calls for olive oil. But there a few such traces of shared experience. As you follow the coast from north to south, everything seems to change, except the presence of the sea.

That sea has given Europe's Atlantic-side peoples a singular and terrible role in world history. Virtually all the large-scale maritime world empires of modern history were founded from this fringe. There were, at most, three possible exceptions. Italy had a brief and modest little empire, built up at intervals between the 1880s and 1930s, in Libya, the Dodecanese, and the Horn of Africa, which could be reached through the Mediterranean and the Suez Canal, without imposing on the Atlantic. Russia had a Pacific empire of sorts, in the Aleutian Islands, with outposts on the west coast on North America, until Alaska was sold to the United States in 1867. Finally, there were the short-lived networks of slave stations and sugar islands founded from Baltic ports, in Courland and Brandenburg, in the seventeenth century.[12]

Not only were virtually all maritime empires founded by Atlantic-side states: there was, effectively, no Atlantic-side state that did not have one. The only possible exceptions are Norway, Ireland, and Iceland; but these states did not achieve sovereignty themselves until the twentieth century and so missed the great ages of oceanic empire building. Iceland is anomalous in almost every way. The Irish, though they had no empire of their own, were participants as well as victims in that of Britain. With a certain delicious *schadenfreude*, Norwegians are rediscovering the guilt of their ancestors' own quasi-imperial past as participants in Danish and Swedish slaving ventures. For the rest, every European state with an Atlantic seaboard has taken to the ocean in the course of modern history with prows set on empire. This applies to relatively tiny and peripheral communities, like Portugal and the Netherlands, and even Scotland, briefly, while it was still a sovereign country, as well as to others, like Spain, Germany, and Sweden, which have only relatively short Atlantic-side coasts and Janus-looks and large hinterlands pulling their interests in other directions.

When receiving an honorary doctorate in his eighties, Salvador de Madariaga, the statesman and scholar who served the Spanish republic in exile, said it was a case of unusual precocity: the same can be said of the maritime imperial career of Europe's Atlantic rim. In this respect, the miraculous thing about 'the European miracle' is that there was no miracle for so long. We western Europeans—as a Galician, whose paternal ancestors lived about as far west in Europe as it is possible to go, I can say this with perfect candor—like to congratulate ourselves on the way our ancestors have shaped the past and present of our continent and, by implication, of the world. Yet, considered from one point of view, Westerners are the dregs of Eurasian history, and the salient they inhabit is the sump into which Eurasian history has drained. A renaissance or three, the medieval expansion of Latin Christendom, the scientific revolution, the Enlightenment, the French Revolution, and industrialization can all fairly be represented as formative movements which started in the West and spread eastwards. In a genuinely long-term perspective, however, Europe's west has been at the receiving end of great transmissions of culture. The spread of farming and mining, the arrival of Indo-European languages, the colonizations of Phoenicians, Jews, and Greeks, the coming of Christianity, the migrations of Germans, Slavs, and steppelanders, the receptions of learning, taste, technology, and science from Asia: all these have been influences exerted from East to West. Many of these movements have left refugees at the Atlantic end of Europe, occupying what, for most of history, have been inhospitable and unpromising shores. There, for hundreds, or perhaps, in some cases, thousands, of years, they remained, without exercising much in the way of seaward initiative.

Overwhelmingly, Europe's Atlantic-side peoples are classifiable today, in the light of their modern history, as maritime peoples. The Atlantic provided them with vocations for fishers and seafarers and regional traders. Once nautical technology permitted, the ocean offered highways of seaborne migration and empire building. Yet the unexplained paradox of western European history is that the call of the sea was long unheard. When they reached the sea, most of these peoples were stuck there, as if pinioned by the prevailing westerlies which blow onto all their shores. Coastwise shipping kept their communities in touch with one another; pelagic hermits contributed to the mystique of the sea; and some places developed deep-sea fisheries at unrecorded dates. But except in Scandinavia the achievements of civilization in western Europe owed little or nothing to the maritime horizon until what we think of as the late Middle Ages.

Meanwhile, western Europe occupied the outer edge of world maps of the time. Scholars in Persia or China, confident in the superiority of their own civilized traditions, thought Christendom hardly worth a mention in their studies of the world. Efforts to expand east and south from Latin Christendom—to landward, into eastern Europe, or via the Mediterranean into Asia and Africa—made some progress but were generally repulsed or compelled to retreat by plagues and great freezes.

The Origins of the Atlantic Turn: Beginnings in Genoa and Majorca

Moreover, when the continuous history of the recorded exploration of the Atlantic began in the late thirteenth century, it is remarkable that none of Europe's Atlantic seaboard peoples took part in it. The European 'discovery' of the Atlantic was an enterprise launched from deep in the Mediterranean, chiefly by Genoese and Majorcan navigators, who unstoppered their sea by forcing their way, against the race of the adverse current, through the Strait of Gibraltar. From there, some turned north to exploit the commerce of Atlantic France, England, and the Netherlands. Others headed south into waters unsailed—as far as we know—for centuries, toward the African Atlantic and the islands of the Madeira group and the Canaries. Along this route, for instance, the Vivaldi brothers of Genoa—the earliest participants known by name—departed in 1291 to seek 'the regions of India by way of the ocean,' anticipating, by nearly two centuries, the very terms of Columbus' project. Maddeningly little is known of them, except their status as members of a prominent merchant family and a chronicler's bare, spare reference to their voyage. They were never heard of again, but they helped to inspire voyages in their wake. One of their successors, the Genoese Lancelotto Malocello, gave a corrupt version of his name to the island of Lanzarote in the Canaries, which a map of 1339 adorned with a Genoese flag. The Canary Islands became as well known to Petrarch—so he claimed, presumably with a little poetic license—in the 1330s as France.[13]

The excitement the African Atlantic aroused at the time can be glimpsed in a series of surviving documents from April 1342. In that single month, at least four voyages were licensed from Majorca, bound for the Canary Islands. That at least one license related to an actual voyage is shown by the chance survival of a claim for wages by a mariner called Guillem Joffre. A detailed account of what may be a fifth expedition of about this time survives in a corrupt version in a printed book of the next century, which describes a fortuitous landfall in the islands by pirates pursuing a galley or fleet of the king of Aragon.[14]

The ships named in the licenses were specifically cogs ('cocas' or 'coques' in the original texts): probably round-hulled merchants' ships, poor performers against the wind, intended to sail with the Canary current. The lexicon of late medieval ship types is extremely muddling: landlubbers wrote most surviving documents and, as they do today, tended to misuse the terms, which gradually interchanged usage and changed meanings. In an ideal world, when we read of a 'cog' we would know a round-hulled, square-sailed ship was denoted, whereas 'caravel' would call to mind a shallower, perhaps more streamlined, vessel, with at least one triangular sail, better adapted for sailing against the wind. But one can never be sure that the writer of a shipping contract or a license or a chronicle meant quite what he said. A classic cog, sailing outward-bound with the trade winds, would not have been capable of returning by the same route. Having made the outward journey normally between February and April, they must have left the islands in October—the most suitable month for the purpose—and swept the sea to the north in search of a favorable wind home.

A gap in the Majorcan archives conceals the next few years' activity, though it seems unlikely that the hectic pace of the early 1340s can have been long sustained. The wage claims of Guillem Joffre make it clear that the voyage on which he was employed was a commercial failure and that its leader died. This may have been a disincentive to other potential explorers, but continued activity during the sparsely documented years is indicated in an allusion in an atlas of the mid-fourteenth century. Beside a picture of a cog off the West African coast, the cartographer reported that a navigator named as Jaume Ferrer was shipwrecked in 1346 in search of the 'River of Gold'—perhaps the Wad Draa, alchemically transmuted, or even the Senegal.

Historians used to think that Atlantic exploration suffered a 'check' in the middle of the century because of the Black Death, the technical insufficiency of ships and nautical aids, and the cumulative effects of the failures and wrecks. Yet when archival records resume in 1351, the traffic seems to have been as brisk as ever. It may be, however, that some of the commercial impetus of the early voyages was lost: most of the Majorcan expeditions of the next generation appear, from surviving records, to have been the work of missionaries.[15]

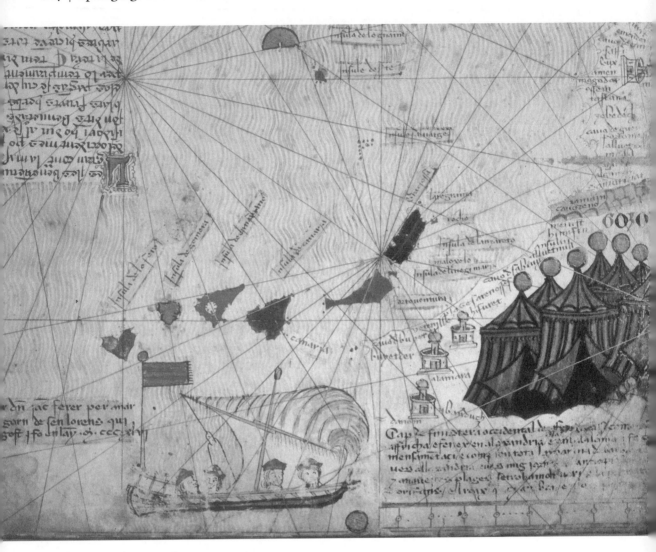

Jaume Ferrer's ship depicted in the Catalan Atlas of Cresques Abraham, 1370s–1380s

Majorca's precocity in Atlantic exploration is not surprising, though Majorcans' role as early leaders in the late medieval Atlantic space race is too often forgotten or ignored. Majorca was itself something of a colonial society and a frontier zone, reconquered from the Moors only a century previously. Briefly, from 1276 to 1343, it was the center of an independent island kingdom, which lived by trade and, therefore, from the sea. Majorca was a center, too, for technical developments in shipping and cartography that helped to make Atlantic navigation practicable on a large scale. Majorca's mapmakers, the most renowned in Europe, were assiduous gatherers of geographical information. Many were Jewish, with access to data from their sea-wide trading links and privileged role as mediators between Muslim and Latin learning. Exploration of the African Atlantic was a natural extension of Majorcans' existing interests in the commerce of the Maghrib. Majorcan shipping, moreover, carried Catalan trade to northern Europe in the late thirteenth and early fourteenth centuries. The dispensations Majorcans enjoyed to trade with the Moors peculiarly fitted them to take part in navigation along the African coast. The island had long been a Genoese staging post for westward navigation. Majorca, finally, was also the home of a school of missionaries, who took a great deal of interest in evangelizing the indigenous inhabitants of the Canary Islands and who maintained a mission on Gran Canaria from 1360 until 1393.

The Canary Islands seem to dominate the documents. They did have some exploitable products, especially the uniquely effective dyestuffs derived from indigenous lichens and the sap of the local 'dragon's blood' tree. The native inhabitants were hunted as slaves. They disappeared so completely in colonial times—exported as slaves, massacred, or assimilated into the immigrant population—that it is hard now to recover any idea of what they were like. Probably they were descendants of the pre-Berber population of North Africa, not dissimilar from such fishing peoples as the Imraguen and Znaga, who survive today in small numbers, clinging to the rim of the Sahara. But they were a modest economic resource: few in number, hard to catch, and—in the face of clerical opposition to their enslavement—hard to hold on to. The Canaries were important not chiefly, at first, for their own sake, but because the winds and currents led there from Iberia. They were of value as a staging post for explorers engaged in a remoter quest: the search for the sources of the Saharan gold trade.

Specie-starved Europeans were highly susceptible to the lure of gold, which traded—as a rough average—for silver at a ratio of 1 to 10 in the mid-fourteenth century.[16] Most of the gold Europeans knew about came across the Sahara, purchased deep in the African interior by Maghribi middlemen, who bought it with salt. The sources were in the Bure region, between the headwaters of the Senegal and Niger and, to a lesser extent, around the middle Volta. But these locations were secrets, guarded from Maghribi and European enquirers by the black monopolists of the West African empire of Mali, through whose lands astride the Niger the trade passed. Procured, according to all accounts—written perhaps from convention rather than conviction—by 'dumb trade,' in which goods were exchanged by being left exposed for collection,[17] the gold generated bizarre theories about its origins: it grew like carrots; it was brought up by ants in the form of nuggets; it was mined by naked men who lived in holes. Wherever it came from, enterprising Europeans wanted to find it.

Enter the Iberians

More surprising than the early Majorcan initiatives is the late start made by the Atlantic-side kingdoms of Portugal and Castile in the exploration of the Atlantic islands. The first really detailed extant account of an expedition survives in a copy apparently made by Boccaccio, dated, perhaps unreliably, 1341. The subject of the manuscript was, at least in part, a Portuguese undertaking, guided by Italian pilots and including, at a lower level, Castilian personnel with mariners 'from other parts of Spain.' Via Italian merchants in Seville, the surviving account reached Florence and ended up in Boccaccio's hands. The humanist's interest in the topic is evident: Boccaccio was concerned to trace the history of language, and the appendix to the document, in which fragments of the speech of the indigenous Canarians appear, was what intrigued him most.[18]

The first recorded flash of official interest in Atlantic exploration by the Castilian crown came a little later, in March 1345, prompted by the pope's attempt to invest Luis de la Cerda, an exiled scion of the Castilian crown, with the right of conquest of an island realm. It was to be called 'the Principality of Fortunia' and to comprise the Canaries and the Mediterranean island of Jalita. Clement VI's motive for attempting to forge such an unlikely realm is unclear; but, had it taken shape, it might have functioned as a launchpad for a crusade into North Africa. Replying to the pope's request for aid with the project, King Alfonso XI of Castile asserted a prior claim to the Canary Islands, which, he declared, had formed part of the perquisites of his predecessors in Visigothic times, while 'the kingdoms of Africa are of our conquest.'[19]

These words were not, at first, backed up by deeds. Aragonese and Portuguese attempts to make conquests in the Canaries are strongly suggested by evidence relating to the 1360s and 1370s. The evidence is, however, highly problematic, because it survives mainly in the form of maps, and maps of the period are notoriously hard to verify and to interpret. Anyone who has ever seen a late medieval mappa mundi or portolan chart will be able to appreciate the sentiments of a Sicilian songster, captured in a mass setting of the third quarter of the fifteenth century: enchanted by the beauty of the maps, he searched them for an isle lovelier than his own, albeit without success. The finest surviving example of the cartography of the period, the Catalan Atlas of the Bibliothèque Nationale, Paris, attributed to Cresques Abraham of Majorca, is as rich and intricate as a spilled jewel casket, resplendent with powerful images of exotic beings and untold wealth. Maps of even greater magnificence, large and more densely illuminated, are recorded but lost. These were royal gifts, intended for ostentation as well as use, but even the more modest and practical portolans would be drawn with grace and adorned with illustrations or, at least, with fine calligraphy and a delicate web of rhumb lines. It was a period in which maps could inspire more music. It was almost certainly a map—perhaps even the Catalan Atlas itself—that in 1402 induced the Poitevin adventurer Gadifer de La Salle to embark on a quest for the mythical River of Gold which led to his ruin. In the late fourteenth century the anonymous author of the *Libro del conoscimiento de todos los reynos* constructed from the legends of maps a fantastic journey of the imagination which reached beyond the limits of the known and even of the accessible world.

Recent scholarship has sorted out sufficiently the problems associated with the relevant maps—their authenticity, chronology, and reliability—to make a few conclusions clear. In 1339 some of the Canary Islands and the Madeira group appeared for the first time on a surviving map. By the time of maps reliably dated to the 1380s, the Canaries are shown almost complete, with the Savage Islands, the Madeira archipelago, and all but two of what look like the islands of the Azores. This was a remarkable achievement, hazardous to the vessels, novel to the technology, and unparalleled in the experience of sailors of the time. Skeptical scholars have doubted whether it was even possible; because the islands identifiable as the Azores are inaccurately placed in terms of longitude, and are accompanied by depictions of other, speculative islands, there is room to question whether the archipelagos of the eastern Atlantic were really known in Europe at such an early date. But detailed analysis of the maps, combined with the logic of the geography of the region, settles the question in favor of a positive conclusion. Because the winds and currents of the Atlantic naturally form a system of ducts, which tend to take ships southwest from the Pillars of Hercules and at most seasons force a wide northward sweep out to sea upon returning traffic, the exploration of the Canaries was necessarily the first phase. The Canaries lay on the outward track of vessels bound for the African Atlantic; the Azores studded their best route home. In the course of return voyages against the wind, navigators who had absolutely no means of keeping track of their longitude increasingly made huge deep-sea detours in search of westerlies that would take them home. This risky enterprise was rewarded with the discovery of the Azores—a mid-ocean archipelago, more than 700 miles from the nearest other land. This was a stage undervalued in existing literature, but of enormous significance: open-sea voyages of a length unprecedented in European experience were now under way: they became something like routine from the 1430s, when Portuguese way stations, sown with wheat or stocked with wild sheep, were established on the Azores.

No further evidence links Castilian voyages with the African Atlantic until the 1390s, when a consortium began to gather in Seville to prosecute opportunities in the region. From 1390 petitioners began to seek royal permission to launch a conquest. According to a tradition recorded in the sixteenth century, King Enrique III entrusted the conquest to a Sevillan gentleman, Fernán Peraza. In 1393 the Peraza family joined that of Guzmán—one of the most powerful aristocratic dynasties of Seville—to mount an expedition. In effect, it was a slave raid, representative, no doubt, of many others of about the same period. According to the account of a chronicler at the royal court, Sevillan and Basque mariners shipped on this voyage, which seized a native chief and his consort on the island of Lanzarote and reported to the king 'how those islands were easy to conquer, if such were his grace, and at small cost.'[20] This was the sort of glib prediction that lured many conquistadores to a terrible fate in the course of Castilian overseas expansion.

From that time onward, there was no activity in the Canaries without some Castilian, and indeed Sevillan, dimension. Nonetheless, of the first conquest to establish a lasting European colony in the archipelago, the leaders and much of the personnel came from France—from Normandy, Poitou, and Gascony. Jean de Béthencourt and Gadifer de La Salle were adventurers attracted by legends of the River of Gold. They seem, at least at first, to have envisaged their enterprise under the French crown. But the exigencies of logistics soon drove them into reliance on Castilian support and patronage. Part of the inspiration and some of the funds came from Robert de Braquemont, Béthencourt's cousin, who was connected, through his sister's marriage, to leading families of Castile, including the Guzmán and Peraza lineages. Seville became the base for the French adventurers' operations. Béthencourt did homage to the king of Castile. His conquests—the islands of Lanzarote, Fuerteventura, and Hierro—became a fief of the Castilian crown.

It was one of those epoch-making accidents that history sometimes throws up. As an undesigned result, Castile had Europe's first Atlantic colony in central latitudes and—more significantly for the future of the world—a base almost athwart the Atlantic trade winds, from where the remoter ocean, and its further shore, could be explored. Castile was in a position to control access to the Atlantic wind system when the era of transoceanic navigation began later in the century. To adapt a famous phrase, without Jean de Béthencourt, Columbus would have been unthinkable. And without the curtain raiser in the Canaries, the drama of Castile's transatlantic empire could never have opened.

Béthencourt's rights eventually passed to the Peraza clan, who added the island of Gomera to the conquests he had won. But the conquest of the most populous islands, with the richest soils, eluded Béthencourt and all his successors for six decades. La Palma, Gran Canaria, and Tenerife proved indomitable. The Perazas' efforts were said to have cost them 10,000 ducats and the life of the promising young heir to the family's fortunes, Guillén Peraza, who fell fighting the natives of La Palma at an uncertain date, probably 1458. 'Weep, ladies, weep,' a perhaps contemporary ballad enjoins,

> If God give you grace,
> For Guillén Peraza, who left in that place
> The flower, now withered, that bloomed in his face.[21]

The tenacity with which native defenders, armed literally with sticks and stones, fought off European armies is a remarkable and ill-understood aspect of the story. Their valor contributed two vital consequences to the story: first, they beat off Portuguese attacks, ensuring that Castile would not have to share the archipelago with another European power; secondly, their resistance to the private efforts of the Perazas ensured that the Castilian crown would eventually commit official resources to the conquest.

Portuguese Exploration in the African Atlantic

The chivalry-steeped world of Gadifer de La Salle and Guillén Peraza was the inescapable context of exploration. The duke of Bourbon, erstwhile chief of La Salle and Béthencourt, was an epitype of chivalric virtue and one of the personal heroes of the infantes of Portugal, who, for most of the fifteenth century, became the leading patrons and proponents of Atlantic exploration. The traditional historiography of Portuguese exploration 'has been plagued,' wrote one of its leading modern students, John Russell-Wood, 'by the cape-by-cape depiction of the building of empire and the founding of innumerable havens by indomitable adventurers.'[22]

Like many princes of the Renaissance, the Portuguese infantes were prepared to invest heavily in 'fame,' because they lived in an age fond of sententious historiography and of appeals to what would nowadays be called 'the judgment of history.' Posthumous renown was a criterion of the good husbandry of political authority, and their chroniclers did the Portuguese dynasty proud. No prince drew more praise than Dom Henrique. He is familiar today as Prince Henry the Navigator, but the name, in the modern sense, is misleading for a patron of navigators who himself never made more than two or three short sea trips on familiar routes between Iberia and Morocco. The soubriquet has been current only since the nineteenth century and was coined, at the earliest reckoning, in the seventeenth.

Henrique's was a world of shabby swagger. His *pourboires* to men of letters, though money well spent, were squeezed out of meager resources. His early fortune seems to have been founded on piracy,[23] his growing competence on a soap monopoly. Although he spoke and wrote of his enterprises as warlike, he struggled to reconcile commercial objectives with the spirit of crusade. Even when he was unable to find gold, or deal profitably in slaves, there were valuable products of the region around the Sahara to be picked up on the coasts his ships traversed: natural dyes in the Canaries, oryx hides, civet musk and gum arabic on the mainland, turtle meat and blood (a supposed cure for leprosy) came from the Cape Verde Islands. His castle at Sagres, commonly misrepresented as a sort of salon of savants, may have been closer in spirit to a prefiguration of the Castle Drogo of Julius Drew, who founded the chain of Home and Colonial Stores, or perhaps—because of the soap—the Thornton Manor of William Lever, who founded Unilever.

He was, in his own way, a *nouvel arrivé*—a royal cadet with ideas above his station. Born a prince, he wished to be a king. Sprung from an impecunious and parvenu dynasty, which had seized the Portuguese crown as recently as 1385, he wanted the sort of wealth that control of the gold trade promised. To make up for the lack of 'ancient riches,' which Aristotle defined as the criterion of true nobility, Henrique saturated himself in the prevailing aristocratic ethos of his day, the 'code' of chivalry.

For at the opposite pole from the image of Henrique the grocer is the equally false, but at least contemporary, image of Henrique the *beau idéal* of romance: an Arthurian figure, surrounded by Merlinesque cosmographers and adventurous knights and squires, riding the waves on missions of knightly and Christian virtue, doing battle with swart paynims, discovering exotic islands, braving supernatural terrors in Seas of Darkness, and fighting for the faith. Henrique certainly shared this self-perception. Largesse and chastity were among his most vaunted personal values. Though he never became a member of a knightly order, one of his positions of profit under the crown was as the administrator of Portugal's richest—the Order of Christ. Henrique treated its goods as his own and its ideals as his aspirations. Contemporaries, whether they loved or hated Henrique, united in endorsing his chivalric image of himself: to friends he was 'great-hearted' and beyond restraint from deeds of derring-do. To enemies he was 'vainglorious' and impractical.[24]

The glamour of great deeds—*grandes fectos*—thrilled him. Henrique commended battle with the infidel as 'more honorable' than war against Christians. Honor and fame, he said, were, after salvation, the great aims of life. He elevated pagan, primitive opponents to the status of 'Saracens'—fit targets for the sword stroke of a crusader—or derogated them to the ranks of the legendary wild men of the woods, the *homines silvestri*, who, commonly in the art of the time, figured as the symbolic adversaries of knights.

Still, it would be rash to take crusading propaganda too seriously. Apart from endowments made late in his career for the study of theology at Lisbon and Coimbra, Henrique never put any resources into spreading the faith. The kingdom whose extension he favored was, to all appearances, one of this world. Remarkably, the only friars who specifically obtained bulls for missionary activities on the Guinea coast—that is, sub-Moroccan Africa—in or soon after Henrique's lifetime were not even Portuguese subjects, but Franciscans of the province of Castile, to whom the Portuguese were 'pirates, Christian in name.'[25]

In a famous analysis of Henrique's motives, the chronicler he employed, Gomes Eannes de Zurara (died *c.*1474), stressed detached curiosity and crusading fervor—which have been accepted as influential by almost all historians, but which are unsubstantiated by any other evidence about Henrique. The scientific adulation he attracted in his day was no more than the equivalent of an honorary degree conferred in our own day by sycophantic dons on a thuggish 'statesman' or successful business 'pirate.'

The one point in his analysis of Henrique's motives where Zurara seems to have spoken with his master's authentic voice appears, ironically, to have been almost universally dismissed by historians.[26] 'The reason from which all others flowed,' according to Zurara, was Henrique's faith in his own horoscope.[27] Mars and Saturn were its dominant influences, with Mars in the seventh house 'of secrets and ambitions.' They destined Henrique to make 'great and noble conquests and to uncover secrets previously hidden from men.' He was indeed profoundly interested in astrology. He composed a book entitled *The Secret of the Secrets of Astrology*, dealing 'briefly,' as a surviving abstract from the library of Columbus' younger son reveals, 'with the virtues of the planets, extensively with their influence on the sublunar world and duly with the art of astrological prediction.'[28]

A good deal of evidence is available to suggest that a sense of destiny drove Henrique. He had—he was convinced—a 'talent' or 'gift' or 'vocatio qua vocatus est,' as ambassadors of King Duarte of Portugal called it.[29] According to the ambassadors' submissions to Pope Eugenius IV, Henrique preferred 'by far to let the talent handed down to him shine forth before the Lord than to bury it in the ground.' The use of the scriptural term 'talent' evokes Henrique's personal chivalric motto and the 'Talent de Bien Faire' that he felt called on to deploy. What did he think this talent was? The ambassadors' memorandum offers further clarifications: 'by amplifying the Christian name'—the phrase can, perhaps, be dismissed as an attempt to endear the infante to the pope—'he might more expressly fulfill the image and likeness of King João, from whom to him, as by hereditary right, that gift was bequeathed.'

A king's heir is a potential king, and Henrique's sense of his filial duty implied a quest for regality. He was, Zurara boasted, the most regal of Portuguese princes. Like his kinsman John of Gaunt, he must be a threat to the crown or seek a crown of his own elsewhere. A memorandum of 1432, addressed to the king from the count of Arraiolos, who knew Henrique intimately and himself played a role in Portugal's Moroccan 'crusade,' made the point vividly. Referring to the infante's desire to conquer Granada or Morocco, the count observed that Henrique might 'have the kingdom of Granada, or a great part of Castile, and have the affairs of this kingdom [Portugal] in the palm of his hand, and the Canary Islands, which you desire.' The same point is suggested by the quasi-regal household of unruly 'knights and squires' whom Henrique maintained at great cost and no little trouble: a surprising proportion of the surviving documents concerning Henrique are pardons addressed to members of his household for violent crimes, especially murder and rape.[30] This entourage was not only evidence of Henrique's pretensions: it also committed him to seeking to fulfill them in order to generate patronage with which to reward his followers.

An illuminating source, generally dismissed by historians because it occurs only in a late and corrupt version, is the account of Diogo Gões, a squire of Henrique's household, who took part in person, under the prince's auspices, in African exploration.[31] Diogo's account of his master's motives is entirely credible: Henrique needed gold with which to reward his followers. The 'sea of sand' that lay athwart the gold road was unnavigable to Christians. Only the 'ship of the desert' could cross it. So Henrique sought a way round it in ships of the other sort.

Europeans attempted land crossings of the Sahara in the fifteenth century. In 1413 Anselme d'Isalguier was reported to have returned to Toulouse from Gao with a harem of negresses and three black eunuchs, though how he got so far into the interior of Africa no one knows. In 1447 the Genoese Antonio Malfante got as far as Touat, before turning back with garnered rumors of the gold trade. In 1470, as we have seen, the Florentine Benedetto Dei claimed to have been to Timbuktu and observed there a lively trade in European textiles. And from the 1450s to the 1480s, Portuguese merchants made frequent efforts to cut across the country from Arguim, via Waddan, heading for the same destination: at least, they seem sometimes to have succeeded in diverting gold caravans to meet them. By the time of the end of their endeavor, communications with gold-yielding areas were open by sea. The intractable nature of the land route, indeed, demanded a seaborne approach.[32]

By implication, Diogo Gões linked the search for gold with an attempt to reenact a traditional strategy, such as Luis de la Cerda had adopted in the 1340s, of trying to link the conquest of the Canaries with the seizure of a Maghribi port, as a terminus for the gold trade. Diogo dates Portuguese sallies against the islands from 1415—the year of the Portuguese capture of Ceuta, in which Henrique played a conspicuous role. And while there is no evidence of sustained interest in the Canaries on Henrique's part before the 1430s, Castilian anxiety about Portuguese interlopers in the islands is documented from 1416. A large Portuguese expedition, allegedly of 2,500 men and 120 horses, apparently inspired by Henrique but paid for by the crown, was launched to defeat in Gran Canaria in 1424. And if Luis de la Cerda could contemplate a principality which included the Canaries and Jalita, there was nothing inherently impossible about ambitions which may have comprehended the Canaries and Ceuta. The attack on Ceuta is traditionally seen as an extension of the 'Reconquest,' or increasingly as part of a widespread Portuguese wheat empire. Ceuta's particular economic importance as a source of coral may also have been influential. The Ceuta expedition belongs at least as much, however, to the history of attempted European interventions in the Saharan gold trade as to any of these contexts.

Without having to rely on Diogo Gões's evidence, we can feel confident that the Canary Islands were Henrique's main objective from the 1430s onwards and that the gold trade was his main motive. Zurara concealed the importance of the Canaries—perhaps deliberately, because the failure of Henrique's efforts to acquire them would have made an unheroic tale, or perhaps because, as he tells us, he covered the events in another chronicle, now lost. But Henrique's correspondence with the popes reveals the archipelago as the focus of his interests.[33] Because the Canaries were evidently understood to be excluded from the series of general crusading bulls issued for Africa to the Portuguese from September 1436 onward, Henrique did not cease to beset the pope with requests to renew his conquest rights.

There were further Portuguese attacks on the islands in 1440 and 1442, and almost continual efforts to reach a peaceful understanding with the natives of Gomera in the 1440s. In 1446 Henrique sought to ban Portuguese vessels from going to the Canaries without his permission. In 1447 he obtained a dubious title to the islands from Jean de Béthencourt's heir, Mathieu de Béthencourt, who no longer had any legal interest to dispose of. Fortified with this specious claim, Henrique made repeated efforts to seize Lanzarote from its settlers and Gran Canaria from its natives between 1448 and 1454, in no case encountering lasting success.

The long-sustained effort in the Canaries cannot have been inspired by caprice. Henrique himself always claimed—as did those who wrote or spoke on his behalf—that he was actuated by religious motives alone: 'more indeed for the sake of the salvation of the pagan inhabitants,' claimed his brother, 'than for private gain, which was nonexistent.' But this claim was disingenuous. For Henrique, as for Béthencourt and La Salle, whose example was before his eyes, the Canary Islands signified a way of outflanking the traditional trans-Saharan gold road, an offshore staging post near the fabled River of Gold—the name is used by Zurara and other sources close to Henrique. He may also have seen them as part of a sort of bifocal dominion, part Canarian and part Maghribi, which would span the presumed route.[34]

The implications of this story subvert the traditional picture of African exploration as Henrique's priority. The much-vaunted Portuguese break-through, with which Henrique's popular reputation is virtually synonymous, was the rounding of Cape Bojador in 1434. This was a product of the effort to secure the Canaries. Coastal toponymy was highly confused, and cartography in the relevant latitudes was imperfectly reliable. It must be doubted whether the Portuguese navigators were consistent in assigning particular names to particular capes. But 'Cape Bojador' probably normally signified nothing more remote than Cape Juby. It had been passed before—probably many times. The Portuguese regarded the Canaries as 'beyond Cape Bojador.' Only in a relatively callow school of navigation, such as Henrique's, can it have seemed significant. If, when Henrique died in 1460, the cape was recalled at all, its memory can hardly have consoled him for his many failures: the Canaries had eluded him; no crown adorned his head; and of the gold of Africa only a few threads had come within his grasp.

Beyond the African Atlantic, Portuguese explorers made several attempts during the fifteenth century to investigate oceanic space. Most, however, doomed themselves to failure by setting out in the belt of westerly winds—presumably because explorers were keen to be sure of a guaranteed route of return. One can still follow the tiny gains in the slowly unfolded record on rare maps and stray documents. An otherwise unknown voyage of 1427 by a Portuguese pilot called Diogo de Silves was recorded on a map: this precious allusion was almost blotted out when George Sand, during one of her winters of dalliance with Chopin, inspected the map and spilled ink over it. Silves established for the first time the approximate relationship of the islands of the Azores to each other, enhancing the failure of sailors in his wake. Before the voyage, maps showed the archipelago strung out from north to south; after his efforts, they began to appear more or less in echelon, reflecting real differences of longitude. Shortly after the turn of the mid-century, the westernmost islands of the archipelago were reached.

Between 1452, when the westernmost islands of the Azores were discovered, and 1487, when the Fleming Ferdinand van Olmen was commissioned to seek, like Columbus, 'islands and mainlands' in the ocean, at least eight Portuguese commissions survive for voyages into the recesses of the Atlantic.[35] Meanwhile, from 1481, at the latest, as we shall see in the next chapter, Bristolian navigators were urgently engaged in their search for the legendary island of Brasil. Attempts from the Azores, such as van Olmen's, were doomed to be turned back by the prevailing westerly winds. Those from Bristol had to succeed, if at all, within a perilously short favorable spring season and, given the conditions of navigation on the far side of the ocean, would find it hard to get beyond Newfoundland.

'Round Africa's Bulge'

Gradually, as success in the Canaries eluded the Portuguese, Africa assumed increasing importance. The great litany of exploratory voyages celebrated by Zurara began in earnest in 1441. By that date, it was doubtless apparent that little or no gold was to be had in the latitudes of the Canaries, which thenceforth became important chiefly as advanced bases 'for the greater perfection,' as Zurara wrote, of Henrique's deeds. It was necessary to continue the search further south, and to exploit the chief resource of the region: slaves. Significant amounts of gold, obtained by truck, did start to reach Portugal from West Africa in the mid-1440s, but the big advances, both in the extent of exploration and in the discovery of gold, came after Dom Henrique's death, as Portuguese explorers worked their way around Africa's bulge.

Toward the end of the prince's life, a navigator of some genius was employed: the Genoese Antoniotto di Usodimare, who sailed up the Senegal and Gambia Rivers, making contact with outposts of the empire of Mali, in the mid–1450s. On at least one voyage he was accompanied by a Venetian with a remarkable flair for reportage. Alvise da Mosto was a Vespucci-like figure, disposed to make exaggerated claims, but his acquaintance with the homeland of the Wolof people of Senegambia seems undeniable and his account is full of authentic observations. The Cape Verde Islands had probably been sighted before; the voyage of Usodimare and da Mosto documented them in detail.

It might be tempting to see the success of these 'mercenaries,' in contrast to the slow progress of Henrique's household knights and squires, as an example of importance, in the making of the Portuguese empire, of foreign professionalism and expertise. But da Mosto, as his account makes clear, was personally interested in exploration and inquisitive about the geography and ethnography of Africa—'very curious to see the world,' as Diogo Gões said—whereas the infante's followers had other priorities, whether crusading, slaving, creating offshore fiefs in island principalities, or hunting for gold.[36]

The most dynamic source of entrepreneurism to appear among the Portuguese in West Africa came from within Portugal itself: the 'privatization' of the right of exploration to Fernão Gomes, a merchant of Lisbon, who commissioned voyages that added 2,000 miles of coastline to the area navigated by Portuguese ships, reaching a point the Portuguese called Cabo de Santa Caterina at 2 degrees north, from 1469 to 1475: it seems an astonishing rate of increase over the tortuous gropings of the lifetime of the so-called Navigator. But conditions were now more propitious. The Portuguese had broken through the most adverse of the coastal sailing conditions of the African bulge and had established colonies in Madeira and the Azores to ease the route home. The profitability of the West African navigations had been established by the trade in gold, slaves, ivory, and malaguetta 'pepper'—a pungent condiment made from Grains of Paradise.

The crown retrieved Fernão Gomes's monopoly in 1475, perhaps in order to confront Castilian interlopers. The navigation of West Africa became the responsibility of the senior prince of the royal house, the infante Dom João. Henceforth, Portugal had an heir and, from his accession in 1481, a king committed to further exploration and exploitation of Africa. João seems to have conceived the African Atlantic as a sort of 'Portuguese main,' fortified by more coastal trading establishments of the sort Henrique had founded at Arguim, because of the hostility of the natives and its suitability as a trading station, in the 1440s. Since then there had been numerous informal and unfortified trading posts set up in the Senegambia region, often by freelance expatriates 'going native' in varying degrees. But João had a militant and organizing mentality, forged in his war against Castilian interlopers on the Guinea coast between 1475 and 1481.

The most important point on the underside of the bulge, both strategically and economically, was around the mouth of the Volta, and west to the rivers Benya and Pra, where there were local sources of gold, while more gold could be traded from upriver. Here the most impressive establishment, the fort of São Jorge da Mina, was erected at João's orders in 1482 by a party of 100 masons, carpenters, and workmen. The inauguration of a new policy of permanent footholds, disciplined trading, and royal initiatives was apparent to the native chief, who expressed a preference for the 'ragged and ill-dressed men' who had traded there before. In European perceptions, São Jorge, which must really have been quite a modest establishment, was a fantasy city of turrets and spires, painted by mapmakers to resemble a sort of Camelot with blacks.

The other prongs of the new policy were the centralization of the African trade at Lisbon in the Casa da Mina beneath the royal palace, where all sailings had to be registered and all cargoes warehoused; and the cultivation of friendly relations with powerful coastal chieftains, like the Wolof chiefs of Senegambia, the Obas of Benin, and ultimately the Manicongos—'kings', as the Portuguese called them—of Kongo. The latitudes of Kongo were hard to penetrate against the Benguela current, but the painstaking voyages of Diogo Cão from 1482 established contact. Cão penetrated the river Zaire and by 1485 had established the shape of the coast to just beyond 22 degrees south.

At the same time João tried to give the entire African enterprise enhanced prestige at home. He took the title Lord of Guinea, emphasizing Portuguese claims in West Africa, doubtless with a wary eye on Christian envy. He also gave enhanced priority to the duty of evangelization which was thought to legitimize Portuguese ambitions. He presided over an extraordinary 'turn-over' in baptisms and rebaptisms of rapidly apostasizing black chiefs. In one extraordinary political pantomime in 1488, he entertained an exiled Wolof potentate to a full regal reception, for which the visitor was specially decked out with European clothes and silver plate.[37] By then Portuguese exploration was on the brink of a new phase, which is part of the subject of the next chapter, in which fleets would penetrate the high Atlantic, round Africa, and open a new route into the Indian Ocean.[38]

Up to that point, the Spanish and Portuguese achievement in the late medieval Atlantic was the fruit of modest miracles of high medieval technology: the compass, the cog, the caravel, and primitive celestial navigation. The navigators based their judgments of relative latitudes on glimpsed appraisals of the height of the sun or the Pole Star above the horizon, with the unaided eye. Most were 'unknown pilots.' Many known by name are recorded only in stray documents or cartographers' jottings. They often had crusading experience, like Gadifer de La Salle, or Joan de Mora, an Aragonese captain in Canarian waters in 1366. They were sometimes penurious noblemen escaping from a society of restricted opportunity at home; or they were adventurers with nothing to lose, embarked on a hazardous mission of social ascent. They sought 'routes of gold', like Jaume Ferrer, or 'routes of spices,' like the Vivaldi brothers, or slaves, like the Perazas and Dom Henrique. Increasingly, like the Guzmáns, they were genuine colonial entrepreneurs looking for cheap land to grow cash crops.

They strove to embody chivalric fable, to win fiefs or create kingdoms, like Luis de la Cerda, the would-be 'prince of Fortunia,' or Jean de Béthencourt, who had himself proclaimed 'king of the Canaries' in the streets of Seville, or the Arthur-obsessed 'knights' of Dom Henrique's affinity. Or else they were missionaries, like the Franciscans of the bishopric of Telde, who sailed to and fro between Spain and the Canaries for some forty years until they were massacred by natives, who, presumably, suspected them of collusion with slavers or conquerors, in 1393. The makers of Iberia's Atlantic destiny came from a world steeped in the idealization of adventure. They aspired to fame and most have been forgotten. But the impulse and direction they gave to overseas expansion had enormous and enduring effects.

The Maritime Turn Elsewhere in the World

Iberia, however, was not the only nursery of explorers, and the African Atlantic was not the only arena of endeavor at the time. The fifteenth century was an era of widely scattered interest in devising new seaborne communications on previously unexploited or underexploited routes. Apart from that of the Chinese,[39] the relatively well-documented examples were those of the Turks and Russians.

The Ottoman Turks were gradually building up the sea power which made them, by the end of the century, potentially world-class maritime imperialists—the most impressive seaward adaptation of a landlubber empire since Rome defeated Carthage. The Turkish vocation for the sea did not spring suddenly and fully armed into existence. From the early fourteenth century, Turkish chieftains operated out of pirate nests on the Levantine shores of the Mediterranean. Some of them allegedly had fleets of hundreds of vessels under their command. The greater the extent of coastline conquered by their land forces, the greater the opportunities for Turkish corsairs to stay at sea, with access to watering stations and supplies from on shore. Throughout the fourteenth century, however, they stuck to undertakings of limited ambition, in small ships with hit-and-run tactics.

From the 1390s, the Ottoman sultan Bayezid I began to build up a permanent fleet of his own, but without embracing a radically different strategy from the independent operators who preceded him. Set-piece battles usually occurred despite Turkish intentions and caused Turkish defeats. As late as 1466, a Venetian merchant in Constantinople claimed that for a successful engagement Turkish ships needed to outnumber Venetians by about four or five to one. By that date, however, Ottoman investment in naval strength was probably higher than that of any Christian state. The far-seeing sultans Mehmet I and Bayezid II realized that the momentum of their conquests by land had to be supported—if it were to continue—by power at sea. After the long generations of experiment without success in set-piece battles, Bayezid's navy humiliated that of Venice in the war of 1499–1503.[40]

In the early sixteenth century, some of the advisers of the sultans Bayezid II and Selim I became obsessed with the need to compete globally against the maritime reach of Spain and Portugal. To collect data about the work of the explorers of those nations became a priority for the sultans' intelligence services. Anxiety about the advantages the Christians were gaining animates the surviving portion of the world map made in Constantinople in 1513–17 by the Turkish admiral Piri Re'is: it includes a detailed report on the findings of Columbus and delineates those of Vespucci. The record shows that when the Ottomans were able to get fleets into the western Mediterranean or Indian Ocean, they could engage Portuguese and Spanish forces with a fair rate of success. The difficulty, however, lay in sustaining efforts in those seas. The Ottomans' heartlands were cut off from them by narrow straits, easily patrolled by their enemies. As for the Atlantic, that was effectively inaccessible. Eventually, the Ottomans became resigned to the impossibility of staking a claim to seaborne empire. 'God,' an Ottoman official told the English traveler Paul Rycaut in the 1660s, 'has given the sea to the Christians,' while reserving the land for the Muslims.[41]

Meanwhile, even Russia began to expand by sea in the 1430s—the period of Portugal's most intense endeavors in the Canary Islands. The evidence is painted onto the surface of an icon, now in an art gallery in Moscow, but once treasured in a monastery on an island in the White Sea. It shows monks adoring the virgin on an island adorned with a golden monastery, with tapering domes, a golden sanctuary and turrets like lighted candles. The glamour of the scene must be the product of pious imaginations, for the island in reality is bare and impoverished, and surrounded, for much of the year, with ice.

Pictures of episodes from the monastery's foundation legend of the 1430s, about a century before the icon was made, frame the painter's vision of the Virgin adored. The first monks row to the island. 'Young radiant figures' expel the indigenous fisher folk with angelic whips. When the abbot, Savatii, hears of it he gives thanks to God. Merchants visit. When they drop the sacred host that the holy monk Zosima gives them, flames leap to protect it. When the monks rescue shipwreck victims, who are dying in a cave on a nearby island, Zosima and Savatii appear miraculously, teetering on icebergs, to drive back the pack ice. Zosima experiences a vision of a 'floating church,' which the building of an island monastery fulfils. In defiance of the barren environment, angels supply the community with bread, oil, and salt. Zosima's predecessors as abbots left because they could not endure harsh conditions. Zosima calmly drove out

The Virgin Mary of Bogolyubovo with St Zosima and St Savatii, with scenes from their lives, 1544–5

the devils who tempted him. All the ingredients of a typical story of European imperialism are here: the more than worldly inspiration; the heroic voyage into a perilous environment; the ruthless treatment of the natives; the struggle to adapt and found a viable economy; the quick input of commercial interests; the achievement of viability by perseverance.[42]

The European Miracle'?

Still, it is one thing to feel the need to change, another to find the means to do so. Historians have scoured Europe for features that might have equipped Westerners to assume the lead in global exploration.

Technology is inescapably an area to search. It would, for instance, have been impossible for explorers to remain long at sea, or return home from unfamiliar destinations, without developing suitable haven finding and direction finding. Most of the technical aids of the period seem hopelessly inadequate to these tasks. It is not surprising that experienced navigators, in regions they knew at first hand, kept close to the coasts and navigated between landmarks. Advice from a treatise of about 1190 represents an early stage of the reception in Europe of the navigator's most rudimentary tool, long known in maritime Asia: when the sun and stars are enveloped in darkness, Guyot de Provins explained, all the sailor need do is place, inside a straw floating in a basin of water, a pin well rubbed 'with an ugly brown stone that draws iron to itself.' The compass was made serviceable in the thirteenth century: balanced on a point, so that it could rotate freely against a fixed scale, usually divided between thirty-two compass points. Other tools for navigators were gradually and imperfectly absorbed in the course of the late Middle Ages, but their reception tended to be delayed and their impact diminished by the natural conservatism of a traditional craft.

Mariners' astrolabes, which enabled navigators to calculate their latitude from the height of the sun or the Pole Star above the horizon, were already available by the twelfth century. Few ships, however, carried them until the seventeenth century. Tables for determining latitude according to the hours of sunlight were easier to use but demanded more accurate timekeeping than most mariners could manage with the sole means at their disposal: sand clocks turned by ships' boys. The so-called 'sun compass'—a small gnomon for casting a shadow on a wooden board—was useful for determining one's latitude relative to one's starting point; but we lack evidence that navigators carried this device.

In view of the dearth of useful technical aids it is hard to resist the impression that navigators relied on the sheer accumulation of practical craftsmanship and lore to guide them in unknown waters. From the thirteenth century onwards, compilers of navigational manuals distilled vicarious experience into sailing directions which could genuinely assist a navigator without much prior local knowledge. Portolan charts began to present similar information in graphic form in about the same period. The earliest clear reference is to the chart that accompanied St Louis on crusade to Tunis in 1270; but perhaps these were mere landlubbers' aid. An experienced navigator would probably have relied on memory, if he was familiar with the location, or, if not, on written sailing directions.

Two conclusions seem clear: technical aids to navigation played little or no part in the work of late medieval explorers; and those that did were borrowed from other cultures. If such technology had been decisive, Chinese, Muslim, and Indian seafarers would have got further faster than any of their counterparts from Europe.

The shipwright's was a numinous craft, sanctified by the sacred images with which ships were associated: the ark of salvation, the storm-tossed barque, and the ship of fools. Much of our knowledge of medieval shipyards comes from pictures of Noah. Atlantic and northern shipwrights built for heavy seas. Durability was their main criterion. Characteristically, they built their hulls plank by plank, laying planks to overlap along their entire length and then fitting them together with nails. Mediterranean shipbuilders preferred to begin with the frame of the ship. Planks were then nailed to it and laid edge to edge. The Mediterranean method was the more economical. It demanded less wood and far fewer nails: once the frame was built, most of the rest of the work could be entrusted to less specialized labor. In partial consequence, frame-first construction spread all over Europe until, by the sixteenth century, it was the normal method everywhere. For ships expected to bear hard pounding, however, in wars or extreme seas, it remained worthwhile investing in the robust effect of overlapping planks.

As we have seen, the ships that performed the earliest miracles of European navigation in the late Middle Ages were mainly of the form called cogs. They were normally round-bottomed and square-sailed—good for sailing with the wind, and therefore for tracing the routes discovered during the fourteenth century: outwards from Iberia into the African Atlantic with the northeast trades, back via the Azores with the westerlies of the North Atlantic. There were no revolutions in what remained a traditional design—only, at best, gradual improvements in maneuverability as a result of tiny incremental improvements in rigging.

In the fifteenth century, ships with at least one triangular sail appeared in the African Atlantic with increasing frequency—and sometimes with two or three, suspended on long yards attached by ropes to masts raked at an acute angle to the deck. These craft, usually called caravels, conferred a big advantage, in two areas. First, on the leg of the voyage between the African coast or the islands near it and the Azores, they could sail close to the wind, tacking within much narrower confines than a conventional vessel when trying to beat their way across the path of the trade winds without being forced too far to the south: typically, caravels could maintain a course only 30 degrees off the wind. Secondly, in combination with hull design of shallower draft than the cogs, the caravels' rigging could help ships to survive and make headway in the region of variable winds and adverse currents beyond the African bulge. In the long run, the cog and caravel types converged in what contemporaries called 'round caravels,' which two features distinguished. The first was a matter of rigging. They relied on square sails to make the most of following winds, but added a triangular sail for use when needed. In hull design, they kept the relatively big, cargo-carrying dimensions of the cog, but slimmed the shape and shortened the draft a little in imitation of the caravel.

Where did this ship type come from? The caravel's resemblance to Arab dhows, which used the same techniques to cope with the hazards of Red Sea navigation, has inspired speculations that the caravel was the product of intercultural exchange in medieval Iberia, but there is no direct evidence for this. Triangular rig and shallow draft were already traditional for Portuguese fishing vessels. The ships typically used by Portuguese explorers of the African Atlantic could have been developed from the fishermen's models, with the addition of decking and with somewhat expanded dimensions—in recorded instances they ranged between 40 and 60 feet, with a recorded capacity of perhaps between 40 and 80 tons—so that they could carry truck out to Africa and bring slaves back.

The biggest problem Atlantic exploration posed for the inventiveness of technicians was water supply. Ships had to stay at sea for unprecedentedly long times and, as they penetrated further along the African shore, they were often off arid coasts. The return course via the Azores could involve three or four weeks without any possibility of replenishing water stocks. Though we know absolutely nothing about how they coped, improvements in water casks must have been made; certainly, Spanish chandlers in the late fifteenth century regarded Portuguese water casks as superior. To improve the durability of shipboard water supplies, the usual recourse was to add vinegar, which acted as a suppressant of harmful microorganisms.

Although technological change played its part in equipping western Mediterranean explorers, it does not on its own explain Europeans' exploring prowess. Shipping technology was far more propitious in Eastern seas. Generally speaking, ships built in the yards of the Indian Ocean had hulls made of planks laid end to end and sewn together, or linked by wooden dowels inserted into the seams, rather than being nailed as was usual in Europe and China. This may seem fragile, but only to minds prejudiced by Western practice. In fact, Eastern hulls were typically more waterproof, thicker, and more robust than those of vessels of European build. Vessels could be hugely bigger, with, on average, more masts, and carrying capacity up to thirty times greater than the biggest European vessels of the day.

A description by a Portuguese seaman of his fleet's attempt to capture a Javanese junk in 1511 demonstrates the advantages of the prey: she was too tall for the Portuguese to board, and her hull, reinforced with four superimposed layers of planks, was invulnerable to artillery. The only way the Portuguese could cope was to snare her rudders and so disable her. This points to a second big advantage of Asian craft: they were equipped with sophisticated steering technology: in the fifteenth and early sixteenth centuries, European ships were still steered by tiller. Finally, Eastern ships—those at least from China or built with Chinese influence—had the advantage of separable bulkheads, which kept them afloat even when rocks or ordnance penetrated part of the hull.

When aware of the insufficiency of an explanation based on technology, enquirers often turn to the assumption that responsibility lies with supposed peculiarities of western European culture. Culture is part of an unholy trinity—culture, chaos, and cock-up—which roam through our versions of history, substituting for traditional theories of causation. It has the power to explain everything and nothing. The Atlantic breakthrough is part of a huge phenomenon: 'the rise of the West,' 'the European miracle'—the elevation of Western societies to paramountcy in the modern history of the world. Thanks to the displacement of traditional concentrations of power and sources of initiative, the former centers, such as China, India, and Islam, became peripheral, and the former peripheries, in western Europe and the New World, became central. Capitalism, imperialism, modern science, industrialization, individualism, democracy—all the great world-shaping initiatives of recent history—are supposed, in various ways, to be peculiar inventions of societies founded in or from Europe. In part, this is because counterinitiatives from elsewhere have not yet been given due attention. In part, however, if allowance is made for traditional exaggerations of Western uniqueness, it is simply true. It is tempting, therefore, to attribute the Atlantic breakthrough, with all its consequences, to something special about the culture of the region concerned.

Most of the cultural features commonly adduced are unhelpful, either because they were not unique to the western European seaboard; or because they are phony; or because they were not around at the right time. The political culture of a competitive state system was shared with southeast Asia, with parts of Europe that contributed nothing to exploration, and, in a sense, with daimio Japan. As a religion conducive to commerce, Christianity was equaled or excelled by Islam and Judaism, among others, including Jainism and some Buddhist traditions, expressed, as we have seen, in Jatakas and in the reliefs of

Borobudur (see figure on p. 36). The tradition of scientific curiosity and empirical method, which certainly seems to have some relevance for exploration which is, in essence, a form of experimental observation, was at least as strong in Islam and China in what we think of as the late Middle Ages (though it is true that a distinctive scientific culture did become discernible later in Europe and in the parts of the Americas settled from Europe). Missionary zeal is a widespread vice or virtue and, though most of our histories ignore the fact, Islam and Buddhism both experienced extraordinary expansion into new territories and among new congregations, at the same time as Christianity, in the late Middle Ages and early modern period. Imperialism and aggression are not exclusively white vices. The explorers of the modern world operated among expanding states and emulous competitors in every continent. Nor is it convincing to appeal to supposed cultural traits to explain the arrest, stagnation, or lack of interest in global exploration of non-European cultures. It is impossible, for instance, to have any faith in 'Confucianism' when it is invoked to explain phenomena as various as Chinese expansion in the eighteenth century, Chinese stagnation in the nineteenth century, and the vigor of the 'tiger' economies of the twentieth century. We should be reluctant to resort to reasoning of this kind to explain the Atlantic irruption of some western European navigators.

Nevertheless, we have seen evidence of one feature of European culture which did make the region peculiarly conducive to breeding explorers. They were steeped in the idealization of adventure. Many of them shared or strove to embody the great aristocratic ethos of their day—the 'code' of chivalry. Their ships were steeds, and they rode the waves like jennets. Their role models were the footloose princes who won themselves kingdoms by deeds of derring-do in popular romances of chivalry—the pulp fiction of the time—which often had a seaborne setting. The hero, down on his luck, who risks seaborne adventures to become ruler of an island realm or fief, is the central character of the Spanish versions of the stories of Apollonius, Brutus of Troy, Tristram, Amadis, King Canamor, and Prince Turian among others, all part of the array of popular fiction accessible to readers at every level of literacy in the fourteenth and fifteenth centuries. The standard denouement provided Cervantes with one of his best recurring jokes, in which Sancho Panza begs Don Quixote to make him governor of an island, with, if it may be, 'a little bit of the sky' above. At the margins, chivalric and hagiographical texts merged. The *Navigation of St Brendan*—the Irish hermit who, as we have seen, according to the legend, explored the western ocean in search of the earthly paradise—popularized the notion that wanderings at sea could ennoble the soul. Columbus made several allusions to the text and frankly included the earthly paradise among the objects of his own travels. The fourteenth-century Spanish romance the *Libro del caballero Zifar* was, in essence, a divinization of the legend of St Eustace, whose seaborne exile led at last to reunion with his cruelly sundered family.

That the sea was a proper field of chivalric endeavor was a commonplace, established by a tradition traceable to the early thirteenth century. It was as if romance could be sensed amid the rats and hard tack of shipboard life. The similarity between a gaily flag-hung ship and warhorse had impressed writers from Alfonso the Wise to Gil Vicente (*c.*1470–1536). The ship must be pictured starlit and with sinuous sail, the horse girthed and caparisoned for knightly combat.

> Digas tu, el marinero . . .
> Si la nave o la vela o la estrella
> Es tan bella.
> Digas tu, el caballero . . .
> Si el caballo o las armas o la guerra
> Es tan bella.
>
> (Sailor, declare
> If ship or sail or star
> Can be as fair.
> Rider, declare,
> If horse or arms or war
> Can be as fair.)[43]

The entourage of Dom Henrique was full of chivalric affectations. The members of his affinity were often little better than desperadoes, déclassé hidalgos exiled from court for crimes of ignominy or infamy. Yet they gave themselves storybook names like Tristram of the Island and Lancelot of the Island. Tristram, a paladin of Madeira, illustrates the gap between the ideals they professed and the behavior they displayed. He lived the romance implied by his Arthurian name, exacting oaths of homage from the cutthroats who came to his island. No incident better captures the tenor of his life than a curious abuse of chivalric conventions in 1452. Diogo de Barrados, a knight of Henrique's service, had been exiled to Madeira, where he served Tristram in his household like a knightly retainer, performing 'honor and vassalage.' Ever since Arthur and Lancelot, lords had tended to encounter sexual trouble with their ladies and household knights. In the present case, Diogo abused his status to seduce Tristram's daughter. The scene, laconically recounted in a royal pardon, in which Tristram chops off the offender's pudenda and flings him into a dungeon, takes us into a strange world of mingled chivalry and savagery.

Maritime romance had other real-life counterparts. The world of Castilian naval warfare is the world of Count Pero Niño, whose chronicle, written by his standard bearer in the second quarter of the fifteenth century, is a treatise of chivalry as well as an account of campaigns. *El vitorial* celebrates a knight never vanquished in joust or war or love, whose greatest battles were fought at sea; and 'to win a battle is the greatest good and greatest glory of life.' When the author discourses of the mutability of life, his interlocutors are Fortune and Wind, whose 'mother' is the sea 'and therein is my chief office.'[44]

From this world Columbus' own father-in-law came. Bartolomeo Perestrelo was the youngest son of a merchant of Piacenza who had made a fortune in Portugal sufficient to enable him to place his children at court or in its vicinity. Bartolomeo's elder brother became prior of a monastery of royal foundation. His sisters became mistresses of the archbishop of Lisbon. Service in Henrique's household gave him an opportunity to make his way as a seafarer and colonizer to the island of Porto Santo near Madeira. Here, after the legitimation of his sisters' children, he was made hereditary captain general in 1446. He died in 1457 and Columbus married the elder daughter of his second marriage at an uncertain date in the late 1470s.[45]

Although fewer texts have survived, chivalric romances in France and England—the homelands of other explorer communities of the fifteenth century—also had seaborne settings. The most important of the lost books was a *Gesta Arthuri*, recorded in sixteenth-century summaries, in which Arthur, finding his home island too small, set sail to conquer Iceland, Greenland, Norway, Lapland, Russia, and the North Pole. This seems bizarre, but was consistent with tradition: in the twelfth century, Geoffrey of Monmouth had included six islands 'in the west' among Arthur's supposed conquests, and many romances located Arthur's last resting place on an Atlantic island. Another text known only through sixteenth-century allusions is the fourteenth-century story of Robert (or, in some versions, Lionel) Machin or Macham, who, eloping with his inamorata, was blown by a storm to the previously unknown island of Madeira.[46]

Columbus himself was highly susceptible to the stimulation of chivalric reading. The most famous incident in the entire history of exploration surely occurred at that moment on 12 October 1492 when a lookout from the rigging of Columbus' flagship cried, 'Land!' Yet despite its fame the episode is shrouded in uncertainty. The lookout's identity is unclear and the priority of his achievement was disputed by Columbus himself, who claimed the reward for the first sight of land on the grounds that he had seen a telltale light the previous night. Columbus' insistence on his claim has been ascribed to dishonesty, greed, and thirst for fame. It becomes easier to understand when we realize that although Columbus' voyage was unprecedented in fact—his route was, as he himself said, one 'by which, as far as we know for certain, no man has ever been before'—it did have a precedent in literature. In a medieval Spanish version of the Alexander romance, the Macedonian king made his own discovery of Asia by sea, and when the land came into sight,

> Díxoles Alixandre de todos mas primero
> Que antes lo vió él que ningunt marinero,[47]

which we might translate, 'To his men said Alexander, the first of all the crew, That he'd seen land ahead ere any seaman knew.' Is it too fanciful to suppose that Columbus, who later called his discoveries a world 'which Alexander had labored to conquer,'[48] might have been influenced by this text? The trajectory of his life so closely resembled the plot of a late medieval romance of seaborne chivalry that it is hard to resist the impression that he modeled it on such sources; in a sense, he plagiarized from them when writing up his own adventures.

Although it is mischievous to accuse other cultures of hostility or indifference to trade and seafaring, the cult of seaborne chivalry did have the effect of ennobling, in Europe, activities which elsewhere had a derogating drag on rank or a depressant influence on social mobility. The Chinese naval effort of the early fifteenth century was undermined by mandarin opposition, which reflected the priorities of a landlubber class. In fifteenth-century Melaka, Muslim traders used titles of nobility and Hindu merchants used the lesser, Sanskrit-derived style of *nina*; but they could not attain the highest ranks. Rulers in that region had hands permanently sullied with traffic, but none dared style himself, like the Portuguese king, 'Lord of Commerce and Navigation.'

It would be a mistake, however, to make too much of these differences or to suppose that maritime Asia was hobbled by prejudices, or that her potential long-range trades and empires were lamed and limited by cultural deficiencies. On the contrary, many Asian states were run by sultans and zamorins with something like entrepreneurial flair. The suitability of traditional societies in the region to be homes of empires and springboards of capitalism is demonstrated in the eventful mercantile and imperial histories of many of them. Europeans' leap into prominence was the outcome not, it seems, of European superiority, but of others' indifference and the withdrawal of potential competitors from the field.

Chinese naval activity, for instance, was aborted after Zheng He's last voyage, probably as a result of the triumph at court of Confucian mandarins, who hated imperialism and depised trade. The Ottoman effort was stoppered by straits: in every direction—in the central Mediterranean, the Persian Gulf, and the Red Sea—access to the oceans was through narrow channels easily controlled by enemies. Overwhelmingly and inevitably, in the face of ice-bound seas, most of Russia's fifteenth-century expansion was landward.

Back to the Wind

These frustrations help to explain western Europeans' advantage. To start worldwide ventures, it was vital to be in the right place. In the age of sail, maritime route finding depended on access to favorable winds and currents. Navigators from the Indian and western Pacific oceans would not have found conditions favorable for long-range navigations outside the area of the monsoons, even had they wished to do so. The only navigable route eastward across the Pacific was an effective dead end until trading places developed on the west coast of America in colonial times. The ways out of the Indian Ocean to the south were laborious and dangerous and led, as far as was known, only to unrewarding destinations. Habitués of the monsoons had no call to experiment in fixed-wind systems.

Inside the fixed-wind system of the Pacific, the most adventurous long-range navigators in the world, the Polynesians, were condemned by their location to sail into the wind. As we have seen, they had probably reached the limits of the expansion possible with the technology at their disposal by the beginning of the last millennium. Their remotest outposts of settlement, in Hawai'i, Easter Island, and New Zealand, were too remote to keep in touch with. When first reported by European visitors in the seventeenth and eighteenth centuries, they had already accumulated hundreds of years' worth of cultural divergence from the lands of provenance of their settlers.

The Atlantic, by contrast, was highway to the rest of the world. To master an oceanic environment, you have to penetrate the secrets of its winds and currents. Throughout the age of sail—that is, for almost the whole of history—geography had absolute power to limit what man could do at sea. By comparison, culture, ideas, individual genius or charisma, economic forces, and all the other motors of history meant little. In most of our explanations of what has happened in history, there is too much hot air and not enough wind.

A trade wind system dominates the Atlantic: a regular pattern, that is, of prevailing winds which blow in the same direction, regardless of the season. From around the northwest corner of Africa, all year round, trade winds curl across the ocean to within a few degrees above the equator, and lead on to the lands around the Caribbean. Thanks to the northeast trade winds, the maritime communities around the mouths of the Tagus and Guadalquivir had privileged access to much of the rest of the world. The prodigious reach of the Spanish and Portuguese empires in the age of sail was in part the result of this good fortune. In the southern hemisphere, the same pattern is roughly mirrored, by winds which link southern Africa to Brazil. Like the northeast trades, these winds become more directly easterly, swinging as they approach the equator. Between the two systems, around or just north of the equator, are the almost windless latitudes called the doldrums. Beyond the latitudes of the trade winds, in both hemispheres, westerlies blow. In the southern hemisphere, they are remarkably strong and constant, affording a fast route around the globe.

There are three big exceptions to the regularity of the pattern. In the crook of Africa's elbow, inside the Gulf of Guinea, a monsoon-like effect sucks wind in toward the Sahara for much of the year, turning the underside of the West African bulge into a dangerous lee shore. In the northern belt of westerlies, a corridor of brief spring variables in the latitudes of the British Isles helps explain why so much of the exploration of maritime North America was launched from Britain. In the far north, beyond the British Isles, the westerlies are less unremitting and there is a counterclockwise series of currents, dominated by the Irminger current, which leads west from Scandinavia, below the Arctic circle. This, as we have seen, makes an intelligible context for the Norse navigations to the Faeroes, Iceland, Greenland, and parts of North America. Other currents could be exploited by navigators anxious to use the system to best advantage. For voyagers to Europe from the Caribbean, for instance, the Gulf Stream, discovered in 1513 by a Spanish explorer in search of the 'Fountain of Youth,' links up with the homebound westerlies of the North Atlantic. Along the coast of South America, the Brazil current leads south across the face of the southeast trades, diminishing the hazards of navigation along a lee shore.

From the northwest edges of the ocean, its wind systems provided easy access to the great windborne thoroughfares of the world. Except for certain Maghribi communities, which remained surprisingly indifferent to long-range seaward enterprise in the critical period, no other Atlantic-side peoples enjoyed a position near the outward path of the northeast trades, and none had the maritime technology or traditions that western Europeans were able to use. Why did the Maghribis not join or preempt the European enterprise? Traditionally, their maritime potential has been underestimated. Because the ocean was a cauldron of the imagination, in which fantastic tales were set, imaginary evocations displaced real experience in most of the literature of the time. Al-Idrisi, the court geographer of Roger II of Sicily, established a tradition that most subsequent writers have followed. 'No one knows,' he wrote, 'what lies beyond the sea . . . because of the hardships which impede navigation: the depth of the darkness, the height of the waves, the frequency of tempests, the multiplicity of monsters and the violence of the winds. . . . No navigator dare cross it or penetrate the open sea. They stick to the coasts.' Yet if high-seas navigation was rarely attempted, it was not for want of suitable ships, men, or spirit. Rather it was the very intensity of coastal activity that inhibited ventures further afield. There was so much trade, migration, and naval warfare that the shipping stock was always fully employed and, as in the Indian Ocean, there was little incentive to develop new opportunities.[48]

On other Atlantic shores, there were no communities interested in rivaling the western European enterprise. The trading peoples of the circum-Caribbean region did not develop means of long-range navigation by sea. The commercial vocation of cities and kingdoms in West Africa was oriented toward river traffic and coastal cabotage.[50] Yet the problem remains: the advantages of an Atlantic-side position had always been available to the maritime communities of western Europe. If position was decisive, why was the Westerners' worldwide maritime enterprise so long delayed, and so suddenly unleashed? That is the central problem for the next chapter.

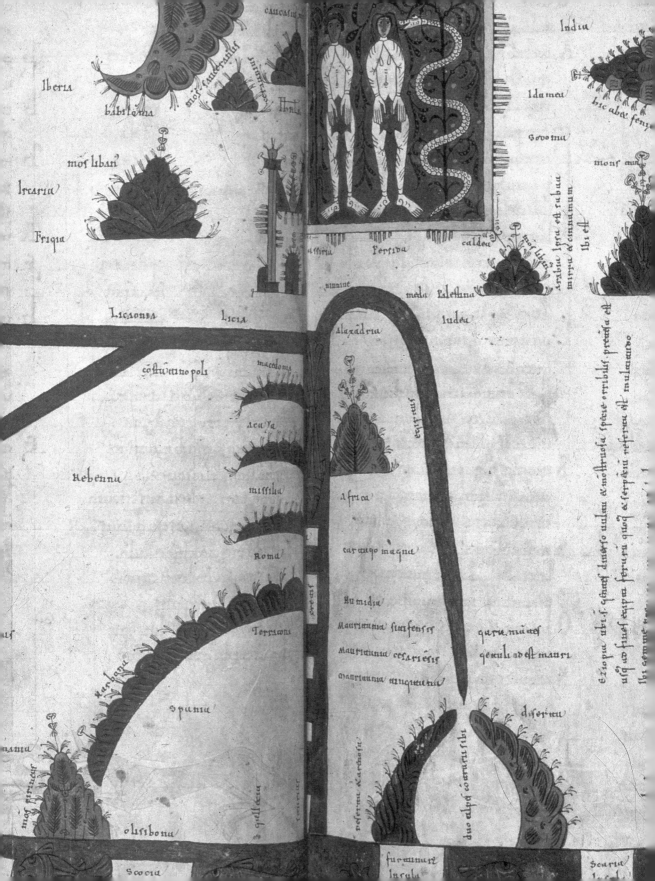

Iberia

babilonia

mos liban̄

Ircaria

Frigia

caucasus mons

mons caudacatus

iuuancipium

Ponta

India

Idamea

Sodoma

mons cau...

Assiria   Persida   caldea

mos liban̄

Arabia igra et rubra
mirra & cinnamum
ibi e͞t

ninue   meda   Palestina

Liconia   Licia   Iudea

alazadria

costantinopoli   macedonia

euptus

Rebenna   acaya

missina   Africa

Roma   cartago magna

numidia

Terraconis   mauritania sitifensis   garamātes
mauritania cesariēsis   getuli ad est mauri
mauritania tingitania

Spania

mabitania   referta kartadfolii?   disertina

duo alpes comarcisti

olissibona

ethiopia ubi.s.gen͞t dinerso uultu a͞mostruosa specie orribilis. precisa est
uisu quod fines extra ferunt͞ quod a serpētu referunt ōt multaucro͞
ibi com me m...?

Scocia   furcunt?
Insula   Searia?

5 Vaulting

The Great Leap Forward of the 1490s

A cabinful: instruments, computations, maps,
Guesswork and lies and credibility gaps,
Travel-tales, half-dreamed and half-achieved, perhaps.

F. C. Terborgh, 'Cristóbal Colón'

AFTER a lecture I once gave in Boston on Spaniards' treatment of the indigenous peoples of their empire, the mayor rose from the audience to ask whether I thought English behavior toward the Irish was not worse. The strength of the Irish legacy in Boston is one of the many signs that make you feel, wherever you go in New England, that you are on the shore of a pond and that the same cultures that you left behind on one side of it have spread to the other with remarkably little change, and remarkably little loss of identity, along the way. In Providence, Rhode Island, the only resident foreign consul is Portuguese: you can buy sweet bread for breakfast or *pasteis de Tentúgal* for tea. A parking lot a few blocks from Brown University was signposted, when I lived nearby, with the words 'Do Not Park Here Unless You Are Portuguese.' Ancestral homes, ancestral grievances, are easily recalled. There are similar patches of Irishness and Portuguese identity dotted here and there all along the coast, mirroring home and looking back across the ocean. They are surrounded with other people's transatlantic reminiscences and continuities. New England is a seaboard civilization: a narrow, sea-soaked coast with a culture shaped by maritime outreach; more than that, it is part of a civilization of two seaboards that face one another.

Small communities span the Atlantic. So does a sense of belonging to a single civilization. When people nowadays speak of 'Western civilization' they mean, essentially, an Atlantic continuum comprising parts of western Europe and much or most of the Americas. The creation of this ocean-spanning world has been a curious departure in the history of civilization. When other civilizations transcended their environments of origin, they did so bit by bit, advancing across contiguous areas or narrow seas, rolling over land or leapfrogging between islands and emporiums. Even the extraordinary and early history of the Indian Ocean as a kernel of civilizations conforms to the pattern, because it happened in an ocean which, unlike others, can be crossed by hopping between harbors or shadowing the coasts. Explorers who found quick ways across it knew where they were going. The projection of people, habits, tastes, ways of life, and a sense of belonging across the breadth of an ocean like the Atlantic—the shores of which are not mutually accessible except by a long journey by open sea or air—was strictly unprecedented when it began.

Of all the problems of Atlantic history, the first is the most perplexing and least understood: the problem of how it started, of how an Atlantic 'meta-Europe' was launched. The peoples of maritime Europe were, for most of history, with few exceptions, remarkably unenterprising in long-range navigation, especially if compared with their enormously more precocious counterparts in maritime Asia, or with Polynesian seafarers. Any convincing explanation of the European breakthrough into Atlantic-wide navigation has to be of the kind Holmes offered with respect to the problem of the dog in the night. It has to explain not only what happened, but also what did not happen; not only the Westerners' sudden breakthrough but also the long period of underachievement that preceded it, the almost ungraspable *longue durée* of near-inertia.

We think of European culture, such as it is, as formed by movements that have unfolded from west to east: Charlemagne's *Drang nach Osten* and those that followed it; a Renaissance or three; the scientific and industrial 'revolutions'; the Enlightenment and the political and social revolutions that followed it; the formation of the European Union. But for most of prehistory and antiquity, the formative movements were exercised in the opposite direction: the spread of farming and metallurgy; the transmission of Indo-European languages; the migrations of Phoenicians, Greeks, and Jews; the communication of learning from 'the east face of Helicon'; the coming of Christianity; the invasions and migrations of Germans, Slavs, and steppelanders. Most of these movements generated refuse and refugees who ended up on the Atlantic rim, where they stayed, surprisingly immobile, as if pinioned by the westerlies that blew onto their shores. I hope I can be excused for returning to this point with insistence that allows no escape. Westerners' long passivity is more remarkable than their eventual awakening. Now Western civilisation is identified with enterprise. Yet for millennia Westerners stared inertly at the sea.

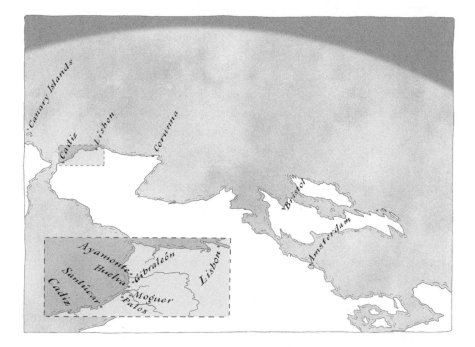

The Atlantic rim of Christendom

By about 1,000 years ago, penetration first by Roman culture and conquerors, then—slowly but thoroughly—by Christianity, turned Europe's Atlantic arc into the outer rim of what historians call Latin Christendom: an impressive civilization, but one which had, it seemed, nowhere to go but westward.

It occupied the ultimate 'water margin'—the edge of world maps at the time. Scholars in Persia or China, confident in the superiority of their own civilized traditions, thought Christendom hardly worth a mention in their studies of the world, or a corner in their depictions of it. Efforts to expand east and south from Latin Christendom—to landward, into eastern Europe, or via the Mediterranean into Asia and Africa—made some progress but were generally repulsed or compelled to retreat by plagues and great freezes. To the north and west, along most of the exposed coast, only a narrow stretch of ocean could be explored by navigators pressed by the prevailing westerlies. Some communities developed local and regional maritime cultures and, in particular cases, fairly impressive deep-sea fisheries: these were schools of experience from which the explorers of the 1490s drew ships and crews. Exceptionally forays were made far into the ocean by the Norse navigators and colonists of the high Middle Ages and the explorers and settlers of eastern Atlantic archipelagos in the fourteenth and fifteenth centuries. Taking advantage in the far north of currents that lead across the ocean, seafarers from Scandinavia and Ireland opened up Iceland to colonization in the ninth century and Greenland in the eleventh. Until the mid-fourteenth century, Icelanders made voyages as far as the North American mainland. The remotest of these precarious links, however, was severed when the Greenland colony was wiped out.

Their buried bones recount the increasing severity of the Greenlanders' lives in the fifteenth century. They went on eating seals—but not, in the final stages of occupation, harbor seals, who dislike summer drift ice. They tried to keep up their stocks of kine while pastures shrank. Pollen studies show the climate was getting wetter. Whether the last colonists were destroyed by the invasions of 'barbaric pagans from neighbouring countries,' or died out, or migrated of their own volition, they seem eventually to have run out of ecological options as the climate got colder and life harder.[1] They were not the only sufferers. For most of the fifteenth century, Europe was a contracting civilization. Recovery from the disasters and contraction of the fourteenth century was slow. Though plagues were less severe than in the fourteenth century, they remained frequent. Though habituated by now to the severity of the climate of their 'little ice age,' western Europeans did not reoccupy the high ground and distant colonies vacated in the previous century. In most places, population increase was modest, and probably did not restore the levels attained before the Black Death. Impersonal enemies—plague, war, and famine—were joined by human foes. In 1396 the failure of a crusade against the Turks marked the beginning of a long period of retreat on Christendom's eastern Mediterranean frontier. Meanwhile, in the northeast, pagan Lithuanians eroded the conquests of the Teutonic Order along the Baltic.

When the Atlantic breakthrough came, it exploded with startling sudden-ness, in a single decade: the 1490s. Or, rather, it was packed into a few years, from Columbus' first transatlantic crossing in 1492 and Pedro Alvares Cabral's landfall in Brazil in 1500. Between them, these voyages achieved two outcomes that reshaped the world.

First, they put Eurasia and Africa in touch with the Americas—joining, in particular, the densely populated central belt of the Old World, from China to western Europe, via south and southwest Asia and the Mediterranean, to the technically advanced and intensively settled parts of the New World in Mesoamerica and around the Caribbean. Instead of an obstacle to the expansion of European peoples along its seaboard, the ocean became a means of access to previously unimaginable empires and trades. The European west was thrust beyond its historic confines. In the short term, in other words, the breakthrough of the 1490s made Atlantic civilization possible. Navigators now knew the routes of reliable, regular communication between the western shores of the Old World and the eastern shores of the New. The Atlantic, which had been a barrier for the whole of recorded history, became a link. New possibilities opened up in consequence: European imperialism in the

Americas, ecological and cultural exchanges across the Atlantic, exploitation of American resources for the benefit of European economies, with the chance to even out existing civilizations' disparities in wealth, which, previously, so favored those of Asia and left Europe's relatively impoverished. Little in the subsequent history of the world can be properly understood except in this context, peculiar to the 1490s, of the power of projection of western European seafaring.

Secondly, the routes pioneered by the explorers of the 1490s cracked the code of the Atlantic wind system. Europeans now had accurate and extensive, though still incomplete, knowledge of how the winds and currents of the north Atlantic worked. More significantly, they had become acquainted with the wind patterns of the south Atlantic. They had found out how to use the southeast trades to cross the ocean in the southern hemisphere, and to reach the belt of strong, fast westerlies that circles the world south of the equator. The immediate effect was to enable them to break into the world's richest and busiest arena of commerce: the Indian Ocean. For the first time, it was possible for merchants to transfer shipping from Europe to that ocean, and therefore to take part as carriers in lucrative intra-Asian trades. This was more profitable— as new research is beginning to reveal—than the much-vaunted direct trade in spices that Portuguese ships now carried around the Cape of Good Hope. A further effect was to give Europeans, potentially, rapid access to the sources of the spice trade in the East Indies, though this was not fully exploited until the seventeenth century, and, ultimately, useful routes into the Pacific as well. The breakthrough of the 1490s, in short, was a concentrated phenomenon, in the course of which a handful of voyages transformed the Atlantic into a potential arena of long-range cultural transmission, all within the space of some seven years, after centuries or millennia of underachievement.

So what made the 1490s special? Historians have shied away from the question. Technology sometimes gets the credit, but no technological break-through coincided with the moment of achievement. Compared with China, much of Islam, south and southeast Asia, and even, in some respects, with Polynesia, Latin Christendom seemed ill-equipped for long-range seafaring. Columbus affected but hardly achieved technical prowess in the handling of navigational instruments and nautical charts. He had a quadrant aboard his flagship on all his transatlantic voyages; but it seems to have served for ostentation rather than use. He really found his latitude by a far simpler method: he used the passage of the guard stars around Polaris to check the duration of the night, subtracted from twenty-four to obtain the hours of daylight and read the results off a printed table. We know this because the mistakes in latitude he recorded in his log correspond to misprints in a surviving copy of the table he used.[2] As far as we know, no navigator made an accurate reading of latitude at sea from a quadrant or astrolabe until well into the sixteenth century.

Nor did maps play any part in the breakthrough. Columbus had a chart with him in his first Atlantic crossing, and he and his co-commander, Martín Alonso Pinzón, made much of it, consulting it repeatedly and at one point, by Columbus' account, altering course in deference to it. Since, however, their route had never been sailed before, the chart can only have been speculative. Other navigators of the time set little store by charts or other aids. They relied on primitive celestial navigation: judging course by feel and experience and calculating their latitude by observing the sun and the Pole Star with the naked eye. Mapping and exploration were mutually nutritive processes, but explorers were slow to recognize the fact. Not until well into the seventeenth century was it normal for cartographic professionals to accompany expeditions.[3]

None of the reasons broached in the last chapter in an attempt to explain western Europeans' exploring prowess helps to account for the timing of the breakthrough of the 1490s. If anything in the culture of the region was responsible, it must have operated over a long period: culture does not unfold by fits and starts but accumulates gradually and endures lingeringly. Competition between states and communities certainly played a part in the events of the 1490s, with different Atlantic-side ports scurrying to grab a share of the fruits of exploration, and Castile, Portugal, and England vying to stake a claim to the potentially exploitable lands that the explorers revealed. But the rivalries were long-standing; they do not explain why the 1490s was such a peculiarly fruitful decade.

The feature of the 1490s which best explains the extraordinary achievements—and which displays, at least, the merit of being indisputably factual—is that it came after the 1480s. That is to say, it was preceded by a remarkably remunerative decade for investors in Atlantic voyages.[4] The deputies of the Portuguese Cortes of 1481–2 extolled the *Wirtschaftswunder* of Madeira and Porto Santo, claiming that in the single year 1480 'twenty forecastle ships and forty or fifty others loaded cargoes chiefly of sugar, without counting other goods and other ships which went to the said islands . . . for the nobility and richness of the merchandise of great value which they have and harvest in the said islands.' In 1482, as we have seen, the fort of São Jorge da Mina was founded on the underside of Africa's bulge to consolidate the diversion of gold into Portuguese hands, while the Casa da Mina centralized African trade. Previously, investors in Portuguese exploration in the Atlantic had rarely, if ever, recouped their outlay. Now it was easy to raise money for new enterprises, chiefly among Italian bankers in Lisbon.

The laborious and costly Castilian Atlantic enterprise, the conquest of the

Canary Islands, began to yield profits in the same decade, as islands were pacified and turned to sugar production. The first mill opened on Gran Canaria in 1484. The financiers of Columbus all had one thing in common: without exception, they were involved in the conquest or commercial exploitation of the Canary Islands. At the nerve center of the monarchs' war effort, scraping contingents together, assembling groups of financial backers, was Alonso de Quintanilla, a treasury official who was one of the most influential architects of policy. He seems to have acquired responsibility for organizing the conquest in 1489, when dwindling returns from the sale of indulgences caused a crisis of finance. He devised a range of expedients, including mortgaging booty and collaborating with Italian capitalists. In doing so, he adumbrated the circle that would later contribute to financing the voyages of Christopher Columbus.

Quintanilla himself was instrumental in arranging the backing for the 'enterprise of the Indies,' as for that of the Canaries. In both cases, key helpers were the Genoese merchants of Seville, Francesco Pinelli and Francesco da Rivarolo. Pinelli had been involved in Canarian finance for as long as Quintanilla, for he had administered receipts from the sale of indulgences on the monarchs' behalf from March 1480. Quintanilla's first personal subvention was made in April of that year. Pinelli went on to acquire the first sugar mill on Gran Canaria and make loans to the conquerors of La Palma and Tenerife. For his part as a backer of Columbus, the monarchs made him one of the first administrators of the Indies trade when it was organized as a royal monopoly in 1493.

Francesco da Rivarolo may have done even better out of the whole affair. His son-in-law was one of the biggest investors in the conquest of Gran Canaria. Rivarolo personally took part in the financing of the conquests of La Palma and Tenerife and became the richest merchant of the archipelago, with interests essentially but not exclusively concentrated in sugar and dyestuffs. He was a mainstay of Columbus, whose fourth voyage he helped to finance and who, at one time, dwelt in his house.

Some non-Genoese of Seville from the fringes of Columbus' world also took a hand in paying for the conquest of the Canaries: the duke of Medina Sidonia, head of the house of Guzmán, whom Columbus saw as a possible patron, and the Florentine Gianotto Berardi, one of Columbus' biggest creditors, who had a share in the earliest years of transatlantic trade. The balance, however, was strongly Genoese. The same is true of the financial circle that sustained Columbus or advanced money for his voyages. There seems to have been sufficient overlap for the conquest of the Canaries and the discovery of America to be seen, to some extent, as the work of the same group of men. The Genoese played, for Castile in the Atlantic, a role similar to that of the

View of Seville between St Justa and St Rufina from the predella of the high altar in Seville Cathedral

Florentines of Lisbon in the impulsion of Portugal into the Indian Ocean a few years later.[5]

Meanwhile, in the north Atlantic, there is good reason to believe that exploration was bringing benefits to merchants in Bristol. After a period when, owing to a Danish royal prohibition on trade with Iceland, northern goods had disappeared from Bristolian port records, the throughput of whaling products and walrus ivory recovered in Bristol in the 1480s. As we have seen, the fact that salt was carried in enormous quantities on an explicitly exploratory voyage in 1481 suggests that rich fisheries might already have been discovered by that date. Money was available for further exploration, even in the cash-strapped economy of western Europe in the 1490s, because the returns of the 1480s had been so encouraging.

If we leave out suppositional earlier journeys for which the evidence is nonexistent or inadequate, four voyages of the 1490s stand out as of trans-cendent importance. The inaugurants were Columbus' two Atlantic crossings of 1493: the first, his return from his more famous 1492 voyage, the second, the journey out on his second ocean-wide voyage from east to west. The year 1492 gets all the hullabaloo, but 1493 was a year of immensely greater significance. All Columbus did in 1492 was to sail as directly westward as he could across the Atlantic until he stumbled into something. The route he took was valueless as a basis for future transatlantic communications: unnecessarily long and laborious. During 1493, however, he established viable, exploitable routes across the central Atlantic and back—routes which would hardly be bettered throughout the age of sail.

The next in the sequence of breakthrough journeys was John Cabot's from Bristol to Newfoundland and back in 1497, which created an open-sea approach to North America, using the easterly winds available in a brief season of spring variables. This route was of little short-term value but ultimately proved to be an avenue to an enormously influential imperial terrain and to the most exploitable of the 'new Europes' created across the world by early modern colonizing movements. Then, beginning also in 1497, Vasco da Gama's first voyage to India discovered a route across the path of the southeast Atlantic trade winds to meet the westerlies of the far south.

In the last years of the decade, the so-called Andalusian and Anglo-Azorean voyages, together with Columbus' own explorations of fragments of mainland coast of the New World, expanded on these achievements. The southernmost-reaching of the Andalusian voyages encountered the Brazil current. Following up in 1500, Pedro Alvares Cabral penetrated so far into the Atlantic along the route Vasco had explored that he struck Brazil.

The simplest approach to this story is the best: looking at each of the voyages in turn.

Columbus

Columbus fascinates mystery mongers who resist the plain and unanswerable evidence of the documents to manufacture fantasy Columbuses of their own—variously Jewish, Spanish, Polish, Scandinavian, and even Scottish to suit the prejudices of the writer. Really, there is no doubt about his identity. We are better informed about him than about almost any figure of comparable social background in his day. Columbus was a Genoese weaver's son with a large, clamorous, and exigent family. Without admitting that fact, you will never understand him. For what motivated him to become an explorer was a desire to escape from the world of restricted social opportunity in which he was born.

Only three routes of upward mobility were available to socially ambitious upstarts like Columbus: war, the Church, and the sea. Columbus probably contemplated all three: he wanted a clerical career for one of his brothers, and fancied himself as 'a captain of cavaliers and conquests.' But seafaring was a natural choice, especially for a boy from a maritime community as single-minded as that of Genoa. Opportunities for employment and profit abounded. And, as we saw in the last chapter, knightly romances with a seaborne setting probably inspired him.

In the 1470s, work as a sugar buyer for a family of Genoese merchants acquainted Columbus with the waters of the eastern Mediterranean and the African Atlantic. In the same capacity he frequented the island of Porto Santo, picked up gleanings from the world of the infante Dom Henrique, and met his future wife, who, as we have seen, was a daughter of one of Henrique's cronies. Columbus also claimed to have visited Britain and Iceland in 1477 and to have sailed down the coast of Africa as far as 1 degree north of the equator in the 1480s; but he was also touched by *folie de grandeur*, and his tendency to exaggerate his achievements should make us wary of accepting his uncorroborated word about anything. Still, by the time he formulated the plan for a crossing of the western ocean, he knew two key facts about the Atlantic: there were easterly winds in the latitude of the Canaries, and westerlies to the north. The makings of a successful round trip were therefore available.

If one discounts legends spun after his death, and his own self-serving account, it becomes possible to reconstruct the process by which he formulated his plan. There is no firm evidence that he had any sort of plan before 1486—only pious deference to unreliable sources makes most historians date it earlier. Nor was the plan ever very clear in his own mind. Like any good salesman, he changed it according to the proclivities of his audience. To some interlocutors, he proposed a search for new islands; to others, a search for an 'unknown continent' presumed, in some ancient literature, to lie in the far Atlantic; to others, he argued for a short route to China and the rich trades of the Orient. Historians have got themselves into a tangle trying to resolve the contradictions. Really, however, the solution to the 'mystery' of Columbus' proposed destination is simple: he kept changing it. The tenacious certainty most historians attribute to him was a myth he created and his earlier biographers enshrined. The adamantine Columbus of tradition has to be rebuilt in mercury and opal.

Indeed, what mattered to Columbus was not so much where he was going as whether, in a social sense, he would arrive. Outrageous claims for noble status and lavish rewards accompanied his negotiations with potential princely patrons for leave and means to make an attempted Atlantic crossing. In the late 1480s, his failure to attract patronage was not, however, solely the result of his egregious demands. None of the objectives he advocated seemed, to most experts, worth investing in. New Atlantic islands might well exist. So many had been found that it was reasonable to suppose that others might await discovery. But new islands remoter than the Canaries and Azores would be less profitable to exploit, even supposing that they were suitable for the cultivation of sugar or of some other product in high demand. The possibility of finding an unknown continent—the Antipodes, as geographers called it—seemed remote. The balance of antique geographical lore was against it. And even if it existed, it was hard to see what good could come of it, compared with explorations that opened a new route to the rich pickings of Asia and the eastern seas. Finally, the idea that ships could reach Asia by crossing the Atlantic was strictly impossible. The world was too large. Ever since Eratosthenes worked it out, savants in the west had known roughly how big the world is. Asia was so far from Europe by the westward route that no ship of the day would be capable of making the journey; supplies would be exhausted and drinking water would go foul while many thousands of miles remained to be traversed.

Yet during the 1470s and 1480s a minority of experts began to entertain the possibility that Eratosthenes was wrong and that the earth was a smaller planet than previously supposed. Paolo del Pozzo Toscanelli, a Florentine humanist, wrote to the Portuguese court urging an attempt to reach China via the Atlantic. Martin Behaim, the Nuremberg cosmographer who, in 1492, made the world's oldest surviving globe, was a member of a circle that thought the same. Antonio de Marchena, a Franciscan astronomer who was prominent at the Castilian court, and who became one of Columbus' best friends and supporters, shared the opinion.

By 1492, therefore, Columbus was focused on and largely committed to the notion that he would lead an expedition to China. He scoured geographical books for evidence that the world is small, and, by misreading much of the data and misrepresenting the rest, he came up with a fantastically small estimate: at least 20 per cent smaller than in reality. He also argued that the eastward extent of Asia had traditionally been underestimated. It would be possible, he concluded, to sail from Spain to the eastern rim of Asia 'in a few days.'

So, after many failures and shifts of pitch, the project he eventually succeeded in selling was for a westward voyage to China, possibly breaking the journey at Japan, or Cipangu, as people called it then, which Marco Polo had located, with exaggeration, some 1,500 miles into the ocean beyond China. Did the patrons who eventually commissioned Columbus to make the voyage believe him? No document commits Ferdinand and Isabella, king and queen of Aragon and Castile, to the same vision as Columbus. His commission referred only to 'islands and mainlands in the Ocean Sea.' The monarchs gave him letters addressed vaguely to 'the most Serene Prince our dearest friend,' which Columbus firmly intended to present to the ruler of China. The monarchs were, however, anxious about the gains Portugal was making as a result of Atlantic exploration. Portugal had access to gold from beyond the Sahara and was investigating routes into the Indian Ocean. Castile had gained no new offshore resources beyond the Canary Islands. When it became apparent that Columbus' project could be financed at no direct cost to the king and queen (the old nonsense about Isabella pawning her jewels to meet Columbus' costs is another myth), there seemed no reason not to let Columbus sail and see what would happen.

The availability of shipping determined his choice of Palos as a point of departure, but the port was in any case well known to Columbus, who had made friends and supporters there. In particular, brothers prominent in the shipping trade, Martín and Vicente Yáñez Pinzón, recruited crew and supplied two ships in a fleet of three. Martín was, in effect, Columbus' co-commander on the first Atlantic crossing.

More important for the success of the enterprise than the choice of Palos was Columbus' decision to sail via the Canary Islands. In part, his reason was simple: most world maps of the time placed the major port of China, Guangzhou, on the latitude of the archipelago. But there was another factor involved, perhaps of greater significance: the nature of the wind system. The Canaries lay in the path of a current that gave ready access, athwart the path of the northeast trade winds. For a navigator with sufficient daring to sail with the wind at his back, or sufficient knowledge to realize that, despite trusting himself to a following wind on his outward journey, he might yet have some chance of finding a suitable homeward wind, the route through the islands represented an irresistible fast corridor westward.

To cross the entire breadth of the trade wind corridor was a daunting enterprise. No one knew for sure how broad it was or what lay beyond it. The intriguing space was left blank on maps, or spotted with speculative islands, or filled, in geographers' imaginations, with lands of classical legend: the Antipodes, an unknown continent, theoretically inferred, which would restore symmetry to an unacceptably disorderly planet by reproducing its configurations on the 'dark side' of the earth; or the Hesperides of one of the labors of Hercules; or a refloated Atlantis; or the Antillia of medieval myth.

Columbus made some show of hawking his ideas around various potential patrons in different European courts—or, at least, he spoke of doing so. But the need to sail via the Canaries really committed him to Castile. As the fifteenth century unfolded, it gradually became apparent that the islands were a worth-while acquisition for the Castilian crown. They yielded slaves and dyestuffs—commodities in growing demand in Europe. From the 1450s, the booming sugar industry of the nearby island of Madeira set an example of the kind of commercial enterprise that might thrive in the relatively irrigable soils of Gran Canaria, La Palma, and Tenerife. Above all, gold was the spur. The race to explore the sources of the West African gold trade gathered pace in the 1470s, when Portuguese commercial interests acquired the rights of exploration that had lain unclaimed since the death of Dom Henrique in 1460. Ferdinand V of

Castile—according to one of his chroniclers—saw the Canaries as the key to communications with 'the mines of Ethiopia.' In October 1477, the crown acquired the rights formerly vested in the Peraza family and their heirs. The struggle to complete the conquest continued to spill much blood and absorb much treasure, until 1496, when the last battle was won on Tenerife. By the time of Columbus' enterprise, however, most of the archipelago was fairly secure in Castilian hands.

The Canaries were a vital part of the context of Columbus in a further sense. They provided him with a starting point for his Atlantic crossing. The port of San Sebastián de la Gomera, from which he set sail on 6 September 1492, was uniquely suited to his purpose. No suitable deep-water harbor was further west, none closer to the path of the northeast trade winds that would provide the power to carry him across the Atlantic. When Columbus made use of it, its security had only recently been established, with the suppression of a native rebellion in 1488–9. The crushing of the rebels left the island in the hands of the widow of Gomera's administrator, Doña Beatriz de Bobadilla, who had probably met Columbus in Cordova in 1486, and who—perhaps by the way—was said to have stirred his affections.

The Canaries—it is worth pointing out—remained strategically significant in Atlantic history—and therefore in the history of the world—for the same reasons that attracted Columbus. Throughout the age of sail, the islands' central position in the Atlantic wind system gave Spain privileged access to the wealth of the peri-Caribbean region of America, where much of the wealth of the New World was concentrated, including, in central America and Mexico, the Pacific-side ports of departure to the riches of Peru and the harbor of return for transpacific missions. The Canaries, in the estimation of a seventeenth-century Spanish king, 'are the most important of my possessions, for they are the straight way and approach to the Indies.' Columbus succeeded where others failed because, sailing under Castilian auspices, he had access to the best route via the islands that unlocked the secret of the wind system, along a wind course that led to exciting and exploitable lands.

Columbus and his early biographers convinced the world that, on the outward voyage, Columbus was alone in his resolution, contending with fearful, ignorant, and mutinous seamen. There is no real evidence for this, though the claim that some of the sailors resented risking their lives 'so that he could make himself a lord' rings true: at least, it captures something true about Columbus' motives. Columbus was prey to anxieties about isolation, and fears—verging on paranoia—of the perfidy of those around him. He was an outsider in all company, a foreigner excluded from the almost ethnic loyalties that divided his crews: the Basques, who rioted together; the men of Palos, who

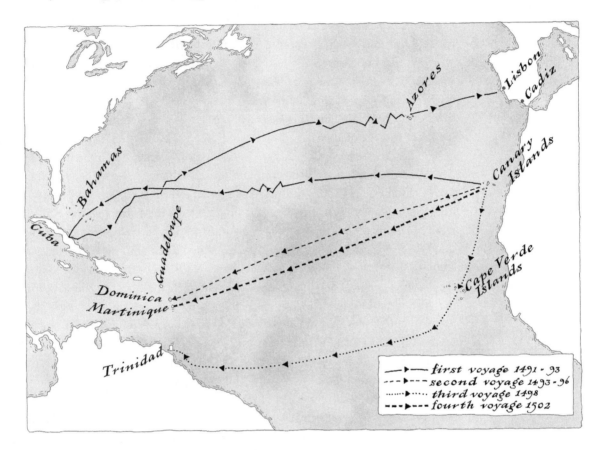

Christopher Columbus' routes to America

owed allegiance to the Pinzón clan. Clearly, however, real concerns about the nonappearance of land overshadowed the first ten days of October. Columbus' strategy was simply to sail due west until he struck land. Really, he almost certainly drifted some way south of his intended course because of the difficulty of calculating leeway, and because of magnetic variation—which Columbus observed but did not know how to allow for. Moreover, toward the end of the voyage, he altered course a little to the southwest, perhaps because Japan lay south of their course according to their chart, or perhaps in response to the evidence of bird flight and cloud formation—those standbys of sailors lost on the open sea.

For these reasons, it is impossible to reconstruct his course with absolute confidence; we therefore do not know exactly where he made his landfall on 12 October 1492. His descriptions of places and courses generally are too vague and too riven with contradictions to be reliable. His accounts of his travels are highly imaginative—almost poetic—and readers who take them literally crucify themselves struggling to make sense of them. All that is certain about the first island he touched when he reached the Caribbean is that it was small, flat, fertile, dotted with pools, and largely protected by a reef, with what Columbus calls a lagoon in the middle, and a small spit or peninsula on the eastern side: this formed an exploitable natural harbor. It could have been almost any of the islands of the Bahamas and Turks and Caicos. The natives, according to Columbus, called it Guanahani. He christened it San Salvador. The island now called Watling is the least bad match for his description.

To judge from the surviving materials, what impressed Columbus most was the natives. This does not necessarily reflect his own priorities, for his first editor, whose extracts from Columbus' papers are almost all we have of the explorer's account of his first voyage, was obsessed with the 'Indians' of the New World. He selected what concerned them and, perhaps, left out much that did not. Four themes are prominent in the narration of the encounter as we have it.

First, Columbus stresses the nakedness of the people he confronted. A reader at the time would have understood that they were 'natural men,' who might not possess legitimate political institutions but who might be naturally good. For classically inclined humanists, nakedness signified the sort of silvan innocence ancient poets associated with the 'age of gold.' For Franciscans, who were the source of the most marked religious influences on Columbus, nakedness was a sign of dependence on God: it was the state to which St Francis himself stripped to proclaim his vocation.

Secondly, Columbus repeatedly compared the islanders to Canarians, blacks, and the monstrous humanoid races which were popularly supposed to inhabit unexplored parts of the earth. The purpose of these comparisons was not so much to convey an idea of what the islanders were like as to establish doctrinal points: the people were comparable with others who inhabited similar latitudes, in conformity with a doctrine of Aristotle's; they were physically normal, not monstrous, and therefore—according to a common-place of late medieval psychology—fully human and rational. This qualified them as potential converts to Christianity.

Thirdly, Columbus insisted on their natural goodness. He portrayed them as innocent, unwarlike creatures, uncorrupted by material greed—indeed, improved by poverty—and with an inkling of natural religion undiverted into what were considered 'unnatural' channels, such as idolatry. By implication, Columbus' 'Indians' were a moral example to Christians. The picture was strongly reminiscent of a long series of exemplary pagans in medieval literature, especially from Franciscan and humanist writers.

Finally, Columbus was on the lookout for evidence that the natives were commercially exploitable. At first sight, this seems at odds with his praise of their moral qualities, but many of his observations cut two ways. The natives' ignorance of warfare establishes their innocent credentials but also makes them easy to conquer. Their nakedness might evoke an idyll, but, to skeptical minds, it could also suggest savagery and similarity to beasts. Their commercial inexpertise showed that they were both uncorrupted and easily duped. Their rational faculties made them both identifiable as humans and exploitable as slaves. Columbus' attitude was ambiguous but not necessarily duplicitous. He was genuinely torn between conflicting ways of perceiving the natives.

Columbus spent the period from 15 to 23 October reconnoitering small islands. His observations of the natives shows that he felt—or wanted to convince himself—that they were, in his eyes, becoming more civilized or, at least, more astute. In one place, they knew how to drive a bargain. In another, the women wore a sketchy form of dress. In another, the houses were well and cleanly kept. Through sign language, or interpreted from the utterances of the natives, indications multiplied of mature polities headed by kings. Though we cannot know where to place these islands on a map of the Caribbean, they occupy an important place in the map of Columbus' mind: serially aligned, leading onward toward the imagined 'land which must be profitable.' In Columbus' imagination, the first big piece of gold reported to him, on 17 October, became an example of the coinage of some great prince.

The same tension of mounting expectations affected Columbus' perceptions of the natural world. He claimed to see hybrid plants that cannot have existed. He noted the abundance of mastic where none grew. He speculated about dyes, drugs, and spices, which, he admitted, he could not identify. He did encounter tobacco—'some leaves which must be highly prized among the Indians'—without at first understanding what it was for. He got around the Caribbean by kidnapping or cajoling native guides to accompany his vessels. The islands were linked by canoe-borne trade and the local navigators had complete mental maps at their disposal, which some of them supplemented, on a later voyage, by laying out a scheme for Columbus, using beans and pebbles.[6]

In his own mind, at least, Columbus was approaching civilized lands and profitable trades. As he approached Cuba on 24 October, he assumed he was about to find Japan or China. When he got there, he took refuge in vague descriptions, unrelated to reality. Everything was of the sweetest and fairest. As it became increasingly obvious that the inhabitants were poor and improbable trading partners, he began to advocate their evangelization, as an alternative justification for his enterprise. He adumbrated a vision of a purified Church peopled by unsullied innocents. Alternatively, the thought that the people could be enslaved to make up for the lack of other marketable goods kept obtruding. This was typical of Columbus, who never found it hard to entertain simultaneously incompatible thoughts.

Dissatisfied with Cuba, he tried to get away from the island, but adverse winds frustrated several attempts. Martín Pinzón, however, succeeded in making off on his own, and remained out of touch until the expedition was almost over. True to form, Columbus suspected his co-commander of disloyalty and seeking private gain. On 4 December, Columbus at last escaped from Cuba and stumbled on Hispaniola. To understand the febrile mental condition that now overtook him a leap of imagination is needed: what must it have been like to be isolated, thousands of miles from home, surrounded by unknown perils, baffled by an unfamiliar environment, for which neither reading nor experience equipped Columbus or any of his men, and surrounded by the unintelligible babble and gestures of captive guides? Not surprisingly in these circumstances, his grip on reality wavered. At first, for instance, he was disinclined to believe the natives' stories of how they were hunted by cannibal enemies (though those stories were, in essence, true). Within a few weeks, however, he was entertaining far more bizarre fantasies: of islands populated respectively by Amazon women and bald men, of the enmity of Satan, 'who desired to impede the voyage,' of the proximity of the fabled Prester John (according to medieval legend, a Christian potentate, dwelling supposedly in the depths of Asia, who longed to join a Western crusade).

On Christmas Eve, when he had still not reestablished contact with Martín Pinzón, his flagship ran aground. The disaster turned Columbus' thoughts homeward. He built a fort from the timbers of the doomed ship and left thirty men to garrison it. On 15 January, he encountered a fair wind for home. Curiously, he began by setting a course to the southeast, but he quickly reverted to what had surely always been his plan: heading north, combing the ocean in search of the westerlies familiar to him from his early experiences of Atlantic navigation. All went fairly well until 14 February, when he ran into a terrible storm, which provoked the first of a long series of intense religious experiences, which recurred at every major crisis of Columbus' life. He expressed a sense of divine election so intense that nowadays it would be regarded as evidence of suspect sanity. God had spared him for divine purposes; he had saved him from the enemies who surrounded him; 'and there were many other things of great wonder which God had performed in him and through him.' After taking refuge in the Azores, he arrived home, congratulating himself on a miraculous deliverance, via Lisbon. There he had three interviews with the king of Portugal—a curious incident which has aroused suspicions of his intentions. Martín Pinzón, from whom the storm had parted him, arrived at almost the same time, exhausted by the exertions of the voyage.

He died before being able to present a report to the monarchs. Columbus had the field to himself.

Opinion was divided on Columbus' achievement. One court cosmographer called it a 'journey more divine than human.' But few other commentators endorsed Columbus' opinions. Columbus had to insist he had reached or approached Asia: his promised rewards from the monarchs depended on his delivering on his promises in that respect. In the opinion of most experts, however, he clearly could not have reached Asia, or got anywhere near it: the world was too big for that. He might have stumbled on 'the Antipodes'—an opinion many humanist geographers entertained with glee. 'Lift up your hearts!' wrote one of them, 'Oh, happy deed! That under the patronage of my king and queen the disclosure has begun of what was hidden from the first creation of the world!' Most likely, Columbus had just encountered more Atlantic islands, like the Canaries. Most of his gifts had a certain exotic allure— captive natives, parrots, specimens of previously unknown flora—but no obvious exploitability. He did, however, have a small quantity of gold obtained from the natives by trade. And he claimed to have got near to its source. That alone made a return voyage worthwhile from the monarchs' point of view.

His course this time led sharply south of Columbus' former track to Dominica in the Lesser Antilles, along what proved to be the shortest and swiftest route across the Atlantic. Once he was back in the Caribbean, Columbus' picture of his discoveries crumbled. First, the stories of cannibals proved gruesomely true, when the explorers stumbled on the makings of a cannibal feast on the island Columbus named Guadalupe. Then, more grisly still, he found on arrival on Hispaniola that the natives had massacred the garrison he left there: so much for the innocuous, malleable 'Indians.' Then, as he struggled to build a settlement, the climate, which he had praised as ideally salubrious, proved deadly. His men grew first restive, then rebellious. There were reports—or were they later embellishments?—of ghostly wailings by night and of shadowy processions of headless men, grimly greeting the famished colonists in the streets.

Faced with intractable problems and daunting horrors, Columbus recoiled from the thankless task of an administrator and turned to what he knew and liked best: further exploration. On 24 April he set out on two quests, both doomed to failure: first, to find more gold; secondly, to prove that Cuba was part of the mainland of Asia. Beyond the spiritual strain induced by his failures on Hispaniola, he became physically exhausted during weeks of taxing naviga-tion amid shoals and reefs between Jamaica and Cuba. Whenever he recalled this period for the rest of his life, the pain came back to sleepless eyes that 'burst with blood,' tortured with watchfulness. He talked of abandoning his post to circumnavigate the world and return home via Calicut and the Holy Sepulchre.

He snatched at any evidence, however implausible, that Cuba was Asiatic: native place names resembled Marco Polo's toponyms; Cuba must be Asia, for he had seen footprints of griffins there. After more than three weeks on Cuba's coast, he summoned the ship's scrivener to record the oath of almost every man—on pain of a huge fine and the loss of their tongues—that Cuba was a mainland, that no island of such magnitude had ever been found, and that, had they sailed on, they would have encountered the Chinese. The men made little attempt to argue with him, partly perhaps because these declarations were obviously valueless, and partly because he had been taxed so much by his grim experiences that he was beyond the influence of reason. When he got back to Hispaniola, he found the situation on the island had not improved. The last exploration he undertook, before returning to Spain in March 1496, was to roam Hispaniola, bloodily imposing obedience on every native community he could track down.

Cabot

By that time, the next explorer to contribute to the Atlantic breakthrough was in England, seeking finance for a crossing of the ocean in northern latitudes. It was a time of increased activity in the north Atlantic by English and Danish traders and pirates. Traditional products—whales, walrus ivory, Icelandic slaves—continued to tempt traders, even when the Greenland trade collapsed.[7] England and Denmark clashed over the Icelandic trade, from which the Danish king tried to ban English merchants, with increased vigor in the 1470s. Excluded, at the same time, from many ports of the north by the Hanseatic League—a confederacy of some of the most successful city republics of the Baltic and North Sea coasts—Bristolian merchants needed new outlets for their energies.

Occasionally in the 1480s, therefore, and perhaps regularly in the 1490s, expeditions sailed from Bristol in search of new islands. Even today, Bristol is about as close as you can get in England to a commune—a city with its own strong sense of identity, like an Italian city republic of the Renaissance, or a Greek polis of the classical period. In the late fifteenth century it was England's second city. Its merchants' wealth endowed huge and sumptuous churches. The maritime community's own church, St Mary Redcliffe, is still the largest parish church in the British Isles, thanks to the munificence of one of the city's richest merchant families, the Canynges, who rebuilt it after devastation by storm in

1445. Bristol's shipyards launched vessels as mighty as any built in Europe at the time. A big increase in the importation of north Atlantic products to Bristol in the 1480s shows the revived trade of the north Atlantic, which such journeys produced or reflected. Some, however, were more than commercial expeditions. They were conscious efforts to explore—to 'serche and finde.'[8] The Bristolians called their objective 'Brasil.' Many late medieval sea charts mark this putative island, without agreeing on where it lay.

How far did the Bristolian explorers get? The voyage of 1481 carried a large cargo of salt, prompting speculation that it must have been bound for the cod fisheries off Newfoundland. A merchant who worked as a Spanish spy—or perhaps an English double agent—wrote to Columbus in 1497, in the apparent conviction that they had 'found Brasil as your Lordship well knows' and what we now call Newfoundland 'in the past.' But unequivocal evidence of a completed transnavigation of the Atlantic occurs only with the work of John Cabot, a Venetian citizen (perhaps Genoese-born), who arrived in Bristol, touting a project for an ocean crossing, some time after Columbus' return.

Cabot reasoned that if Columbus could get to Asia or, at least, to some useful destination, across the breadth of the ocean at 28 degrees north, where the globe was relatively wide, a much shorter crossing might be possible further north. He therefore importuned merchants in Bristol and the king in London for the right and means to make the voyage. 'A man like Columbus,' reported the Spanish ambassador in England in 1496, was proposing 'another enterprise like that of the Indies.' His objective, according to the Milanese ambassador, was 'an island which he calls Cipango . . . where he believes all the spices of the world have their origin, as well as the jewels.' In March of that year, Henry VII granted to Cabot and his sons dominion under the crown of any lands they discovered 'which before this time were unknown to Christians' and not already claimed by another Christian king. Strictly speaking, it was a worthless concession, since Henry had no right to dispose of anybody's land, Christian or not.

Cabot sailed in what all sources call a 'small ship.' Between 20 May and 6 August 1497, he explored a stretch of coastline which, he reckoned, lay between the latitudes of Dorsey Head in Ireland and the mouth of the Garonne—roughly from 46 to 51 degrees north, before turning back and retracing his previous course along the coast. This would confine virtually the entire voyage to the coast of Newfoundland—which makes sense, since any ship reaching the southern tip of Newfoundland would begin to encounter adverse currents. He insisted that 'he has discovered mainland 700 leagues away, which is the country of the Great Khan.' He reported a rich cod fishery and speculated on the availability in the vicinity of exotic flora, including logwood and silk. According to an account of a few years later by his fellow Venetian Pasquale Pasqualigo, Cabot spent his £10 reward from the king on swaggering apparel and behaved with the usual chivalric impulses: promising to bestow the governorship of islands on his crew, down to his Genoese barber.

The king was, or now became, an investor in Cabot's efforts, contributing £20 in customs revenues from the port of Bristol to the costs of his second voyage, granting Cabot the right to requisition up to six ships, providing at least £221 16s. toward the cost of ships, and encouraging some recruits for the crew: 'John Cair going to the new Isle' received 40s. from the royal purse in April 1497. London merchants also took a hand in providing funds, according to a London chronicler. It seems overwhelmingly likely, however, that Cabot's main backing, especially on his first voyage, came from Bristol merchants. That, after all, was what the explorer went to Bristol for. In the next generation, the head of the Thorne family, one of the leading merchant dynasties of the city, claimed to have inherited an exploring urge 'from my father' and another Bristolian merchant, Hugh Elyot, who were 'the discoverers of the Newfoundland.'[9] The many investors in the search for Brasil constituted an obvious constituency from which Cabot could draw support.

He disappeared on his next voyage, never to be seen again, together with four of his five ships: the last returned to Ireland, badly storm-damaged. 'He is believed to have found the new lands nowhere but on the very bottom of the ocean,' commented Polydore Vergil, the Italian humanist whom the English employed as a court historian. But Cabot's effort was not barren of consequences. It was followed up by Portuguese and Bristolian navigators, sometimes in collaboration, so that by 1502, a great extent of coast was revealed, probably from Hudson Strait to the southern tip of Nova Scotia. However, the material rewards of exploration in the region seemed negligible, and, for most of the next three or four decades, efforts to follow up Cabot's initiative were sporadic. Columbus had found far richer pickings. Meanwhile, even more alluring economic prospects opened as a result of the perseverance of Portuguese explorers of the south Atlantic.

Da Gama

In the summer of 1487, Bartolomeu Dias left Lisbon with three ships and a commission to find the ocean route around Africa. At first retracing Cão's coast-hugging route[10] he subsequently, with great daring, turned away from the coast, perhaps in around 27 or 28 degrees south, in an attempt to use the prevailing southeasterlies in order to penetrate the high ocean and try to find a favorable wind. He succeeded in encountering westerlies, which carried him to a landfall some 300 miles east of the Cape of Good Hope, at what is now Mossel Bay. This was a major contribution to knowledge of the wind system of the south Atlantic. Dias sailed on to about as far as Cabo Padrone, or Fish Point, before turning back. The expedition seems to have been exceptionally well provisioned, suggesting that the detour into the open sea was planned in advance.

No follow-up efforts were recorded for the next ten years. Historians have always professed to find this puzzling, and commonly resort to the assumption that other voyages, of which the records have been lost, 'must have' taken place in the interim, or that a policy of secrecy obscured them. Alternatively, factional squabbles at the Portuguese court may have arrested progress and paralysed exploration. Really, however, the simplest explanation is the best. Bartolomeu Dias's findings must have been discouraging. He would have reported the adversity of the current at and beyond the Cape of Good Hope. The fact that he was unable to get very far along Africa's eastern coast suggests that he appreciated the dangers and difficulties. Indeed the sixteenth-century writer João de Barros, who became the official historian of Portuguese exploration, and who is generally well informed, says that Dias's description of the fury of the sea in the region of the Cape 'created another legend of dangers,' like those that had deterred explorers of the African coast in the time of the infante Dom Henrique.[11] Dias actually named the cape the Cape of Storms. 'Good Hope' was a label devised for propaganda purposes to make the discovery seem more auspicious.

It is apparent, moreover, that the Portuguese were deterred by doubts about whether the Indian Ocean was accessible by sea in any case. Ptolemy had treated it as landlocked, and European merchants active in the Indian Ocean in the fifteenth century did nothing to dissipate those doubts. Many itineraries of the time survive for Abyssinia and the approach to the Red Sea via the Nile, but little evidence has survived of the routes Europeans frequented beyond those points. The most spectacular exception is the account of the oriental odyssey of Niccolò Conti, which became the subject of a famous book, the *De Varietate Fortunae* by Poggio Bracciolini, in 1439. The commonplace business of a Venetian merchant took Conti to Damascus, where, in 1414, he seems to have decided to investigate the sources of the spice trade via the Persian Gulf. Taking the generally favored route out, via Ormuz, he covered most of the established shipping lanes of the Indian Ocean as far as Java and perhaps Saigon, though omitting the links between India and East Africa.

The change of fortune which led, indirectly, to Conti's fame occurred when he returned to Cairo via the Red Sea in 1437. During a two-year wait for a passport, he was obliged to abjure his faith, and saw his wife and children die in an epidemic. When he finally got back to Italy, he went to Florence, where the pope was presiding over a General Council, to seek absolution for his abnegation of Christianity. The occasion of the council had brought together humanists and cosmographers from Italy and the Greek world, and Conti's story found a ready audience. Poggio represented it as a moral tale 'of the fickleness of fortune,' yet it was a success as an example of the traditional genre of travel literature. Twenty-eight fifteenth-century manuscripts of the work survived. Pope Pius II relied heavily on Poggio's book in writing his own compilation of world geography, especially for material on Burma and China. Conti's accounts of the Ganges and the Irawaddy influenced the most comprehensive attempt to map the world, Fra Mauro's in Venice in the 1450s.

One other voyage of the same kind generated a surviving narrative. In spring 1494, the Genoese merchants Girolamo di Santo Stefano and Girolamo Adorno set off up the Nile to Keneh, turning aside to make a seven-day caravan journey to the Red Sea at Kosseir. They experienced the infamous dangers of navigation on that sea, taking thirty-five days to get to Massawah, which they recognized as 'the port of Prester John.' The remotest points on their Indian Ocean itinerary were Pegu, in Burma, where Adorno died, and Sumatra, where Santo Stefano, faced with confiscation of all his goods, was saved by an official who could speak Italian. Despite shipwreck at Cambay, Santo Stefano made it home via Ormuz by taking service with Syrian traders. Like their recorded precursors, he and his companion were not really explorers, but travelers on recorded routes, who stopped short of the Spice Islands. Their news, in any case, came too late to serve the Portuguese effort.

Rather than relying on travelers' reports, meanwhile, the Portuguese crown commissioned intelligence of its own. Pedro de Covilhão, the chosen agent, joined the service of Afonso V of Portugal from that of the duke of Medina Sidonia at a time of war between Portugal and Castile. He conducted diplomacy on behalf of João II before being sent, in 1487, with a companion, Afonso de Paiva, on a triple mission: to find the route to the land of spices; to verify the navigability of a passage from the Atlantic to the Indian Ocean; and to make contact with Prester John, the legendary Christian potentate then generally identified with the Negus of Abyssinia. The travelers made for Alexandria and Rhodes, disguising themselves as honey merchants. From Cairo, they joined the Red Sea at Toro, or El Tur, and sailed its length, via Suakim, to Aden. There they parted. Covilhão headed east in search of the spice lands. Afonso de Paiva turned south seeking Prester John.

Our only surviving account of Covilhão's journey was pieced together, some thirty years later, from an old man's memories. It contains romantic episodes, which are subject to doubt, and complexities that perhaps arise from confusion. It seems unlikely, for instance, that he really traveled up and down the Nile four times, or that he visited Mecca and Medina in disguise, making his way from there to Cairo, via St Catherine's monastery in Sinai. On the other hand, it seems probable that he reached Ormuz and Calicut and investigated the route from southern Asia to East Africa as far south as Sofala. At some point in his travels—reportedly but implausibly in Cairo—he heard of Paiva's death and decided to continue the mission to Prester John in person, first dispatching to Portugal a favorable report on the trading prospects.

Clearly it made sense to hold back further efforts to double the Cape of Good Hope until Covilhão's report became available. Unfortunately, however, his report never reached Portugal. Opinion at court havered between factions keen on further exploration and opponents who wanted to continue to concentrate on Africa. The death of Dom João in 1496 and the accession of his cousin Dom Manuel surely played some part in resolving the impasse. Manuel's imagination was alive with images of messianic kingship and millenarian expectations of the end of the world. Ever since the twelfth century, anticipations of an imminent 'age of the holy spirit,' preceded by the cosmic struggle of a 'last world emperor' against Antichrist, had dominated the prophetic tradition in western Europe. Columbus and other courtiers flattered Ferdinand the Catholic with the notion that he might be the last world emperor, with a mission to lead a crusade, capture Jerusalem, and lay Mecca waste. Manuel was equally susceptible.

The choice of a leader for the expedition fell on a surprising individual. Vasco da Gama is a hard character to approach. Materials from his hand are trivial business letters in unrevealing officialese. Even in his grandeur, when he became admiral, count, and viceroy, he remained silent and almost unsung. Biographers have therefore tended to fall back on legend: a golden legend of trailblazing among lesser breeds, and a black legend of a ruthless, leech-like imperialist. In reality, Vasco was neither hero nor villain but an irascible provincial with no stomach for the court: an *hobereau*, an upcountry gentleman, catapulted into unaccustomed magnificence; a xenophobe improbably trans-planted to the tropics; a frustrated adept of the Renaissance cult of fame, trying to enhance commerce by bloodshed.[12] He was also a fall guy made good. He was plucked from obscurity and entrusted with responsibility for the voyage, thanks only to the acquiescence of a court faction who hoped he would fail. How the voyage was financed is one of the most obscure aspects. All we can say for certain is that the crown raised backing, largely from Florentine commercial houses in Lisbon.

A few years later, João de Barros, composing his history of Portuguese endeavors in Asia from materials no longer extant, left a memorable account of Vasco's leave taking at court. If Barros is right, the king's parting words were steeped in the traditional language of feudal obligation, and sprinkled with implicit admissions of greed. His object in seeking to increase the royal patrimony, he claimed, was to be able to reward his lords and gentlemen. 'The discovery of India and those lands in the Orient' was 'the most profitable and honorable enterprise and worthy of most renown.' He hoped that the Portuguese would spread Christianity there—and get the credit for it—as well as 'seizing from the hands of the barbarians' kingdoms 'with many riches' and 'those eastern riches so celebrated by ancient writers, part of which, by way of commerce, has made Venice, Genoa, Florence and other Italian cities into great powers.' The credentials Vasco received are further clues to the objectives he had in mind. They included letters addressed to Prester John and to the ruler of Calicut. The Portuguese were seeking, as one of Vasco's captains famously declared when they arrived in India, 'Christians and spices.'[13]

Vasco set off on 8 July 1497, with four square-rigged ships: the caravels stayed at home, except for a supply vessel, chosen to be able to shift back and forth among the main ships. This was a solid gesture of confidence that the voyage would be made with following winds. On his outward journey from the coast of Sierra Leone, Vasco spent over three months crossing more than 6,000 miles of open sea—by far the longest journey ever made out of sight of land.

He made landfall at the Bay of St Helena on 4 November. Initially friendly relations with local people broke down in a volley of spears, which drove a shorebound reconnaissance party back to the ships on 16 November. Two days later, 'we beheld the cape . . . but were unable to get round it, for the wind blew from the SSW.' At last, on 22 November, 'having the wind astern, we succeeded in doubling the Cape.' By the time they reached Mossel Bay, the store ship was unserviceable and had to be broken up. They made little headway at first, but on 12 December 'met a great storm and ran before a sternwind' and within three days were beyond the Cabo do Recife, where the last marker erected by Bartolomeu Dias indicated the former limits of Portuguese exploration. Here they were pinioned by the current, which, from 17 to 20 December, persistently forced them back on their course. At last, however, as they approached KwaZulu-Natal, 'it pleased God to allow us to make headway.'

Wherever they stopped along the coast, they encountered Khoikhoi herders; everywhere, suspicion or active hostility on both sides clouded relations with them. Not until 10 January, when the explorers anchored at the mouth of the river Inharrime, did they find natives they regarded as 'good.' The descriptions left by members of the expedition—of a densely populated country, rich in copper, tin, and ivory, with courteous, hospitable people, and many 'lords' and 'kings'—reflects the explorers' heightened expectations as they got close to where they imagined the great civilizations of Asia awaited them—just as Columbus had changed his perceptions of the natives of the Caribbean as he convinced himself he was close to the gorgeous East.

This time, however, the heightened expectations were justified. When the explorers reached the region of the Zambezi, where they were inside the trading arena of the Indian Ocean, they noted the silk and satin in local chiefs' attire, and met people well acquainted with ships at least as large as their own. From Mozambique Island northwards, they used local pilots to help them navigate. Effectively, the pilots were prisoners, flogged if they appeared to mislead their abductors. These practices—which Vasco da Gama evidently considered necessary—contributed to deteriorating relations with the Muslim communities dominant on the coast. On 14th April, however, they found a relatively hospitable reception in Malindi, where the locals were used to trading with Christians: indeed, there were Christian merchants' ships from India in the harbor when da Gama arrived.

Here, the expedition acquired a pilot willing and able to take them across the Indian Ocean to the great pepper market of Calicut. The contemporary

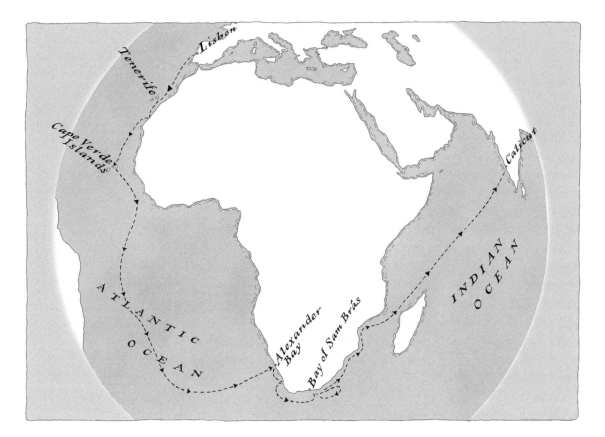

Vasco da Gama's voyage to India

sources variously call him a Christian, a Muslim, and a Gujarati. Some early sixteenth-century accounts give him the name of Molemo Cana or Molemo Canaqua. Molemo is a corrupt version of a word that just means pilot; Cana or Canaqua may be a version of a personal name, or an attempt to render a Swahili term meaning pilot. We can be certain of one thing: he was not the famous Arab hydrographer ibn Majid, with whom a tenacious but mistaken historical tradition identifies him, but who cannot have been anywhere in the vicinity at the time.

Still, Muslims who, from the late sixteenth century onward, blamed ibn Majid for showing Europeans the way across the ocean were not entirely wrong. The sage's sailing directions, written toward the end of the century, fell into Portuguese hands. Ostensibly, they were designed for pilgrims to Mecca. 'For how long,' exclaimed Ibn Majid, 'have we sailed in ships from India and Syria, the coasts of Africa and Persia, the Hejaz and the Yemen and other places, with the fixed intent of not being turned aside from the direct route to the desired land, either by worldly possessions or by human agency.' Really, however, the main market for ibn Majid's work was probably in commercial circles. This was the first instance of what became a normal—but little-remarked—habit of European explorers in the Indian Ocean: they relied on local guidance to find their way around.

Thanks to the services of their newly acquired pilot—whoever he was—the expedition crossed the ocean with the monsoon in only twenty-three days. On 20 May, Vasco anchored a couple of miles outside Calicut. From the first, his mission went awry. Ignorant of Hinduism, the Portuguese mistook the local culture for an unfamiliar form of Christianity. When he obtained an audience before the ruler, Vasco had gifts of contemptible value in local eyes: cloth, hats and coats, ewers, butter, honey, and a little coral. The courtiers derided him and said their master would accept only gold. Da Gama insisted he was an ambassador; the locals treated him as a trader—and a poorly supplied one at that. After negotiations dominated by mutual suspicion, one of Vasco's lieutenants obtained what appeared to be a contract of sorts—unless, as seems likely, it was a forgery made to cover Vasco's failure. 'Vasco da Gama,' wrote the ruler of Calicut to his Portuguese counterpart, 'came to my land and I rejoiced at that. In my land, there is much cinnamon, and much cloves and ginger and pepper and many precious stones. And what I want from your land is gold and silver and coral and scarlet cloth.'[14]

On 29 August, the Portuguese set sail for home. This time, in their haste to escape, and their unwillingness to trust local goodwill, they failed to respect local knowledge. It was the wrong season. The winds were still blowing onshore. After a pause for repairs in the Anjediva Islands, it took the fleet until 7 January 1499 to get back to Malindi. The voyage cost the lives of nearly half the crew, and crippled the survivors with scurvy. Over the whole course of the expedition, the strain on his men's endurance was such that over half were lost. At one point the ships were reduced to active crews of only seven or eight men, and one ship had to be abandoned, in January 1499, near Mombasa, for want of survivors to sail it. The two surviving ships made it back to Portugal in July and August respectively.

Vasco had made almost every mistake imaginable. His famous track, far into the south Atlantic, deserves to be commended as an open-sea excursion of unprecedented duration for a European navigator. But it was a demonstration of audacity rather than ability. Vasco can be presumed to have made the detour in order to find winds that would carry him beyond the Cape of Good Hope. Instead, he missed his latitude, made his easting too early, and fetched up on the wrong coast of Africa. He then had to confront adverse currents, which drove him back and almost defeated him. Though he arrived in the Indian Ocean by a new route, he crossed it along a shipping lane known for centuries, relying on a local guide. When he got to India, he prejudiced the future of European missions and commerce in the region by mistaking Hindus for Christians and offending his hosts so severely that, by report, 'the entire land wished him ill.' On his way back, he recklessly defied local knowledge and risked the outcome of the adventure by trying to depart for the West in August, against prevailing storms, to the peril of the expedition.

The reasons traditionally said to have made Vasco's exploit memorable have vanished under scholarly scrutiny. Western imperialism in the Indian Ocean in Vasco's wake is now seen as a feeble affair and the 'Vasco da Gama era' is regarded as not much different, in that part of the world, from the era that preceded it. Indigenous empires and trading states remained dominant and largely unaffected by Europeans scurrying and worrying at their edges.[15] At least until well into the seventeenth century, European sovereignty was confined to spots which hardly modified the overall picture and outside which colonization was a 'shadow' presence, 'improved' at private initiative.[16] Even in the eighteenth century, 'the equality of civilisations' was little compromised, according to the current scholarly consensus, by Western intrusions into Asia.[17] The European merchants who penetrated the ocean by way of the Cape of Good Hope are now seen as similar to their ancient and medieval predecessors, who usually came by way of the Nile and the Red Sea. They fitted into the existing framework of trade, served regional markets and suppliers, and caused, at worst, local and temporary disruptions.[18] Only in the seventeenth century, as we shall see, did the situation change radically, because the Dutch East India Company pioneered a new, fast route across the ocean, enforced monopolies of key products, and, late in the century, moved directly to selective control of production as well as of trade routes. To ascribe this revolution to Vasco da Gama seems impertinent.

Finally, the belief that the Cape route wrenched East–West trade out of its historic pattern by diverting commerce from the traditional Eurasian routes has long been exposed as mythical. The volume of trade along traditional routes continued to grow, together with that of the new route, almost throughout the sixteenth century, as world demand and supply expanded in the key products: pepper and exotic spices, aromatics and drugs. Traditional trade continued to flow through time-honored channels until well into the seventeenth century. It now seems incontrovertible that the first casualty of the new era—the intercontinental caravan routes of central Asia—suffered not so much from Portuguese competition as from political turmoil of the late sixteenth and seventeenth centuries deep in the interior of Asia.[19] For 100 years after Vasco's achievement, no European rival bothered to emulate it. Seventeenth-century crises in the spice trade are now generally blamed on the Dutch, for whose depredations Vasco da Gama incurs, at most, a rather remote and indirect responsibility.

Nevertheless, Vasco's voyage deserves part, at least, of the reputation it acquired. It was a stage in the globalization of trade. It was an occasion of unprecedented cultural encounters. It opened a new route for the exchange of influences between the ends of Eurasia. It made it possible at last for shipping from Europe to take part in the lucrative trades that throve within the Indian Ocean. To a lesser extent, it stimulated direct trade between Europe and Asia. Adam Smith ranked it with Columbus' discovery of a route to America as one of the most important events in history, and rightly so, for it made possible the long, slow process by which European economies, enriched by the pickings of the Orient, began to catch up with those of the Indian Ocean rim. It may not have changed much for the peoples and powers of the Indian Ocean, who barely noticed the poor barbarians from Portugal, but it transformed Europe, bringing Europeans into closer touch with the gorgeous East than ever before, and putting the newly emerging Atlantic world in touch with older, wealthier civilizations.

Cabral, Vespucci, and the Andalusian Navigators

Da Gama's voyage confirmed the dominance of southeast trades in the central south Atlantic. It was presumably in order to find the shortest route across these crosswinds that the next voyage out, Cabral's in 1500, attempted a different approach, leaving the Old World directly from the Cape Verde Islands and using the northeast trades, instead of the south equatorial current, to make as much southing as possible. This route, followed on the basis of da Gama's own reports and advice, led directly to Brazil. The fleet that accomplished it was a prestigious assembly of 1,200 men in thirteen ships, whose lavish caparisons decked the Tagus 'like a spring garden in bloom,' designed to impress the Eastern potentates with whom it was expected to trade. The assurance of huge profits, thanks to da Gama's precedent, made recruitment and investment easy. Cabral was a gentleman of the court, as were most of the captains of the individual vessels. His mood of confidence was such that once out of Lisbon on 8 March, Cabral stopped neither for victuals nor for water until he sighted Brazil on 22 April.

The next leg of Cabral's journey exposed the hazards as well as the advantages of the south Atlantic wind system. The expedition was now beyond the root area of the westerly winds, and the season, by the time of his departure on 2 May, was unpropitious. The plan was to make for Mossel Bay, identified by

Dias and da Gama as a suitable anchorage on the southern shore of Africa. Probably in the dangerous high-pressure zone north of Tristan da Cunha, a tempest struck the fleet, sank four ships, and scattered the rest. The sundered squadrons were not reun.'+ed until they had rounded the Cape and reached Mozambique.

Cabral's arrival in Brazil was almost certainly a fortuitous event. Rumors of islands and mainlands in the south Atlantic had circulated at least since the 1440s. Columbus had actually demonstrated the existence of a large land mass inland of the Orinoco delta in 1498, on his third transatlantic mission, which is worth dwelling on for a moment. In Columbus' mind, it was to be a voyage of self-vindication. His discoveries, he speculated, would prove to be 'another world, which the Romans and Alexander and the Greeks had striven to conquer.' His voyages would prove as important as King Solomon's to Ophir, or Alexander's supposed discovery of Ceylon, or 'the Emperor Nero's to the sources of the Nile.' He tried a new course across the ocean, via the Cape Verde Islands, which proved relatively slow and made landfall at Trinidad. The first recorded European reconnaissance of part of the American mainland followed, along the southern coast of the Paria peninsula, into the bay where copious fresh water from the Orinoco and the San Juan flows. 'I believe,' he concluded, 'that this land which your Highnesses have now ordered to be revealed must be very big, and that there must be many other such lands in southern parts, of which nothing has ever been known before.'

His misreadings of the altitude of the Pole Star led him into further, less felicitous speculations. The closer he approached to what we think of as South America, the wider the radius the star seemed to describe around the pole. He decided that he must be sailing uphill.

> And I concluded that [the world] was not round in the way they say, but is of the same shape as a pear, which may be very round all over but not in the part where the stalk is, which sticks up; or it is as if someone had a very round ball, and at one point on its surface it was as if a woman's nipple had been put there; and this teat-like part would be the most prominent and nearest to the sky; and it would be on the equator, in this Ocean Sea, at the end of the Orient.

Columbus found a further conclusion irresistible. 'The end of the Orient' was, traditionally, the most favored location for 'the earthly paradise.' The fresh water he had observed must be the discharge from its fabled rivers. 'And if it is not from Paradise that it flows, the marvel is even greater, for I do not believe any river so big and so deep is known anywhere else in the world.' Perseverance would get him close to Eden:

I believe that if I were to continue along the line of the equator, as I climbed into the higher part, I would find the mildness of the atmosphere very much enhanced and much greater variation in the position of the stars and a change in the nature of the waters. Not that I suppose that it would be possible to sail to where the altitude attains its highest point, nor that one could ever climb up there. For I believe that this is where the earthly paradise is, which no one can reach save by God's will.[20]

When he reached Hispaniola, his mismanagement of the rebellious garrison led to his disgrace and his return to Spain in chains to face charges of gross neglect of duty. The monarchs suspended his monopoly of navigation along the routes he discovered and opened the way to the New World to interlopers. There were plenty of professional mariners in ports around the Guadalquivir, especially among Columbus' shipmates, who were willing to try to follow up his achievements. First in the field, in May 1499, was Columbus' former henchman Alonso de Ojeda, accompanied by Columbus' future confidant Amerigo Vespucci.

Vespucci, who was born in Florence, probably in 1454, was the son of a rich notary. Showing little aptitude for study in childhood, he was obliged to devote himself to trade and became, in the 1480s, a trusted employee of the Medici. In 1489 his employers commissioned him to enquire into the advisability of undertaking business in Seville in partnership with Gianotto Berardi, whom we have already met as one of the explorer's key financial backers. Vespucci moved to Seville, where he became Berardi's colleague, agent, and—as Berardi's will says—'special friend.' The political convulsions of Florence and the collapse of the Medici bank left Vespucci committed to his life in Seville. From 1496 he had contracts for supplying the Indies fleets. He could not have made the voyage commonly ascribed to him in 1497: documents prove his presence in Seville almost throughout that year. His career as an explorer began only—as far as we know—when he sailed in Ojeda's company.

The expedition made initially for Margarita, which Columbus had discovered on his voyage of 1497. They then traveled west along an unknown stretch of coast, rounded San Roman point, and made their first discovery: the Gulf of Maracaibo. A native village built over the water obscurely reminded Vespucci of Venice. Hence the name Venezuela became attached to the entire coast. They reached Cabo de la Vela before turning north and returning to Hispaniola. Vespucci's own account includes claims that he made a detour on his own initiative as far as the mouth of the Amazon but there is no corroboration of this.

Columbus blamed Ojeda for robbing him of 'his' pearl fisheries. In fact, Ojeda missed the pearls and died in poverty. The benefit fell to the Guerra

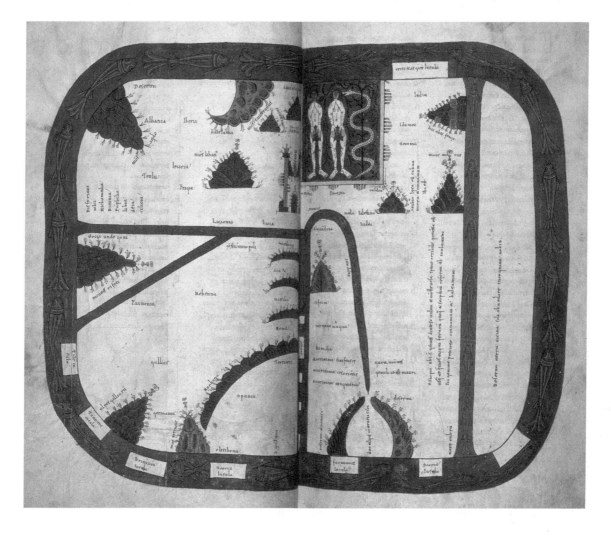

The Beatus map from the Commentary on the Apocalypse of Saint John of Beatus of Liebana, 1109, showing a fourth continent, which Beatus considered to be inhabited. The earthly paradise, with Adam and Eve looking suitably abashed, is in the extreme Orient

brothers of Triana, purveyors of hard tack to the Indies fleets, who were well placed to muster capital for further exploration. The active partner in their scheme was Pero Alonso Niño, a shipmate of Columbus, who led a pearl-fishing expedition to Margarita in 1499. In the event, the voyage added little or nothing to the tally of exploration, but in January 1500 a further effort, headed by Rodrigo de Bastidas, got beyond the limit of Ojeda's voyage and explored the Gulf of Uraba. Because of the ravages of termites, Bastidas's fleet was obliged to run for Hispaniola, where it sank on arrival.

Meanwhile, other privately financed voyages contributed to the exploration of the coast of Brazil. Vicente Yáñez Pinzón arrived on a course similar to Cabral's in January 1500. Pinzón's four caravels sailed from Palos on

18 November 1499, and skirted the Cape Verde Islands on the southern edge of the trades. Fortunate to be carried at speed by 'a terrible high sea,' they arrived off what they called Cabo de Consolación only twenty days out from the Cape Verde Islands. If Pinzón hoped to get around Columbus' presumed mainland to the south, he was deterred by the inauspicious trend of the coast, for he turned west to reconnoiter the mouth of the Amazon. By the time of Cabral's landfall, Pinzón was working his way back north along the coast. His achievement cannot have influenced Cabral.

He got back to Spain, via Hispaniola, in September 1500. By then, a similar enterprise had unfolded under Alonso Vélez de Mendoza, an impecunious hidalgo, who may have sailed further south than Pinzón, probably discovering the mouth of the present Rio de São Francisco. A third voyage, by Diego de Lepe, another citizen of Palos, made its landfall south of Pinzón's but gleaned no new data.

Vélez de Mendoza's illustrates how such voyages were financed. It was conceived in a chivalric and romantic spirit. Its objectives included a search for the earthly paradise. Yet Mendoza needed hard-headed backing. Antón and Luis Guerra, ships' victuallers who specialized in providing squadrons for Hispaniola, provided two caravels. Mendoza obtained another on credit. The Guerra brothers safeguarded their stake by seizing slaves and dyewood on the Brazilian coast. The originator of the enterprise was left penniless.

Ultimately, Vespucci eclipsed the fame of these rivals and threatened that of Columbus. He was an unreliable witness, who picked colleagues' brains without acknowledgment and who shuttled with dubious loyalty between Spanish and Portuguese service. He was also, however, an investor and chronicler for voyages of genuine achievement. Unhappily, his descriptions are so vague, his sailing directions so amateurish, and his calculations so wild that it is impossible to be sure by what routes he sailed or how far south he got. Nonetheless, on a voyage probably of 1501–2, he reached a harbor he called Rio de Janeiro, extending knowledge of Brazil, and encouraging successors to continue the reconnaissance of South America.

None of these privately financed voyages, however, solved the riddles of the nature of South America and its relation to Asia. Pinzón was convinced that he was on a giant promontory of Asia, as was Vespucci, despite his use of the phrase 'Mundus Novus.' He also shared Columbus' view that the world was small. These errors and problems endured into the new century. The explorations that righted and solved them are the subjects of the next chapter. First, however, we should look at the world beyond the Atlantic, and endeavors beyond those of the Europeans of the Atlantic rim, to see what other explorations were afoot in the 1490s.

The World Around Columbus: Exploration Outside the Atlantic

Long-range military reconnaissance was the closest thing to exploration on the Atlantic scale anywhere else in the world. Although Andean chronology in this period is extremely uncertain, it seems likely that the Inca empire grew enormously in that decade, covering more than 30 degrees of latitude, from Quito to the Bío-Bío, encompassing almost all the sedentary peoples of the Andean culture zone. Stories current in early colonial times credited Tupac Inca Yupanqui, the ruler responsible for the southward extension of the frontier, with exploration by sea and the discovery of 'Isles of Gold' in the Pacific. In the same period, Ahuitzotl ruled the Aztec *Grossraum*; documents almost certainly copied from Aztec archives attributed to him the conquest of forty-five communities, in campaigns spread over 200,000 square kilometers, from the river Pánuco in the north almost to the present Guatemalan frontier.

The ambition of these expeditions was hard to exceed. However, the most prodigious case of long-range military action in the world in the fifteenth century was that of Muscovy. During the reign of Ivan the Great, the extent of territory nominally subject to Moscow grew from 15,000 to 600,000 square kilometers. He annexed Novgorod and wrenched at the frontiers of Kazan and Lithuania. It was in the northeast, however, that his armies ventured into little-known territory, along a route explored by missionaries in the previous century, following the river Vym toward the Pechora. The object of this thrust into the 'Land of Darkness' was the effort to control the supply of boreal furs—squirrel and sable—for which there was enormous demand in China, central Asia, and Europe. In 1465, 1472, and 1483 Ivan sent expeditions to Perm and the Ob with the aim of imposing tribute in furs on the tribespeople who lived there. The biggest invasion was that of 1499, when the city of Pustozersk was founded at the mouth of the Pechora. Four thousand men crossed the Pechora on sleds in winter and made for the Ob, returning with 1,000 prisoners and many pelts. Ivan's ambassador in Milan claimed that his master received 1,000 ducats' worth of fur in annual tribute.

Sable was black gold and Russia's northeast frontier was an icy El Dorado. The region remained occluded by myth. When Sigmund von Herberstein served as the Holy Roman Emperor's envoy to Moscow in 1517, he picked up some of the stories of monstrously distended giants, men without tongues, 'living dead,' fish with men's faces, and 'the Golden Old Woman of the Ob.' Nonetheless, by comparison with the previous state of knowledge, Russian

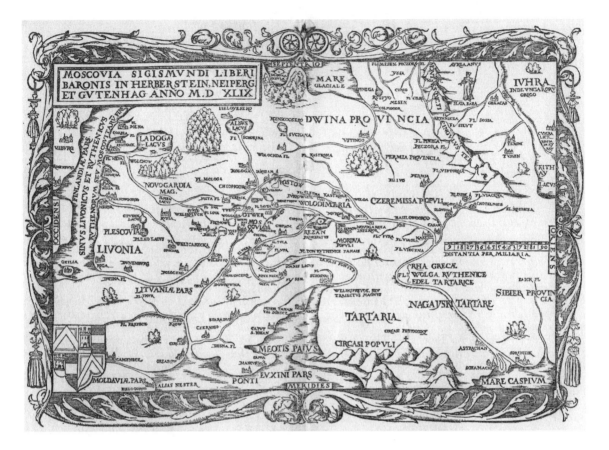

acquaintance with the boreal north and with Siberia was transformed by the new contacts.

Apart from these marginal cases of landward explorations by military expeditions, the record of exploration in the rest of the world in the relevant period is conspicuous by its paucity. The most startling and significant cases of arrested development are to be sought in maritime Asia and around the Indian Ocean and its adjacent seas. Until the 1490s, any well-informed and objective observer would surely have acknowledged these regions as homes to the planet's most dynamic and best-equipped exploring cultures, with the most impressive records of long-term, long-range achievement. In that fateful decade, rivals from western Europe leapfrogged ahead, while the powers that might have stopped them or outstripped them remained inert.

At the western end of the Indian Ocean, for instance, the Ottomans, as we saw in the previous chapter, were confined or limited by their geographical position. The Egypt of the Mamelukes, similarly, exchanged embassies with Gujarat, exercised something like a protectorate over the port of Jiddah, and

Map of Russia, from Sigmund von Herberstein's Rerum Moscoviticarum Commentarii, *1549. The Golden Old Woman appears toward the right, at the top*

initiated trade with India via the Red Sea; but, because of that sea's hostility to navigation, Egypt was ill-placed to guard the ocean against infidel intruders. Abyssinia ceased to expand after the death of the Negus Zara-Ya'cob in 1468; after defeat at the hands of Muslim neighbors in Adel in 1494, hopes of revival dispersed: survival became the aim. Persia was in protracted crisis, from which the region would emerge only in the new century, when the boy prophet Ismail reunited it. Arab commerce ranged the Indian Ocean from southern Africa to the China Seas, without relying on force of arms for protection or promotion. In southern Arabia, yearning for a maritime empire would arise later, as we shall see, perhaps in imitation of the Portuguese, but there were no signs of it yet.

In the central Indian Ocean, meanwhile, no Indian state had interest or energy to spare for long-range expansion. Vijayanagar maintained trading relations all over maritime Asia, but did not maintain fleets. The city that housed the court underwent lavish urban remodeling under Narasimba in the 1490s, but the state had ceased to expand and Narasimba's dynasty was doomed to overthrow. The Delhi of Sikandar Lodi, meanwhile, sustaining traditionally landward priorities, acquired a new province in Bihar, but the sultan bequeathed to his heirs an overstretched state that tumbled easily to invaders from Afghanistan in 1525. Gujarat had a huge merchant marine, but no long-range political ambitions. Its naval power was designed to protect its trade, not force it on others. There were of course plenty of pirates. Early in the 1490s, for instance, from a nest on the western coast of the Deccan, Bahadur Khan Gilani terrorized shipping and, for a time, seized control of important ports, including Dabhol, Goa, and Mahimn near present Bombay.[21] But no state in the region felt the temptation either to explore new routes or to initiate maritime imperialism.

Further east, China, as we have seen, had withdrawn from active naval policy and never resumed it. In Japan in 1493, the shogun was under siege in Kyoto as warlords divided the empire between them. Southeast Asia was between empires: the aggressive phase of the history of Majapahit—formerly an imperial state in Java—was in the past; Thai and Burmese imperialism were still underdeveloped and, in any case, never took on maritime ambitions. There had been maritime empires in the region's past: Srivijaya, the Java of the Sailendra dynasty, the Cholas in southern India in the eleventh and twelfth centuries, and Majapahit in the fourteenth, all tried to enforce monopolies on chosen routes. But at the time Europeans burst into the ocean around the Cape of Good Hope, no indigenous community felt the need or urge to explore further, and nothing like the kind of maritime imperialism practiced by Portugal, and later by the Dutch, existed in the region.

Europe's conquest of the Atlantic, in short, coincided with the arrest of exploring and imperial initiatives elsewhere. This did not mean that the world was instantly transformed, or that the balance of wealth and power would shift quickly to what we now call the West. On the contrary, the process ahead was long, painful, and interrupted by many reversals. Yet that process had begun. And the Atlantic-rim communities that had launched it—especially those of Spain and Portugal—retained their momentum and continued a dominance in exploration that lasted for most of the next three centuries. The tasks of the next couple of chapters are to examine and explain their achievements and their limits.

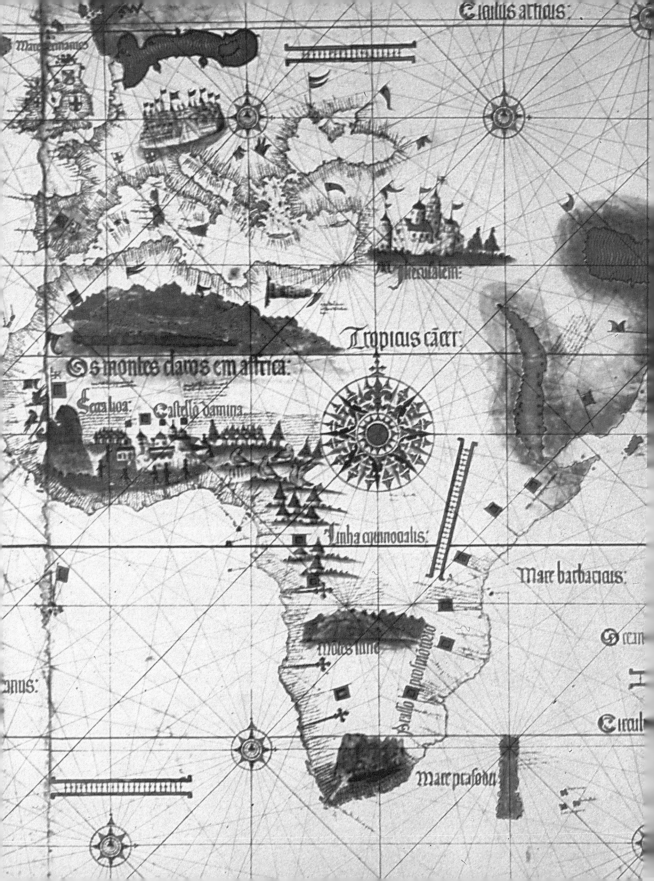

6 Girdling

Connecting Global Routes, c.1500–c.1620

> The ebbs of tides and their mysterious flow,
> We, as arts' elements, shall understand,
> And, as by line, upon the oceans go,
> Whose paths shall be familiar as the land.
>
> Instructed ships shall sail to quick commerce,
> By which remotest regions are allied,
> Which makes one city of the universe,
> Where some may gain and all may be supplied.
>
> John Dryden, 'Annus Mirabilis'

FOR Juan Ponce de León, the ex-governor of Puerto Rico, it was a chivalric and romantic escapade. It was also, perhaps, an attempt at personal rejuvenation. In February 1512, frustrated by one of the many dismissals that punctuated his career in the Spanish bureaucracy in the New World, he applied to the crown for permission to search the waters north of the Bahamas. His aim was to find a fabled island: Bimini, or Bermendi. Columbus had reported its existence—or, at least, native rumors of its existence, which he picked up in Hispaniola. It was, according to Columbus, a place full of gold: the sort of nonexistent place natives might well have directed him to if they wanted to get rid of him. By the time the island appeared on a map in 1511, it had acquired another reputation as the location of the Fountain of Eternal Youth—a classical myth, apparently confirmed by, or confused with, native legends. Ponce set off in March 1513 and landed the following month at what he thought was an island: really, it was the continental coast of North

America, at what he reckoned was about 30 degrees north. The name he gave it—Florida—stuck. To that extent, the seeker of eternal youth achieved eternal fame.

He did not find his fountain. An excursion to the southwest on his return from Florida took him to what he identified as Bimini: perhaps a part of the Cuban coast; perhaps the extremity of Yucatán. There was no fountain there either, or among the Bahamas, which he combed thereafter. But he did make a far more practical discovery. Off the coast of Florida, on 21 April, his ships encountered an adverse current so fierce that it drove them back. They had entered the path of the Gulf Stream, the current that curls from the Caribbean along the North American coast, before turning east to cross the Atlantic and warm the western coasts of northern Europe. Ponce's pilot, Antonio de Alaminos, remembered it and used its power to escape from the vengeance of a thwarted superior a few years later. It was the perfect vehicle on which to hitch a ride from the region of Spanish colonization in the Caribbean to the zone of westerlies in the North Atlantic. Western Europeans' picture of the Atlantic system of winds and currents was now complete.

This left two great tasks for oceanic exploration: to crack the wind code of the Pacific, as European navigators of the late fifteenth and early sixteenth century had done for the Atlantic; and to learn how to use the still little-explored southern portions of the Indian Ocean, beyond the monsoons. Both of these tasks proved long and laborious. We can look at them in turn, before broaching the other achievement of the explorers of the age—the coasting and internal exploration of much of the Americas.

Decoding the Pacific

The enormous dimensions of the Pacific demanded real resolve of any navigator who proposed to find routes back and forth across them. No one before the sixteenth century had any incentive to make the effort. No Asian seafaring people had any business with anyone in the Americas. In the northern Pacific, Aleut fishermen knew the waters that lapped both continents but had no interest in developing exchanges of trade or culture across them. In the latitudes sailed by Polynesians, the distances were too vast for the available technology. As we have seen,[1] Hawai'i, Easter Island, and the Chatham Islands represented the furthest limits of Polynesian navigation, and even within the world encompassed by Polynesian voyages it proved impossible to maintain permanent routes of contact.

Early in the sixteenth century, however, people arrived in the Pacific who had a strong reason to want to cross it. Probing eastward from India, Portuguese merchants and diplomats established contact with all coastal and island regions of southeast Asia and with China between 1502 and 1515. Most importantly, they reached the Moluccas, the source of the world's most costly spices: nutmeg, mace, and cloves. Theirs was a privileged route, with plenty of stopping places in useful markets. By treaty, it was closed to subjects of the monarchs of Spain, who therefore needed to find another way to the riches of the East. For them, the obvious approach was across the Pacific, from their outposts in the New World.

The story of how Western minds adjusted to the vastness of the Pacific is inseparable from two others: the debate over the size of the world, and the conflict between Spain and Portugal over the delimitation of their respective spheres of navigation. Columbus had initiated the first, by casting doubt on ancient, agreed, and—as it turned out—roughly accurate assumptions about the dimensions of the globe. One of my favorite fictions, by the twentieth-century Galician writer Rafael Dieste, tells of a student who had the impertinence to say, 'It's a small world.' After his indignant landlord boxed his ears he revised his opinion: 'The world isn't as small as they say.' Sixteenth-century opinion followed a similar trajectory. On the one hand, the experience of explorers seemed to shrink the planet. Columbus' apparent success seemed—at least to some geographers—to vindicate his calculations and force scholars to revise their estimates downward. The world-girdling voyages that followed made so much accessible that distances seemed to dwindle. Globe makers gave their customers the curious sensation of being able to cup the world in their hands. Carlos Borja, thanking his famous uncle Francis, the Jesuit general and future saint, for a gift of a globe in 1566, said that it made him realize how small the world was.

On the other hand, over the same period of time, explorers continually encountered evidence that challenged their tendency to underestimate. Though cartographers stubbornly ignored the fact, and optimistic adventurers chose to resist its implications, it was increasingly obvious that Columbus had got nowhere near to Asia. America was revealed, bit by bit, as a wide continent, and the Pacific as a defiantly broad ocean. In 1546 Sebastian Munster's map showed a narrow New World, lying just off the coast of 'India.' No map fully evoked the vastness of the ocean until well into the seventeenth century. The story of this chapter is a story of the unshrinking of the image of the world. But, as we shall see, the process was painfully slow and stubbornly opposed.

Envisaging the Pacific: The Problem of Scale

Wishful thinking was partly responsible. So many explorers sustained Columbus' quest for a quick route from Europe to Asia; so few could bear the heartbreak of admitting it was impossible. Politics also played a part. When Spain and Portugal divided Atlantic zones of navigation between them, in the Treaty of Tordesillas in 1494, they did so by drawing a meridian through the ocean. They left open the question of whether the line of demarcation extended all round the world, or whether it stopped at the Poles. But the question could not be indefinitely postponed. As Portuguese explorers ventured ever further east, and those of Spain reached ever further west, they were bound to meet, and their rights in their discoveries would depend on where the line lay between their respective spheres.

We still do not know exactly when or how the extension of the Tordesillas line—the Tordesillas anti-meridian, as scholars call it—came to be accepted as the proper basis for an agreed solution. The original treaty was clearly confined to the Atlantic. At the time, the leading Spanish court geographer, Jaime Ferrer, assumed that the Spanish zone would cover the whole of the western ocean 'as far as the furthest point of the Arabian Gulf.' Of course, he assumed that there was only one ocean in the world and had no inkling of how a whole continent lay in between.[2] By Ferrer's interpretation of the treaty, Portuguese seafarers would be confined to Africa, and Spain would have a monopoly over access to most of maritime Asia. Asian markets would be approachable only via the west. In 1497, in another Spanish gloss on the treaty—which some scholars believe Columbus himself wrote—the Spanish zone is said to extend 'as far as the point at which land belonging to a Christian ruler is found' ('fasta donde avía o oviese príncipe cristiano'): in Columbus' mind, this meant the Cape of Good Hope.[3]

Despite many speculations to the contrary,[4] documents that envisage a prolongation of the Tordesillas line around the entire world have not come to light for any time before 1512. In June of that year, Juan Díaz de Solís received orders from the crown for a westward voyage to Asia. He was instructed to ascertain whether Ceylon 'was in the part which belonged to Spain' and then to go to Melaka or perhaps the Moluccas ('Maluque' in the original) 'which falls within the limits of our portion' ('que cae en límites de nuestra demarcación').[5] Confirmation occurs in a letter of 30 August of that year from the Portuguese envoy in Castile, informing his king that Solís was sure that 'Melaka lies four hundred leagues inside the Castilian portion.'[6] Solís's orders state that, according to the best information the monarchs of Castile had at the time, 'the line of demarcation should run through the middle ("la demarcación se debía hacer en medio") of the island of Ceylon. The reasoning behind this is made explicit. Ceylon, the monarchs believed, lay 120 degrees 'of longitude to the east of our meridian' ('por longitud de nuestro meridiano a la parte oriental'). It is not clear what they meant by 'our meridian'; but wherever that was, it would obviously have been ridiculous to suppose that the Tordesillas line was another 60 degrees further west.[7] If 'our meridian' was that of Toledo— the most likely choice—the best estimate made in Spain in the sixteenth century located the Tordesillas line 43 degrees 8 minutes to the west.[8] Rui Faleiro, a Portuguese pilot whose views were influential at the Castilian court in the second decade of the century, was convinced that the Moluccas lay on Castile's side of the line. The notion of an anti-meridian was clearly in the air, even though no one knew where to place it.

Penetrating the Pacific: The Voyage of Magellan

At the time Solís received his instructions, the question was becoming urgent, because of the places mentioned and muddled in the documents: Ceylon— modern Sri Lanka—was the world's main source of cinnamon. Melaka, seized by Portugal in 1511, commanded the straits that led between Malaya and Sumatra, toward most of the Indonesian archipelago, where some of the world's most valuable products beckoned. The Moluccas, the 'Spice Islands' par excellence—especially the islands of Ternate and Tidore—produced most of the world's cloves, nutmeg, and mace. The Portuguese, having already got as far as Melaka, and established privileged trading relationships almost wherever they went, were now poised to reach the final prize.

Afonso de Albuquerque, Portugal's viceroy in the east, was already hard at work gathering intelligence on the Spice Islands. In 1512 the name of Francisco Rodrigues first appears in the records—mentioned in April as having obtained a large fragment of a Javanese pilot's map. In August of that year he was appointed to accompany the fleet then in course of preparation for a voyage to the Spice Islands on the grounds that 'he possesses excellent knowledge with which to make maps.' The expedition left toward the end of that year, with three vessels and 120 men. 'No more ships or men,' wrote the expedition's chronicler, 'went to New Spain with Christopher Columbus, nor to India with Vasco da Gama, because the Moluccas are no less wealthy than they, nor ought they to be held in less esteem.'

The expedition turned back from Banda before reaching the Moluccas— satisfied, perhaps, that ample cloves, nutmeg, and mace could be obtained

Francisco Rodrigues's drawing, probably of Adonara, in the Lesser Sunda Islands, Indonesia

without going further afield. But one of the fleet's captains, Francisco Serrão, was shipwrecked en route and was able to make his way by local shipping to the island of Ternate, where production of those spices was concentrated. He negotiated the basis of a Portuguese monopoly, which remained almost unbroken for the rest of the century. Rodrigues, moreover, brought back outstanding maps and profile drawings of islands along the route—presumably copied from Javanese prototypes—and data on the entire journey from the Bay of Bengal to China.

For Spain, meanwhile, the problems of getting to the Moluccas were twofold: first, the Americas were in the way; secondly, if traditional calculations of the size of the globe were anything to go by, the distance to be traversed was excessive. Fernão de Magalhães, whose name is most familiar in Anglicized form as Magellan, claimed to have the means of dispelling or defeating both problems. He was a gentleman adventurer, a knight errant already addicted to seaborne deeds of daring. His fellow countrymen shunned him when he insisted that it would be easier to get to the Spice Islands via the Atlantic than through the Indian Ocean: Portugal already had a satisfactory route to Asia. In October 1517, he abandoned his efforts in his homeland and transferred his allegiance to Castile.

Magellan shared Columbus' picture of a small world and assumed that the wealth of Asia lay only a short way beyond America. As for the intervening hemisphere, it did not daunt him. He would sail, he declared, 75 degrees south if need be; and if he still found no way around the Americas, he would defy the

Treaty of Tordesillas, turn eastward, and sail to the Spice Islands 'by the route of the Portuguese.'

Consistently with the established practice of the Castilian crown, the voyage had to be privately financed, and the backers—bankers in Seville—indemnified by grants of considerable prospective rights in the results: a fifth of the profits of any trade, for a term of ten years, and the governorship of conquered lands. Magellan, in consequence, was doomed in advance: compelled to find exploitable lands and undertake their conquest, however impracticable.

He set off from Sanlúcar de Barrameda on 20 September 1519, with five ships and 250 men. He chose Portuguese companions, pilots, charts, and water casks: Castilians still had little experience of long open-sea voyages across the south Atlantic. Even so, the crews mutinied after enduring the crossing of the doldrums and again when Magellan prudently decided to winter on the Patagonian coast before continuing southward into unknown waters in worsening weather. When they finally found the longed-for strait that led westward to the Pacific, they had in effect already failed: the strait was too southerly to be a convenient gateway to Asia. It was also a maze-like web of channels which tortured explorers. When they entered it, they took seven weeks to navigate it, in the face of bitter winds, short rations, and threatening coasts. The hardships of the crossing provoked another mutiny.

Nevertheless, the delays and privations Magellan endured had one happy outcome: he arrived in the Pacific at just the right moment to get the best of the southeast trade winds that would carry him across the ocean. He used the Humboldt current to make a quick dash north along the Chilean coast into warmer latitudes, before turning west on what he believed would be an easy voyage: wind-assisted, across a narrow ocean, punctuated by islands. In fact, he faced ninety-nine days at sea. By the time they sighted Guam on 6 March 1521, the explorers were reduced to chewing on the leather casings of the sails with mouths swollen by scurvy. Their water was putrid. Their biscuit, decayed and wormy, 'stank of rats' urine.'

On the 9th, Magellan set sail again, believing that he had missed the Spice Islands and was approaching China. Seven days later, he sighted Samar in the Philippines. A few weeks later, the fatal temptation to imperial adventurism claimed his life in battle, fighting for one local raja against another on the nearby island of Mactan. From there, by a tortuous route, the remainder of the expedition made its way to the Spice Islands, arriving in the sultanate of Tidore on 6 November 1521. At terrible cost, they had reached the expedition's declared objective.

Magellan's world voyage, by Battista Agnese, 1545. Though Magellan proved the vastness of the Pacific, Agnese was one of the few mapmakers to register the fact

Troublesome as the passage was, it by no means represented the worst the Strait of Magellan could inflict. A follow-up expedition in 1525 took four-and-a-half months to get through and recommended the abandonment of the route. Explorers who tried it again at intervals during the rest of the century had similarly discouraging experiences. No serious attempt to find another south Atlantic route to the Pacific was renewed for nearly 100 years; and in 1615, when the Dutch explorers Jakob Le Maire and Willem van Schouten found the way round Cape Horn, they were actually looking not for a link between the oceans but for the fabled southern continent supposed to lie beyond the reach of previous expeditions.

Magellan's journey, for all its heroism, had solved nothing. Its survivors got back to Spain by completing the first recorded circumnavigation of the world: but so what? The feat had a certain journalistic éclat but it was the Pacific leg of the journey that was really important, because it was altogether new; yet, on the evidence the expedition and the follow-up voyage brought home, the route was unexploitable: it was too long, too slow, and fatally flawed, because it led only one way across the ocean. The task of finding a practicable, two-way route across the Pacific remained.

Decoding the Winds: The Voyage of Urdaneta and Its Context

Moreover, not even Magellan's voyage, which dramatically revealed the intimidating breadth of the Pacific, could convince cartographers and mariners of the truth about the size of the globe. Had people known the calculations of longitude Magellan and his pilots made, they might have made an impact. Of the surviving computations, one set, made by Francesco d'Albo, is remarkably accurate, another yields an underestimate but quite a high one. Magellan himself thought that a degree on the surface of the earth represented 17½ leagues—about 70 miles; so, if anything, he is likely to have ended up greatly overestimating the size of the world if he kept anything like an accurate record. But he died on the voyage and, unfortunately, the set of figures published in the aftermath of the voyage were those of Antonio Pigafetta, which were consistently underestimated, perhaps for political reasons.[9]

In 1524 Hernando Colón was able therefore to maintain unchanged the opinion for which his father was notorious: the circumference of the world was only 5,100 leagues at the equator.[10] And almost all maps continued to represent the Pacific as much narrower than it really is. During the negotiations between Spain and Portugal that followed Magellan's voyage, both parties seem to have taken it for granted that the Moluccas lay in the Spanish zone, defined by the Tordesillas anti-meridian.[11] This implied a narrow Pacific and a small world.

In the 1560s, when the question of the location of the anti-meridian was again under review, some of the leading cosmographers in the field, such as Pedro de Medina (author of a leading handbook for navigators), Alonso de Santa Cruz (the consummate cartographer), and Andrés de Urdaneta (the most renowned Pacific pilot of the day), continued to believe that the Moluccas lay within the area assigned to Spain.[12] This is surprising, because Santa Cruz was also a believer in the 17½ league degree, while Urdaneta had unrivalled practical knowledge. Yet their sincerity is beyond question, as both were perfectly willing to point out that by the Treaty of Zaragoza of 1529, the Moluccas and even the Philippines had been reassigned to Portugal.[13] The pilots who made the voyage from New Spain to the Philippines tendered estimates of the distance as between 1,550 and 2,260 leagues: the real figure is of the order of 2,400 leagues. Back in Spain, the geographer Sancho Gutiérrez, reviewing the figures for the king, treated them with contempt: professional pilots, he thought, were sloppy, ignorant, and unscientific. He reduced the figure to 1,750 leagues.[14] He probably thought that seamen exaggerate—which they do, usually, but not in the case of sixteenth-century estimates of the size of the Pacific.

Meanwhile, exploration of the Pacific was largely confined to voyages originating in or bound for the Spanish colonies on the Pacific coasts of New Spain and Peru. A viable eastbound route was not hard to find. In 1527 one of the conquerors of Mexico, Álvaro de Saavedra, demonstrated that it was possible to get to the Philippines in a few weeks by using the prevailing north-westerlies to skirt the doldrums to the north. The only problem was that, having completed the journey, he could find no way back. Less than a decade later, Hernando de Grijalva led a similar effort from Peru, disfigured by mutiny and ending in shipwreck. Again the voyage seemed to show that the Pacific was a one-way ocean, traversable only from west to east.

Spanish navigators in the Pacific needed to accumulate nearly three more decades of experience before they could break the impasse. In 1564 the most knowledgeable of them was Andrés de Urdaneta. For a figure of primordial importance in the history of the world, he is woefully undercelebrated. Despite leaving plenty of writing of his own, he remains maddeningly elusive. His career began in the follow-up voyage to Magellan's, in 1525, when he was 17 years old. He took part not out of the dreams or despair that drove so many of his contemporaries to sea; he was an educated young enthusiast for cosmography. His account is candid about the inadequacies of his superior officers, two of whom had sailed with Magellan yet still mistook a Patagonian river mouth for the entrance to the strait. His mentors repaid his skepticism with confidence: throughout the voyage, he tended to get delicate or demanding jobs. He demonstrated his competence by surviving shipwreck in the labyrinth of Magellan's strait, finding the rest of the fleet and effecting the rescue of his fellow castaways. He brought back a daughter by a woman of the Indies and an account of the voyage, which, though pardonably egotistical, shows consistently the good judgment for which contemporaries generally commended him for the rest of his life.

He spent most of the rest of his youth in the Indies, working as a navigator or discharging administrative offices on shore. When he could, he turned down commands, perhaps from modesty, perhaps from the bitter experience of seeing so many fail, so many die, or perhaps from the stirrings of religious vocation, which led him to vows as an Augustinian in 1553 and to ordination as a priest in 1557. In some ways, his progress in cosmography and his acute moral sensibilities unfitted him to serve Spanish interests. He felt obliged to point out that, after the Treaty of Zaragoza of 1529, which set aside the question of the anti-meridian and allotted the Moluccas and, by implication, the Philippines, to the Portuguese zone of navigation, Spaniards had lost the interest, and perhaps the right, to continue to roam the Pacific; when officials begged him to resume transpacific exploration, he declined to do so. But he emerged on the orders of the king to resume the search for a return Pacific route in 1560. 'Although I am now over fifty-two years of age and in poor health,' he wrote,

> and owing to the hard labors of my earlier years intended to spend the rest of my life in retirement, yet having in mind the great zeal of your Majesty in all that concerns the service of our Lord and the spread of our holy Catholic faith, I am ready to face the labors of this voyage, trusting solely in the help of God.[15]

On Urdaneta's recommendation, the evangelization of the Philippines, not commercial advantage, was defined as the purpose of the voyage: this would forestall accusations that Spain was treaty breaking in waters rightly assigned to the Portuguese zone.

'Next to faith in the help of our Lord,' ran the orders addressed to the commander of the expedition, 'it is confidently believed that Fray Andrés de Urdaneta will be the chief agent in discovering the return route to New Spain, because of his experience, his knowledge of weather in these regions and his other qualifications.'[16] He realized that timing was the key to success. It was vital to leave the Philippines with the benefit of the summer monsoon and make a rapid transition northward to catch the Japan current, continuing as far as necessary to meet the north Pacific current and turn east for home. With a short turnaround time in Manila, the feat was possible. In November 1564, he began the attempt, reaching the Philippines in February and beginning the return voyage on 1 June 1565. The quest for a west wind took him to beyond 39 degrees north. The 11,000 miles he crossed made his journey the longest ever undertaken on the open sea without a landfall. It took four months and eight days to get to Acapulco. Everyone aboard was nearly prostrate with scurvy and exhaustion. Urdaneta's subordinate Alonso de Arellana actually preceded him to Mexico by two months, having got separated from the flagship by a storm. But the plan was Urdaneta's and the credit is justly his.

Mastery of the Pacific had been achieved by daring of the same kind that mastered the Atlantic: willingness to sail with the wind at one's back, with no certainty of finding a homeward wind. But once viable routes back and forth across the ocean had been opened up, inertia set in. Overwhelmingly, through-out the seventeenth century and for most of the eighteenth, ships stuck to the known sea lanes and crossed the Pacific with the known winds. To some extent, this was understandable: the wind system is so regular and so reliable, the ocean so vast and—over much of its breadth—so empty that it made little sense to spend time off the beaten track. In partial consequence, the ocean remained mysterious. Its size still defied measurement. Incautious optimism continued to lead seamen to grief. Most of them continued to reject the facts about the extent of the ocean into the 1590s.

Mastering the Extent of the Ocean: Mendaña and Quirós

The effects were obvious from the 1560s to the early 1600s, during the Pacific odysseys of Álvaro de Mendaña and Pedro Fernández Quirós. Their inspiration was of a kind already familiar to readers of this book: romance, fable, fiction, myth. Inca legends of 'Isles of Gold' combined with convictions of the existence of a 'great unknown southern continent' and the notion that the islands of the Amazons and King Solomon's mines lay in the southern sea.[17] In 1567 the governor of Peru ordered an expedition under Álvaro de Mendaña to search for these unlikely delights. Mendaña was a voracious visionary, who hoped to evangelize undiscovered peoples and found a colony he could rule himself. His pilot, Hernando Gallego, was full of exaggerated notions of the island we now call New Guinea, which Portuguese navigators had discovered, approaching from the Indian Ocean. Adopting a project already advocated by Urdaneta, he hoped to secure that large and promising land for Spain. Their divided aims contributed to leading the expedition astray.

They started from Callao, on the rim of the world known to Spaniards. Its residents stared out over a barely charted ocean. One might think it was so far from the heartlands of the Spanish monarchy, and, indeed, from most other Spanish colonies, as to satisfy the most determined wanderlust or accommodate the most evasive migrants. But frontiers attract the restless and there never seems to be a shortage of paladins anxious to go that bit further.

They set sail on 19 November 1567. Almost from that moment, changes of mind and of direction warped their purposes and frustrated their efforts. By the end of December, they seem to have abandoned the search for the fabled islands and to have headed for where they thought New Guinea lay. By mid-January they were running out of drinking water and had found no land. On 7 February, however, they stumbled on an archipelago southeast of New Guinea. The natives were hostile. There was no evidence of the presence or proximity of any exploitable resources. In the circumstances, the name 'Isles of Solomon' was an alluring promotional device, calculated to evoke associations with the mines of Ophir and to connect with legends of the 'Isles of Gold' supposedly known to the Inca. The discovery lay an estimated ninety days' sail from Peru, but with unreliable means of measuring distance and checking latitude, and no means of verifying longitude, no one could say for certain exactly where they were. 'Nor is longitude fixed,' the expedition's chief pilot admitted, 'except by such estimation as each one may make.'[18]

It is not, perhaps, surprising, that it took twenty-five years to raise finance and get leave for another expedition to the islands. Mendaña, however, cherished the dream and never gave up the attempt. On his second journey he recruited 400 potential colonists in a venture to a destination the whereabouts of which no one knew for sure. They sailed from Callao on 9 April 1595. Many took their wives with them, including Mendaña, whose formidable mate, Doña Isabel Barreto, was to prove herself as tough as any of the men on board.

The baffling recklessness of the venturers is clinched by the fact that they were unable to find their islands. After three months, they were still far off their destination. Some said the isles 'had fled away, or that the Adelantado had forgotten the place where they were to be found, or that the sea had risen and covered them. . . . Either we have passed them or they do not exist, for by this road we shall go round the world, or at least we shall come at last to Great Tartary.'[19] The pilot who wrote those words was wrong: because they ludicrously underestimated the distance to be traversed, they had not yet got anywhere near the Solomons. Eventually, lost in the vastness of the Pacific, the voyagers attempted to colonize Santa Cruz, a little to the east of the Solomons. There the usual disasters of early modern Europeans in the tropics over-whelmed them: deadly sickness, want of food, and deteriorating relations with the natives. They began with embraces, continued in abuse, and ended in bloodshed: the usual sequence in the 'cultural encounters' of the age. Forty settlers or more died in a single month.

After Mendaña's death, Doña Isabel rallied the survivors and led them to the Philippines, through the privations of what has been called 'one of the classic horror stories of maritime travel'.[20] 'The sick became rabid,' said a witness. Some begged for a single drop of water, 'showing their tongues, pointing with their fingers, like Dives with Lazarus.'[21] They arrived 'in such state,' the chief pilot reported, 'that it could only have been the mercy of God which brought us there, because had we been relying on human strength and resources we should not have been able to cover a tenth of the journey.'[22] By then, over three-quarters of the complement were dead.

How can we explain a 'spirit of adventure' so egregious, so ill-disciplined, so adventurous, so indifferent to suffering, so profligate with lives? A clue to the foolhardiness that animated the explorers of the day can be found in the life and work of the Portuguese chief pilot of the expedition, known by the Castilian version of his name as Pedro Fernández de Quirós. Undeterred by the horrors of the voyage, he devoted most of the rest of his life to an attempt to repeat it. His efforts, too, were doomed to frustration. The Solomon Islands proved irrecoverable; but he set a new objective for himself: the Terra Australis, the unknown continent postulated in the great South Sea.

No one knows why so many geographers of the sixteenth to eighteenth centuries believed in the existence of this gigantic will o' the wisp, which remained a fixture in European maps until the late eighteenth century, when Captain Cook finally disproved its existence. As an eighteenth-century wit remarked, 'If they know it for a continent, and know it for a southern continent, why do they call it an unknown southern continent?' Speculation is rife that the belief represented unrecorded mapping of Australia, or even of Antarctica, by 'secret' Portuguese navigations or 'ancient sea kings' or imaginary Chinese rovers. Misguided symmetry seems in part responsible. Most advocates who gave their reasons claimed that the planet would seem disorderly and unbalanced if a disproportionate amount of land were concentrated in the northern hemisphere.

Quirós did not find Terra Australis. He did, however, find an island which he initially mistook for it and which he called La Australia del Espíritu Santo. On 13 May 1606, he celebrated by founding a new Order of Chivalry. He had planned the event before sailing and had come prepared for it. 'To this end,' wrote the expedition's chronicler,

> he made some crosses of blue silk, in varying sizes, for all those who came in the said fleet, whether white or black or Indians, and even one for the native brought from the island of Nuestra Señora de Loreto. He ordered that all should wear the insignia on their breast, making them all Knights of the Holy Ghost, by which name they were to be called.[23]

Knighthood was conferred on all the crew, down to the white trash and the black cooks. 'And so,' according to the expedition's accountant,

> at Whitsun he gave crosses of blue taffeta to all . . . to the great delight of the majority, and even to their amusement, because even two negro cooks were rewarded by such largesse, great liberality and munificence, for their gallantry and courage. Besides on that day he granted them their liberty, although they did not belong to him, and what is more they afterwards continued in the self-same state of slavery.[24]

The expedition's Franciscan chaplain, who in this respect was more worldly than Quirós, was equally alert to the comic possibilities of this quixotic burlesque. 'It was a marvellous thing,' he remarked, 'to see such a diversity of knights, for truly nothing like it has ever been seen since the world began, because here there were sailor-knights, grummet-knights, ship's page-knights,

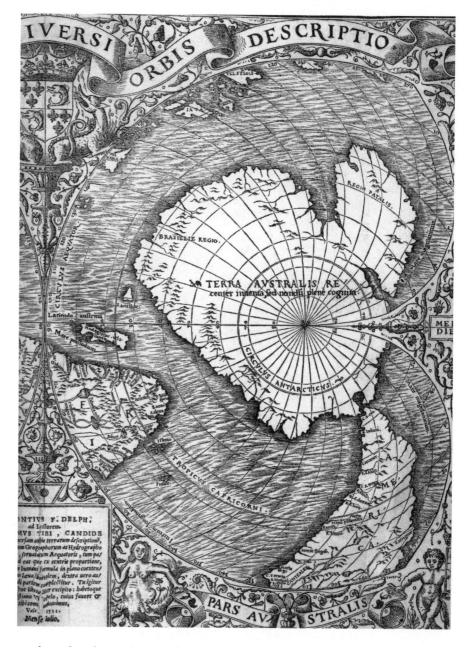

Terra Australis

mulatto-knights and negro-knights and Indian-knights and knights who were knight-knights.'[25]

The expedition had set out in the year Don Quixote was published: a reminder that the satire of Cervantes only bit because real-life adventures were still being inspired by chivalric romance. Explorers still modeled the trajectory of their lives on storybook heroes who performed gallant deeds in glorious

ships that fly over the waves like steeds. In the books, the favored denouement—usually a fade-out in the arms of some princess—generally happened
on an island fief. Sancho Panza's plea to be 'governor of some island' echoed
the heroes' romantic ambitions. Mendaña was said by his mutinous crew
to have risked their lives to make himself a marquis, much as Columbus'
grumblers blamed him for sacrificing them to his wish to become a lord.[26] The
spirit of knight errantry fed exploration; the quixotic impulse helped Spain's
empire grow at the edges. Chivalric self-perceptions did not just inspire
madcap exploits. They helped to make the consequent sufferings bearable—for
the reality endured by an explorer like Quirós could hardly have been tolerable
without some psychological strategy of escape. Chivalric fantasy was a useful
form of mental opiate.

The Indian Ocean

Maritime Asia

Pacific explorers touched the frontiers of Portuguese navigation from the
Indian Ocean in east and southeast Asia. After Quirós's departure from Espíritu
Santo, his more level-headed colleague Luis de Torres sailed along the southern
coast of New Guinea, sighting Australia on the way and entering the zone of
Portuguese navigation. But his report languished, almost unremarked, for over
a century and a half. As early as 1526, Jorge Meneses, blown off course during a
voyage from Melaka to the Spice Islands, had preceded Torres in New Guinea.
The first Spaniards to reach Yap in the Caroline Islands found that the natives
already knew some words of Portuguese.

These were traces of the outposts and spearheads of voyages promoted by
Portuguese authorities in Melaka and Goa in the attempt to exploit commerce
with the extremities of the Orient. The choice as Portugal's first emissary to
China fell on Tomé Pires, an apothecary of the royal household, who had
arrived in the Indies in 1511, probably to supervise the shipping of medicinal
drugs. After a year in the job he found himself, as he informed his brother,
'more rich than you can imagine.' After experience as a merchant in Java and
a collector of botanical specimens in the South China Sea, he sailed for China
in 1516. Repelled by storms, he tried again the following year. Once he got to
China, the fastidious protocol of the empire defeated him. He incurred the
contempt the Chinese naturally felt for 'barbarians' from afar and was unable
to inaugurate a relationship with the Chinese throne that was satisfactory
to Portugal. His fate is uncertain. He seems never to have got away from
China. But his detailed report of his journey reached home and Portuguese

persevered—informally and illegally—in sailing to China and creating trading networks there, where their activities gradually won official acceptance. Meanwhile Portuguese trading ventures fanned through southeast Asia.

In the 1540s contact with Japan began. Fernão Mendes Pinto, who sailed the seas of maritime Asia for thirty years from 1528, claimed to have been the first European in the country. But his romance of his own life was full of invention. He was the Portuguese Sinbad, whose storm-studded career was a chronicle of shipwrecks. The hand of God always rescued him from capricious fortune, as his life constantly reenacted the triumph of Christianity over paganism. He was also a talented satirist, whose sense of humor was so animated by irony that readers never know when to take him at his word. He was certainly an important early source of information about Japan. His accounts of the superior, pitying, condescending attitude the natives evinced toward the Western barbarians ring true. In one anecdote, he relates a dumb show performed by a daimio's daughters, in which the Portuguese were lampooned for both their poverty and piety: they were shown expecting the Japanese to take an interest in their crude wooden reliquaries, much to the amusement of the audience. It seems unlikely, however, that Mendes's first visit to Japan can have occurred before 1546. In that case, Diogo Zeimoto and his companions preceded him by two or three years. They were bound for China from Siam when—either blown by a tempest or deflected by official prohibitions on foreign traders—they fetched up in islands previously unknown to them at Tanegashima, south of Kyushu. Japanese sources confirm that they introduced the use of firearms (which Japanese craftsmen rapidly succeeded in copying successfully).

The Ocean Crossing

While striving to extend the range of their commerce eastward, Portuguese explorers took little trouble over improving their route from Europe to the Indian Ocean. Here inertia ruled. For 100 years after Vasco da Gama's voyage, navigators in his wake largely contented themselves with doing more or less what he had done: skirting the east coast of Africa after rounding the Cape of Good Hope, and crossing the ocean with the monsoon to a Malabar port or to Goa. To some extent, this is unsurprising. Monsoonal routes were reliable. And they were fast in one sense: the winds ensured rapid passage across the open sea. But they cost merchants a great deal of turnaround time. If you missed the wind, you had to idle in port for up to half the year. Moreover, to get to the monsoonal zone of the Indian Ocean by the route Vasco da Gama had pioneered, or returning from it, ships had to skirt the bone-strewn coasts of

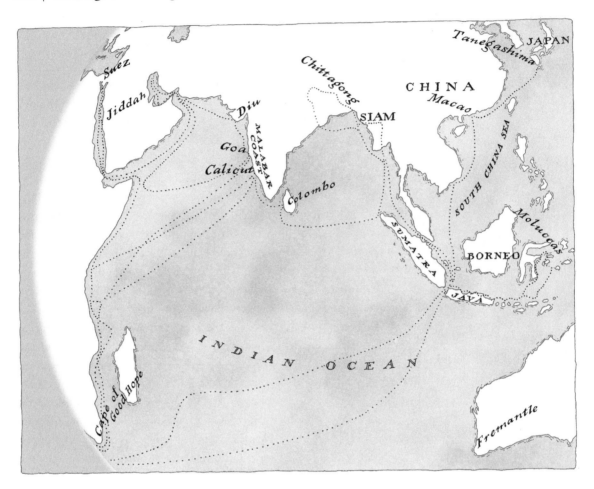

Natal, where tempests tore into lee shores in spring and early summer, and
Portuguese writers bemoaned 'the tragic history of the sea.'

In 1512 the naval commander Pedro de Mascarenhas attempted an
emergency dash across the ocean to reinforce Goa, across the face of the
southeast trade winds, using the southerlies to force his way north, and discovering the Mascarene Islands in the process. But this route only worked
during the summer monsoon; and it involved more time at sea than Portuguese
merchantmen cared for. So the route along the east coast of Africa as far as
Mombasa continued to prevail, until, in the late sixteenth century, adventurous
explorers began to look for a way round them.

In 1997 I attended a curious ceremony on the esplanade of Fremantle,
Western Australia, where a bust of Vasco da Gama was unveiled in honor of
the five hundredth anniversary of the start of the voyage that first brought

Portuguese and Dutch
navigations in the Indian
Ocean, 1498–1620

European ships to the Indian Ocean. The aboriginal dancers obligatory at every Australian event performed with characteristic vitality. A group of singers from the local community of Portuguese descent sang old Madeiran folk songs. The mayor made a speech. At the time, an exhibition in the local museum featured a magnificent Dutch shipwreck, 300 years old, raised from the nearby sea bottom—one of many Dutch wrecks of the period that strew Western Australia's coasts. There are no Portuguese wrecks. The mayor, however, did not mention the Dutch. He simply extolled the greatness of Vasco da Gama, who was worthy, he thought, to be an honorary son of the town, and of the Portuguese navigators who succeeded him in opening up the neighboring ocean to European commerce. He exceeded the evidence, however, in ascribing the European discovery of Western Australia to Portuguese seafarers. 'How come,' a member of the audience asked him, 'if the Portuguese were here first, our coast is strewn with Dutch wrecks, but not one Portuguese?' 'Ah,' the mayor replied, 'that just shows how much better the Portuguese were at navigation.' Later, I asked him why he had said that. 'You see, Felipe,' he replied, twinkling at the joke, 'there are no Dutch votes in Western Australia, but we have 7,000 voters of Portuguese descent who are proud of their ancestry.'

The truth is that though Portuguese navigators may have occasionally glimpsed Australia, as Torres did, they had no call to go there and their established routes did not lead there. With the Dutch, it was different. They were latecomers to Indian Ocean navigation. Only in the 1590s did Dutch merchants conceive the ambition to break into Eastern trade and curtail the Portuguese monopoly. At the time, they were in the midst of a long civil war between the United Provinces in the northern and eastern Netherlands, that wanted to be an independent republic, and the southern provinces, which remained loyal to the hereditary ruler—who happened also to be king of Spain and Portugal. Though the United Provinces lacked natural resources, they had two inestimable advantages: a defensible homeland, which Spanish armies could never quite conquer, and a great deal of surplus shipping, which could earn fortunes in the Indian Ocean, where shipping was always in demand, if they could get there.

Interest in the possibility ignited in the 1590s, when Jan van Linschoten, a Dutch servant of the archbishop of Goa, published a brilliant account of the Indies and the options for trade. At first, the Dutch had no option but to follow the routes the Portuguese—and the indigenous explorers for centuries previously—had run out. But this was clearly unsatisfactory. It exposed Dutch ships to risk of attack; it condemned them to sea lanes where the Portuguese already controlled many of the most desirable ports and emporiums; and it conferred no competitive advantage. What the Dutch really needed was a route that was faster and cheaper to operate than their rivals'. From 1602 control of Dutch navigation to the Indian Ocean was the responsibility of a joint stock company with a monopoly granted by the state: the Vereinigde Oost-indische Compagnie.

In 1611 one of their most trusted captains, Hendrik Brouwer, who was later to govern the Company's operations in the East, put into operation an idea that seems to have occurred to him during previous voyages via the Mascarenes. Instead of turning to cross the Indian Ocean diagonally from the Cape to the Indies, he used the strong westerlies south of the Cape to get a long way east with favorable winds, before turning north and making straight for the Sunda Strait. Gradually, over succeeding years, Dutch captains experimented ever more boldly with this strategy, until by the 1630s it became routine practice to follow the westerlies almost as far as the Australian coast, and speed for the strait with the Great Australia current. The wrecks of ships on the coast of Western Australia are the results of miscalculation in a period when it was impossible to measure longitude at sea. But the profits were so enormous that the risks seemed worth taking.

This was an enterprise of breathtaking daring. The danger of shipwreck was sporadic: the problems of hunger and thirst during such a long ocean crossing, nonstop from Holland to Java, were constant, and help to explain why the Dutch developed the Cape of Good Hope as a way station from 1652. The opening of the new Indian Ocean route was an unsung episode of enormous importance for the history of the world. The Dutch gained the competitive advantage they sought. Holland's Golden Age became affordable. A growing proportion of the world's spice trade, which the Portuguese had never been able to shift out of its traditional grooves, spilled into European hands. The western European economy, long outclassed by those around the Indian Ocean and in maritime Asia, began to catch up.

The Western Rim

Meanwhile, on the western rim of the ocean, Portuguese explorers brought more of the African interior into the web of the routes they traveled. The least productive of their efforts focused on the Red Sea. The monsoons connected maritime Asia with East Africa and the Red Sea, but the latter had an evil reputation with sailors. Ibn Majid, writing toward the end of the sixteenth century, warned that it contained 'many hidden places and things.' His Portuguese successor João de Castro, in 1541, thought that 'this sea presents more hazards to navigation than the whole of the great ocean.' There was not much scope for developing the sea's connections with the outside world: the Portuguese never sought or obtained the welcome here that enabled them to operate successfully further east or further south: religious animosity closed the ports to them.

The opportunities were much greater, however, on and beyond the edges of the Islamic world in East Africa. When the Portuguese occupied Sofala in 1506, they controlled the outlet to the sea from the great inland empire of Monomotapa, which stretched from the Limpopo to the Zambezi and handled enormous wealth in the form of salt, ivory, and, above all, gold. Exploration of the routes into the interior fell in the first instance to António Fernandes—a carpenter by trade, who had helped to build a fort on Kilwa. He was one of the criminals who earned their pardons by accepting exile to Africa. Like many escapees from Europe, he basked in acceptance in Africa. 'The blacks,' according to a contemporary report, 'adore him like a god. . . . If he goes to any place where there are wars, hostilities are suspended for love of him.'[27] His first expedition, from 1511 to 1514, took him to Manica and across Mashonaland to the Zambezi and from there to the courtly center of the ruler of Monomotapa at Chatacuy. In 1515 he set off up the river Buzi and sent back reports of places in the depths of the interior. The trading fairs of Monomotapa became well known to Portuguese merchants in the 1530s and 1540s. In the following decade, the Portuguese chronicler João de Barros was able to describe the ruins of Great Zimbabwe from his compatriots' reports.

Meanwhile, Ethiopia—the other great indigenous empire of East Africa— also became relatively well known to some Portuguese. Relations between this Christian kingdom and Europe had never been quite severed. European merchants had occasionally visited the kingdom on their way to the Indian Ocean via the Nile and the Red Sea. In Venice, Fra Mauro had mapped Ethiopia in unconvincing detail in 1459. Ethiopian clergy were often to be seen in Rome in the late fifteenth and sixteenth centuries.[28] In 1493 Pedro de Covilhão, pursuing his orders to investigate the limits of the Indian Ocean,[29] had settled in the country. But contacts were sporadic until 1520, when a Portuguese embassy was selected to accompany an Ethiopian envoy home. The Franciscan Francisco Alvares traveled with the embassy and wrote an awestruck account of what he called the land of 'Prester John'—the figure of medieval fable who supposedly ruled a great Oriental empire and who would one day unite with Latin Christendom to smite Muslim enemies. In reality, Ethiopia was more needful of help than able to provide it. Pagan, pastoralist migrants eroded its frontiers, while Muslim invaders crossed them from the Adil region to the empire's west. From 1541 to 1543 a Portuguese task force— initially 400 warriors strong, with 130 slaves—intervened to help save the country from Muslim conquest. The fame of their exploits inspired missionaries to follow them. In the early seventeenth century the Society of Jesus was particularly active in attempting to persuade Ethiopia's rulers to abandon their heresies.

Their most remarkable contributions to exploration were the discovery of the source of the Blue Nile by Fr Pedro Páez in 1618, and the search for a route 'which we hope God will keep open' from Gojam to Mogadishu by Fr António Fernandes in 1613. Fernandes's endeavor was part of an increasingly desperate effort to improve the beleaguered empire's communications with the rest of the Christian world. Beyond Kambatta, he entered terrain barely known to the Ethiopians themselves and never again visited by Europeans until the nineteenth century. But he was captured by Muslims and sent back to Ethiopia. He told the Order's historian that

> in the depths of that vast and savage wilderness he thought of himself as an ant in a great meadow . . . going along with the grain of wheat or millet he carried without fear of being trodden on or crushed, and without regarding the purposes of other travellers. . . . I think the Father had this attitude not only on that journey but throughout his life.[30]

Outlining the Americas

The navigators who made the great Atlantic breakthrough of the 1490s had been looking for a quick way to Asia. Instead, they stumbled on a Stone Age obstacle course. It took a long time to appreciate the potential of the New World, longer still to work out how big it was and where its limits lay. In the mid-sixteenth century, cartographers in Europe were still unsure whether it

Portuguese routes in East Africa in the sixteenth century

was a vast peninsula of Asia, as Columbus had believed, or a discrete hemisphere surrounded by seas. Equal uncertainty surrounded its southward extension as, until the early seventeenth century, no one knew for sure whether the land south of what came to be known as the Strait of Magellan was a small island or, as most cartographers assumed, a vast continent stretching toward the South Pole.

The Caribbean and the Lands Around It

Columbus began the long job of tracing the outline of the Americas. He relied on native guides who were already adept at navigating the Caribbean, along trade routes that encompassed every island and met the coastal trades that linked central Mexico to Yucatán and the Mississippi delta.

On his second transatlantic voyage, in 1493, Columbus added the Lesser Antilles from Dominica northward to the catalog of islands he had already made. He also explored most of the coasts of Cuba and Jamaica. Obsessively, anxiously, as we saw above,[31] in his desperate desire to vindicate his claim to have reached Asia, he made his men swear that Cuba was part of a mainland—a promontory of China—but most of them did so with glaring mental reservations. On his third crossing from Spain, in 1498, Columbus really did discover mainland, and correctly identified it as such, when, after making his first landfall at Trinidad, he observed the fresh water flowing from the mouth of the Orinoco. Here he coined the phrase 'Another World' to designate the 'very large landmass' he still saw as in some sense part of Asia—a world 'Alexander and the Romans laboured to conquer.'[32] He followed the coast as far as the island of Margarita before returning to Hispaniola.

Over the next few years, followers, henchmen, and rivals continued his work of exploring the coast. By the end of 1501 they had got as far west as Darién, and probably much beyond the Tropic of Capricorn to the south, confirming that the newly found land was indeed of continental dimensions. They continued to cling to the hope that they were in or near Asia. Columbus' colleague Vicente Yáñez Pinzón, for instance, wondered whether he had found the Ganges when he reached the mouth of what we now call the Amazon in 1499. Vespucci, Columbus' disciple, who was probably the first European to cross the equator on the coast of the New World in the same year, thought he was 'at no great distance' from the Indian Ocean.

On reflection, Columbus seems to have concluded that the Asia he sought must lie beyond the lands he had already found. In 1502 he therefore sailed west from Hispaniola, making the first recorded crossing of the Caribbean. He scoured the coast from Honduras to Darién, seeking a 'strait,' experiencing the visions of personal encounters with God that afflicted or comforted him at times of stress, amid terrible tropical rainstorms. Among the side effects were the discovery of Veragua, with its tantalizing, inaccessible deposits of gold, and an encounter with a Maya trading vessel: these were the first signs that the mainland of the Americas might repay close investigation. Eventually, when he had reached the limit of earlier explorations, Columbus turned away. By then, his ships were riddled with teredos and only just reached Jamaica before foundering.

Thereafter, seekers of the strait that eluded Columbus looked for it further north, and completed the picture of the Caribbean and the Gulf of Mexico in the process. A map in a work of 1511 shows the coastline incomplete; a sketch made by a participant in a voyage of 1519, though very crude, reflects knowledge of the complete outline as far as Florida.

The North American Atlantic Coast: Seeking a Strait

By then, Portuguese loggers and Spanish explorers had taken the search along the coast of South America as far as the River Plate. In the following year, Magellan continued the search and really did find a strait at last—at 52½ degrees south, over 5,000 miles from where Columbus had sought it. As we have seen, however, the strait of Magellan was hardly the longed-for route of access to Asia.

There was still a chance, however, that a passage to Asia lay across the north Atlantic. At the time of Magellan's voyage, European navigators had still largely neglected latitudes between Florida and Nova Scotia. Many maps of the time show the coast as continuous. This assumption was probably based on reports by fishermen and on an inference from a reconnaissance made in 1508–9 by John Cabot's son Sebastian: his shadowy account of it makes it impossible to reconstruct, but wherever it was he went—and he certainly explored further than his father both to north and south along the Atlantic rim of the New World—he found no open water leading westward. On the other hand, most cartographers regarded the question as unresolved, showing a blank beyond the northern limits of Spanish exploration.

The question of whether any opening had been missed was resolved by voyages commissioned to find a westward route to Asia in 1526—the year of an influential world map by Vespucci's nephew which showed a way to India between the 'Land of Cod' and the 'Florid Land.' French capital now entered the exploration market. Lyon was a center of the silk trade; so the prospect of a short route to China was of special interest in that city, where Florentine mercantile and financial houses were well represented. A Florentine adventurer, Giovanni da Verrazano, therefore went there to raise money for his project of seeking a strait north of Florida. The king of France provided a ship.

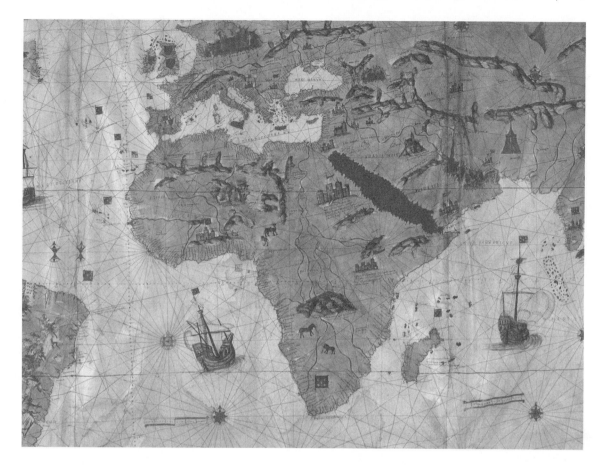

*Juan Vespucci's
Planisphere, 1526, detail.
The map exemplifies, and
perhaps fortified, belief in a
narrow New World and a
passage through it from
the northwest Atlantic*

Verrazano discovered, by his own account, 'a new land, never before seen by anyone, ancient or modern'—implicitly excepting the people who lived there. The land blocked the site of the expected passage to Asia. He tried to make up for the disappointment by some rather unconvincing promotional writing. The land was 'adorned and clothed' with useful trees. It 'partook of the nature of the Orient.' It was full of hospitable people, at least at intervals. It looked as if it had gold, 'to which land of such appearance has every disposition.' It was full of game. Verrazano established the existence of a continuous coastline. He also initiated a new myth: that North America was a narrow continent and that the Pacific lapped it, at its closest point, only a short way from the eastern shore of the continent. Rounding Cape Lookout, he claimed to be off an isthmus only a mile wide, 'where from the ship we could see the Oriental Sea . . . which, no doubt, surrounds the shores of India, China and Cathay.' Presumably, the shallow islets of the Carolina Outer Banks deluded him.[33]

Meanwhile, the king of Spain sent an expedition under yet another Portuguese renegade, Estevão Gomes, who had accompanied and deserted Magellan, to 'go and explore eastern Cathay as far as our island of Maluco.' Gomes reported no way through between Cape Breton and Florida, which was well known, about as far north as Cape Fear, from Ponce's efforts and those of failed colonizing ventures that followed in his wake.

The only remaining prospect of a short sea route from Europe to Asia now lay in the far north, through the abominable hazards of icy Arctic waters. In the years after John Cabot's voyages,[34] Portuguese reconnaissances of the coasts of Labrador, Newfoundland, and, perhaps, Nova Scotia had impressed mapmakers, but not backers of further voyages, except in England, which was the realm best placed for access to these bleak lands and deceptive waters. Robert Thorne, merchant of Bristol, whose father had been among John Cabot's financiers, made the point in a petition he addressed to Henry VIII of England in 1527. To reconnoiter the 'north parts . . . is only your charge and duty.' Thorne subscribed to a theory widely espoused at the time and inherited from late medieval geographers: that the Arctic Ocean was navigable and traversable via the North Pole. One of the sources cited by sixteenth-century cartographers in support of the theory was the now lost work of a fourteenth-century English friar, recounting his voyages to the Pole.[35] This was an unfortunate basis on which to begin the task of Arctic exploration. John Rut, sent to put the theory to the test in 1527, turned back at about the fifty-third parallel for fear of ice.

The English assault on the Northwest Passage began in earnest only in the 1570s, when English envy of Spain and Portugal became acute. Realization dawned that the realm had lagged behind its rivals in exploiting the opportunities of empire and trade. Toward 1577, the Welshman John Dee, physician, astrologer, and Renaissance magus, who flitted between the courts of Elizabeth I of England and the Holy Roman Emperor Rudolf II, was working on a book in celebration of the maritime vocation of what he called, presciently, 'the British Empire.' The surviving frontispiece hints at what the work—now mostly lost—was like. The queen stands in the prow of a ship named 'Europa,' perhaps because Dee saw Elizabeth as the potential liberator of Europe from the Spanish yoke. The queen's hand reaches to grasp a laurel crown held out by Opportunity—a damsel atop a tower, like Rapunzel in the story—with invitingly loose hair, waiting to be grasped. On the sea shore, Britannia kneels, praying for a navy. Rays from the divine tetragram impel the ship. Sun, moon, and stars cast benign influences. St Michael descends, sword in hand, with hostile intent, toward the Spaniards who occupy the New World.[36]

Dee's was one of many works of lobbying and propaganda designed to coax

Frontispiece of John Dee's General and Rare Memorials pertayning to the Perfect Arte of Navigation*, 1577*

Britannia into attempting to rule the waves, and, in particular, to challenge Spanish preponderance by exploiting England's privileged access to boreal seas. The propagandists invented, or compiled from others' inventions, an imaginary history—which, like so many falsehoods, proved in the long run more powerful than facts—of English navigation in the north Atlantic, which allegedly gave England a prior claim to disputed northern lands and routes, attributing to King Arthur the conquest of Iceland, Greenland, Lapland, Russia, and the North Pole.[37]

The strategy was doomed to frustration. The English tend to be self-congratulatory about their maritime traditions. They date their empire from Elizabeth's reign, whereas really it is the failure of England at sea that is the conspicuous and curious feature of the history of the age. They represent Elizabeth's reign as their epoch of national greatness, whereas really, by the standards of the rest of western Europe—of Spain or Italy or even France or the Netherlands—England was a realm of lightly gilded savagery and serious underachievement. England had all the prerequisites for maritime empire: easy access to the sea; a seafaring tradition; the direct experience of imperialism in Ireland. In the previous century, moreover, the English had lost their continental empire—the provinces of France controlled by the English crown. This might have released energy for seaward expansion. Yet despite these advantages, England's empire remained unlaunched until the seventeenth century. The problem is another dog-in-the-night problem: why did this bitch not bark?

A great deal of English energy was expended exploring ice-bound culs-de-sac. The White Sea to the north of Russia and the straits that lead to Hudson Bay—two major theaters of English endeavor in the sixteenth-century search for northern routes to Asia—were navigable for only two or three months a year. This was not enough time for ships to get in and out and still have time to engage in further exploration. Beyond these waters, the only way to make progress was to accept the constraints of the enclosing ice and to drift, trapped, with the current. But this was a long business, for which ships at the time were ill-equipped, having neither the space nor the means to keep supplies fresh for long. In view of the problems, it is not surprising that the effects of English efforts were modest.

At about the time Dee was at work, Martin Frobisher was already at sea on his way to find—so he hoped—a Northwest Passage north of Labrador. In three voyages from 1576 to 1578 he found the entrance to Hudson Bay, dismissing it as a mistake, but bestowed the name of 'Frobisher Strait' on what we now call Frobisher Bay. It was another mistake. An even worse mistake was to gather iron pyrites in the belief that they were gold and exhibit them on returning to England to an incredulous public. This discouraged further attempts until 1585–7, when John Davis, in a renewed bout of wishful thinking, reported 'clear water to the West' in Davis Strait.

The promises Frobisher and Davis held out were belied as soon as exploration resumed under Henry Hudson, Robert Bylot, and William Baffin between 1610 and 1616. It took Dutch interest to rekindle dormant English hopes of finding a passage, for it was under Dutch auspices that the quest was renewed. Hudson already had considerable experience of boreal waters, having sought the fabled passage to the North Pole at the behest of the Muscovy Company in 1607–8 and concluded that it was impossible. He seemed to the Dutch East India Company to be the ideal captain to find a Northwest Passage, if there was one. As we have seen, the Dutch were building to a frenzy of activity at the time, seeking any means of gaining a competitive advantage in the spice markets of the East—sponsoring new attempts along the route pioneered by Magellan, and looking for faster ways of circumventing monsoonal seas. The decision to commission Hudson was part of a three-pronged strategy.

His first voyage across the Atlantic in 1609 merely confirmed the nonexistence of a passage in the region bounded by the modern states of Maryland and New York, where his backers hoped that previous explorers might have missed a vital inlet. By following the river named after him, he established what in later years became a promising route for fur traders between the Atlantic and the fur-rich forests in the vicinity of the Great Lakes. On the way back to Holland, he was arrested by the English and imprisoned as a traitor; his best way out of his predicament was to make his next voyage at English behest.

In 1610 Hudson set off, with orders from the London merchants who backed him to seek a passage at about 61 degrees north. His course led him into Hudson Bay, where, with rations running short, and no ice-free passage out, he was forced to spend the winter, immured by ice in the southernmost extension of the bay. When the summer thaw failed, at first, to free the ship, his men mutinied and cast him adrift. Ravaged by scurvy, starvation, frostbite, and violence at the hands of the Inuit, the handful of survivors included Robert

Bylot, who inherited the mantle of his former master. A voyage in 1612 under the command of a naval officer, Thomas Button, was immeasurably better provided for than Hudson's and proved that a ship could winter in Hudson Bay and survive. After that, Bylot led a further series of expeditions in search of a passage.

His greatest contribution lay in recruiting a navigator and surveyor of unsurpassed genius, William Baffin, to the cause. The voyages they made in 1615 and 1616 were full of false dawns, when their deprivations and dangers seemed time and again about to be rewarded with success. In 1615 they roused high hopes of a passage through Foxe Channel, before having to admit defeat. The following year they exceeded 77 degrees north before accepting that Davis Strait, too, led them only to impenetrable ice. 'I dare boldly say (without boasting),' Baffin concluded, 'that more good discoverie has not in shorter time (to my remembrance) been done since the action was attempted, considering how much ice we have passed, and the difficulty of sailing so near the pole.'

Baffin admirably summed up the prospects for further exploration. There was plenty of food in the Arctic for sailors equipped and able to hunt it down. The seas he had explored made excellent whaling grounds, which could be profitably exploited in summer. As for finding a strait, that was more problematical. Possible routes blocked by ice in winter often proved equally inaccessible in summer because of the way the melting ice and snow fed offshore swells. 'Doubtless there is a passage,' he believed—perhaps approachable via Hudson Bay, or perhaps via Davis Strait. But to find it a ship would need to winter repeatedly in the ice. And that task proved beyond any ship or crew of the time.[38]

Meanwhile, England had scant energy to spare for colonizing other accessible parts of the Americas. English colonies promoted by Sir Walter Ralegh at Roanoke Island between 1585 and 1587 failed: natives, provoked by the newcomers' rapacity and violence, wiped out the first; the settlers of the second disappeared without trace and were never located. Yet from 1602 to 1607 reconnaissances from private English venturers sought suitable sites for new colonial ventures along the coasts of New England, experimenting with three different transatlantic routes: they might follow Cabot's to Newfoundland before dropping south—but even in the most favorable season this counted on unreliable winds and faced adverse currents; or they might follow Columbus, by what became the preferred route, taking the northeast trades to the Caribbean before using the current to head north; they even tried to cross the north Atlantic directly in the face of the wind.

Not until 1607 did a new colony take shape at nearby Jamestown on the mainland. The English had no serious plans to make the colony productive. They still expected to find great riches, lost civilizations, or a route to the Pacific not far off. Unsurprisingly, therefore, the first colonists here proved to be a feckless lot, who depended on their precarious and sometimes coercive friendship with the local Powhatan Indians for food. But there was one man of energy and vision among them. Captain John Smith was, in part, a fantasist who lied his way into esteem and wrote self-aggrandizing romances in praise of his own adventures. He was also the first American tough guy: a self-important tyrant whose real personality—bloody, bold, and resolute—has been sugar-crusted by a cloying Disney myth. He claimed to be able to charm goods and girls out of the Indians. But his real means of making them feed the colony was terror. Most of his abundant energy went on keeping the colony alive. But he also conducted some modest exploratory forays. In 1607 he traveled up the James River to the falls beyond the lodge of the Powhatan ruler. He was unable to discharge what he later claimed were his secret instructions—'not to return without a lump of gold, a certainty of the South Sea or one of the lost colony of Sir Walter Raleigh,' but he did acquire an Indian map and the information that the interior of the country was mountainous.[39] The following year he explored Chesapeake Bay as far as the Susquehannock and, pursuing Indian reports of a 'shining big sea water' in the interior, followed the Potomac to beyond the present site of Washington DC. The best that can be said for English efforts in Virginia is that French efforts to create colonies on the Atlantic coast of North America were equally modest and those of Spain hardly more successful. None made productive probes into the interior.

The Pacific Coast

While the northern limits of America remained shrouded in ice, and if the north Atlantic coasts were inhospitable to bases for further exploration, the western edges of the continent seemed to vanish in the distance that separated them from explorers' bases. Emerging from his strait, Magellan stayed close to the Chilean coast for about three weeks. Exploration of the rest of the Pacific coast of South America proceeded from the north. The first recorded expedition, by Pascual de Andagoya in 1522, aimed, according to his later recollection, 'to discover the chief of Peru and the coast beyond the Gulf of San Miguel.'[40] This may reflect hindsight; but native navigators would surely have given the Spaniards some foreknowledge of what lay in that direction and Peru or 'Biru' seems to have been a name the natives of what are now Nicaragua and Panama gave to Andean lands. Beyond Peru, coastal navigation encountered a serious obstacle: the Humboldt current is extremely arduous to sail against. When Pedro de Valdivia invaded Chile in the 1540s and again in the 1550s, when he reached the river Bío-Bío by land, his supply vessels had difficulty keeping up with him. In 1557–8 Juan Ladrillero lost half his fleet trying to pick his way through the rough-hewn islands that line much of Chile's Pacific coast. At that time, it took ninety days to get from Callao to Valparaiso—longer than needed to get from Spain to Mexico or the Indian Ocean, or to span the whole of maritime Asia from Arabia to China. The only way to make the colonization of Chile viable was to find a better, faster sea route. Traditionally, the discovery of such a route is ascribed to the effects of Mendaña's first Pacific voyage of 1567, which improved knowledge of the wind system. It seems more likely, however, that pilots simply stood out ever further to sea to avoid the Humboldt current, gradually learning where best to alter course for the coast. Detailed charting of the complexities of the southern Chilean coast had to await the work of Pedro Sarmiento de Gamboa—an *uomo universale* of exceptional talent as a navigator, historian, and propagandist—who, in 1579 to 1580, scoured the islands, swept the Pacific as far as the Chatham group, and worked his way through the Strait of Magellan from west to east. His voyages were part of an attempt to make the Pacific secure against incursions by English, French, and Dutch pirates by finding suitable sites for fortifications and naval bases.

Meanwhile, starting from the Spanish colonies in Mexico, exploration of the Pacific coast of North America made little progress. The Spaniards were unimpressed with the poverty and nomadism of the natives to the northwest of New Spain and were more interested in finding a route across the Pacific to the Spice Islands, which, Cortés hoped, would be 'very easy and very short.'[41]

After Cortés himself had put to sea and sighted the tip of Baja California in 1533, in 1539–40 Francisco de Ulloa reconnoitered the coasts of most of that province: he proved it to be a peninsula, but cartographers forgot or ignored the fact, and continued, in some cases, to show it as an island for another 200 years. They were, perhaps, misled by the term 'California'—borrowed from a popular work of chivalric fiction, in which it was the name of an island of Amazons, located near the earthly paradise. The influence of chivalric fable on explorers still showed no sign of abating.

Shortly after the expedition's return, Hernando de Alarcón followed Ulloa's route into what was then called the Sea of Cortés with the aim of provisioning an overland expedition, which was then in the vicinity of the Mogollon Rim. Alarcón ventured 90 miles up the Colorado River. As usual the Spaniards were being wildly overoptimistic, and seriously deluded about the dimensions of their discoveries, in hoping to effect a junction with a force which they expected to find close at hand but which was by then many hundreds of miles away.

As yet, no one in New Spain had any idea what lay north of Baja California. In 1542–3 an expedition led by Juan Rodríguez Cabrillo embarked on a survey of the coast, against the current, through terrifying weather, and, after the commander's death, perhaps got as far as Oregon, or 43 degrees north by the pilot's reckoning, covering nearly 1,000 miles, before turning back. Regular Spanish voyages coasted the region in the sixteenth century, in pursuit of Urdaneta's transpacific route from the Philippines. But the silk-laden galleons from there rarely took the risk of stopping or turning aside to explore until they got to Mexico. An exception occurred in 1587, when Pedro de Unamuno explored Morro Bay with the intention of locating a suitable stopping place for galleons, should one be needed short of their destination. Sir Francis Drake called on the same coast in 1578 during his piratical escapade in the Pacific, when he cheekily took possession of what he called Nova Albion for England. Whether he added anything to knowledge of the coast is doubtful, and hinges on whether a bay he reported was San Francisco Bay, which previous explorers had missed, or Drake's Bay, which Cabrillo had already observed. The arguments are too perfectly poised to settle. But Drake's vagueness in reporting what he saw ought to disqualify him as a discoverer.

Exploring the Americas from Within

While the outline of the Americas remained patchy in Westerners' mental maps, selective forays into the interior of the continent gradually contributed to growing awareness of how big it was. Two kinds of routes led the explorers: cross-country marches, usually of relatively short duration, overland through barriers of mountains, forests, and deserts, and the causeways of great river systems, by which the hemisphere could be deeply penetrated and, in some places, almost crossed. Until nearly the end of the century, almost all the explorers' efforts needed rumors of wealth to trigger them: of rich kingdoms, or productive mines.

The Overland Marches

The first such rumor inspired Vasco Núñez de Balboa to seek the realm of Dabeiba along the San Juan valley in 1512. He had fled to Urabá—the remotest place in the Spanish monarchy, a precarious outpost on the mainland at the neck of Central America—to escape his debts in 1510. He moved to a more promising site at Santa María la Antigua in Darién, where a viable colony took shape under his leadership. His first exploration took him south to within sight of the Andes. His second, from September 1513 to January 1514, crossed the isthmus of Panama from Carreta and made him the first European 'to gaze on the Pacific.'

Dabeiba proved to be a myth. But, as similar myths seemed to breed, so did plausible reasons to believe them. In the 1520s and 1530s Spanish conquistadores proved that the realities of America could exceed even the fictions of chivalric romance. Mexico and Peru really did have gold-rich kingdoms to conquer. From here, in the 1520s and 1530s, exploration radiated into the interiors of the Americas.

Hernán Cortés landed with what was supposed to be a reconnaissance force at Veracruz in August 1519. Abjuring the authority of his superior in Cuba, he constituted his men as a civic community and had himself elected mayor. It was a reflex action. When Spaniards met on a wild frontier they founded a city, just as Englishmen, in similar circumstances, would found a club.

Beaching his ships, Cortés proceeded 'with no fear that once my back was turned, the people left in the town would betray me.' Rumors of Aztec wealth steeled a resolve, which, with the ships grounded, was literally to conquer or die. 'Trusting in God's greatness and in the might of their Highnesses' royal name,' 315 Spaniards struck inland to seek Motecocuma 'wherever he might be.' The route was consciously chosen to penetrate the most inaccessible patches of the Aztec world, where the Aztecs' most reluctant tributaries and most defiant enemies would be found. The Spaniards climbed from Jalapa by a pass 'so rough and steep that there is none in Spain so difficult,' emerging with the conviction that they were now in the Aztec realm. 'God knows,' wrote Cortés, 'how my people suffered from hunger and thirst and . . . hailstorms and rainstorms.'[42] They fought their way through the land of Tlaxcala, where their courage was rewarded by the alliance of the fiercest pocket of resistance to the Aztecs between Mexico and the coast.

The thread by which their morale hung frayed quickly. They were thousands of miles from home. They were cut off from hope of help and knew that if a force followed them from Cuba it would be to punish them, not to assist. They were surrounded by a hostile and awe-inspiring environment and hundreds of thousands of menacing 'savages' whom they could not understand. They had to breathe an unaccustomed, rarefied atmosphere; to endure extremes of heat and cold; to eat a debilitating diet without the red meat and wine that Spaniards considered essential for health and high status. They were at the mercy of native guides and interpreters who might choose to betray them at any moment. At Cholula, Cortés resorted to terror. To preempt, he said, an Indian conspiracy, but, more convincingly, to alleviate the Spaniards' stress, he massacred, by his own account, more than 3,000 people.

He is overrated as a conqueror. A coalition of indigenous peoples overthrew the Aztecs. The successful alliance seems to have been contrived not so much by Cortés as by his indigenous mistress, who was also his interpreter and the only person really in a position to know what was going on on the diplomatic front. Native representations of the conquest show her center stage, conducting negotiations and even directing operations.

As an explorer, however, Cortés deserves renown. Of course, he was as dependent on indigenous help for what he achieved in route finding as for what he achieved in war; but his efforts extended the existing routes of contact between the world's civilizations in world-changing fashion. Until then Spanish outposts in the New World had been of marginal importance: only modestly productive, barely significant for the lives of most people in Eurasia. Cortés put them in touch with one of the world's most populous and productive regions. The great belt of rich sedentary civilizations that stretched across Eurasia could now begin to exchange culture and biota with those of the Americas. A line of communications—still imperfect, still precarious—was beginning to bind the world together.

Francisco Pizarro conquered Peru in conscious imitation of Cortés. The usual fantastic ambitions animated the conquistadores. The illiterate Pizarro was to be 'governor, captain general and adelantado' of conquered Peru. His henchman Diego de Almagro, an outcast born out of wedlock, was to be 'a nobleman of some recognized seat.' Hernando de Luque, who fixed the expedition's finances, was to be a bishop. To win these rewards, they had to go through appalling hardships. Though the partners launched their enterprise in 1524, it was not until January 1532 that Pizarro began to climb the Inca highlands, along the Cira and Piura Rivers, with only 185 men. When he met Atahualpa at Cajamarca in November 1532, he relied on surprise and cold steel to overcome odds of over fifteen to one. With Atahualpa as his prisoner, he could deter counterattack and gather a ransom in gold.

He followed the Inca road that skirted the high Andes to the west, before crossing from Cajatamba to Jauja and beginning, toward the end of October, the descent on the Incas' valley capital at Cuzco. Inca roads led Diego de Almagro south from Lake Titicaca in 1535 and Pedro de Valdivia to Chile in 1541. By the same means, Diego Rojas crossed the Chaco and began the conquest of Tucumán in 1543.

Meanwhile, in the late 1520s Spanish explorers of the River Plate estuary picked up rumors of what became known as the city 'of the Césares' after the brothers who first sought it or recorded the reports. Adventurers looked for it at intervals for more than a quarter of a century, in places from Colombia to Patagonia. The most promising potential location was in the northern Andes, where persistent reports located a kingdom of fabulous wealth. Here, three river valley routes from the Caribbean, along the rivers Magdalena, Sinu, and San Juan, converged. So, in the 1530s, did rival bands of conquistadores.

One approached from the east. Charles V had granted Venezuela to a firm of German bankers, the Welzers. In September 1530 their representative, Nicholas Federmann, found himself in command at Coro, with 'so many men, inactive and unemployed, that I determined to make an expedition to the South Sea' and 'do something profitable.' This showed how ignorant explorers were of the continent that lay before them: it was ludicrously overambitious to hope to reach the Pacific from Coro. He got mired in the mud of the Venezuelan llanos and mistook it for the seashore. His superior commander, Ambrose Alfinger, meanwhile set off on an exploration of his own—which lasted for three years and cost him his life—as far as the rivers Magdalena and Sagramoso. But Federmann did not give up.

There really was a gold-rich, sedentary, and partly urban civilization in the Colombian plateau around Bogotá: that of the Muisca. In 1537 a party exploring inland from Santa Marta stumbled on it while hoping to open an overland route to Peru. For two years, they had the run of the place, amassing treasure and native textiles. Then, in 1539, Federmann arrived in the same spot, clad only in skins, having lost half his force, originally 300 strong, during the rigors of the ascent of the Andes from the east. A third force, pressing northward from Peru, arrived a few months later, inaugurating a seven-year lawsuit over the division of the spoils.

The discovery of three gold-rich civilizations—Aztec, Inca, and Muisca—naturally excited more cupidity. The focus of the search now shifted to the lowlands of Venezuela and Amazonia, where explorers sought to confirm suspicions of the existence of El Dorado—literally, 'The Gilded Man'—a chief, supposedly ritually dusted with powdered gold prior to bathing in a lake, into which many rich artifacts would then be plunged.[43]

It may seem odd that explorers should scour the lowlands for lost civilizations, when the previous finds had all occurred in highland environments. But impressive sites near the eastern foot of the Andes seemed to point explorers eastward. Inca gossip, based on respect for trading partners in the forests, may have helped. The lowlands probably did enclose societies that built large settlements, farmed intensively, and generated a surplus for trade. Early explorers of the Amazon reported such societies, and archeological finds in recent years have tended to bear them out. Turtle and fish farming and the large-scale production of bitter manioc gave the lowlands the potential to support populations unattainable by the forest Indians of today. In the second half of the sixteenth century, there was scarcely a written report from Spaniards

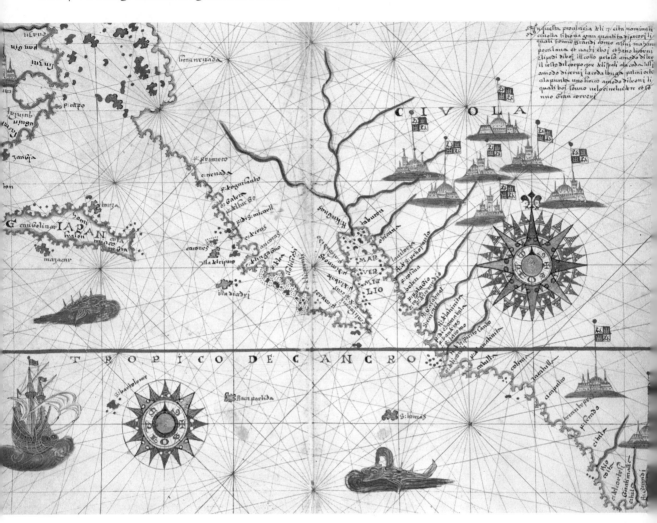

posted east of Coro that did not mention El Dorado, now generally relegated to the mysterious tableland of Guiana. Here, in the seventeenth century, the search continued.

North America had equally persistent legends of similar kinds. In 1539, a missionary's black servant, reconnoitering ahead of his master in search of unknown peoples north of Mexico, left before his death a report garbled by delirium and inflated by the hopes of those who heard it. Cíbola, he claimed, was one of seven great cities in the North American interior. It was bigger than Tenochtitlán. Its temples, in rumors spread by Chinese whispers, were smothered in emeralds.[44] The effect of the news can be seen in the map made in Catalonia by Joan Martínez nearly forty years later: a richly gilded compass points straight from Chihuahua and Sinaloa into a colorful region of domed,

Map of the southwest coast of North America from the atlas of Joan Martínez, 1578, showing the legendary seven cities of Cíbola

spired, and turreted cities which did not exist. Cíbola gave its name to the whole reputed galaxy of seven.

In April 1540, Francisco Vázquez de Coronado led an expedition of 200 horsemen in search of them, ahead of a support column of 1,000 slaves and servants, driving pack mules and herds of livestock for food. Cíbola was said to lie beyond mountains, so they simply headed upstream until they reached the watershed of the Mogollon Rim, then followed the rivers down. With his supplies lagging far behind, Coronado led his men into extremes of hunger in the highlands. Some of them died, poisoned by greenery they chewed on the trail. After two months they reached a populated region. The Indians they called Pueblo, because of their well-built settlements, were sedentary farmers. They were 'good people,' the Spaniards reported, 'more devoted to agriculture than war,'[45] but their material culture fell well short of the reputed marvels of Cíbola. They possessed no emeralds—only turquoise in small amounts.

The Great Plains were close. At the Pueblo settlement of Hawikuh, Coronado first heard of what he called 'the country of the cows'—the American bison.[46] He first saw a buffalo tattooed or painted on the body of a member of an embassy which brought buffalo-hide shields, robes, and head-dresses from people who lived near the edge of the grasslands. Following the emissaries to their home town of Tziquite, Coronado acquired a charismatic guide who 'talked with the devil in a pitcher of water.'[47] This guide could speak a smattering of Nahuatl—or perhaps he just belonged to the people later called Comanches, whose language had common roots with the Aztecs'. Lured by talk of a state with canoes of forty oars and prows of gold,[48] Coronado pressed north to a supposedly rich, urban culture called Quivirá. Never out of sight of the buffalo, he rode on 'plains so vast that in my travels I did not reach their end, although I marched over them for more than three hundred leagues.'[49]

The Spaniards' reports reveal a region where life depended on the herds of bison. The natives ate nothing else. They dressed in buffalo hides tied with thongs of buffalo leather. They slept in buffalo-skin tents and wore moccasins of the same material on their feet. They impressed the visitors with their fearless and friendly greetings, but their table manners embodied Spanish ideas of savagery. They swallowed raw meat, 'half-chewed, like birds'; they drank fresh blood from vessels made of buffalo guts. They drank with relish the half-digested contents of buffaloes' stomachs. For explorers seeking what they hoped they would recognize as a great civilization, the disappointment was intense.

After five weeks of fruitless searching in 'lands as level as the sea,' Coronado decided that his guides were trying to lose him. But Indians he met continued to wave him northward when asked for Quivirá. He took a bold decision in the best conquistador tradition. Sending most of his force and all the camp followers home, he headed north by the compass with only thirty horsemen. They lived off buffalo, heaping mounds of buffalo dung as they went, to serve as markers of the way home.

They finally found Quivirá in what is now Cow Creek, Rice County, Kansas, on the edge of a zone of relatively long grasses, which thickened as the prairie descended to low altitudes. The vaunted 'cities' were turf lodge settlements of the 'racoon-eyed,' tattoo-faced Kirikiri, who farmed patches of plain with difficulty in villages that had gradually spread west along the Arkansas River. Coronado transformed their world: he brought horses into it. With horse and spear, he was able to kill 500 buffalo in a fortnight. Though natives on foot could achieve multiple kills in pits, the horsemen's prowess as hunters was of a different order. It was a revelation of the future—a future still surprisingly distant, for it was more than a century before the horse became the universal companion of man on the plains.

Hernando de Soto approached the same region from another direction. He had served with Pizarro in Peru and expected easy riches. His conquistador's windfall gave him the capital with which to fund an expedition of his own. The idea of seeking another fortune in Florida was not original. Spaniards had penetrated the interior of what is now the North American 'deep south' before, in 1528, under Pánfilo de Narváez. They found no treasure, and the few who survived emerged 'naked as we were born, with the loss of all we had . . . so skeletal that we looked like death.'[50]

Soto thought he could do better. Impatience and profligacy scarred his methods. He landed near Tampa Bay in May 1539. His 400 soldiers and over 200 horses threaded their way through swampland into the country of the Appalachee, seizing chiefs for ransoms so petty that they enraged those who received them as much as those who paid them. After wintering in what is now Florida, he crossed the Blue Ridge Mountains and descended the Alabama as far as Mabila, just north of present-day Mobile. Here the previously agreed plan called for the force to return to the coast and take ship at Pensacola Bay, where a fleet was waiting to make a rendezvous. But Soto still hoped for some great treasure. The well-built settlements in which the Indians lived, the artistry of their shell work and copper work, and the skill with which they crafted the small amounts of gold they possessed all convinced him that he must be on the fringes of some rich civilization. He turned aside and led his men toward the northwest.

The region Soto traversed was scattered with settlements rich enough to encourage the explorers but too poor to satisfy them. 'De Soto,' reported one of his disaffected followers, 'because his purpose was to find another treasure like that of Atahualpa, lord of Peru, would not rest content.' The expedition seemed to wander purposelessly. 'Neither the governor,' complained one of the men, 'nor anyone else knew where they were headed other than to find a land so rich that it would satisfy their desires.'[51]

Almost wherever they went, plagues seemed to have preceded them—probably caused by diseases the Spaniards carried, to which the natives had no immunity. Turning inland to investigate rumors of what they understood to be a sea, Soto's men reached the vastness of the Mississippi at Quizquiz. They crossed on rafts and pursued the course of the Arkansas as far as the place where Little Rock now stands, attempting, without success, to terrorize natives into producing gold. Disillusioned by the poverty of the inhabitants and the ferocity of their resistance, the Spaniards abandoned the expedition in the spring of 1542. Soto died—apparently naturally of 'flux'—in May of that year. After failing to find an overland route back to Mexico, his men turned back to follow the Mississippi to the coast on rafts they built themselves.

The experiences of the early 1540s were so disenchanting that the North American south was neglected for most of the rest of the century. Only in the 1590s did interest in exploring the region really revive. By then, the inhabitants of New Spain had resigned themselves to the fact that the region concealed no rich civilizations; but it began to seem worth conquering to exploit the relatively modest potential ranchland and farmland of New Mexico. In 1595 Juan de Oñate began to plan an expedition of 500 men. He would establish a colony in New Mexico and explore outward from there with the aim of opening a route to the Pacific: as usual, he was making outrageous under-estimates of the sort of distances that might be involved, and clearly had no inkling of the vastness and hostility of the terrain that separated New Mexico from the ocean.

Just to reach and feed his proposed colony, Oñate had to assemble thousands of livestock—his herd covered a space 3 miles square—across hundreds of miles of desert and mountains, including one 60-mile stretch so much worse than the rest that it was uninvitingly known as the Jornada de la Muerte, the March of Death, or, later, the Jornada del Muerto, or Dead Man's March. Numerous accounts of the expedition survive. The most vivid was left by Gaspar Pérez de Villagrá, who described the sufferings of a route through defiles up rock-strewn slopes and over dunes where the glare was so fierce that his eyes roasted and seemed to burst from their sockets. The horses were blinded and stumbled helplessly. The men breathed fire and spat pitch. In a particularly harrowing passage, Villagrá described his escape from the hostile pueblo of Acoman. He got stuck in a pit in the snow. He then trudged on for four days through storms, thirst, and hunger, until he felt compelled to eat his dog, his last surviving companion. Touched by loyalty, or frustrated by want of cooking equipment, he was unable to carry out his resolve but the dog died anyway. 'Leaving him stretched out and his blood ebbing away, I swallowed a bitter gulp and went in search of the stroke of fortune that might finish the dregs of life that were left to me.' He vanquished these suicidal thoughts, but almost killed himself by overindulgence when he reached water.

Villagrá's is not, of course, a disinterested narrative. It was a collective plea for recognition and royal rewards, made on behalf of the writer and his fellow campaigners, a record addressed to the king, of sufferings undergone 'for nothing more than to serve you and to please you.' One canto is headed, 'Of the excessive travails suffered by soldiers in the new discoveries and of the bad recompense their services receive.' There is, however, no reason to doubt the outline of facts Villagrá conveys. Most of them are confirmed in other accounts and official documents.

What elevates this work to a level of discourse beyond the merely believable is not its content but its form. For this catalog of horrors, which culminates in a particularly repulsive story of massacre and countermassacre in the conflict with the Indians of Acoman, is entirely written in heroic verse with strong echoes of Vergil. The poem actually begins with the line 'I sing of arms and the heroic man.' That line occurs often enough in other self-consciously heroic poetry of the time, and Villagrá's classical allusions must have seemed appropriate in a world of humanistic values. He managed to cram references to Rome, Carthage, Circe, Cineas, Pyrrhus, the Favii, the Scipii, the Metelli, Pompey, Sulla, Marius, Lucullus, and the Trojan horse into the space of a few lines.[52]

Villagrá used chivalric romance, too, to reimagine the realities of the campaign. He describes the expedition as including

> fair ladies, duennas and damsels, as perfect, discreet and lovely as they were noble, charming and prudent; and . . . gentlemen of fine appearance, each competing with the rest in as great an array of liveries and trappings as the most curious courtiers are accustomed to don to distinguish themselves in the most colorful and lofty court at high feast-time.[53]

This can hardly have been literally true, but with the aid of a literary imagination the writer could see himself as a knight and the expedition as knightly companionage. He went further. At one point in the story, an Indian woman called Polca turned up at the Spanish camp in search of her husband, whom she believed to be a prisoner there. The sergeant on watch ordered her to pass unhindered:

> The sergeant saw how gracious and polite
> She was, how calm and frank and fair
> And ordered all to grant her, without let,
> The freedom due to all unblemished beauty,
> As courtliness for gentleness commands.

Don Quixote met Dulcinea. The true squire recognized the noble squaw. The expedition tended to become—as an impatient viceroy of New Spain remarked—'a fairy-tale.'[54]

The Great River Routes

Alongside the cross-country routes that penetrated mountains, deserts, forests, and prairies, great rivers conveyed explorers to new, and often to unsuspected or unintended, destinations. The Americas are deeply cleft by great river systems: the Orinoco, the Amazon, and the Paraguay–Paraná were causeways across much of the continent in the south. In the north, the St Lawrence and the Great Lakes invited explorers from the Atlantic into the depths of the interior. However, the Mississippi–Missouri—not only a vast system but also, for most of its length, a remarkably navigable one—was relatively neglected until well into the seventeenth century.

At the end of 1541 the first Spanish voyagers arrived on the Amazon: fifty-eight men, borne on a raft built on the spot, with nails battered out of scrap metal, and a few canoes scrounged or stolen from Indians. They were part of a typical ill-fated expedition in search of chimerical wealth: the 'land of cinnamon' supposed to lie inland from Peru. Desperate for food, they reached the Amazon by toting and paddling down the Napo River. 'It turned out,' wrote Fray Gaspar de Carvajal, 'otherwise than we all expected, for we found no food in 200 leagues.' Indeed the assumption that the rainforest was an abundant environment undid many European explorers: in reality, the forest floor is largely bare of plants edible to man.[55] Instead, Carvajal continued, 'God gave us a share in a discovery new and unheard of,' the first recorded navigation of the Amazon from its junction with the Napo to the Atlantic Ocean.

The adventure unfolded by accident. The navigators did not intend to abandon the companions they left starving back at camp. At first, as the distance mounted between them and their base, they were driven on by hunger. Then, when their search failed, they were too weak to turn back against the current. For days the torrent bore them. They were unable to reach the banks. Fray

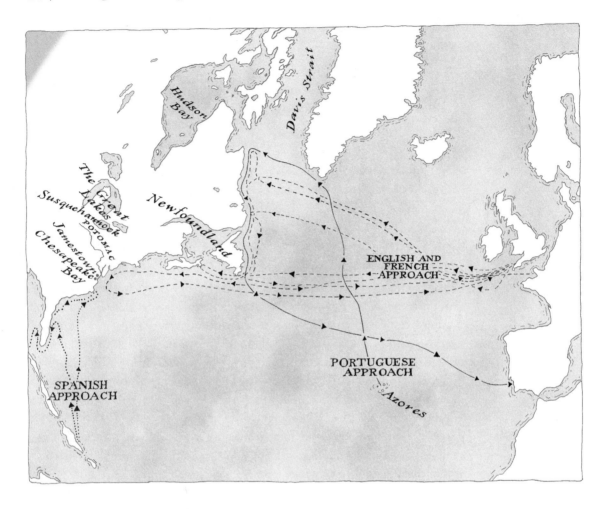

Gaspar said mass 'as they do at sea', without consecrating the host in case it should be lost overboard. On 8 January 1542, after twelve days afloat, they made the shore and were fed by Indians who took pity on them. This gave them the strength to decide to continue the navigation as far as the sea and to build a brig for the journey. Their biggest want was of nails. Two soldiers with engineering experience were deputed to build a forge. They made bellows out of the old boots of men who had died of hunger. They burned wood to make charcoal for smelting. By collecting up every bit of metal they had, apart from essential weapons and ammunition, they made 2,000 nails in twenty days. Thus the Iron Age came to the Brazilian rainforest.

They had to postpone building their brigantine until they got to a place with better food supplies. They never developed expertise in finding their own food, but, coming to a densely populated stretch where the Indians practiced

Approaches to North America from Europe, c.1496–c.1513

turtle farming, they secured ample provisions of turtle meat, supplemented by 'roast cats and monkeys.' Here it took thirty-five days to build the vessel and caulk it with Indian cotton soaked in pitch, 'which the natives brought because the captain asked them for it.'

The vessel soon became a warship. For much of May and June the voyagers battled their way through hostile canoes, relying for most of the time on crossbows for defense, since powder would not stay dry. During this time, they lived on supplies seized in sallies against natives on the shore. On 5 June, they experienced the encounter that gave the river its name. In one village they found a fortified sanctuary, presided over by carvings of jaguars. 'The building was something worth seeing and, impressed by its size, we asked an Indian what it was for.' His explanation was that there they adored the insignia of their female rulers. Further downriver, the Spaniards picked up rumors which they interpreted to mean that there was a powerful empire of female warriors to the north, seventy villages strong, rich in gold, silver, salt, and llamas. The story must have been created by leading questions from the Spaniards and garbled native replies. Soon after the expedition emerged from the Atlantic, after an estimated 1,800 leagues' voyage downriver, stories were circulating in Europe about the Spaniards' heroic battles with the Amazons. In 1544 Sebastian Cabot decorated his world map with a scene of the supposed fight with the nonexistent females.

The Orinoco proved to be a tougher proposition. In the 1530s explorers attempting the ascent of the river could not get beyond the rapids at the confluence with the Meta. Further exploration—though sporadically attempted—was not achieved until the 1580s, when the legend of El Dorado lifted Spanish eyes toward the Guiana highlands. Antonio de Berrio, heir of one of the conquerors of Bogotá, devoted his wealth to the search for the fabled kingdom. Descending from his home at Chita, northeast of Bogotá, he began a methodical exploration of the river system in 1584, following the Orinoco as far as the junction with the Ventuari, which flows precipitately from the Guiana highlands. He crossed the watershed and descended the river along the northern edge of the highlands, founding a settlement at Santo Tomé, near the mouth of the Orinoco, as a base for further exploration. His son Fernando carried on the work, struggling upriver as far as he could get and exploring, one by one, the tributaries that cascade into the Orinoco from the south. These vain labors never yielded any riches or even a viable route of trade to link Venezuela with New Granada. The exploration of the river system was incomplete until in 1647 Miguel de Ochogavia, 'the Columbus of the Apure,' conquered the last of the Orinoco's Andean tributaries, celebrating his achievement in doggerel:

> I came, I saw, I conquered and returned in glory
> From Orinoco—crystals cleft and fear allayed.
> To God I dedicate, in thanks, my wondrous story,
> To you, my readers, all the benefits to trade.[86]

The first European discovery of the River Plate is much disputed. Vespucci claimed it. It might have been the work of Portuguese or French woodcutters, who frequented the Brazilian coast in search of logwood. In 1516 Juan Díaz de Solís turned into the river mouth in the vain hope of a short route to the Pacific but did not get far. Of the first European to penetrate the interior of South America via the River Plate we have scant information. Arraigned for insubordination during Díaz's expedition, Alejo García was marooned on an island near the estuary and heard of a rich kingdom inland, ruled by a 'White king' amid 'mountains of silver.' Had knowledge of the Incas reached Indians so far from the Andes? Or was this another of the rumors Spaniards excited by their own leading questions? At an uncertain date, in the early or mid-1520s, García returned to seek his fortune. His wanderings can no longer be reconstructed with any precision: his course is known only from reports Spaniards later gathered from Indian informants. But he penetrated almost to Peru and amassed a legendary treasure that inspired subsequent explorers. He died in the Chaco region, probably at the hands of the natives, during his return, adding legends of his own wealth to the myths of Indian riches.

Attempts to emulate him met the same end and added little or nothing to the outside world's knowledge of the region until 1541. In that year, Domingo de Irala was in command of the Spanish outpost of Buenos Aires. Learning of the massacre of the latest party to advance upriver, he took a bold decision of the sort typical of successful conquistadores. He abandoned his base and established a new settlement way up the Paraná at Asunción, where he forged an understanding with the local people. Meanwhile, a relief expedition was under way. Alvar Núñez Cabeza de Vaca led it. He was among the most talented Spanish commanders in the New World, author of a remarkable account of his own adventures from 1528 to 1536. He had been enslaved by Indians on the Texan coast when an expedition intended for the exploration of Florida came to grief. With three other Spaniards and a black slave, he escaped and set off in an attempt to find a way back to Mexico. A combination of personal charisma and medical skill gave him a reputation as a holy man. At the end of his seven-year odyssey he arrived at the Spanish frontier in Sinaloa with 600 Indian followers. He now brought the same determination to the problems of the Paraná.

Arriving in March 1542, he established an advanced base the following year at Puerto de los Reyes, from where parties fanned out in the hope of finding

Alejo García's lost treasure. Compelled to return empty-handed to Asunción in April 1544, he found the restless conquistadores increasingly hard to manage: 'the devil himself,' he reported, 'could not have ruled us.' In 1546 he submitted to Irala's demand 'to go inland to see if we could find gold or silver.' After forty-three days' hardship, with no rations left, they drew lots to decide whether to go on. 'Chance determined we should proceed'.[57] Fighting hostile Indians for most of the way, they struggled on for another forty-two days, when they encountered outposts of the viceroyalty of Peru. The new cross-continental route they had opened proved to be of enormous utility to the Spanish empire, creating an exploitable link between Peru and the Atlantic.

In North America, neglect of the Mississippi made it impossible to create the kind of network of river routes that was emerging in South America. The usefulness of the St Lawrence, however, as an important causeway toward the interior emerged relatively early. Here, as in the cases of the river routes of South America, legends of rich kingdoms became the explorers' main inducement. In 1534 the king of France commissioned Jacques Cartier to 'undertake a voyage on behalf of this kingdom to the New Lands to discover certain islands and countries where there are said to be great quantities of gold and other riches.'[58] Spanish success in Mexico and Peru were obviously the trigger; the project Verrazano had begun was, at best, now a secondary part of the French agenda. His first voyage was discouraging. Reconnoitering the coasts of Newfoundland, he explored the Gulf of St Lawrence in what seemed to him 'the land God gave to Cain.'[59] Three events, however, made a return visit desirable. First, Indian traders offered Cartier impressive furs—the black gold of the north—sometimes stripping them off their backs in exchange for hawks' bells. Secondly, he established friendly relations with Donnaconna, the chieftain whose people dominated the lower St Lawrence, who allowed him—after some negotiations which, presumably, neither party fully understood—to erect and adore a cross emblazoned with the arms of France. He was even allowed to take two of the chief's sons back to France, where, Cartier hoped, their good reception would earn him further favor on his return. Finally, Iroquois he met told Cartier of a gold-rich realm they called Saguenay, upriver from the estuary that lay at the head of the gulf.

So in 1535 he returned and began to ascend what is now known as the St Lawrence, which, said his Iroquois informants, 'comes from such a distance that no man has been to the end.' In some ways, his experiences of the river were positive. Natives he met continued to urge him toward the supposed riches of Saguenay. The material culture of Iroquoian peoples seemed selectively impressive: they practiced agriculture and built permanent settlements. The town of Hochelaga, on the site of present-day Montreal, had 2,000 inhabitants by Cartier's reckoning in streets arrayed with perfect geometry. People he met were uniformly welcoming, generous, and favorably impressed by the novelties Cartier brought: Christian rituals, tin truck, the noise of guns, and the music of trumpets. The abundance of game, fish, and fur impressed the French in their turn. On his return he explored a feature he had noted on his first voyage: a strait between Newfoundland and Cape Breton, which ensured a faster, safer passage to the St Lawrence via the islands of St Pierre and Miquelon, which still belong to France.

Yet in other respects the voyage was disappointing to participants and baffling to historians. Cartier's account makes it quite clear that according to his Iroquois guides the 'way to Saguenay' lay up the Saguenay River, a tributary which flows into the St Lawrence from the north with a fierce rush through deeply cleft rock. Cartier seems to have convinced himself that he could get to Saguenay by continuing along the less daunting waters of the main river. Moreover, despite the goodwill Cartier had invested in the entertainment of the Indian princes, whose command of French enormously improved his communications with the locals, friendly relations with the natives proved hard to sustain. His hosts clearly did not want Cartier to advance beyond Quebec into the territory of their enemies. He lost confidence in their offers to guide him and proceeded without their help. On his way back upriver, he imitated the Spanish conquistadores by taking Donnaconna prisoner—not to control him so much as to get him back to France, where his tales of Saguenay would surely raise more capital for further voyages. He proved an effective publicist, acceding to every wishful French thought about the fabled realm: it produced pepper and pomegranates and was peopled by monsters from European fables. The most serious problems arose from the need to winter in Canada. The ships were bound in river ice 12 feet thick. The stores froze. The men suffered from scurvy until they accepted Indian remedies. Cartier made at least one more trip along the St Lawrence, to establish a colony at Quebec, and perhaps a second to evacuate it when it proved unsustainable. The settlers found no evidence of the existence of Saguenay along the tributaries of the St Lawrence.

So it seemed, for the time being at least, that the St Lawrence led nowhere. Until the development of the fur trade in the next century and the establishment of viable settlements at Quebec and Montreal, exploitation of the North American interior was frustrated by the lack of centers of instant wealth of the kind Spain exploited in New Spain and Peru.

But, as in Spain's dominions, expectations in France of what the New World had to offer gradually changed. By the end of the sixteenth century, hopes of instant riches in the form of gold and silver lapsed: the glories of the Aztecs, Inca, and Muisca receded into the past. The furs Cartier had observed came to

(Right)
*Babylonian world map,
c.600 BC. Babylon is at
the top, within the circular
band of the ocean. The
parallel lines represent the
Euphrates. Beyond the
sea, the wedge-like shapes
represent lands legendary
or little known*

(Below)
Polynesian exploration

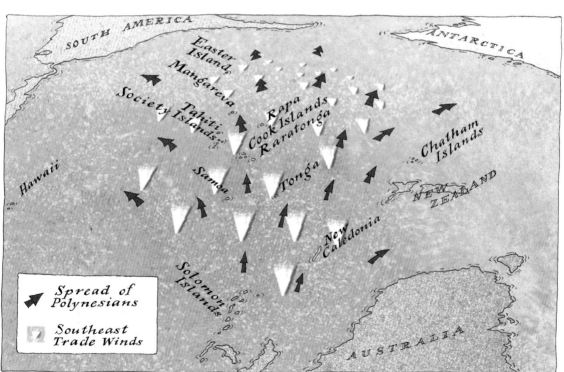

 Spread of
Polynesians

Southeast
Trade Winds

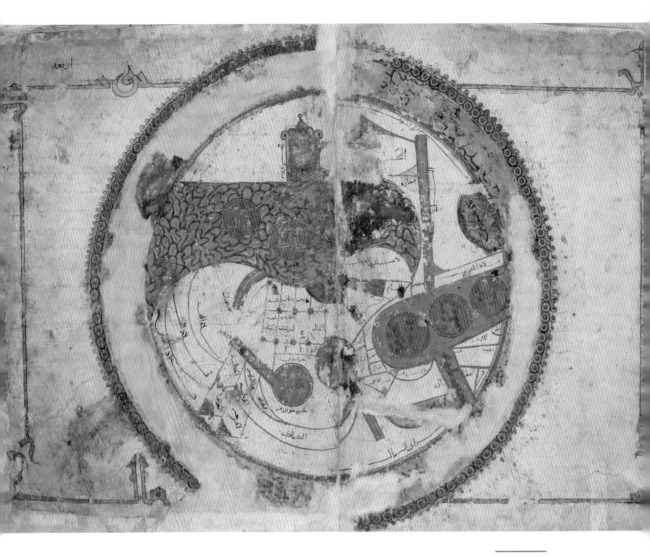

The world according to
the Persian geographer
al-Istakhri, 1193. South
is at the top. Europe is
a small triangle in the
bottom right hand corner.
The mapmaker's Persian
home is central

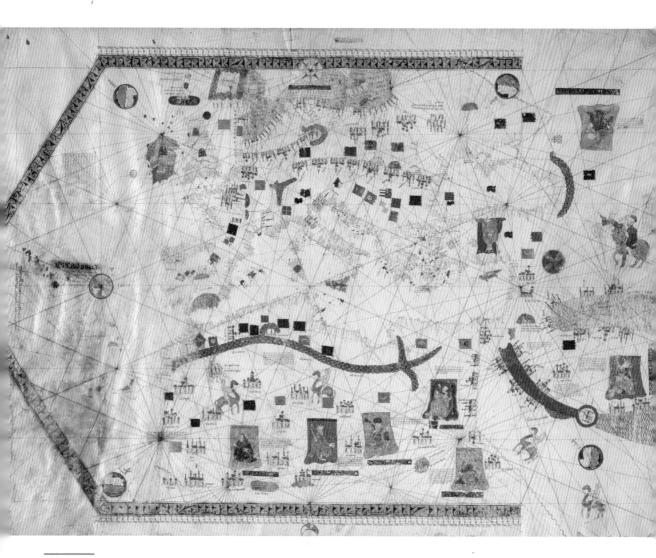

Islands visited by the
Portuguese explorer Diogo
de Silves appear in a map
by the Majorcan cartog-
rapher Gabriel de Vallseca,
1439. This was the first
time the Azores appeared
aligned from northwest to
southeast. The remains of
the ink blot George Sand
made are visible

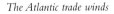

Castile and the
Atlantic winds

The Atlantic trade winds

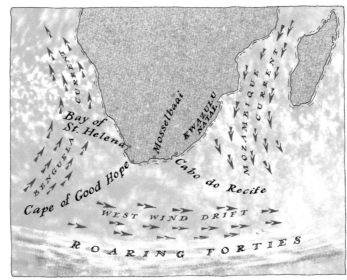

(*Above*)
The Lisbon waterfront from Civitates Orbis Terrarum *by Georg Braun and Franz Hogenberg, c.1572*

(*Right*)
Rounding the Cape of Good Hope: winds and currents

(*Above*)
*The mappa mundi of
Fra Mauro, a monk from
the monastery of San
Michele in Murano, 1459.
Replete with explorers'
information, the map
shows the Indian Ocean
accessible via the southernmost cape of Africa*

(*Facing page, top*)
*Made in Lisbon and
purchased in 1502 by the
duke of Ferrara, this map
was informative as well
as decorative, including
remarkable (and perhaps
partly speculative) extents
of American coastlines, and
the Caribbean according
to the latest information
at the time*

(*Facing page, bottom*)
*Mercator's double-
hemisphere world map,
1587, with conjectured
southern continent*

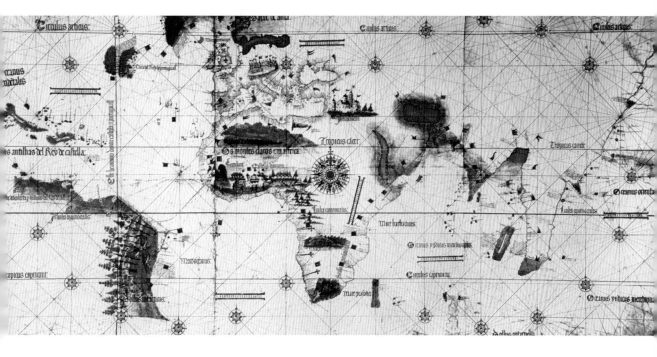

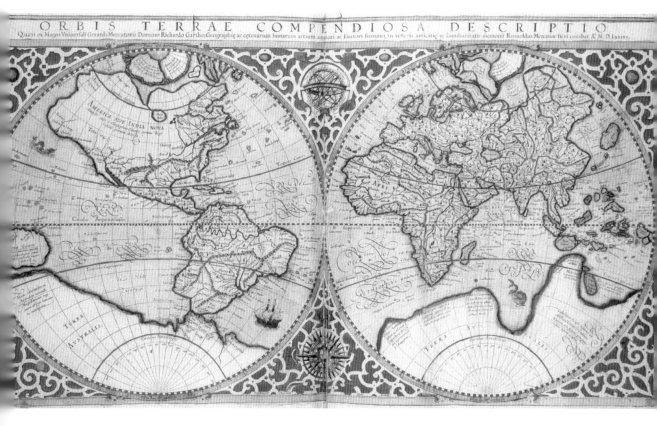

ORBIS TERRAE COMPENDIOSA DESCRIPTIO
Quam ex Magna Vniuersali Gerardi Mercatoris Domino Richardo Gartho, Geographiæ ac cæterarum bonarum artium autori ac fautori summ; in veteris amicitiæ ac familiaritatis memoriã Rumoldus Mercator fieri curabat Aᵒ M. D. lxxvii.

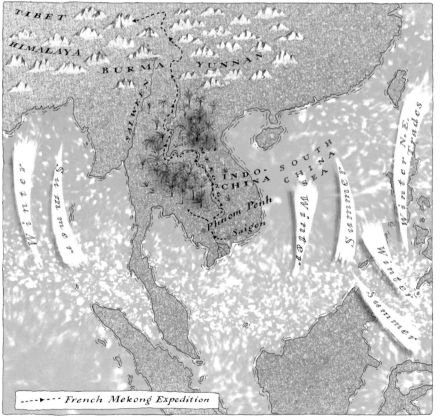

(*Above*)
*The German naturalist
Alexander von Humboldt
(probably the figure picking
a flower) setting out to
climb Mount Chimborazo,
June 1802*

(*Left*)
*Southeast Asia:
monsoonal system and
inland communications*

seem attractive enough to renew efforts to found a colony. Between 1598 and 1600 fur traders set up trading posts on the St Lawrence as far as the Saguenay, but merchants of Honfleur and Saint-Malo disputed the right to exclusive trade and the settlements foundered or perished. In 1600, however, the picture changed when merchants of Dieppe entered the field; the crown granted a monopoly to a consortium from Honfleur and Dieppe; and the promoters made a felicitous choice of governor for their new colony in the person of Samuel de Champlain.

During the years he spent intermittently in charge of French operations in Canada from 1603 to 1616 he gave high priority to further explorations. He made the first ascent of the Saguenay, and explored tributaries of the St Lawrence to the south. In 1609 he pursued the course of the Richelieu River as far as Ticonderoga and obtained from the Indians a pretty accurate picture of what lay beyond as far as the Atlantic coast: this was important, as the route along the Richelieu and Hudson valleys was to play an increasingly important role as a highway of the fur trade. He made contact with the Huron, who became the staunchest indigenous allies the French could hope for, and fought alongside them against other Iroquoian peoples who were their enemies. He surveyed the coasts of what are now Nova Scotia, New Brunswick, and New England as far as Cape Cod in greater detail than had previously been attempted. Finally, in 1615–16, following up reconnaissances he had previously ordered, he followed the St Lawrence to Lake Huron, crossed country to lead an attack on hostile Iroquois on the east bank of Lake Ontario, and returned to explore much of the east bank of Lake Huron. From Indian informants, he pieced together a fairly complete and accurate picture of all the Great Lakes except Lake Michigan.

Even in the seventeenth century, colonization on the St Lawrence was always sparse and ecologically fragile. When, as we shall see, French exploration opened access to the interior via the other great river system of North America—that of the Mississippi and Missouri—it proved hard to attract colonists. French North America therefore never prospered as the English colonies along the Atlantic seaboard did. In the long run, however, the river routes came into their own.

The Indigenous Guides

Wherever it happened in the world, the exploration of new routes of cultural exchange depended on western European initiative. Explorers from a few points of provenance in western Europe—mostly from Spain and Portugal, some from England, France, Italy, Germany, and the Low Countries—led it. Yet it was not, of course, an exclusively European activity. Europeans rarely mention them, but native guides were the transmitters of otherwise unrecorded previous explorations.

Columbus made use of men 'of very subtle intellect who navigate all those seas, and it is a wonder how good an account they give of it all' in canoes, some of which were bigger than European vessels of eighteen banks of oars. 'And with these they navigate all those islands, which are innumerable, and they do business with their goods. I have seen canoes of this kind with seventy or eighty crewmen aboard, each with his own oar.'[60] He was perfectly frank about his dependence on local navigational skill and geographical knowledge. His motive for seizing native captives, he admitted, was chiefly 'to take them and get information of what to expect in these places.'[61] According to a story told by Bartolomé de Las Casas, Columbus' first editor, two of the Indian captives who accompanied Columbus back to Spain were able to demonstrate the relationship of islands he reported by arranging beans on a dish.

Around the beginning of October 1526, Pizarro's pilot Bartolomé Ruiz descried what looked like a galley in the distance as he reconnoitered the coast of what is now Ecuador between San Mateo and San Francisco. On closer inspection, it turned out to be a balsawood raft, laden with colored shells intended as payment for the gold, silver, and textiles of the Chibcha civilization. This coastal trade extended along the Pacific shores of what is now Panama, carrying the copper that Panamanian and Nicaraguan goldsmiths gilded expertly to the amazement of Spaniards who saw their work.[62] Although documentary evidence is lacking for trade in the opposite direction, there were turquoises in the jewel work of people as far south as Chile, even though no mines of those stones were known at the time south of the Mogollon Rim. One way or another, perhaps by emporium trade, they seem to have traveled that far.

In Florida, Ponce de León found a native who spoke Spanish to guide him away from the peninsula. Cortés used maps, as well as guides, to obtain a picture of the Mesoamerican world and to lead his largely Nahua armies to Honduras and Guatemala. Vasco Núñez de Balboa was said to have the benefit, thanks to a native chief, of 'a sketch of the land.' In Mesoamerica, the Spaniards were surrounded by mapmaking cultures. The map Alonso de Santa Cruz or an associate made on the basis of information supplied by members of Hernando de Soto's expedition of 1539–43 has more detail and greater accuracy than can reasonably be accounted for except on the basis of indigenous mapping. An elderly local informant sketched the course of the Colorado River for

Hernando de Alarcón during his search for Coronado in 1540. Meanwhile, some of the landward explorers collected a Zuni painting on skin of a group of settlements in the neighborhood of Hawikuh and sent it back to Spain. Informants set down 'a report of all the country' of the Chesapeake for Sir Ralph Lane during the English interlude in Virginia in 1585. An Indian named Nigual made a surviving sketch map of New Spain for Francisco Valverde de Mercado in 1602. Iroquois used sticks to give Cartier an impression of the course of the St Lawrence between the rapids. John Smith's ability to map Virginia was extended beyond the range of his own and his companions' explorations 'by information of the Savages.' Powhatan himself drew 'plots upon the ground,' illustrating for Smith the nature of the country far to the west. Indians drew portions of coastline for Bartholomew Gosnold in 1602 and Samuel de Champlain in 1605. When Champlain met the Huron, 'I had much conversation with them regarding the source of the great river, and regarding their country . . . They spoke to me of these things in great detail, showing me by drawings all the places they had visited.'

Asian cartographers made a similar input into the work of European explorers. According to an admittedly late tradition, Vasco da Gama's Muslim pilot drew 'a chart of India in the fashion of the Moors' with 'meridians and parallels' and Vasco obtained another indigenous map from the Samorin of Calicut. The vague and speculative outline of Japan in European maps was transformed in 1580, when Jesuit mapmakers worked with indigenous models. Even in places where indigenous cartographic traditions are unrepresented in surviving maps, European explorers betray their dependency in their own accounts. The extraordinary fidelity with which Francisco Rodrigues mapped the coasts between the Bay of Bengal and the Banda Sea, on slight acquaint-ance, would be inexplicable save by reference to indigenous maps, and early Portuguese maps of eastern seas can safely be assumed to incorporate informa-tion from them. In 1512, a Javanese map, which was said to include data from Chinese maps or sailing directions, was dispatched to the court of Portugal by Afonso de Albuquerque, who called it 'the best thing I have ever seen.' It was lost in a shipwreck in 1513. On his way to China, Tomé Pires saw local charts of the route to the Moluccas 'many times.' The influence of Javanese maps may help to explain one of the unsolved riddles of early modern European cartog-raphy of Australasia: the presence and persistence of a large island called 'Java la Grande,' with an outline puzzlingly similar to that of part of the north coast of Australia from the 1530s—long before any record of a European discovery of Australia: this would make sense if it were copied from Javanese maps. Although Australia was not frequented, as far as we know, by Javanese shipping, it is incredible that Javanese seamen did not know of its whereabouts, not far from their homeland across a monsoonal sea. A chief from the Ladrones showed Urdaneta the way to the Philippines.[63]

Exploration, therefore, relied on native guides and native maps. But Europeans must be given some credit for meshing the native routes together. As far as we know, no native Americans previously took any interest in maintaining contacts across the hemisphere, let alone with the world beyond. The Incas and Aztecs knew nothing of each other. Cultural transmissions northward from Mesoamerica reached, in some respects, as we saw in earlier chapters, to the North American southwest, the Mississippi valley, and even the Great Lakes; but they were the results of intermittent, frequently mediated exchanges that proceeded between emporiums. In some cases, they took generations or even centuries to unfold. The people Alejo García met on the Atlantic coast may have had some shadowy inkling about the Inca—but until he arrived among them, none of them seems to have tried to get to Peru. As a result of the achievements of European explorers of the sixteenth century, all these regions, for good or ill, came into regular touch not only with each other but also with parts of Europe and Africa; thanks to Urdaneta, Mexico became linked to the further shore of the Pacific.

In the Pacific, no indigenous people had previously created transoceanic routes. In the Indian Ocean, though Europeans could contribute nothing to the inward exploration of monsoonal seas, the forging of links to Europe and the creation of a new, unprecedentedly fast fixed-wind route from the Atlantic to the Sunda Strait were new developments for which Europeans alone were responsible. Only European ships, or those Europeans built, traversed the Atlantic.

Clearly, the world was entering a new phase of its history, in which Westerners would play, for the first time, a major role in taking productive initiatives. This should not be mistaken for evidence of European superiority. By comparison with most Indian Ocean peoples, the explorers were, if anything, inferior in some of the key technologies. Obviously, there were no disparities in intelligence or aptitude. Global route forging was a European specialty only because Europeans needed to engage in it in ways uninteresting to peoples elsewhere who were richer or more self-sufficient. They needed the resources to which empire gave access. They needed an entrée into trading zones where they could sell their shipping services. They needed access to a diversity of environments to make up for the relative poverty of their homelands. As a result of their explorations, and those of their successors, the rest of the world became an offshore resource for Europe—exploitably reachable. A region once marginal to the great themes and currents of global history became the nodal point of global routes of exchange and began to gather the tethers that bound the world.

7 Connecting

Global 'Reconvergence', c.1620–c.1740

> Lo, soul, seest thou not
> God's purpose from the first?
> The earth to be spann'd, connected by network,
> The races, neighbors to marry and be given in marriage,
> The ocean to be cross'd, the distant to be brought near,
> The lands to be welded together.
>
> Walt Whitman, 'Passage to India'

SCIENCE stumbles into our story. Partly owing to the new data accumulated during the exploration of the world, Western science registered leaps in the seventeenth century that science in other parts of the world could not match. Westerners became the coordinators of global knowledge, curators of museums, makers of maps, recyclers of data among other cultures. Western explorers still depended on local guides and indigenous maps. But their role was increasingly dominant. They gathered, standardized, and charted the work of pathfinders all over the world, drawing control of the routes of global exchange into their hands like reins.

Jesuits were the preferred cartographers of the Chinese imperial court from the second decade of the century. Increasingly, as the century wore on, cultures formerly preeminent in science deferred to Western works. By the end of the century, 'wise men from the West' ran the imperial observatory in Peking, the king of Siam was taking lessons in astronomy from Jesuits, Japanese artists were copying the frontispieces of Dutch scientific books, and Koreans were imitating Western maps.

Meanwhile, in the West, science and exploration touched: each began to affect the other, albeit in still limited ways. Exploration remained adventurous, romantic, suffused and inspired by legend; but science equipped explorers with ever more exact methods of direction finding and route recording. This is a story best told in three phases: first, how science changed the way explorers worked; then what they did; and, finally, how explorers' work changed science.

The Reform of Navigation

Until the seventeenth century in the West, seamen's memories had to operate selectively. In a work of 1545, Pedro de Medina, the most learned cosmographer of his day, explained how he had often seen pilots

> return from our Indies after experiencing great danger, having been even on the point of death, and yet soon after their arrival they forget it like a dream and then they prepare to return as if it was a pleasure. This is not out of greed but the result of divine will; because if the dangers were recalled no one would navigate.[1]

Even so, practiced seamen relied on experience to find their way at sea: squinting at the sun or scanning the night sky to judge whether they were on a familiar latitude, remembering features on shore and even the feel and appearance of the open sea to help them retrieve their routes. In consequence, fifteenth- and sixteenth-century navigators were surprisingly innocent of technology.

This is hard for modern readers to accept, partly because navigation today is heavily dependent on scientific devices, and partly because historians of the subject have long insisted on the transforming nature of the new direction-finding instruments and techniques that became available in the period. It is one thing, however, to invent new technologies or devise new techniques; another to get them adopted by practitioners of a traditional art. According to Columbus, the navigator's art resembled prophetic vision.[2] He wielded his quadrant like a magic wand—not for practical use but for specious effect. He almost certainly could not make it work. On the contrary, everything we know about his calculations of latitude suggests that they were made by using traditional stargazing to calculate the duration of the day and reading the results off a table that listed latitudes by the hours of daylight throughout the year. The instruments were there to boost his credibility with an impressionable crew.

As time went on, and instruments gradually became more familiar aboard ship, they lost even that magic. According to William Bourne, writing in 1571 and renowned for his expertise in his day, 'ancient masters of ships . . . derided and mocked' as 'star-shooters' the modish-minded who used newfangled astrolabes or quadrants. Even for him—and he was perhaps the nearest thing to a scientific navigator you could find in England at the time—navigation was

Pedro de Medina (1493–1567) depicted demonstrating the astrolabe

little better than guesswork.[3] Although, from the evidence excavated from shipwrecks, the numbers of astrolabes and substitute devices seem to have grown in the sixteenth century, they were still regarded as rare arcana, or impractical toys.

Still, scientific navigation did spread, slowly and gradually, to become normal in high-seas environments by the early seventeenth century. This was perhaps more a consequence of exploration than a cause: the result of the new opportunities for long-range trade that explorers opened up. More trade generated more demand for navigators. The old way of schooling them, by apprenticeship and long experience, could not produce enough experts. Spain and Portugal established official training colleges for navigators in the early sixteenth century. From 1508 Spain had an official—the *piloto mayor*—permanently employed to examine and license pilots. From the 1550s, the Spanish crown began to create a series of professorships 'of the art of navigation and cosmography' for particular regions and seas. Other countries created similar institutions in the seventeenth century when they established long-range commercial and imperial enterprises of their own. Professional schooling required a generalized curriculum. Textbooks for navigators multiplied.

The Rise of the Chart

Mapping and exploration were mutually nutritive projects, but it took a long time for them to become aligned. The portolan charts of the Middle Ages, which survive in something like abundance, may not have been much used by navigators, whose traditional preference, established before portolan charts became available, was for written sailing directions. The history of the development of the sea chart is so obscure that we cannot even be sure that this type of document was evolved for mariners' purposes: it may have been a visual aid to illustrate—for the enlightenment of passengers, landlubbers, and such interested parties as merchants—the data pilots preferred to carry in their heads or in ruttiers.[4]

In the sixteenth century explorers showed little interest in mapping their findings. Until well into the seventeenth century, the ruttier—written sailing directions—seems to have prevailed over the chart as the form in which seamen liked to get navigational information. In many recorded cases, this was also the form in which explorers preferred to collect it. The prejudice in favor of ruttiers was tenacious. Even Lucas Janszoon Waghenaer's *Spiegel der Zeevaerdt* of 1584—a work that did much to recommend the serviceability of charts for the coasts of Europe from Zeeland to Andalusia—still contained sailing instructions in traditional form, while the charts the author supplied remained relatively sketchy. *Le Grand Insulaire et pilotage*, which the French cosmographer royal André Thevet was compiling at the same time, was a book of charts and ruttier combined.[5]

Nor was the preference for ruttiers irrational. They could provide vital information that surviving sea charts of this period rarely or never carried, concerning, for example, currents, winds, hidden hazards, landmarks, depths, anchorages, port facilities, and the nature of the seabed. Hydrography was still in its infancy in the late sixteenth and early seventeenth centuries, and for coastal navigation charts could be dangerously misleading. Writing in 1594, John Davis regarded a chart as part of the indispensable equipment of a navigator, but warned, 'A chart doth not express that certainty of the premises which is thereby pretended to be given.'[6] On long voyages, unless in a very approximate fashion, charts could not help mariners establish their course, because of magnetic variation; nor could they help seamen determine their position on a grid, because of the difficulty of finding and representing lines of latitude and longitude. Charts could and did illustrate and complement ruttiers; they could not easily replace them.

Soundings, made by dropping a weighted line until it hit the seabed, which were the items of information that pilots wanted most on unfamiliar shores, only began to appear on charts around 1570. The practice was very slow to become generalized, spreading from the English Channel to the North Sea, Baltic, and Atlantic coasts of Europe generally in the 1580s and 1590s, but not appearing on charts of coasts in regions of exploration until the Dutch introduced the practice with charts compiled on the basis of their first voyage to the East in 1595–7. It gradually became general practice in the seventeenth century, in Portuguese charts of Brazil, for instance, in 1610 and the Gulf of Cambay in 1616, and growing rapidly thereafter. The inclusion of coastal profiles followed a similar course.[7]

For all these reasons, from the point of view of the navigator and therefore, a fortiori, of all seaborne explorers, charts were not particularly user-friendly ways of recording information. They only became so very gradually and relatively late, as their accuracy increased. Not until after 1600, when Edward Wright had worked on the basis constructed by Mercator and popularized the results, was a consistent projection suitable to the needs of mariners available.[8] From early in the sixteenth century, the Spanish crown provided for a master map of Spanish discoveries and standard charts of how to reach them, to be kept under lock and key in Seville and updated according to seafarers' reports. This admirable scheme does not seem to have worked. The *padrón*, as it was called, was rarely, if ever, up to date. For most of the time, indeed, no standard map existed; and navigators who wanted charts bought them from commercial chartmakers: no standard charts survive for any time during the sixteenth century.

The surveying techniques that made accurate scale mapping and chart-making possible were, in great part, developments of the seventeenth century. Seventeenth-century inventions included the telescope, which was immensely useful to traditional navigators because it brought the stars nearer and made, for instance, the passage of the Guard Stars around Polaris easier to time. The telescope-enhanced quadrant was invaluable: the quadrant was a fairly simple device for obtaining latitude by measuring the height of the Pole Star or the sun above the horizon, and the addition of a telescope made it easier to operate at night. The filar micrometer, hairs attached to a telescope lens, made it possible to measure the distance between celestial bodies at a given moment with previously unattainable accuracy. The technique of triangulation was unpracticed by explorers until well into the century: without it, long distances could only be estimated, even on land. Although—or perhaps because—seasoned navigators, as we have seen, had skills we have now lost and could make impressive judgments of relative latitude by observing the sun or Pole Star with the naked eye, technical aids for estimating latitude before the seventeenth century were very inadequate: the mariner's astrolabe or simplified versions of it, such as the quadrant and backstaff. Refinements added before the 1620s added only marginally to the precision and reliability of the results.

During the seventeenth century, thanks in part to these innovations, it became normal for cartographic professionals to accompany expeditions. The early seventeenth century was a transitional period, when the chart began to take over the role of the ruttier and to become an indispensable navigator's aid. The pace of chartmaking quickened. In 1602–3 and 1606, Bartholomew Gosnold and Martin Pring returned from their reconnaissances of parts of the North American coast with newly sketched charts that have not survived, as far as is known, but are the subjects of allusions in other documents.[9] Quirós and Luis de Torres were accomplished mapmakers in a technical sense, however much fantasy distorted the maps of Quirós. In 1605 James Hall, pilot of an expedition Christian IV of Denmark dispatched to Greenland to search for evidence of Old Norse colonies, produced a series of coastal profiles and included soundings in detailed charts of coastwise exploration northward to 68½ degrees north. They survive only in presentation copies embellished for the king's own perusal.[10] Among the maps produced in the first years of an enduring English presence in Virginia were Robert Tindall's scale charts of the navigation of the James River of 1607–8.[11] William Baffin acquired well-merited renown as a chartmaker on his Arctic voyages.[12] Champlain was an excellent cartographer.[13] Pedro Páez[14] made only sketch maps of the Blue Nile, but they became part of the detailed mapping the Jesuits in Ethiopia put together.[15]

'The Demonstration of the Fordes, Rivers, and Coast.' Illustration from the charts of the west coast of Greenland drawn by James Hall on the Danish expedition in 1605

The early seventeenth-century breakthrough in the mapping of northern Siberia and the Barents and Kara Seas is a hint of a new era. Here, both Dutch and Russian expeditions seem to have been accompanied by cartographic specialists. Almost every extension of the routes navigated by Dutch vessels in the eastern Indian Ocean and western Pacific in the early seventeenth century is documented on individual ships' charts.[16] As late as 1622, Portuguese navigators used the ruttier format to keep their instructions for route finding between Nagasaki and various ports in China and southeast Asia.[17] Yet by that date, not only were the Portuguese producing serviceable charts of the seas around Japan for shipboard use, but Dutch navigators were also making an attempt—albeit, as we shall see, not a very successful one—to map the archipelago's coasts as they traversed them as part of a systematic campaign to chart all the waters their shipping frequented.[18]

This phenomenon, which we can fairly call the rise of the chart, affected and was affected by seaborne exploration. As well as an aid to navigation, the chart at last became the standard form in which new information was recorded. Thomas Blundeville in 1613 reckoned that every navigator had an obligation to record his course on a chart 'that you may more readily direct your ship again to the place whereunto you would go.'[19] Over the next couple of decades, the responsibility of explorers to map their findings seems to have been widely assumed. In Hudson Bay in 1631–2, Thomas James and Luke Foxe evidently accepted detailed chartmaking as part of the job during their frustrated attempts to prosecute the quest for a Northwest Passage.

Yet, despite their increasing detail and reliability, charts were still sirens in one respect: if used injudiciously, they could land ships on the rocks. The calculation of longitude remained, in effect, beyond the science of the time. It resembled other Faustian yearnings of the age, like the search for the Philosopher's Stone, the Fountain of Youth, the squared circle, and the secrets of hermetic tradition. Apart from estimation of distance traversed—a method subject to the alarming accumulation of error—the most commonly used shipboard method in the late sixteenth century was based on the erroneous assumption that longitude was related to magnetic variation.[20]

Tradition passed on no theoretically satisfactory method, except by recording the time difference between two places at the moment of an eclipse. As the Spanish cosmographer Alonso de Santa Cruz pointed out in 1556, the unreliability of clocks made this method hopeless. The insufficiency of the technique was exposed in the early 1580s, when astronomers commissioned by Philip II of Spain tried to fix the longitude of places in Spanish America. Calculations made for Mexico City varied by more than 10 per cent either way. Those for Panama were wrong by about 20–5 per cent. In 1584 the king announced a lavish prize—6,000 ducats a year for the winner and his heirs in perpetuity, with a further 2,000 ducats a year for life and an additional one-off gratuity of 1,000 ducats, equivalent in all to a handsomely noble income—to anyone who could supply the want of a reliable longitude-finding device.

No progress was made in the quest until Galileo, with the aid of the newly invented telescope, made the first observations of the moons of Jupiter in 1616. The regularity of the moons' motions made them a reliable point of reference in checking the passage of time. With careful monitoring and scrupulous recording, they could serve as means of verifying the difference in time, and therefore in longitude, between any two places. As well as greater accuracy, they provided a further advantage over the method that depended on eclipses. They were always available for observation when the sky was clear, whereas eclipses had to be awaited. By 1636, when Galileo completed his tables of the movements of the moons, all that was wanting was a reliable means of chronometry to make it possible for differences in longitude to be accurately recorded on land. Twenty years later, Christiaan Huyghens's pendulum clock completed the array of the necessary technology.

For shipboard purposes, however, none of these advances made much difference. Ships at sea were rarely stable enough to read the heavens accurately enough for Galileo's method to work. The motion of a ship affected the setting of a pendulum. Changes in the climates the ship might traverse shrank pendulums and distorted the mountings. So, even within a single climatic zone, did the damp and the routine but unpredictable alternations of the weather. Coasts continued to surprise navigators and shipwrecks stacked up on inopportune shores.

The Endurance of Myth

Cartographic tradition, in any case, was full of siren songs. Misleading speculations tempted explorers toward putative destinations that did not exist or were imaginatively located on maps. The myth still beckoned of an open-water passage to the North Pole.[21] The Golden Old Woman of the Ob, a mythical creature—a boreal El Dorado, perhaps?—who appeared on the most influential sixteenth-century map of Russia, summoned explorers to boreal Siberia. The prospect of an ice-free route to east Asia lured European navigators into ice-bound seas. In the furthest south, the land of Terra Australis lay invitingly. Eldorados and other fabled treasure lands still proliferated in the American interior. A Northwest Passage supposedly still lay around them. So, at the start of the century, did a narrow Pacific.

Sometimes the myths had classical authorities to back them or legendary exploits to encourage them. Usually, they were the results of theoretical or political agendas allied to wishful thinking. The North Pole had to be in clear water to vindicate the principle that all seas were navigable—a principle espoused with scientific fervor by empiricists who rejected equally invalid but older myths of 'seas of darkness' and 'boiling oceans' that would impede human ambition and humble human arrogance. A Northwest Passage was necessary because the oceans of the world had to be unimpeded. A narrow Pacific was necessary to confine the world to credible dimensions, to maintain symmetry with the Atlantic, and to guarantee the right to the Moluccas of the king of Spain. Theorists could infer the existence of Terra Australis from the known facts of how land and water were distributed across the face of the planet.

Paradoxically, science nourished speculation. The rise of science is commonly hailed as one of the great features of the history of Europe in the seventeenth century. But observation is fallible and experience can mislead. Cloudbanks, bird flight, the appearance of the sea, and the presence of floating objects can all generate 'discoveries' of nonexistent islands. The stimulus of wishful thinking acts to multiply islands in the minds of seamen in need of land. So does excessive caution in the case of navigators oversensitive to potential hazards. Imaginary islands pullulate in maps because of well-attested principles of the history of cartography: it is safer to have too many islands on your chart than too few. Owing to the difficulty of proving a negative, it is easier to introduce speculations than to excise them. The islands of Rica de Oro and Rica de Plata, which occur frequently in seventeenth-century maps, not only would have conferred imaginary riches on anyone who took their names literally, but they would also have been useful to Spain, or to pirates intent on raiding Spanish galleons: they were usually located well east of Japan, not far from the course ships normally followed from Manila to Acapulco.[22] Poor observation by a navigator sailing north from Acapulco in 1602 entrenched the notion that California was an island.[23]

Sixteenth-century promoters made speculative maps showing wide-open seaways around northern America in an attempt to encourage explorers and attract investors. Michael Lok, one of the most assiduous promoters of the idea of a Northwest Passage, attached great importance to the evidence of a map attributed to Verrazano's brother. Mercator reproduced the myth on his maps.[24] The navigable North Pole was another fable that deluded Mercator, who devoted an insert to it in his world map of 1569. Spurious reports recorded in the late sixteenth century indented the map of the Pacific coasts of America with inlets knows as the Strait of Anian or the Strait of Juan de Fuca, which pointed invitingly eastward. Together with the Northwest Passage, the realm of Quivirá, and the cities of Cíbola, the strait is prominent on a printed map dedicated to North America by Cornelis de Jode in 1593.

The biggest intruder from myth to the map was Terra Australis. On Abraham Ortelius' world map it seemed to embrace the world. On Mercator's it resembled the jaws of some macroparasite, ready to devour other lands. On Jodocus Hondius' version, it resembled a hand reaching to grasp the other continents. Quirós bore much of the responsibility. He strung together portions of the coast of New Guinea with bits of the coasts of islands he had reconnoitered, creating a partial outline of a putative continent.

Explorers' reports sometimes fed back into fantasy and spattered maps with mirabilia. The line between exploration and adventure, or between explorers' reports and travelers' tales, has never been exactly fixed. Travel literature existed to depict a world of wonder, not reduce it to easily classifiable facts. Exploration, unfolding an ever more diverse world, whetted public appetite for curiosities. Fictional travels became cartographers' sources, just as in the fifteenth century chivalric romances had been mistaken for accounts of real journeys. The economics of exploration encouraged exaggeration. It was a capital-intensive business, which returned only sporadic profits. To get renewed backing, explorers tended to inflate their reports, especially of exploitable finds.

It is perhaps not surprising, therefore, that the new science of the seventeenth century hardly got explorers much farther. Myths still dominated their objectives. Fables still inspired their actions. They still saw North America as an obstacle on the way to an elusive Asia. The Pacific remained a sea unloved for its own sake but rather explored in the search for 'unknown' lands or routes elsewhere. The explorers who traversed Siberia did so in pursuit of dreamlands that did not exist. We can look at each of these theaters in turn.

America: The Elusiveness of Asia

By the 1630s, it was evident that even if a Northwest Passage existed through Arctic waters, it would be seasonal, at best: laborious, ice-ridden, and subject to the hazards of blockage in conditions of deadly cold. To optimists, it looked more attractive to seek a North American isthmus—a narrow neck of land, like Panama, with a western shore that could serve as a springboard for trade with China. Of course, north of the area already appropriated by Spain, North America was uniformly broad. But no one yet knew that for certain. Gradually, over the century as a whole, French explorers probing west from the Great Lakes and English expeditions out of Virginia and New England shared the disillusionment.

The English Shores

Having failed to find the South Sea when they first got to Virginia, the English took little further interest in exploring inland until French navigation on the Mississippi alerted them to a possible missed opportunity. They remained convinced, however, that only a narrow continent lay ahead of them: 'the happy shores of the Pacific,' according to a servant of the Virginia Company writing in 1651, lay 'in ten days' march from the head of the James River, over those hills and through the rich adjacent valleys.' In 1670 John Lederer, a German physician who traveled inland as far as the Catawba River, claimed—among much other fantasy or error—to have met Indians from California. In 1671, on the governors' orders, English deerskin traders accompanied a party of Totero Indians across the Appalachians and, as reported in the diary of the journey kept by Robert Fallam, convinced themselves that they could see the Pacific in the distance as they began the descent of the Tug Fork River toward the

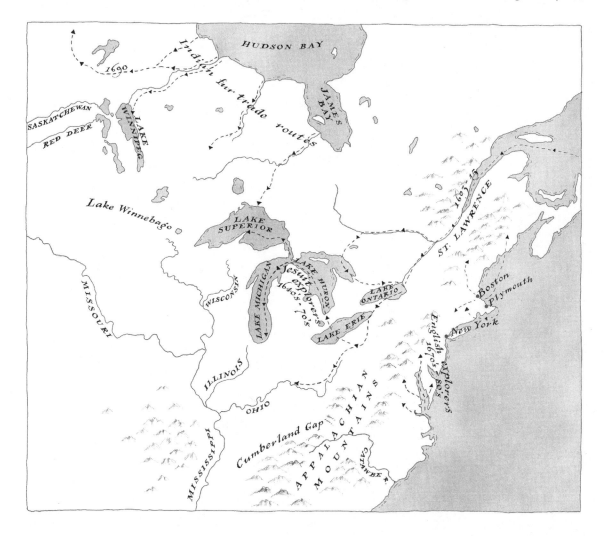

French and English explorations in North America (north), seventeenth century

Ohio. But in 1673–4 the discoveries of a trader's servant, George Arthur, had a dispiriting effect. Separated from his master, he lived with the Tomahitan Indians. From their base near the headwaters of the Alabama he traveled far and wide with their war parties as far north as the Ohio Valley via the Cumberland Gap, then unknown to the English, and along the Alabama River almost to the coast in the south. The vastness of the continent was crushing English hopes of crossing it easily and quickly.

From their North American colonies, the English were equally sluggish. New England was oriented toward the sea—a narrow, sea-soaked coast with a culture shaped by maritime outreach. Indeed the first attempt at Sagadahoc in 1607 to found a colony was commercially inspired, along the lines of Portuguese trading posts on the coast of Africa; but the hoped-for trade never

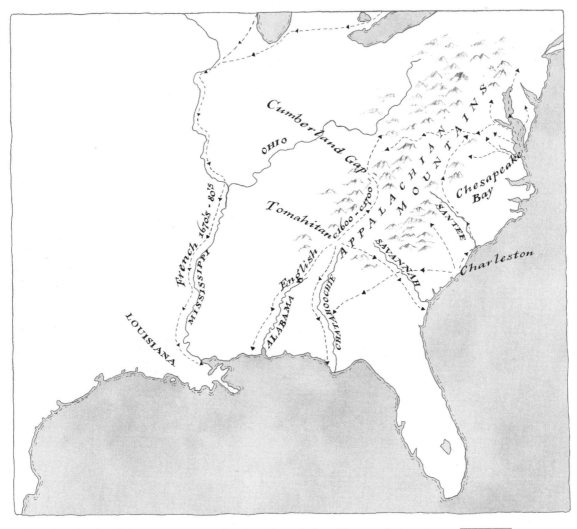

French and English explorations in North America (south), seventeenth century

materialized. The first permanent settlement, founded at Plymouth in 1620, was of dedicated farmers struggling to coax crops out of the rock-strewn soil; but fishing and shipping rapidly became the main sources of wealth. In 1627 a group of eight colonists assumed responsibility for the Plymouth Colony's debts in return for a monopoly of trade.

At first, the export of furs brought merchants business, if not always much profit. Most of New England, however, was poorly placed for access to the fur trade; even in the mid-1640s New Englanders had no idea of the location of the Great Lakes; all the fur seekers' upriver expeditions had led only toward ground controlled by French middlemen. Supplying settlers with imports at inflated prices was a better business for the merchants. In Boston, for instance, in 1639, Robert Keayne was prosecuted for profiteering: 'taking above six pence in the shilling profit . . . and in some small things two for one.' In 1664, according to a critical observer of merchants' methods, 'if they do not gain Cent per cent they cry out that they are losers.'[25] Anyone who still believes that Puritanism favored capitalism should turn to the records of tension within the New England elite between the godly and the greedy.

Attempts to found native industries—iron foundries, textiles manufac-tories—failed: only distilling proved profitable. The merchants had no choice but to become dealers between distant markets. They also took fish, timber, spirits, and sugar products, and, for the Caribbean, temperate foodstuffs from home, and swapped them for slaves, sugar, and wines. In 1643 the first five voyages initiated what became a pattern, selling salt fish and pipe staves in Spanish, Portuguese, Canarian, and African ports; from 1644 the Caribbean colonies became New England's most important trading partners. In the eighteenth century, when New England finally did become a center of trade with China, the routes led round Cape Horn, not across America.

Inhabitants of New England did show some interest in exploring routes of contact inland with colonies on the St Lawrence and the Great Lakes, but New York had an advantage in that respect, because of the Hudson River. As a result of all these constraints and distractions, New Englanders added nothing substantial to the stock of knowledge of routes deeper into the interior until 1692–4, when Albany traders probed the Ohio valley. By then, however, French explorers had already established that the continent, though of unknown breadth, was too big to be easily traversable and concealed no exploitable isthmus.

In some ways, it is surprising that French explorers should have made such a significant contribution. The tracks of Indian fur traders and trappers led west from Hudson Bay and the Great Lakes, but the quickest and most economical routes favored the English, who held the bay, rather than the French, who dominated the lakes. The incentive to push west tempted reconnaissance par-ties of both nations into the prairies, where explorers tried to keep interest alive by renewing the quest for a route to the Pacific; but the prairies were of no interest to the commercially minded. Squirrel and beaver pelts were salable; those of American bison were not. Further north, in the fur-producing environment of the boreal forests, the incentive to keep exploring was much greater. In 1690, for instance, the Hudson's Bay Company sent one of its most enterprising young traders, Henry Kelsey, with a party of Cree trappers west along the Saskatchewan as far as Red Deer River. His mission was to find fur-rich peoples and encourage them to come to Hudson Bay to trade. Kelsey's own motives were of good old-fashioned adventure and self-improvement—'to understand the natives' language and to see their land.' His route led him away from the fur country into the prairie, and its results—deemed commercially valueless—were ignored.

La Salle and the Mississippi

Meanwhile, on the French frontier, Jesuit and Franciscan missionaries jostled the fur traders and trappers known as *coureurs des Bois*. Sometimes, the two professions seemed to shade into one another: some of the same tastes and urges impelled both vocations. The leading figures in French exploration of the Mississippi, Louis Jolliet and René-Robert de La Salle, both studied to be Jesuits, but abandoned the religious calling for the fur-trading life. Missionaries and *coureurs* alike needed to look ever further afield in search of new people for commerce or conversion. Bit by bit, they advanced the frontier known to Europeans in the region. Lake Michigan, for instance, unknown to Champlain[26] even by report, was revealed in 1634. It was to serve as a sort of launching bay for further, long-range expeditions. But long-range expeditions depended in their turn on capital investment and political authorization: for that level of support, the lure of a quick route to Asia was still needed.

At Lake Michigan, Jean Nicollet, an associate of Champlain's with a penchant for Indian company and an invaluable talent for picking up Indian languages, heard tell of the Mississippi. He also learned from Indians that the mighty river swept on to the sea. The notion that the sea in question might be the Gulf of Mexico does not seem to have occurred to the French: the Pacific was the only sea their minds were set on. Even so, it was not easy to get beyond the region of the lakes. Most Iroquoian peoples mistrusted the French and fought them implacably. Not until the 1670s was it possible for Europeans to travel in the region beyond the confines of French forts with anything like security, and even then the dangers of falling into hostile hands were considerable. Jesuits, who were the paladins of exploration in the region, were not concerned with trade routes, but could afford to take their time, exploring the region thoroughly, getting to know its people, mapping its terrain, and advancing, step by step, the frontier of evangelization.

So it was not until 1673 that Europeans began to sail the Mississippi. In that year, the government of New France commissioned Louis Jolliet to find a route from the Great Lakes to the river. With the help of Jean-Jacques Marquette, a Jesuit priest whom he recruited at St Ignace, the Jesuit mission on Lake Michigan, he made light of the work: the Wisconsin River proved to be the key. But once on the Mississippi, the explorers found the experience dispiriting. The river led south, not west, as they had hoped. Worse still, the Missouri met it, flowing from the west: 'a river of considerable size,' the explorers noted, 'coming . . . from a great distance.' Evidently there was plenty of continent astride the longed-for route to the Pacific. They got as far as the junction with the Arkansas before turning back. 'Judging from the direction of the course of the Mississippi,' they concluded, 'we believe it flows into the Gulf of Mexico.' There was no point in proceeding. They were approaching areas of well-established Spanish control. Heeding advice from Indians they met, they returned along the Illinois River, reaching Lake Michigan overland from its headwaters to where Chicago now stands.

René-Robert de La Salle, however, thought their efforts worth following up. The Mississippi was, at least, a highly navigable river and therefore potentially a route of communications and an axis of the great empire La Salle envisaged for France in the American interior. In 1681–2 La Salle began canoeing down the great river in Indian craft, via the Illinois, and reached the Gulf of Mexico in April 1682. He conducted a ceremony of possession overlooking the sea. He had pioneered a potentially important route from the lakes to the gulf.

In a way, La Salle was only just in time to forestall the English. By the last years of the seventeenth century, English deerskin traders from Charles Town, a recent foundation on the coast of North Carolina, were penetrating the Mississippi valley in search of wares. But La Salle's efforts never really paid off. France was densely populated compared with other colonial centers, such as Spain, Portugal, and England. But it never generated as many colonists as its rivals—never, indeed, enough to establish a permanent presence in continental North America outside the St Lawrence valley. The region La Salle tried to open up was never attractive enough or accessible enough to overcome the stay-at-home preferences of his countrymen. The beginnings of the empire he envisaged were inauspicious. When he reached the Gulf of Mexico, he measured his longitude with the aid of a broken compass and an unserviceable astrolabe. In 1684, therefore, when he tried to return to the mouth of the Mississippi by sea, he was unable to locate it. His ships were wrecked. His crew fell out with one another. Their attempts to reach Spanish areas failed. Most of those who survived their own violent dissensions died in battles against Indians. A handful struggled overland to reach a French outpost on the Arkansas, near the junction with the Mississippi.

Though a failure as a colonist, La Salle had made an important contribution to exploration. Together with the priest who was one of his closest collaborators Louis Hennepin, and his loyal lieutenant Henri de Tonti, he had helped to demonstrate that North America enclosed 'a very great country.' Tonti scoured the environs of the Mississippi as far as the Cadoquis in search of his friend. After La Salle's death he continued exploring east of the river, filling in gaps on the map as far as the Alabama. Hennepin, a Franciscan missionary among the Iroquois, who accompanied La Salle along the Illinois, turned north to explore the Mississippi upriver. As a captive of the Sioux from April to June 1680, and a companion of their hunting parties, he was able to sense and hear about the immense expanses of territory that lay west of the great river. He became the eloquent publicist of the future of what he called Louisiana.

The Spanish Southwest

The French and English were not alone in clinging to the hope of finding a nearby Pacific shore. Spaniards in New Mexico nourished similar illusions. Juan de Oñate hoped that the colony he founded in 1598 might be near the Pacific. In the early years of the new century, expeditions he led westward as far as the Colorado River dispelled this hope. But the prospect remained that the Colorado might in time become the axis of a colony with privileged access to the ocean, and handily placed for trade with China. These hopes depended on the abiding belief that California was an island. The intervening region, however, was unattractive, except to missionaries, and native 'rebellions,' as the Spaniards called them, disrupted the mission frontier and delayed its advance.

Systematic exploration of the region between Pimería Alta and the Pacific was the work of Fr Eusebio del Kino, the Jesuit paladin responsible for extending Christendom into the wilderness of what is now the US southwest. Missions appeared: at Dolores in Sonora in 1687 and Tucson in Arizona and Caborca in Sinaloa in 1700. Kino's tireless journeys made two routes familiar: across the desert from Caborca to Yuma, linking the valleys of the Concepción and Gila Rivers; and along the Gila and Colorado to the head of the Gulf of California. Even then, his conviction that California was not an island was slow to take root in official perceptions, and misrepresentations continued on maps.

Kino dreamed of reaching China overland from California, on the assumption that only a short strait, if any, would have to be crossed on the way. But the chimera of a short route to Asia was at last receding. Jean Nicollet had wandered from Lake Michigan to Lake Winnebago in a Chinese silk robe in the expectation that he would meet Chinese—or at least someone who would recognize the product for what it was. As late as 1670 John Lederer expected to see the South Sea from the crest of the Blue Ridge Mountains of Virginia; the following year, Robert Fallam and his companions thought they had done so. In 1671 La Salle was being heavy-handedly ironic in naming his house on the St Lawrence 'La Chine,' and even the optimism of the English in Virginia ebbed soon afterwards.

Into Amazonia

So by the end of the century, explorers in North America were really only just beginning to appreciate their continent for its own sake, or to accept that their work was to investigate its own internal routes and inherent resources. In South America, where exploration was more advanced and El Dorados were becoming exhausted, realism was quicker to set in. This was a disincentive to further exploration. The main work of the seventeenth century consisted in finding improved routes between far-flung colonies. The development of the Orinoco river system[27] is one example. Efforts in Amazonia constitute another.

The Amazonian world described by Francisco de Orellana's expedition had vanished. Dense populations had receded from the riverbank—winnowed, in all probability, by diseases Orellana's men left behind them. Exploration along the Amazon revived only as the result of an accident in 1637. At the time, the Franciscans were investing much effort in an attempt to evangelize the upper Amazon. It was dangerous business. Missions, scattered through country where communications were fragile and few, tended to be short-lived, sometimes revoked because of problems of supply, sometimes extinguished in massacres by volatile Indians, who suspected the missionaries of collusion with conquistadores, slavers, and expropriators of Indian land. Two Franciscan lay brothers, Domingo de Brieva and Andrés de Toledo, joined an expedition along the Napo from Quito, and helped to establish a mission station at San Diego de Alcalá among the Encabellados Indians. They then became detached from their companions and, in a voyage that echoed Orellana's navigation nearly 100 years before,[28] sailed, 'borne on by divine inspiration and driven by want of food,' to the Portuguese zone and the river's mouth.[29]

The Portuguese responded by sending them back home as guides for a major upriver expedition by Pedro de Teixeira, who was the officer responsible for clearing the Amazon of foreign intruders. At the time, Philip IV was king of both Portugal and Spain; but the Portuguese remained unwilling to share their empire even with the most closely allied outsider. The ascent took a year; the scale of Teixeira's task force—in nearly fifty canoes—posed huge problems of management and supply. But they arrived safely. The authorities in Quito equipped them with chartmakers and official reporters; by the time they got back to Belem, at the end of 1639, they had the river well mapped.

But for the revolution that sundered the crowns of Spain and Portugal in 1640, the Amazon might have become a trans-American highway at once. Instead, missionaries, approaching from the Spanish colonies in the equatorial Andes, and slavers, invading from Portugal's Brazilian outposts, made slow, small inroads. Missionaries were vulnerable. Roque González de Santa Cruz and

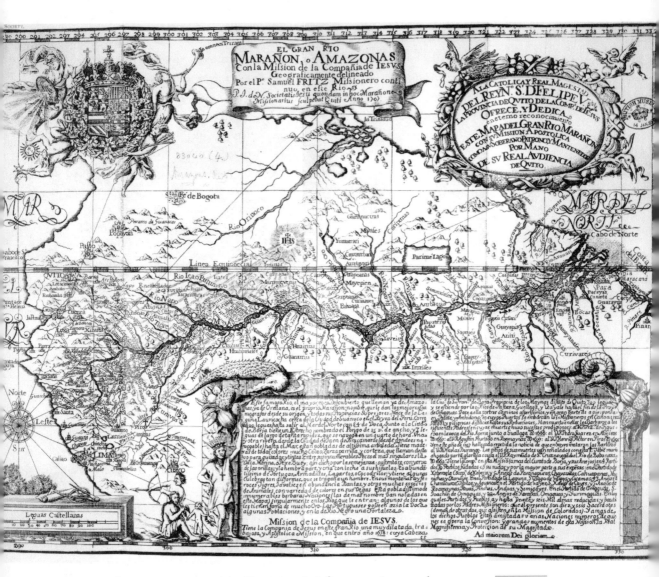

two companions were martyred in Caaro in 1628 for reproving a polygamous chief. Ramón de Santa Cruz died mapping the Archidona in 1662. Francisco de Figueroa was killed by slavers on the Ucayali in 1685. Yet they were undeterred. Fr Samuel Fritz conducted a heroic mission on the middle Amazon in the face of Portuguese slavers from 1686 onward and produced the best map yet made in Amazonia. The 'paradise' or 'godly republic' of autonomous missions the Jesuits constructed in the interior cost many martyrdoms. The missionaries' foes, *the bandeirantes* of São Paulo, were also talented pathfinders. Big, burly men, in quilted armor, bristling with arms and shaded by hats of roughly woven reeds, they raided deep inside Amazonia, confidently terrorizing the Indians and defying 'divinely guided bullets' from guns the Jesuits—despairing of peace by any other means—smuggled into native hands. In 1650, for instance, António Raposo Tavares led an expedition across the Paraguay to the eastern flank of the Andes and down the Amazon, perhaps adding to knowledge of the Rio Negro.

Imagined Lands, Inspired Straits: The Pacific Quests

In 1639–40 the Dutch became uniquely privileged among European traders in Japan. The Japanese government's long-maturing hostility to Christianity culminated in the expulsion of all who refused to trample on the crucifix: foreigners' willingness was tested in annual ceremonies. The Dutch, commercial in their priorities and, in most cases, iconoclastic in their religion, were happy to oblige. Spaniards and Portuguese were not.

From their perch on the Japanese coast, the incentive to explore nearby seas became irresistible to the Dutch. Abel Tasman began his career as the favorite explorer of the Vereinigde Oostindische Compagnie (VOC), the Dutch East India Company, sweeping the ocean east of Japan in 1639 as far as 175 degrees west. Maarten Vries reconnoitered north of the archipelago in 1643. The results were highly misleading. Cartographers continued to scatter nonexistent islands liberally through the region explored by Tasman, while Vries seems to have been an incompetent observer whose reports disfigured maps with weirdly misshapen versions of northern Japan and the coasts of northeast Asia for generations to come. Though it is hard to make sense of what he claims to have seen, he appears to have conflated the Kurils into two large lands, which he called Staaten Land and Compagnie Land: the former a substantial island, the latter perhaps a continent

At about the same time the VOC attempted to extend the range of Dutch trade and navigation in the zone of the westerlies that took their ships across the Indian Ocean from the Cape of Good Hope on their way to the Spice Islands. This did not necessarily mean finding Terra Australis. At the time, the Dutch were much more interested in a route to the cone of South America, which they saw as the soft underbelly of the Spanish empire. Antonis van Diemen, who was in charge of the VOC's operations in the East, hoped 'the better to be assured of a passage from the Indian into the South Sea.' In van Diemen's opinion the result would be that 'the Company will be able to do great things with the Chileans . . . to snatch rich booty from the Castilian in the West Indies, who will never dream of such a thing.'[30] In 1642 Tasman was appointed to proceed beyond the meridian of the Great Australia current, where Dutch ships normally turned north,[31] to learn what lay beyond.

He bypassed Australia to the south without realizing it was there and found the southern shore of Tasmania. From there he continued on his former route, stumbling on New Zealand, coasting much of the western shore of both islands, and missing the strait between them. The encounter was a great novelty for the Maori as well as for the rest of the world: as far as we know this was a land unrecorded in the geographies of any people outside the islands. Even in Polynesia, its existence was remembered only in myths. If he had respected his orders, Tasman would have continued in search of Chile; but he chose instead to follow the coast to the north; this suggests that he may have thought he had found Terra Australis and that there was therefore no point in sailing south. When he reached the northernmost point of North Island, he again forbore to continue but simply asserted an open passage east of New Zealand before turning for home. Approaching the known region of European navigation in the Pacific from an unaccustomed direction, he saw Tonga and made the first known sighting of Fiji by a European.

The following year he charted the north coast of Australia from west to east as far as the tip of Cape York. Like most of the rest of the world, he remained ignorant of the explorations of Luis de Torres, who, as Quirós's second-in-command, had found the strait that now bears his name. Tasman therefore thought he had merely penetrated an enormous gulf in the coast of a huge land mass comprising Australia—or New Holland, as the Dutch called it—and New Guinea.

The finds were disappointing. The parts of Australia Tasman saw offered no useful products. Their inhabitants were 'only poor naked beach-runners,' said van Diemen,[32] or, according to the Englishman who left the first description of them in 1699, were 'the miserablest people in the world . . . And setting aside their human shape, they differ but little from brutes.'[33] As for New Zealand, Maori were dangerously inhospitable—they clubbed to death sailors who approached them on Tasman's first contact—and their islands lay on no route of trade. The hoped-for route to Chile remained speculative. The directors of the VOC lost interest in continuing to look for it. 'We do not expect great things from the continuation of such explorations,' they insisted, 'which more and more burden the Company's resources . . . The gold- and silver-mines that will best serve our purpose have already been found: we mean our trade over the whole of the Indies.'[34]

Only the English showed any appetite for following up Tasman's achievements and even their interest took a long time to mature. They penetrated parts of the Pacific off the tracks of established shipping as they sought safe harbors in which to lie in wait or surprising directions from which to pounce on the major sea lanes. Islands accrued from their unreliable reports. In 1690 one of them rescued three others on Juan Fernández. They reported land at 27 degrees 20. This report was perhaps the result of a mistaken sighting of the islands of San Ambrosio and San Felix. But it encouraged the search for Terra Australis. In 1699 the British navy sent William Dampier to Australia. This engaging former pirate owed his command to his success as a publicist. His voyage yielded no new information and opened up no new routes, although with his characteristic flair he wrote it up well and made a literary success of it. Dampier noted that 'it is not yet determined whether it is an island or a main continent; but I am certain that it joins neither to Asia, Africa, nor America.'[35]

South Sea fever was about to ignite and 'South Sea bubbles' to rise. In 1701 the last Habsburg king of Spain died; in the ensuing war of succession, the trade of the Spanish empire seemed up for grabs. Legitimate investors, who coveted the pirates' profits, were willing to put money into Pacific exploration. In 1721 Jacob Roggeveen made another attempt to locate the elusive southern continent and to attempt to verify pirates' reports. He was inspired, so legend relates, by the deathbed entreaty of his father, who held an unexploited charter to trade in the South Seas; he certainly sailed at the behest of the Dutch West India Company, which was nigh moribund. The Atlantic route to the Pacific would be a lifeline—if only it led somewhere exploitable.

Roggeveen tried to ease his way into the Pacific around Cape Horn by heading south to escape the westerlies. Once in the Pacific, he ran into icebergs and turned north, lured by pirate fables. From Juan Fernández he headed west into a navigational black hole—an uncharted region, off the lines of established seaways. There he found Easter Island, the most remote inhabited island in the world. From there, after further searching, he followed the route of the great Polynesian voyagers in reverse, via the Society Islands and Samoa, never before reported by European seafarers, to Batavia. The officials of the Dutch East India Company imprisoned him for attempting to infringe their monopoly. The pirates who had misled Roggeveen were, he concluded 'plunderers of truth, as well as of the Spaniards' wealth.'[36] Not all of his men agreed, arguing when they got home that if they had lingered to explore further among the Society Islands they would have found Terra Australis. So Roggeveen did not dispel the legend, except in his own mind. But he had scoured previously unfrequented stretches of ocean and identified much that was new to Westerners' knowledge.

For an oblique but brilliant light on the state of Pacific exploration at the time, no reader could do better than turn to the fiction Jonathan Swift wrote in the early 1720s: *Travels into Several Remote Nations of the World by Lemuel Gulliver.*

Swift was the subtlest yet most savage of satirists. At one level, his book spoofs the travel genre, as Gulliver survives a series of shipwrecks stranger than those of any Sinbad. At another, he practices traditional moralizing, using noble savages and moral 'monsters' as exemplars with which to berate fellow humans, fellow Christians, and fellow citizens. His own people, the British, emerge as 'the most pernicious race of little odious vermin that nature ever suffered to crawl upon the face of the earth.' At a further level, he traduces his pet hates: especially politicians, scientists, and South Sea speculators. Finally, he lampoons the world: when he at last encounters humans, 'I never beheld in all my travels so disagreeable an animal, or one against which I naturally conceived so strong an antipathy.' The map that accompanies an early edition locates his journeys in the Pacific. It shows the lands 'discovered' by de Vries. Laputa—Gulliver's 'floating island' inhabited by cloudy-headed philosophers—lies to their east. Brobdingnag, a land of giants, is a peninsula at the northeastern extremity of America. All Gulliver's travels were imaginary, but all his recollections revealed truths. The Pacific was a sea where anything could happen, of blanks and blarney, fancies and falsehood, latitude and lies.

Crossing Siberia: Eldorados in the Ice

While Swift was writing, Russians were approaching the presumed region of Laputa and Brobdingnag from Siberia. The conquerors of Siberia conquered rivers rather than lands. The rivers run from south to north. They make good causeways into the fur-rich forests from settlements in the plains, but poor trans-Siberian routes. Travelers who used them faced laborious portage between the Taz or the Ob and Yenisei, waiting for snow to make the ground traversable with sleds. For explorers—traders, trappers, or cossack mercenaries—the deal was simple. Each explorer contracted with the state for a certain number of sable pelts and kept the surplus, if any. As he went, he interrogated the natives about what lay ahead. The next river was always the best by repute.

In the 1620s the Russians were stymied in the region of Lake Baikal. The Buryats' determined resistance forced them to look elsewhere for routes eastward across the Tunguska Plateau toward the Lena. The best route involved a grueling struggle upstream against the Nizh Tunguska to find the upper Vilyuy, which flows into the Lena. The new arrivals reduced the native Yakut horse herders of the Lena valley to tribute and reached the river delta by 1633. The Lena was a great, navigable artery; it also watered good grazing land where Russians could stock up food for onward expansion. The terrain beyond the valley, however, was the most hostile Russians had yet encountered in Siberia, with mountains and tundra stretching who knew how far.

The Struggle to the Anadyr

In the 1630s they concentrated most of their efforts on this front along two routes—navigating up the Aldan, around the edge of the plateau, while sending seaborne probes, financed by hunters of walrus ivory, along the Arctic shore in purpose-built craft. The koch was a light, flat-bottomed vessel, with a draft of 5 or 6 feet, and usually about 60 feet long. Curved sides deflected ice. Oars for inshore work supplemented the single square sail. On the Alazeya River in 1640, the navigators first met Chukchi herders. In 1644, in the region of the Kolyma delta, they encountered 'walking' Chukchis for the first time—the most isolated of what the Russians called 'small peoples' of the north. Here the Chukchi lived in huts along the sea—earth huts in winter, summer huts of whalebone under stretched hides—and ate wild reindeer, seals, whales, and sturgeon. In the easternmost of the Chukchi lands were people distinguished by walrus tusk ornaments stuck through their lips.

The first Russians to trade with them noticed how they rejected walrus products: clearly these were people with ample sources of walrus ivory. That made their lands worth exploring. The incentive was fabled riches: the realm of Pogycha, 'a new land beyond the Kolyma' first reported in 1645,[37] was supposed to be full of walrus ivory and sable with a mountain of silver and a pearl-filled lake. The Anadyr River—supposedly rich in sable—became a target. Kolyma became a magnet: Russian authorities issued 404 passports for the region. In the late seventeenth century, the amount of fur it yielded in tax and tribute was consistently the highest in Siberia.[38]

Petitions written by Semen Dezhnev, a peasant turned fur hunter, evoke life on this frontier at the time. They dwell on his hardships in imperial service. He complains repetitiously about the cost of salmon nets—literally vital for explorers in the region, who had little or no other source of food. He denounces unremittingly the thanklessness of officialdom, the unfairness of unsalaried life in the service of the tsar, and the obstructiveness of ice, which impeded his first voyage in 1647. When the tribute system failed to yield expected returns in fur, it was the result, according to Dezhnev, of wars between the native tribes, or ruthless, reckless overexploitation by Russian conquistadores. The blood they shed pointlessly alienated natives and frustrated his efforts as an explorer. His life seems compounded of 'great want, impoverishment and shipwreck.'[39]

His main purpose, it seems, was to find the mouth of the Anadyr to facilitate the trade in sable pelts as well as 'to look for other new rivers and any place where the sovereign's profit might be made.'[40] In the summer of 1648 Dezhnev sailed from the mouth of the Kolyma on the furthest-reaching expedition yet. He embarked on a laborious journey, taking from early June until late September to negotiate the hazards of the Arctic coast. The ice that year was exceptionally favorable, clinging to the shore rather than breaking into the icebergs that crushed and crunched most ships. Even so, only two or three of Dezhnev's seven koches survived. He reached the remotest extremity of Siberia and rounded the cape now named after him, though whether he sighted it is a matter of doubt: his descriptions of the coast are too vague. He shows no awareness of having passed through a strait. He continued to explore beyond the mouth of the Anadyr. His was therefore the first recorded navigation through the strait that separates Asia from America. But he assumed that the Kamchatka stretched east to join the New World.

The year after Dezhnev reached the Anadyr, a rival party of explorers arrived overland from the Kolyma valley. According to Dezhnev, they prejudiced the entire operation by tyrannizing the natives. The conflict that ensued was a deterrent to further efforts. Dezhnev's efforts to extend his search overland to find 'new people and bring them under our sovereign's exalted hand' failed for want of native guides. The significance of his find therefore failed to register. He returned with few sables, many wounds, a tale of hardships, and no definitive information about the geography of eastern Siberia. Knowledge of his expedition got buried in official reports in Tobolsk and failed to reach geographers in St Petersburg or Moscow. Eight attempts to repeat his voyage between 1649 and 1787 all failed because of ice or hunger.[41] Most late seventeenth-century and early eighteenth-century maps of Siberia show the northeast extremity of the country shading vaguely into impassable ice, and remain noncommittal on the question of whether the ice shrouded a land link to America.

The Search for 'Dauria'

Meanwhile, the Russians on Lake Baikal at last succeeded in imposing tribute on the Buryats who lived on its eastern banks. The fact that the Buryats had silver diverted efforts for a while to a search for its source in some supposed mine: really, however, the silver ultimately came from China by way of trade. Ivan Moskvitin reached the Sea of Okhotsk from the Lena valley in 1639, crossing the Dzhugdzhur Mountains and descending the river Ulya. He picked up rumors of riches in 'Dauria' on the river Amur to the south, which inspired his superiors at Yakutsk to send Vasily Poyarkov to find them. Poyarkov found the Amur and followed it to the sea. But he committed every outrage in the conquistador repertoire along the way, torturing and massacring people too poor to satisfy his extortions, and allegedly feeding his force with the carcasses of Daur tribespeople, whom he killed because they refused to feed his men.

Russians were unwilling to abandon the illusion that an advanced civilization still awaited discovery in this region. In 1655 the unruly archpriest Avvakum Petrovitch departed for Siberia as an exile. At Yeniseisk he was ordered to join a new expedition to the 'Kingdom of Dauria.' The terrible sufferings to which his duties condemned him make his report of the expedition spellbinding. Not only had he, along with his fellow explorers, to face the rigors of adverse rivers, grueling terrain, and the hostile climate, but he also incurred his commander's wrath for insubordination and spent a winter imprisoned in a hideous dungeon, while the wounds inflicted on him by scourging festered, and he grew emaciated for want of food. The outline of the expedition is simple to recount. Anafasy Pashkov, with 300 men, was to report on the region between Lake Baikal and China, impose tribute on the inhabitants, seek valuable minerals, and establish relations with China and other neighboring countries. In case no agrarian peoples should be found in the region, he was also to establish a farming settlement to grow food for future armies and expeditions. He was enjoined to observe moderation in his dealings with the natives, maintain discipline among his men, and practice self-restraint. His forty boats set off along the river Angara in July 1656. Having crossed Lake Baikal, they began the ascent of unruly rivers—the Selenga and Khilok—hauling their equipment from broken banks, to Lake Irgen. There they built 170 rafts, which they hoisted onto their backs, and made for the river Ingoda, which flows into the Shilka. They reached Nercha in June 1658.[42]

In the late seventeenth century Siberia became a route to China for Russian couriers and even ambassadors. In 1689 the Russians were compelled, in the face of superior Chinese strength, to accept a border north and west of the Amur; but China neither could nor would police its claims in remoter parts of eastern Siberia, where Russia retained a free hand.

The Effort to Place America

The unresolved question of where Siberia ended remained important for Russia's main design: the accessibility of a potential Pacific empire. It mattered just as much to western Europeans: if there was an Arctic passage yet to be discovered around the northern coast of North America, the effort of finding it would be unrewarded if Siberia blocked it at its western end. Conversely, if clear water lay between the Pacific and the Arctic, through what most maps of the time called the Strait of Anian, it might be possible to approach the fabled Northwest Passage from the east. Plenty of texts held out hope of such a consummation. Most were spurious. For instance, although the Spanish crown gave it no credence, a work appeared in 1626 under the name of a respected Spanish navigator, Lorenzo Ferrer Maldonado. The author claimed to have sailed in 1588 via Davis Strait, through 290 leagues of unfrozen sea, at nearly 75 degrees north, in February, and to have returned in June with temperatures as warm as those of Spain. He got as far as a strait between Asia and America. Here he met Lutheran traders with a cargo of silks, brocades, pearls, gold, and porcelain. Plenty of readers were happy to suspend their critical faculties in favor of such claims.

In 1724 the Russian emperor, Peter the Great, resolved to turn to 'a matter which has been on my mind for many years.'[43] He was dying from fever contracted when he waded into the Gulf of Finland to rescue drowning sailors. Deathbed conviction inspired his vision. Although he spoke of 'finding a passage through the Arctic Sea,' his scheme, once formulated in writing, was more equivocal. Explorers were commanded to sail from Kamchatka, at the eastern edge of his empire, to map 'land which lies to the north, which, since no one knows where it ends, it seems is part of America' and find 'the place where that land might be joined to America.'[44]

Peter's admirals gave the job to Vitus Bering, a Danish-born officer in the Russian navy—one of the many Westerners who took advantage of the opportunities for preferment in Peter's Russia. Anna, Bering's wife, was evidently the driving force of the family: a wife and mother whose sacrifices for husband and children were all the fiercer for the egotism that impelled them. Snobbery made her harry her menfolk into unrealistic ambitions. She networked relentlessly, belaboring every potential patron she knew—and many she didn't. Her political nous never matched her *folie de grandeur*, and most of her efforts disappeared in the mole holes of the court and among the warrens of faction. Bering's aims were a permanent appointment and a country estate. Instead, he wrote in 1740, 'I have been in this service for thirty-seven years and . . . I live like a nomad.' Adventuring was the only way out of the world of restricted social opportunity that confined him.

In March 1725, shortly after Peter's death, Bering set off to cross Siberia overland to Kamchatka along the 60-degree parallel. To officials in Moscow, the task looked easy; victims of their own propaganda, they imagined Siberia as a teemingly rich region, scattered with populous Russian settlements. A compilation of Siberian history, written a few years before, illustrates this view. The author, Semen Remezov, was an official in Tobolsk, the gateway town to Siberia, and had undertaken a good deal of intelligence-gathering work, involving ethnographic and geographical researches. The frontispiece of the book shows rays of light emanating from the eye of God to illumine Siberia, touching eighteen spired and turreted cities, of which Tobolsk occupies pride of place, alongside the legend 'He shall dwell in righteousness and cities shall arise in the Lord.' Really, however, Siberia's 'cities' were ramshackle outposts choked by surrounding wilderness, more suited to the text inscribed on the open Bible that also graced the frontispiece of the Remezov Chronicle: 'Where two or three are gathered in my name, there shall I be with them.'[45]

Tobolsk, the starting point of Bering's trans-Siberian journey, was the first disappointment. He expected to be able to recruit soldiers from the garrison and carpenters and smiths. The settlement was so short of manpower that the governor would allow him few more than half his needs. Many of the recruits he got at Yeniseisk were 'lame, blind and riddled with disease.'[46] Okhotsk, the terminus of his journey on the Pacific coast, had only eleven huts. To get there, he faced a 6,000-mile journey that took three years. Horses died for lack of grass. The explorers stretched corduroy roads over boggy terrain. The intricate courses of the rivers they had to cross meant that they sometimes had to ford six crossings in a single day. They inched through a dynamic environment, 'like pebbles in the swift waters of a stream.'[47] Fifteen men died. Scores deserted. When they arrived, the pressure on the native population of Kamchatka—the exactions of supplies and sleds, dogs and men—caused a rebellion. Following orders, Bering built a ship and put to sea in the summer of 1728. The true extent of Siberia emerged as Bering charted 1,000 miles of coast to the east. Reaching to almost 68 degrees north, Bering decided—without really knowing—that water must separate Russia from America. The truth is that he had not gone far enough to test the hypothesis.

His second expedition, which began in 1733, had far more ambitious aims: to explore the Arctic coast with a view to establishing a sea route to the East; to find the way to America via Siberia; to open trade with Japan; to explore a new, 'shortest' route from Irkutsk to the Pacific; to establish a route for a viable postal service between the extremities of the Russian empire; to report on the geology, geography, ethnography, flora, and fauna of Siberia; 'and generally to learn everything that is of scientific interest.'[48]

The size of the expedition—3,600 strong in two parties—strained the resources of the road. Numbers grew as it got deeper into the wilderness, because they needed manpower to build boats and bridges. At Tobolsk, they requisitioned the labor of a sixth of the population. At Yakutsk there were only twenty-four houses in which to billet the expedition. While Bering's picky, prickly professors demanded comfort, forced labor had to be intimidated against desertion. 'We set up a gallows every twenty versts' with 'exceptionally good effect,' but nothing could stop Siberians' 'ungodly drinking.' By 1739 Bering had to abandon efforts to find a short route to the Pacific and open a usable postal route. From Okhotsk in July 1738 he reported that many men

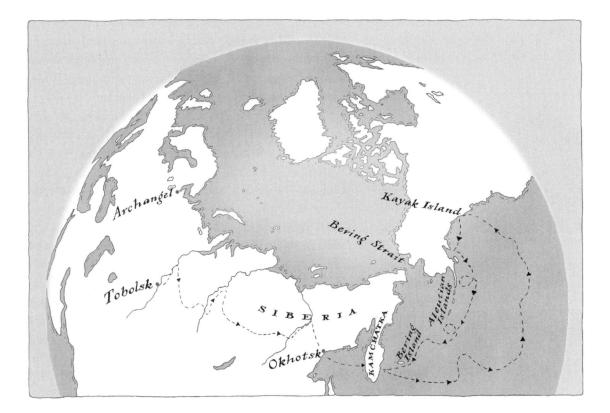

Efforts to sail around the Arctic coast and to map it, when seaborne
expeditions failed, by means of overland surveying parties, took a terrible toll in
lives. Bering summed up the results:

lacked clothes and shoes; 'while transporting provisions they became very
emaciated and in wintertime some hands and feet were frozen by the severe
cold and because of such difficulty and the lack of other victuals many can
barely walk.'[49]

Bering's journeys to Alaska, 1728–1741

> There are certain learned persons who maintain that one ought to sail
> right out from the coast and cross the Icy Sea nearer the Pole, it being their
> opinion that by that means one would reach open water. . . . I am unable to
> understand it. . . . I have never heard or read of anyone being farther north
> than a latitude of 82 degrees; and what those had to endure in the way of
> effort and privations before they came back again is, indeed, a most harrowing
> tale.[50]

The proposed trade route to Japan proved equally elusive. Bering sent ships
along the line of the Kurils and they reached Japan, but their effort to
reconstruct the route the following year met with failure: they discovered

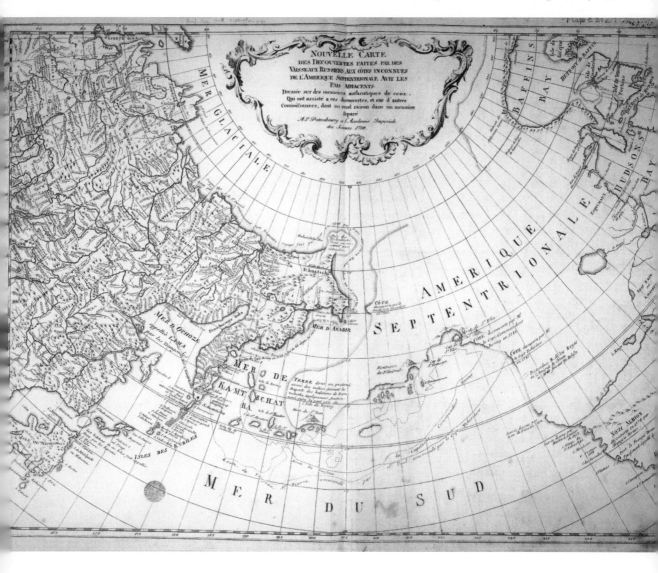

NOUVELLE CARTE
DES DECOUVERTES FAITES PAR DES
VAISSEAUX RUSSIENS AUX CÔTES INCONNUES
DE L'AMERIQUE SEPTENTRIONALE AVEC LES
PAIS ADIACENTS.
Dressée sur des memoires authentiques de ceux,
Qui ont assisté a ces decouvertes, et sur d'autres
Connoissances, dont on rend raison dans un memoire
separé.
A S.t Petersbourg à l'Academie Imperiale
des Sciences 1758.

Russian map of Alaska showing the Danish explorer Vitus Bering's two expeditions in 1728 and 1741

Sakhalin—fog-bound and barren—instead. Readers back home doubted whether they can ever have got to Japan at all.

One task remained. They built and provisioned two ships. In May 1741, Bering sailed from Kamchatka in search of America. Instead of going northeast, where the shortest route really lay, he began by searching in a southeasterly direction, where false or imaginary sightings of land by earlier explorers led him to hope that some unknown arm of America extended. 'My blood still boils,' wrote a survivor, 'whenever I think of the scandalous deception of which we were victims.'[51] They tacked between the Aleutian Islands. When Bering eventually stumbled on Kayak Island, off the coast of America, in mid-July, he was clueless about where they were, striving comically to communicate with natives using dodgy word lists purportedly of Algonquian and Iroquoian. The same on the homeward journey with the Aleuts.

He knew it was a mistake to sail for home so late in the season, but there was nothing else he could do. He knew it was risky to return by an unexplored route, but he let his officers overrule him. He knew it would be fatal to anchor off Bering Island—but, racked by sickness, he was powerless to countermand his subordinates, submitting to the madness of 'minds as loose from the storm as teeth from scurvy.' He shared Cassandra's tragedy—that of prophets proved right because their prophecies are disregarded. He followed 'the shortest route but the longest manner, by bumping into islands,' according to Georg Steller, the expedition's resident botanist, the smock-frocked scientist whose modesty is a counterfoil to Bering's ambition. The relations of commander and scientist were satisfyingly consistent with the canons of drama. When Steller presented a strategy based on local knowledge in the vicinity of the straits, Bering dismissed his views, muttering, 'Who believes Cossacks?' The ill-matched pair were condemned to share a cabin, where Steller felt he 'took up too much space' and forever feared the fate of the scientific specimens Bering contemptuously threw overboard for want of room.

On the way home, the expedition became an epic struggle against nature. They waged war on scurvy—hopelessly, resignedly, even to death, while abundant unknown cures were at hand. Storms pounded them with waves 'like shots out of a cannon.' Bering, who had taught his children a religion of trust in God's providence, made his men subscribe to a votive offering to be divided between Lutheran and Orthodox churches if they survived; but 'curses accumulated during ten years in Siberia would allow no granting of a prayer.' When the ship foundered, they built another. They fed themselves on Bering Island by beating seals to death for their nauseating flesh. 'When the cranium is broken into little bits, and almost all the brains have gushed out and all the teeth have been broken, the beast still attacks the men with his flippers and keeps right on fighting.' Misfortune reconciled Bering with Steller. Steller nursed Bering in his last illness and became something of a guardian of his memory. On 8 December 1742, he died, as his physician certified, from 'hunger, thirst, cold, vermin and grief,' half-smothered in sand against the unbearable Arctic winter, surrounded by crates full of his court clothes and wigs: 'He died like a rich man,' according to the embittered eulogy pronounced by his second-in-command, 'and he was buried like the ungodly.'

Bering's story excels fiction for human interest and farce for human foibles. He had overmighty ambitions. Dreams of grandeur made him desert his Danish homeland for Russian service and risk his life for the tsarina's reward in the uncharted corner of the world that now bears his name. Nemesis harried him toward his death. Bering's was a breakthrough era in scientific knowledge of the boreal world, not only because of his own discoveries, but also because of the survey he commanded of the Arctic coast from the White Sea to Kamchatka, and the expedition of Pierre-Louis de Maupertuis to Finland to determine the length of a degree on the surface of the globe near the Arctic Circle.[52] The last irony is that Bering's discoveries blended, in the geography of the Enlightenment, with muddled data from apocryphal voyages. The effects of his work only became enshrined in uncontested maps nearly half a century after his death.

Africa: Slaving and Exploration

Although little exploration got recorded in seventeenth-century Africa, that does not mean it did not happen. On the contrary, the tramp of armies and slave coffles drove paths through the forests. The range of commercially inspired journeys grew with the stimulus to trade that slave wealth brought. New, ill-documented routes were forged. From Lagos, for instance, canoes traveled to Allado for salt, which was also sent inland, over 200 miles, to supply markets in Oyo. This was a new trade, for formerly Oyo had relied on salt extracted from vegetables. Allado was also an emporium for beads from Yoruba lands, reexported to the Gold Coast, where traders from Dahomey also found a market for beans and horse tails with which sword pommels were decorated. Markets attracted thousands of people at Jakin and Savi.[53] There were comparably large and busy trading centers at Gongo in the kingdom of Congo.

Most of Africa's internal routes, however, remained unfrequented by visitors from outside the continent or, indeed, from outside adjacent localities. In the late 1670s and early 1680s, Jean Barbot, a Huguenot slave trader, was on the West African coast compiling data for a book he intended to write for the benefit of fellow travelers to Africa. He consulted 'the most intelligent Europeans who had resided long in Guinea' and 'the discreetest of the natives to whom I could explain my meaning.'[54] But he could learn little about the interior at any point, 'none of the Europeans dwelling along the coast ever having ventured far up the land, that I could hear of.'[55] Other notices of the interior were typically vague and culled from the reports of native merchants. In most of the continent, Europeans who made significant inland journeys were few.

In West Africa, a rare exception occurred in 1701, when the council of the Dutch trading post of Elmina decided on 'a venture never before undertaken' and appointed an ambassador to a kingdom in the interior. David van Nyendael visited the Asante court of Otumfuo Osei Tutu I, to establish trade relations and congratulate him on his recent victories against his former over-lord, Ntim Gyakiri of Denkyira. Van Nyendael stayed in Kumasi for almost a year and returned to Elmina in October 1702, seriously ill. He died eight days later, before he could prepare his final report on his mission in Kumasi. He left only fragmentary letters, including a description of Benin, published by Willem Bosman, his colleague at Elmina, a few years later; but owing to his untimely demise most of what he might have told the world about contacts with Asante remained obscure.

Ethiopia, Mwene Mutapa, Congo, and Angola, where Portuguese explorers had already penetrated, remained, for Europeans, the best-known regions of sub-Saharan Africa. All the missionary and military establishments of the Portuguese fringe looked seaward—Congo and Angola toward Brazil, Ethiopia and the Swahili coast to Goa—but it was still possible for inroads to be made into the continent. In 1623–4 the Jesuits of Goa in India were encouraged to attempt to explore new routes into Ethiopia via East African ports, because 'Moors came who traded with Christian Abyssinia and could act as guides.' The project involved reattempting the routes pioneered unsuccess-fully by Fr António Fernandes.[56] Jeronimo Lobo, one of two fathers assigned to make the attempt, was under no illusions as he set out from Goa.

> And truly there were few among those who said farewell to us who could promise us long lives. For the undertaking was extremely risky, never before attempted or imagined; the lands were unknown, and the people were savage and had never before dealt with Portuguese people; the road, when such existed, could not fail to have an infinite number of mishaps in store for two foreigners with white skin penetrating the interior of Africa where every-one's skin was the colour of coal; and the culture, food, mountain ranges, wildernesses and deserts were the last of our concerns.[57]

He could find no guides. Fever and fear of the 'savage' Gallas who bestrode his path overcame him. Besides, 'there is no route that way,' asserted Manoel de Almeida, the Jesuit who knew Ethiopia best, because of 'the windings' of the roads, and the political obstacles strewn where 'petty kings and rulers are as numerous as the days of travelling.'[58] The explorers were obliged to return and resume the usual route via the Red Sea and Massawah. Meanwhile, another Jesuit party attempted a route via Zeila—apparently in error, misled by a mis-take in a letter from the Ethiopian court. Their journey ended in martyrdom at the hands of Adelian tribesmen. The flow of data shrank, first because the incursions of Galla and Muslims increased Ethiopia's isolation, and increasingly because the rulers' collaboration with Portugal broke down: the Jesuits, increasingly intolerant of Ethiopian heresies, became unwelcome in the land.

From Mwene Mutapa, the information that reached the outside world was even more fragmentary. Between 1608 and 1614 Diogo Simões Madeira, captain of the fort of Tete, continued the search for the mines of Mwene Mutapa, supposed to lie in the vicinity of Chicoa. Since the monarch was understandably loath to specify their whereabouts, Simões revived the project of conquering the kingdom; but memories were still vivid of the defeat the Portuguese suffered at their previous attempt in the 1570s, and in 1622 the crown called the project off. Succession struggles multiplied; the kingdom fragmented. Opportunities increased for Portuguese adventurers—'men who would be kings'—to found private fiefdoms. But most of them had little interest in broadening the region's range of contacts with the outside world. The prospect receded of finding routes across Mwene Mutapa to link the Indian Ocean with the deep interior of Africa.

Nor was much achieved by Portuguese probes inland from the Atlantic coast of Angola. From Benguela prospectors in search of sources of copper and rumored gold hardly punctured the mysteries of the interior. From Luanda, however, military expeditions, diplomatic missions, and missionary efforts did gather information and reach ever further east. Andrew Batell, for instance, as a mercenary, captive, and pedlar, spent years in the interior of Luanda and wrote a description of his experiences, published in 1610. In the mid-century, the court of Queen Njinga of Ndongo was a magnet. This formidable virago, who affected, as it suited her, Christianity and paganism, female wiles and masculine attire, devoted most of her long life to a struggle for control of the kingdom she inherited. Missionaries pursued the queen's court ever further into the interior as strategic needs displaced her court eastwards, reaching as far as Matamba in 1656.

Meanwhile, Capuchin missionaries arrived in the kingdom of Congo in 1645 and founded missions all over the country: in Sona Bata and Sanda, south of the Zaire, not far from present-day Kinshasa; in the uplands of Bamba, which divide the valleys of the Mebridege and the Cuanza, and beyond on the river Dande; in Unanda, an isolated spot in what is now the province of Uige. Mateo de Anguiano, historian of the Order, who collected and collated the missionaries' reports in 1716, evoked the difficulties:

> the heat of the sun, the corruption of the air; the foodstuffs, insufficient and inedible; the frequent lack of drinking water; the great distances that separate human settlements; the absence of any native breed of horses; the asperity of the tracks, where there are no taverns or inns and which are more like goat-tracks than proper roads, and which, being narrow and little frequented,

sprout hard grasses, half a pike's length high and thick as our European canes. It all makes you very weary. Breathing becomes difficult. For us, who go unshod, it is very troublesome, for at every step we take the tufts of needle-grass punish our feet. Bleeding is usually the only remedy available for the fierce diseases that afflict the blood. . . . The rains are copious and normally they start in May and continue until September. Ferocious winds precede them, with horrendous storms and skies so black that they depress the spirit, and this happens every day.[59]

In 1727, for the first time, a European mapmaker broke the convention of speculating injudiciously in order to fill in embarrassing gaps. Most of his map of Africa was shockingly blank. Just as *Gulliver's Travels* seemed to demonstrate the limitations of Pacific exploration, so another fiction demonstrated the ignorance of sub-Saharan Africa that still prevailed in Europe in the early eighteenth century. In 1740 the *Histoire de Louis Anniaba, roi d'Essénie en Afrique sur la côte de Guinée* referred to nothing recognizably African. The continent, as depicted in that work, was undifferentiatedly exotic. The people were not even black: the plot of the novel hinged on episodes of mistaken identity, similar to those provoked by the Albanian disguises that the heroes of *Così fan tutte* wore.

The Map of the World

Still, though the achievements of seventeenth- and early eighteenth-century exploration were modest, they had important effects. Our mental map of the world began to take shape. The story can be said to have begun with the opening of the Paris Observatory in 1669, or perhaps with the foundation of the institution's parent organization, the Académie Royal des Sciences, established by Colbert in 1666 for the correction and improvement of maps and charts. It was an example of the sort of state initiative in the scientific world with which we are familiar today, with research treated as a form of investment, directed, in a practical spirit, toward 'wealth-creating' objectives, rather than being pursued for its own sake. The members of the Académie, however, included the cosmographical avant-garde of the time, and their work soon came to transcend its utilitarian remit. The most conspicuous figures, in the early years of the new institution, were Jean Picard and Christiaan Huyghens.

Picard was a driving force in the creation of the Académie, recommending suitable scholars to Colbert and helping, where necessary, to lure them to France. His early life is obscure. His first profession was said to have been that of a gardener, which perhaps should be interpreted *lato sensu* to include horticulture and botany. Like many men of scholarly proclivities in his day, he embraced a clerical vocation—or, at least, a career in the Church—and eventually became prior of a college of canons in Rille. The turning point in his life came with a more secular revelation. In 1645, at the age of 25, he assisted the great astronomer Gassendi in an observation of an eclipse of the sun. He became Gassendi's devoted pupil and succeeded to his master's chair of astronomy in 1655. He pioneered the use of the lens in the measurement of angles and, exploiting the efficiency of the pendulum clocks that Huyghens developed, he proposed a new method of determining the apparent positions of stars in relation to their passage of the meridian. He justified his combined callings of astronomer and priest by working to improve the exactitude of the calendar of the Church. When his *Connoissance des temps* appeared in 1679, it was advertised as 'a collection of holy days and festivals'; but it contained so much astral information useful for checking latitude and longitude that no aid to navigation surpassed it until the publication of the *Nautical Almanac* in 1766.

Huyghens was first destined for the law. But his mathematical precocity, which attracted the attention of Descartes, deflected him into a new career. His *De Circuli Magnitudine Inventa* of 1654 proposed the most exact value yet achieved for π. Like Picard, he realized that advances in the science of astronomy demanded technical innovations. His new methods of grinding and polishing lenses enormously enhanced the clarity of telescopes and made him, in 1655–6, the first observer of the Orion nebula and of clear images of the rings and satellites of Saturn. The need for exact measurement of time to complement astronomical observations inspired his work on the pendulum clock. After moving to France, he worked mainly on the problem of the nature of light and on the construction of enormous telescopes with long focal distances. In 1681, however, he returned permanently to Holland, disenchanted by professional and perhaps personal differences with colleagues. He developed a theory of the shape of the world as an oblate spheroid, 'flattened' at the poles but 'bulging' at the equator: it was bitterly disputed but, as we shall see in the next chapter, ultimately vindicated by the Académie.

In 1669 the personnel of the Académie was enormously enriched. A great Italian astronomer, henceforth to be known as Jean-Dominique Cassini, joined the staff. He was born Gian Domenico Cassini in the Savoyard county of Nice in 1625. At the time, the region belonged, culturally and politically, to the world of northern Italy. Cassini went to school with the Jesuits of Genoa. His early inclinations were supra-rational—poetic, mystical, and astrological—rather than scientific as we now understand the term. But common routes of entry into science in early modern Europe lay through astrology and even magic. Perusal of Pico della Mirandola's indictment of astrologers persuaded

Cassini to burn his astrological notes and turn instead to the disinterested study of astronomy. He was still only 25 when he took up the chair of astronomy at Bologna, vacated by the death of Galileo's apologist, Cavalieri. Cassini kept Bologna in the astronomical avant-garde. He constructed a new meridian line, still marked in brass in the floor of the north aisle of the cathedral, and invited leading astronomers from around Europe to observe his attempts to verify Kepler's hypotheses about apparent variations in the speed of motion and in the size of the diameter of the sun.

Jean-Dominique Cassini (1625–1712)

Cassini's *Novum Eclipsium Methodum* of 1659 linked his work on the sun to one of the most perplexing problems of the cartography of his day: the establishment of longitude. Cassini proposed disciplines which would improve readings by making the comparative timing of eclipses on different meridians more accurate. In 1665 he made the first of a series of discoveries of previously unknown moons of Jupiter. In 1668 he published his *Ephemerides*, or tables of the motions of Jupiter's satellites. This completed a work Galileo had begun: providing a celestial standard for the exact measurement of time. His astronomical work did not prevent him from achieving a distinguished reputation in other fields: as a theorist of hydrography and hydraulic engineer in the service of the pope and of the senate of Bologna; as a calculator, like Picard, of the ecclesiastical calendar; as a pioneer of blood transfusions; as an expert on the physical properties of liquids; and as a surveyor of the frontiers of Tuscany and the Papal State, with a view to fixing the border. But it was his contribution to the problem of longitude that made his services indispensable to the cartographic project Colbert was launching in France. His adscription to the Académie was not uniformly happy. He fell out with Picard, who had championed his summons to France, and he alienated Huyghens. But his own endeavors, in expediting the project and marshaling the data, more than made up for the dislocations he caused to his colleagues' morale.

In the years after Cassini joined, the work of the Académie became focused on two enterprises: the fixing of the location of important places around the world by latitude and longitude; and the response to Colbert's demand that

France be mapped with improved accuracy. In the west tower of the Paris Observatory, Cassini laid out the third floor as a vast map, 24 feet in diameter, with meridian lines and lines of latitude spread over it at intervals of 10 degrees. Teams of observers combed the world.

As previously unknown longitudes were verified by means of Galileo's technique and Huyghens's invention, the relevant places were marked according to their coordinates. When he visited the work in progress, Louis XIV could stamp on the world and pinpoint places with toecap accuracy.

In some ways, the obsession with enmeshing the world in a grid of reference was curiously antiquated. It had originated at a suggestion of the second-century Alexandrian cosmographer Claudius Ptolemy. Since the rediscovery of Ptolemy in the Western world in the fifteenth century, scholars had held it up as an ideal method, without much practical hope of ever seeing it accomplished. Cassini's floor map presented a distorted picture of the world, determined by the dimensions of the Observatory tower and unable to convey any visual impression of the distances between the places marked. Yet it was a genuine scientific breakthrough, unexcelled in importance in the history of cartography. For the first time, the world was being mapped to scale on the basis of verifiable assumptions.

Data came in from all over the world. Cassini briefed expeditions to Cayenne and Egypt, Cape Verde, and the island of Guadelupe. Jesuit missions in Madagascar, Siam, and China made observations to the common end. Halley reported from the Cape of Good Hope and Thévenot from Goa. The main discrepancy which emerged arose from the apparent retardation of pendulum clocks in the vicinity of the equator, despite the sedulous means devised by Cassini to compensate for changes in heat and humidity.

Maps reflected their work. In 1702 the election of the cartographer Guillaume de L'Isle augmented the body of savants. He was said to have been able to draw maps illustrating the settings of ancient history from the age of 9. He came under Cassini's influence, and, at the age of 25, resolved to reform the existing cartographical corpus by constructing new maps on grids created with scientific readings of longitude as their basis. In 1700 he published an epoch-making series of world maps and maps of the individual continents, in which for the first time the Mediterranean was given its true length. His total output of 134 maps literally charted the Académie's progress in gathering accurate data on the coordinates of places all over the world.

De L'Isle died in 1726, but his ambition of correcting the maps of the world was inherited by a young man, born in 1697. The chance discovery of a map when he was 12 years old inspired Jean-Baptiste Bourguignon d'Anville with a lifelong devotion to cartography. He demonstrated the scholarly fastidiousness for which he became famous when he withheld from publication, on grounds of its imperfection, a map the Prince Regent, the duc d'Orléans, commissioned from his hand. In 1727 his famous map of Africa, mentioned above, appeared. Over the next few years he illustrated with maps the *Histoire de Saint-Domingue* of Charlevoix, the *Oriens Christianus* of Le Quieu, and the great Jesuit compilation on China edited by du Halde. In 1744, in his *Analyse géographique d'Italie*, he proposed a reduction in the perceived size of that country, by analogy with the revelations about France disclosed in the Académie's surveys. When a survey of Italy by triangulation began under the auspices of Pope Benedict XIV, d'Anville's opinion was confirmed. Critically piecing together cartographical traditions and the observations of others, he constructed astonishingly accurate versions of remote places. An explorer of 1782, for instance, found his map of the Moluccas admirable. Savants who accompanied Napoleon to Egypt in 1798 relied on d'Anville's map. In a total of 211 printed maps and seventy-eight other printed works, he mapped the world without ever leaving France.

The Académie's other great project was the Survey of France. This work has a place in the history of exploration because of the contribution the surveyors made to the science of mapping and, therefore, of recording and retrieving explorers' routes.

The state of knowledge of the map of France before the Académie's work is best assessed with reference to the leading work in the field at the time: that of Nicolas Sanson the elder. Sanson was the founder of a tradition passed on through his sons and pupils to all the greatest mapmakers of late seventeenth- and eighteenth-century France. Born in 1600, and educated by Jesuits in Amiens, he felt shocked, as a mere schoolboy, at the inadequacy of the maps available to assist perusal of classical texts and, in particular, of Caesar's Gallic War. He made his own map of ancient Gaul in his teens but his antiquarian interests were essentially amateur. It was not until 1626 that financial embarrassment caused him to publish the map for profit. It caught the attention of Richelieu, who made Sanson tutor in geography to the royal household and Géographe du roi. His sons were distinguished and productive geographers: the elder was killed in the Fronde at the age of 22 but the younger, Guillaume, survived to produce works of his own on geographical theory and successive new editions of his father's maps until the end of the century.

Sanson's own maps were necessarily of a traditional type: compilations from existing works rather than new essays based on scientific evidence. The Académie's attempt to improve on the map of France really began in earnest only in 1669—a decade before the publication of the last edition of Sanson's version—when Picard set out to establish the meridian of Paris. He worked along the traditional route north to Amiens, along which Jean Fernet had attempted to measure the length of a degree using an odometer attached to his carriage wheel, 144 years before. He used the odometer to measure the distance traversed on the face of the earth, while verifying his latitude by using a quadrant to measure the elevation of the Pole Star. Like Fernet, Picard used a quadrant to check his latitude as he went along, but improved its sighting by the addition of a telescope. The rough-and-ready odometer was dismissed in favor of surveyors' triangulation techniques for measuring distance. From the extremities of a baseline measured with rods or cables, in conditions of stable temperature, an apex could be selected with a theodolite and the distances between all three points could be computed by trigonometry from the angle subtended.

Parallel with Picard's triangulation, the Académie ordered a further trial survey by the engineer David du Vivier. In 1671 publication of the results began, with Picard's new calculation of the length of a degree: assuming the world to be a perfect sphere, he reckoned the value of a degree to be the equivalent of 111.2099 kilometers at the equator. By 1678 his and Vivier's map of the triangulations they had carried out between Paris and Amiens was complete and available to the public in engraved form. Over the next few years the Académie concentrated on establishing the true longitude of points along the coast, and incorporating the results of well-conducted coastal surveys into an accurate map of the country's seaboard. The results seemed to show that France was considerably smaller than Sanson envisaged.

The Shape of the World

The major cartographical problem thrown up by the Académie's program was that the length of a degree did not appear to be uniform, suggesting that the world could not be a perfect sphere. The Survey of France proceeded slowly and fitfully, and some discrepancies might be expected as techniques improved, but the results seemed consistently to show values for the length of a degree lower in the north of the country than in the south. This fueled speculation that the world might be elongated between the poles—a prolate spheroid rather than a perfect sphere. Jean-Dominique Cassini's heir and successor Jacques Cassini adopted this conclusion in 1718, and it appeared to be confirmed in a specific experiment carried out along a perpendicular drawn to the meridian of Paris between Paris and Saint-Malo in 1733. The results were the consequence of error but they seemed to confirm that the length of a degree at that latitude was too small for a spherical world. Such findings conflicted with the Académie's own data from equatorial climes, where pendulum clocks had been found to slow down. J.-D Cassini had been inclined to dismiss these as the result of misreadings, but again the phenomenon seemed too consistent for that: it demanded a general explanation. Newton and Huyghens, the greatest authorities on the nature of the pendulum, agreed that it was the result of the distension of the surface of the globe toward the equator, so that the center of gravity of the planet was relatively further away, and the pull on the pendulum relatively less, in low latitudes than in high ones. The doctrine of centrifugal force offered a plausible explanation for such a distortion. So, whereas the surveyors of France were inclined to suppose that the world bulged at the Poles, the hierophants of gravity postulated an oblate spheroid, with flattened Poles and distended equator.

The debate was to be settled by an elaborate and expensive experiment under the Académie's auspices. Two simultaneous expeditions measured the length of a degree as accurately as possible at the practical extremities of the alleged variations: one at or almost on the equator, the other in Arctic Lapland, as far north as conditions would permit. Neither expedition was able to operate in propitious conditions.

The equatorial explorers operated under the leadership of Charles-Marie de La Condamine, with the assistance of two ingenious Spanish officers, António de Ulloa and Jorge Juan, beginning in 1735. They endured a long journey to Quito, where the expedition was riven by internal dissension and impeded by the formidable terrain. Their results took nearly ten years to obtain, at the end of which La Condamine concluded that he might as well never have gone to Quito at all but could have conducted his experiment with greater ease at Cayenne. Juan's and Ulloa's accounts appeared relatively quickly and proved influential in an unanticipated respect: despite the austerely scientific nature of their enquiries into geography, geology, hydrography, and climate, they illustrated their work with stunningly beautiful diagrams that incorporated romantic representations of American landscapes: the first stirrings of what was to be a long story—the nourishing of European romanticism with images of America.

Meanwhile, in the Arctic, Maupertuis had already effectively resolved the issue about the shape of the earth. He got as far north as he could by sea, up the Gulf of Bothnia, then trekked inland to find ground high enough for triangulation. In December 1736, at Tornio, close to the Arctic Circle, he began to measure his base line, some 12 miles long—'the longest base line that ever was used, and in the planest surface, seeing that it was upon the ice of the river that we were to measure it.' The measuring rods were made of fir wood, because of all available materials it was least likely to shrink with the cold. The Swedish army lent a detachment of soldiers to carry them. 'Judge what it must be like,' he wrote,

> to walk in snow two feet deep, with heavy poles in our hands . . . in cold so extreme that whenever we would take a little brandy, the only thing that could be kept liquid, our tongues and lips froze to the cup and came away bloody, in a cold that congealed the extremities of the body, while the rest, through excessive toil, was bathed in sweat.[60]

It would have been practically impossible to achieve total accuracy under such conditions, but Maupertuis's readings were overestimated by less than a third of 1 per cent. His findings were enough to convince the world that the planet was indeed an oblate spheroid—squashed at the Poles. On the frontispiece of his collected works, he appears in a fur cap and collar over a eulogy that means 'It was his destiny to determine the shape of the world.'

Like many scientific explorers seared by experience, Maupertuis ended disillusioned by science but inspired by nature. He set off believing that every truth was quantifiable, and that every fact could be sensed. He ended as something of a mystic. 'You cannot chase God in the immensity of the heavens,' he concluded, 'or the depths of the oceans or the chasms of the Earth. Maybe it is not yet time to understand the world systematically—time only to behold it and be amazed.' In the *Letters on the Progress of the Sciences*, which he published in 1752, the next experiments for science to tackle, he felt, would be on dreams and the effects of hallucinatory drugs—'certain potions of the Indies'—as the only way to knowledge of what lay beyond the universe. Perhaps, he speculated, the perceived world is illusory: maybe only God exists, and perceptions are only properties of a mind 'alone in the universe.'

Maupertuis's experiences raised deep uncertainties in his own breast about the value of science. But the controversy over the shape of the world, at least, was over. Newton was proved right and Jacques Cassini wrong. Indeed, inaccuracies in the explorers' calculations tended to exaggerate the distortion of the globe. La Condamine's figures for the length of a degree was 110.92 kilometers instead of the correct 110.567. Maupertuis's was 111.094 instead of the figure of 110.734 which, in strict accuracy, should have been yielded in the latitude at which he was operating. The doubt thrown on former surveys dented the Académie's prestige. But the glory of obtaining an important result restored it.

Under the next head of Cassini dynasty, César-François Cassini de Thury, the Académie quickly made the necessary adjustments in former findings. In 1740, with the advantage of the results of Maupertuis's expedition, albeit not yet that of La Condamine, Cassini and his great-uncle Maraldi published an interim map of the whole of France on the basis of the Académie's findings so far. It appeared in eighteen sheets, on an average scale of 1:878,000. Though the final version on a small scale (1:86,400) would not be ready until 1789, the interim map was enough to excite the envy of states, and arouse the ambition of cartographers, all over Europe.

The discoveries of explorers had transformed the way Europeans pictured the world. They confirmed the vastness of the globe, disclosed the existence of a 'New World' in the western hemisphere, and swept animal, mineral, and plant specimens of the diversity of creation into the 'wonder rooms' of European collectors: these collections, formed to inspire awe, came to stimulate research and became the first modern museums. The widening range of contacts between cultures now linked almost all the coastal peoples of the world. Even formerly isolated shores in the Asian Arctic, Australia, and New Zealand were now part of the web of routes. Lines of communication now crisscrossed the oceans. The next tasks were to fill in the gaps between the sea lanes, especially in the Pacific, and to open links with still-sundered cultures, especially in the African and American interiors.

Endeavour River where we repair'd the Ship

Cape Bedford

Cape Flattery

Pt Lookout

Turtle I.s

H

Eagle I.

Lizard

3 Isles

Turtle Reef

T

I.s of Direction

4
8
10
16
10
20
18
10
12
14
16
12
9
14
12
14
10
14
5
7
10
16
16
14
28

8 Deepening

Enhancing the 'World-Picture', c.1740s–c.1840s

Was it not for the pleasure which naturally results to a man from being the first discoverer . . . this service would be insupportable.

Cook, *Journal of the voyage of the Endeavour*

What helps it to harass the ship, the rigging and crew in these turbulent seas beating to windward, if to satisfy the government and the public that no land is left behind, it will not suffice the incredulous part of the public if the whole Ocean were ploughed up?

Johann-Reinold Forster, *Resolution Journal*

When I was but thirteen or so
I went into a golden land.
Chimborazo, Cotopaxi
  Took me by the hand.

   .   .   .   .

I dimly heard the Master's voice
And boys far off at play.
Chimborazo, Cotopaxi
  Had stolen me away.

Walter J. R. Turner, 'Romance'

WHAT good came of all this exploration? It was a question *philosophes* found irresistible. Progress was their almost irresistible answer. But Diderot, the secular pontiff of the Enlightenment, the editor of the *Encyclopédie*, did not agree. In 1773 he wrote a denunciation of explorers as agents of a new kind of barbarism. Base motives drove them: 'tyranny, crime, ambition, misery, curiosity, I know not what restlessness of spirit, the desire to know and the desire to see, boredom, the dislike of familiar pleasures'—all the baggage of the restless temperament. Lust for discovery was a new form of fanaticism on the part of men seeking 'islands to ravage, people to despoil, subjugate and massacre.' The explorers discovered people morally superior to themselves, because more natural or more civilized, while they, on their side, grew in savagery, far from the polite restraints that reined them in at home. 'All the long-range expeditions,' Diderot insisted, 'have reared a new generation of nomadic savages . . . men who visit so many countries that they end by belonging to none . . . amphibians who live on the surface of the waters,' deracinated, and, in the strictest sense of the word, demoralized.

Certainly, the excesses explorers committed—of arrogance, of egotism, of exploitation—showed the folly of supposing that travel necessarily broadens the mind or improves the character. But Diderot exaggerated. Even as he wrote, the cases of disinterested exploration—for scientific or altruistic purposes—were multiplying.

If the eighteenth century rediscovered the beauties of nature and the wonders of the picturesque, it was in part because explorers alerted domestic publics to the grandeurs of the world they discovered. If the conservation of species and landscape became, for the first time in Western history, an objective of imperial policy, it was because of what the historian Richard Grove has called 'green imperialism'—the awakened sense of stewardship inspired by the discovery of new Edens in remote oceans. If philosophers enlarged their view of human nature, and grappled earnestly and, on the whole, inclusively with questions about the admissibility of formerly excluded humans—blacks, 'Hottentots,' Australian Aboriginals, and all other peoples estranged by their appearance or culture—to full membership of the moral community, it was because exploration made these brethren increasingly familiar. If critics of Western institutions were fortified in their strictures and encouraged in their advocacy of popular sovereignty, 'enlightened despotism,' 'free thinking,' civil liberties, and human 'rights,' it was, in part, because exploration acquainted them with challenging models from around the world of how society could be organized and life lived.

Of course, the tally of atrocities, despoliation, expropriation, and abuse continued. At the same time, however, exploration did become a form of benign frenzy. Those who engaged in it did so increasingly for its own sake, as if they could not resist it. Profit and power began to slide from the foreground of European explorers' motives. So, to some extent, did evangelization. And some of the less malignant vanities Diderot identified—curiosity, ennui, escapism—

increasingly took over. To some extent, the old spirit abided in new forms. Explorers no longer drew their inspiration directly from tales of chivalry, but they still responded to some of the urges of knight errantry: social ambition, lust for adventure, and what Captain James Cook called the 'pleasure of being first.' Some of the same myths that impelled earlier generations of European explorers were still around, working their magic on susceptible minds.

The Persistence of Myth

The Pacific, for instance, still stretched between myths: the 'unknown continent' of Terra Australis in the south and the rumored sea passage around America in the north.

The tenacity of the Terra Australis myth is remarkable in view of the lack of evidence to support it, but understandable in view of the logic summoned in its defense. Pierre-Louis Moreau de Maupertuis, one of the most renowned men of science of his day,[1] put the case succinctly and comprehensively in 1752:

> Everyone knows that in the southern hemisphere there is an unknown space where there may be situated a new part of the world greater than any of the other four . . . Nowhere else on the globe is there a space as vast as this, but rather than being totally occupied by a continuous sea, there is much more probability that one will find there land.[2]

A world disproportionately awash with ocean—a world such as we really inhabit—seemed to defy every principle of order and symmetry, such as rational minds expected from a divine creator.

On the assumption that Terra Australis existed, it would have been a dereliction of duty and a waste of opportunity to leave it unknown. Alexander Dalrymple, the British navy's chief hydrographer, envisaged Terra Australis as 'sufficient to maintain the power, dominion and sovereignty of Britain, by employing all its manufactures and ships.' Charles de Brosses, a lawyer who was one of the most tireless propagandists for exploration in the southern seas, expressed larger and, to some minds, even more compelling reasons for seeking the fabled continent: 'What comparison can be made between the execution of a project such as this and the conquest of some ravaged little province?'[3]

Similarly, the myth of the Northwest Passage survived every disappointment in the effort to verify it, and defied every argument against it, however convincing. In 1731, for instance, an armchair promoter, the Irish MP Arthur Dobbs, argued that evidence of a tide flowing from the northwest corner of Hudson Bay was inexplicable unless 'we suppose a Western Ocean flowing in at a Straight.'[4] This was unwarranted reasoning. The Hudson's Bay Company men knew well enough that there was no way westward out of the bay: one of them, James Knight, had lost his life in the ice trying to prove it as recently as 1719. But Dobbs convinced the navy to renew the quest and, when they failed, prosecuted it with a private company. There was a market for data about the passage, and merchants obliged. Charlatans came forward with claims to knowledge of the interior of America; spurious voyages by suppositious seamen were called in aid. Not even the failure of both expeditions inspired by Dobbs in the 1740s could quench expectation, though it did shift the search for the mouth of the strait to the Pacific 'where,' wrote Henry Ellis, one of the most active promoters of the scheme, in 1750, 'it is probable the weather is milder, and the Seas clearer of ice' and 'the Passage, if such there be, more visible.'[5]

Instances accumulated of an impressive paradox: the more people learned about the world, the further their credulity stretched. Every discovery fathered a dozen speculations. Long-standing myths persisted and new ones multiplied, which proved, in their turn, hard to disprove. According to various theoretical geographers of the eighteenth century, for instance, Australia was split by straits or smothered in an inland sea; North America was traversed, if not by a Northwest Passage, by a chain of navigable waterways which crossed the continent almost without interruption. Australia must have a river like the Amazon. The Nile must conform to ancient descriptions, however ill-informed, and the Niger to those of the Renaissance; the riches of ancient Mali must be concentrated in Timbuktu; there must be liquid seas around the Poles.

Would-be myth busters or verifiers of myth had two big practical problems to sort out before their projects could advance much further: we need now to look in on their efforts. The first problem was longitude blindness, which left explorers blundering into rocks and shores in ignorance of their exact location; the second was scurvy, which condemned travelers out of reach of fresh food to pain, lassitude, and death.

Longitude

One incident displays perfectly the limitations of even the most reputedly reliable of traditional longitude-finding techniques.[6] On 9 November 1769 Mercury passed across the face of the sun while Captain Cook was in New Zealand. Cook therefore had an ideal opportunity to determine his longitude by timing the eclipse. He was, moreover, one of the most punctilious hydrographers the world has ever known. Even so, he placed New Zealand well to the east of its true position. At the best of times, the eclipse method could not be relied on. In overcast conditions, it was impossible; on a moving ship, it was impractical.

Toward the end of the seventeenth century, the invention of the reflecting octant—a quadrant-like instrument combined with a telescope—had held out new promise. This instrument used magnification to increase the accuracy of readings of the relative position of celestial bodies, 'and though the instrument shall shake by the Motion of your Ship at Sea,' wrote Newton, sketching such an invention in 1672, 'yet the Moon and Stars will move together, as if they really did touch one another in the Heavens; so that an Observation may be made exactly at sea as at land.' In the first couple of decades of the eighteenth century, refinements and streamlining produced an improved instrument, the double reflecting quadrant, and a handier version, the sextant, which became the companion of navigators on every open-sea voyage.

This was an invaluable latitude-finding device because it enabled the navigator to measure the elevation of the sun or the Pole Star with absolute confidence. In theory, it could also be used to pinpoint longitude. With a sextant, a seaman could tell the time with perfect accuracy by measuring the distance between the moon and selected stars. The navigator could then compare the time observed at his location with tables that showed the time for the same lunar distance at some standard meridian, such as that of the Paris Observatory, or that of its English counterpart, founded in 1675 at Greenwich.

It took a long time to compile those tables. They were ready by the 1760s and published in 1766 by Britain's astronomer royal, Nevil Maskelyne. Annually from then, the *Nautical Almanac* tabulated the angles measurable between sun and moon, or between pairs of small stars, at three-hourly intervals for different longitudes. But even as this technique was perfected, a new, foolproof method was already beginning to supplant it.

The prize offered by the British government was the spur. In 1714, after a series of disasters at sea, the Board of Longitude was established to award prizes for trustworthy marine devices for finding longitude. If tested to the Board's satisfaction, a device accurate to within 1 degree would command a prize of £10,000. £15,000 would be awarded to a method correct to within 40 minutes. If, on a voyage across the Atlantic between a British port and the West Indies, an invention could guarantee a result accurate to within half a degree—that is, 2 minutes of time or 30 nautical miles—the prize would be £30,000. Results like these would transform safety at sea: for the first time ever, navigators would know with reasonable certainty when they were approaching dangerous shores. The most obvious solution was a time-keeping device, if only one of sufficient reliability could be invented. A chronometer that could resist the motion of a ship, the effects of varied climes, the threats of humidity and corrosion, and variations in gravity and problems of friction would enable a navigator to keep an accurate check of the time at a standard meridian.

John Harrison—the inventor who was to solve the problem—was 21 years old when the Board was set up. His childhood fascination with clocks is well attested. When he was 12 he reputedly kept a watch under his pillow to study its motion and listen to its tick. By 1728, in pursuit of the Admiralty's prize, he had already invented two potential components of a sound marine chronometer: a pendulum of combined brass and steel, in which the different rates of shrinkage and expansion of the two metals canceled each other out; and the 'grasshopper' recoil escapement, which was virtually frictionless. He produced his first chronometer in 1735, eliminating the pendulum altogether in favor of two mutually corrective balances. This 'Number One' chronometer was probably accurate enough to win the Board's prize. But emulous competitors and self-interested critics strewed the way. Professional astronomers, such as Maskelyne, found it hard to believe that a craftsman like Harrison could improve on the efforts of scientists like themselves. An impartial test proved hard to arrange.

At first, Harrison's innovations secured little improvement. At length, however, his 'Number Four' chronometer enhanced both the performance and the convenience of his earlier efforts. Instead of a cumbrous piece of machinery, he produced a readily portable invention, resembling a large pocket watch, which needed no special means of suspension but could be stowed in a box and consulted at a glance. When tested in 1761 on a transatlantic voyage, it proved accurate to within 1¼ minutes of longitude or 5 seconds of time. After five months at sea and a bad passage home from Jamaica, it was still only 1 minute 54½ seconds out, or 28½ minutes of longitude, or 18 statute miles. By the 1770s the device had passed all tests and began to be adopted as standard sea-going equipment.

Coping with Scurvy

Meanwhile, the struggle for the other prerequisite of progress—a preventive and cure against scurvy—continued at an even more painful pace. Henry Ellis[7] reported the symptoms.

> Our men when first seized with it, began to droop, to grow heavy, listless, and at length indolent to the last degree: a tightness in the chest, pains in the breast, and a great difficulty in breathing followed; then ensued livid spots

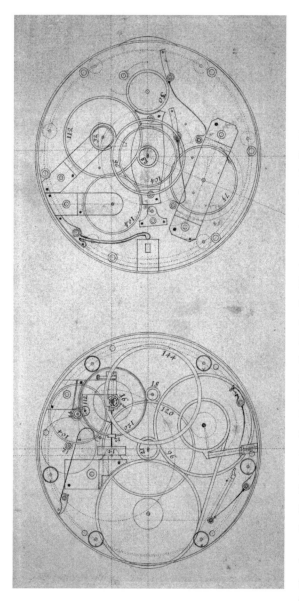

upon the thighs, swelled legs, contraction of the limbs, putrid gums, teeth loose, a coagulation of the blood upon and near the backbone, with countenances bloated and sallow. The symptoms, continually increasing till at length Death carried them off, either by a flux or a dropsy.[8]

Sufferers, moreover, could not easily take food and succumbed to starvation. Lassitude accompanied the affliction and could be fatal in itself in the exigent conditions of exploration. Old wounds opened and bled, worsening the patients' weakness.

The apparent links between scurvy and sea voyages misled physicians, who assumed that humidity or salinity must be the causes of the disease. Association with crowded shipboard conditions encouraged belief that it was contagious or infectious. Henry Ellis blamed drink. The notion that fresh victuals might help arose in the late sixteenth century, thanks in part to Renaissance humanism. Readers of Galen—and that ancient Greek authority still had many devotees in the medical profession—noted his recommendation of lemons as a 'warm' fruit. More influential was the knowledge Spanish physicians accumulated in the New World, where they saw plenty of scurvy cases and had access to the pharmacopoeia of ethnobotany.

In the 1560s, the Franciscan Fray Juan de Torquemada vividly described the horror of treating men in agony, who could not bear to be touched or clothed, and who wasted for want of solid food. He recommended a native remedy—a couple of ingestions of wild pineapple: 'and God gave this fruit such virtue that it reverses the swelling of the gums and makes them grip the teeth, and cleans them, and expels all the putrescence and pus from the gums.' As early as 1569, Sebastián Vizcaino noted on transpacific voyages that 'there was no medicine . . . nor any other human cure against this disease; or if there was such a cure it was fresh food alone and plenty of it.' By the end of the century, Spanish physicians regularly prescribed fruit, especially lemons and oranges.

John Harrison's Number Four chronometer, showing the movement of his longitudinal timekeeper. The illustration was designed and drawn by Harrison c.1760–72

For Spanish crews it was relatively easy to get fresh fruit, because they had free access to the harbors of their far-flung empire. For less privileged nations, it was harder. A crisis in the history of the disease occurred in 1740–4, when George Anson lost almost 1,400 out of a complement of 1,900 men during a voyage around the world. Scurvy was only the worst of a plague of deficiency diseases that visited the voyage, including beriberi, blindness, 'idiotism, lunacy, convulsions,'[9] but Anson's experience provoked at last a systematic inquiry into how to treat it. James Lind, a naval surgeon who had seen service in the West Indies, tried out a large selection of the remedies previously proposed on a sample of twelve patients at sea, including such unpromising suggestions as seawater, 'gutts of elixir of vitriol'—drops of a solution of sulfuric acid—and an ominous mixture of garlic, mustard, radish, quinine and myrrh.

> Their cases were as similar as I could have them. They all in general had putrid gums, the spots and lassitude, with weakness of the knees. They lay together in one place . . . and had one diet common to all, viz., water gruel sweetened with sugar in the morning; fresh mutton-broth oftentimes for dinner; at other times puddings, boiled biscuit with sugar, etc., and for supper, barley and raisins, rice and currants, sago and wine, or the like. Two of these were ordered each a quart of cider a day. Two others took twenty-five gutts of elixir of vitriol three times a day, upon an empty stomach, using a gargle strongly acidulated with it for their mouths. Two others took two spoonfuls of vinegar three times a day, upon an empty stomach, having their gruels and other foods well acidulated with it, as also the gargle for their mouth. Two of the worst patients . . . were put under a course of seawater. Of this they drank half a pint every day, and sometimes more or less as it operated by way of gentle physic. Two other had each two oranges and one lemon given to them every day. These they ate with greediness, at different times, upon an empty stomach. They continued but six days under this course, having consumed the quantity that could be spared. The two remaining patients took the bigness of a nutmeg three times a day of an electuary recommended by a hospital surgeon, made of garlic, mustard seed, *Radix raphana*, balsam of Peru and gum myrrh; using for common drink, barley water well acidulated with tamarinds; by a decoction of which, with the addition of cream of tartar, they were gently purged three or four times during the course. The consequence was that the most sudden and visible good effects were perceived from the use of the oranges and lemons; one of those who had taken them, being at the end of six days fit for duty.[10]

The cider drinkers showed a slight improvement. Everybody else got worse.

Lind had discovered a cure, but not a preventive; for there was still no way of preserving oranges and lemons at sea for long enough to secure the health of the crews. Nor was it clear from his work that citrus fruits would work for all patients: the theory of humors retained a residual hold on physicians' minds and universal cures were distrusted as quackery.

During the 1750s and early 1760s, at least forty publications appeared in Britain alone with proposals for dealing with the disease. Richard Mead, who studied Anson's records and recollections, despaired of a solution: he concluded that sea air was irremediably unhealthful. Tar water was widely recommended for no apparent reason. Lind's own proposal was to issue rations of concentrated lemon juice; but the process destroyed the ascorbic acid and cost more than the Admiralty was willing to pay. John Huxham advocated the addition of cider to ships' rations, but the modest beneficial effects of this beverage vanished when it was stored aboard ship. Gilbert Blane realized that the therapeutic properties of fruit juice needed to be fortified to endure at sea and suggested adding alcohol: this kept the decoction drinkable but did not restore its effectiveness. David MacBride advocated unfermented malt, which, recommended by its cheapness, was adopted by the Royal Navy but was utterly inefficacious. It had the enthusiastic endorsement of Johann Reinhold Forster, the shipboard physician of Cook's voyage of 1772–5, though for the printed edition of his journal the recommendation was deleted.[11]

A surgeon with experience of Russian Arctic exploration advised 'warm reindeer blood, raw frozen fish, exercise,' with any edible greenstuff that might come to hand.[12] During his Pacific odyssey from 1785 to 1788 Jean-François de La Pérouse put his faith in breathing 'land air,' and mixing molasses, 'wort, spruce beer and an infusion of quinine in the crew's drinking water.'[13] 'Spruce beer' was an invention of Cook's, made of an extract from the Newfoundland spruce, mixed with molasses and pine sap and laced with spirits. It contained virtually no vitamin C.

The only vegetable food which retains reasonable quantities of ascorbic acid in a pickled state is sauerkraut, a food peculiar to Dutch ships among the navies of the early eighteenth century, but one which seemed to do good. In the 1760s and early 1770s Captain Cook's experiments convinced him of the virtues of this nostrum, which, thanks to Cook's matchless reputation, became standard-issue rations for long voyages. Cook virtually eliminated deaths from scurvy, after zealous trials of all the recommended remedies. His success was assisted by his regime of cleanliness, enforced by iron discipline. But until a way was discovered to preserve the juice of citrus fruits cheaply and without destroying the ascorbic acid, every substitute was of limited value. The only effective remedy was to replenish with fresh supplies at every opportunity and to eat as much greenstuff as could be encountered wherever a ship could land, ravaging desert islands for the barely edible weeds sailors called 'scurvy grass.' By the time of the voyage of Alessandro Malaspina, the most ambitious scientific expedition of the eighteenth century, from 1789 to 1794, scurvy was virtually banished from the fleet, thanks to the conviction of the medical officer, Pedro González, that fresh fruits—especially oranges and lemons—were the essential remedies. Only one outbreak occurred in the entire course of the journey, during a voyage of fifty-six days between Acapulco and the Marianas Islands. Five men, who were weakened by dysentery contracted in Mexico, went down with the disease and only one exhibited serious symptoms. After three days ashore on Guam on a diet rich in vegetables, oranges, and lemons, he was up and about.[14] Yet other navies, which lacked the Spaniards' advantage of a large colonial empire with frequent ports of call, remained desperate for alternative diagnoses and easier cures. As late as 1795, when Spanish crews were getting the benefit of assiduous treatment with citrus fruits, George Vancouver attributed an outbreak of scurvy aboard his ship to the men's 'pernicious' practice of eating fat with their beans, though he took the opportunity of feeding grapes, apples, and onions to the crews when they reached Valparaiso.[15] The issue of lemon juice rations to English sailors began the following year.

'Scurvy grass' (Oxalis enneaphylla), *so called because it was often the only source of greenery available to mariners in extreme southern latitudes. Engraving from Malaspina's expedition of 1789–94*

The science of the disease was still not understood. Nor was it always practical to have fresh victuals to hand in mid-ocean and mid-desert or in ice-bound seas. Scurvy was not conquered; but it was now containable within limits that allowed explorers to undertake longer journeys than ever.

The Pacific: Beyond the Wind Corridors

As the problems of longitude and of scurvy receded, the length and range of explorers' efforts increased. The late eighteenth-century acceleration in Pacific exploration is a case in point. The Pacific was now an arena of unbridled competition between Britain, France, Spain, and Russia. In 1756 Charles de Brosses published *Histoire des navigations aux terres australes*, recommending 'more ample discoveries and a means of establishing a settlement.' He favored international cooperation, but conflicting interests limited the chances of that. The conclusion of the Seven Years' War in 1763 meant that all the European nations with interests in the region found those interests redoubled, while peace diverted to exploration ships and men formerly fully occupied in war. For Spain the Pacific was a dangerous frontier—the soft underbelly of an immense empire. For Britain it was an ocean of commercial opportunity. For the French, who withdrew from most of America at the end of the Seven Years' War, it represented the prospect of a new start in empire building. For Russia, imprisoned in the irony of an immense country, virtually landlocked, obstructed by ice, and penned in and pinched by narrow straits, the Pacific represented a unique route to seaborne expansion.

The results became immediately apparent. Until the 1760s, Pacific crossings stuck to routine routes and predictable trajectories. In 1765, for instance, John Byron, on a British naval expedition, ignored orders to undertake new exploration and crossed the Pacific as quickly as he could. But progress in longitude finding and antiscorbutic treatments gradually freed navigators to undertake new risks. In 1767 Philip Carteret struck south of the usual trans-pacific route from Juan Fernández and showed that Terra Australis did not lie in the previously uncharted ocean west of Easter Island. His commander, Samuel Wallis, made the first landing on Tahiti—the men at first mistook the island for 'the long wished for southern continent'[16]—and reported the sexual hospitality for which the island became famous or notorious. A French expedition was hard on his heels. Louis-Antoine de Bougainville was candid about his motives. 'Seeing that the North was closed to us, I thought of giving to my country in the Southern Hemisphere what she no longer possesses in the northern one.'[17] The political results were modest: on his way, he established a French fort on the Malouines, or Falkland Islands, but was obliged to return it to Spain in April 1767; but he reestablished contact with the New Hebrides, first reported by Quirós,[18] and he continued west as far as the Great Barrier Reef, where he was forced aside to New Guinea.

Ten years of revolutionary progress followed. Investigation of the myths of Terra Australis and the Northwest Passage became the objectives of an explorer of exceptional skill and determination, the British naval officer James Cook. After experience on the coal carriers of his native Yorkshire, he had joined the Royal Navy as an able seaman. Service in the north Atlantic in the Seven Years' War drew attention to his uncanny gifts as a coastal surveyor and chartmaker. In 1769 he went aboard an old Whitby collier to observe the Transit of Venus from Tahiti, which astronomers in London advocated as the best scientific vantage point. He returned with an explorer's vocation as intense as any the Pacific had seen since the days of Quirós,[19] and conceived the ambition to sail 'not only farther than man has been before me but as far as I think it possible for man to go.'[20]

On that first voyage, Cook's work in New Zealand was a labor of un-precedented accuracy and efficiency. He sighted New Zealand on 7 October 1769. Over the next six months he charted 4,500 kilometers of coastline. He collected data for an outline of the entire coast over 117 days' sailing at about 32 kilometers a day along the coast at a reasonable distance offshore, while taking compass bearings and making rough sketches of the shoreline and prominent features. A sextant could measure the angle between selected points. The distance between various points was measured by log line—a knotted cord trailed through a seaman's fingers at the stern of the vessel. The ship's speed was calculated by counting the number of knots that slipped through his fingers in the course of a minute. The ship then sailed along the coast to a point where several landmarks were visible at once, and the procedure was repeated.

Cook also produced what was called a running survey—the fruit of about fifty-eight days spent at anchor carrying out meticulous surveying work to provide detailed maps of all the harbors and anchorages *Endeavour* found, to save the ships of future visitors from going aground. On shore he used triangulation. Cook transferred his results daily to a 'compilation sheet' plotted to scale. Surviving examples use 10 or 16 inches to represent 1 degree of longitude. In cramped and unstable shipboard conditions converting these sheets to a series of graduated charts was a slow business, and they were com-pleted only after the *Endeavour* returned to Britain.[21] Cook also undertook a remarkably thorough exploration of the east coast of Australia, narrowly escaping shipwreck on the Great Barrier Reef. His report of his landing at Botany Bay in April 1770 inspired a new imperial venture: the colonization of New South Wales.

In the Pacific, especially when they turned away from the great wind corridors, Europeans needed native help. Though Cook gave him little credit, Tupaia, the Polynesian sage who accompanied him, was a vital guide. His character—shrewd, ingenious, proud, and obstinate—could make him hard to work with. He named over seventy islands when he first met Joseph Banks and charted seventy-four of them, though Cook found the chart hard to under-stand. Cook found him 'to know more of the geography of the islands situated in these seas, their produce and the religion, laws and customs of the inhabitants than anyone we had met.'[22]

In two further voyages of Pacific exploration he ranged the ocean with a freedom never before attained. He crossed the seventieth parallel north and the seventy-first south. By charting New Zealand, the west coast of Alaska, and the east coast of Australia, he delineated the extremities of the Pacific. He filled in most of the remaining gaps in the map, accurately locating the island groups of Polynesia, Melanesia, and the Hawai'ian archipelago. He brought a

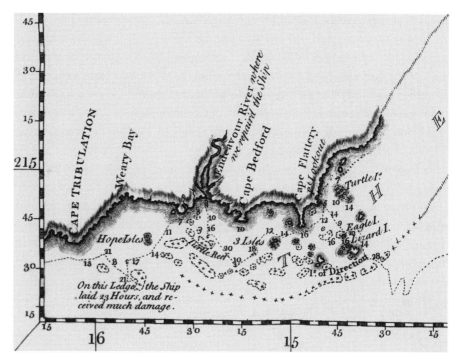

Chart engraved for a vulgarization of the time, after James Cook, of the Endeavour river area, now Cooktown, in Queensland, where Cook's ship was repaired after being damaged on the Great Barrier Reef

new precision to cartography, using John Harrison's exquisitely accurate chronometer as the 'faithful guide' of his second and third voyages. He fairly exploded the myth of Terra Australis or, at least, pushed its possible location into latitudes 'doomed to lie for ever buried under everlasting snow and ice.'[23] In the early 1770s French and Spanish expeditions had proved that there was no unknown continent north of or around the fortieth parallel south; Yves-Joseph de Kerguelen, indeed, reported that he 'had the good fortune to discover the southern continent'[24] at 50 degrees south, but it was only a tiny island. So in 1773–4 Cook went further south—to beyond 71 degrees, criss-crossing the ocean to be sure to have missed no land of substantial dimensions.

On his return, he teased potential successors:

> I had now made a circuit of the Southern Ocean in a high latitude, and traversed it in such a manner as to leave not the least room for the possibility of there being a continent, unless near the pole, and out of the reach of navigation. . . . That there may be a continent, or large tract of land, near the pole, I will not deny; on the contrary, I am of the opinion there is; and it is probable that we have seen part of it.[25]

In reality, he had seen only icebergs. But he had proved that Terra Australis did not exist on the scale previously expected. If there was a southern continent, it lay in uninhabitable latitudes. 'Thus I flatter myself,' he continued, 'that the intention of the voyage has in every respect been fully answered . . . a final end put to the searching after a Southern continent, which has at times engrossed the attention of some of the maritime powers for near two centuries past and the geographers of all ages.'[26] If anyone, he added, 'should have the resolution and perseverance to clear up this point by proceeding farther than I have done, I shall not envy him the honour of the discovery; but I will be bold to say, that the world will not be benefited by it.'[27]

In his next voyage, Cook returned to the remaining mystery: the Northwest Passage. He took an entirely new route, directly north from the Society Islands. On the way he found Hawai'i in an extraordinary 'black hole'—a gap around which Pacific exploration had swirled but which it had never penetrated. At least, no 'discovery' of Hawai'i had ever been reported in the annals of European exploration, but the inhabitants had a few iron artifacts. 'We were driven,' Cook concluded,

> to a supposition of a shipwreck of some Buccaneer, or Spanish ship, in the neighbourhood of these islands. But when it is recollected that the course of the Spanish trade from Acapulco to the Manilas is but a few degrees to the southward of the Sandwich Islands, in their passage out, and to the northward, on their return, this supposition will not appear in the least improbable.[28]

Cook continued through the Bering Strait until ice turned him back at over 70 degrees north. His comment on the Northwest Passage was similar to the conclusion he had already drawn on Terra Australis. 'I give no credit,' he wrote, 'to such vague and improbable stories, that carry their own confutation along with them.'[29] He pointed out that explorers had exploded all possibility of an inlet as far as 52 degrees north; and that the fantasies of linked rivers and lakes were incredible to any explorer of experience.

The voyage culminated in Cook's death—battered in an altercation with natives back on Hawai'i in an episode that arose from a misunderstanding still ill-understood. Was he the victim of a sudden misunderstanding or a divine sacrifice? Had he offended the natives by his importunity, or had he infringed some ritual of which he was ignorant?

His achievements, in any event, overflowed the map of the Pacific. By rigorous standards of hygiene and nutrition aboard ship he contributed to the suppression of scurvy. He mooted the colonization of Australia and New Zealand. His ships brought back sketches and specimens of creation—human, botanical, and zoological—which helped to equip the science of the age of reason and stimulate the sensibilities of the age of Romanticism. The kangaroo George Stubbs painted in 1772—a reconstruction from a pelt Cook brought

Kangaroo, *by George Stubbs, c.1771–2*

home—seemed to scent the possibilities, sniffing quizzically over a hazily limitless landscape.

Cook was the spearhead of an enormous scientific invasion of the Pacific by late eighteenth- and early nineteenth-century expeditions from France, Spain, and Russia. Between them they acquainted the European public as never before with the dimensions and diversity of the ocean. It was now possible to conceive it as a geographical unit, though it could not begin to become an economic zone until the power of the steamship made its proportions manageable.

In 1785 Jean-François de Galaup de La Pérouse set off—it is hardly an exaggeration to say—to check for what Cook might have missed. La Pérouse's plan began by paying tribute to his predecessor:

> But although this voyager, famous for all time, has greatly increased our geographical knowledge; although the globe he travelled through in every direction where seas of ice did not halt his progress, is known well enough for us to be sure that no continent exists where Europeans have not landed; we still lack a full knowledge of the earth and particularly of the Northwest coast of America, of the coast of Asia which faces it, and of islands that must lie scattered in the seas separating these two continents. The position of several islands shown to lie in the southern ocean between Africa and America, whose existence is known only from reports made by the navigators who discovered them, has not yet even been determined; and in eastern seas several areas are still only roughly sketched out. Consequently a great deal remains to be done by a nation that is prepared to undertake the completion of the description of the globe. The Portuguese, the Spanish and the Dutch in earlier times, and the English in the present century, have opened up new routes to navigation; and everything seems to invite the French who share the empire of the seas with them, to perfect a work of which, until now, they have only done a small share.[30]

La Pérouse ranged widely but achieved little. On the Northwest Passage, he already agreed with Cook that 'this passage is but a dream.'[31] He penetrated

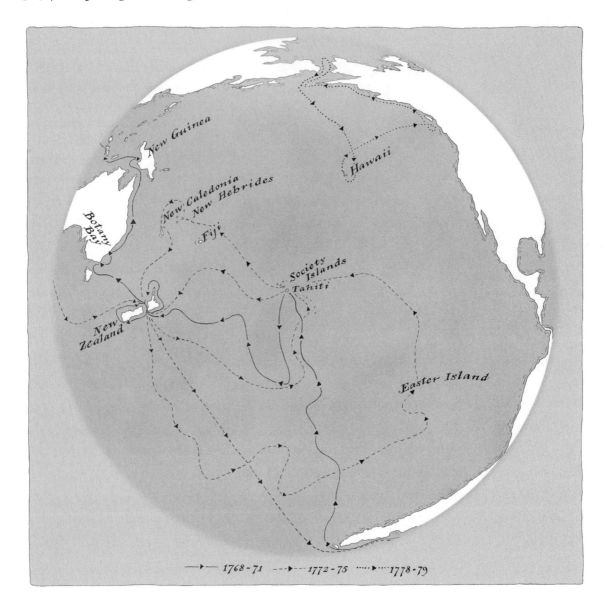

New Guinea

Hawaii

New Caledonia
New Hebrides

Botany
Bay

Fiji

Society
Islands
Tahiti

New
Zealand

Easter Island

——▸—— 1768-71   --▸--- 1772-75   ┄┄▸ 1778-79

every part of the Pacific—then vanished as thoroughly as the crew of the *Marie Céleste*. Louis Antoine d'Entrecasteaux was sent to look for him in 1791–3. He combed the ocean and added previously unrecorded islands—Rossel, the Trobriands, the Entrecasteaux Isles—to the map; but he died in the attempt, together with many of his crew, smitten with scurvy and dysentery. No clue emerged about what happened to the lost explorers.

Pacific expeditions of Captain Cook

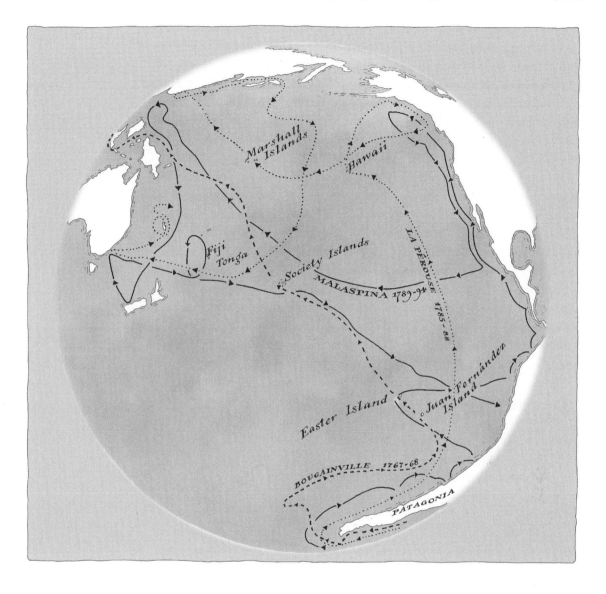

*Cook's French and
Spanish rivals*

Meanwhile, the active nature of French and British interventions in the
Pacific stung Spain into emulation. This was not solely or even primarily
because Spaniards feared or resented foreigners' intrusion into an ocean they
formerly had largely to themselves. It was the scientific profile of the French
and British explorations that really evoked a response in Spanish minds. The
Spanish monarchy of the day spent incomparably the biggest scientific budget
of any European state. The New World empire was like a vast laboratory for

experiments and an enormous repository of specimens. Carlos III loved every aspect of physical and mechanical science, from clockmaking to archeology, from ballooning to forestry. In the last four decades of the eighteenth century, an astonishing series of research missions traversed the Spanish empire. Botanical expeditions to New Granada, Mexico, Peru, and Chile gathered up much of the florilegium of America. The most ambitious of all the expeditions was the voyage to the Americas and across the Pacific led by a Neapolitan subject of the Spanish crown, Alessandro Malaspina.

He sailed in 1789 with explicitly scientific and avowedly moral goals: 'the progress,' he said, 'of navigation, of geography, and of humanity.' Some of the leading scientists of the day accompanied him. The quest for study collections of botanical, zoological, chemical, and physical specimens was entrusted to the Spaniard Antonio Pineda, Luis Neé, a Frenchman by origin, and the Czech Thaddeus Haenke. Experts in mineralogy and medicine were also aboard. In addition, various naval officers who took part were experts in the hydrographic tasks assigned to the expedition. All the participants shared the various tasks and contributed to the less specialized jobs, garnering the ethnographic and linguistic data available on the coasts of the Americas and among the islands of the ocean.

The scientific work was impressive: in the Museo Naval, Madrid, more than 300 journals and logbooks survive, 450 albums of astronomical observations, 1,500 hydrographic reports, 183 charts, 361 views of coastal elevations, and more than 800 drawings, mainly of botanical and ethnographical materials. Neé collected almost 16,000 plants and seeds for the Real Jardín Botánico. The expedition made important contributions to the study of volcanoes and thermal springs. The ethnographical discoveries were of great value for the debate about the 'noble savage' and for the development of a concept of a moral community inclusive of all humankind. As Dolores Higueras of the Museo Naval has pointed out, the data the Malaspina expedition generated amounts to the greatest accumulation of scientific materials of its day.

How, then, did this outstanding contribution to the science of the Enlightenment become cloaked by obscurity and almost unstudied until the late twentieth century? The Malaspina mission was more than merely scientific. Malaspina was also charged with reviewing the political and economic state of the Spanish empire.[32] As a liberal of the Enlightenment, Malaspina made predictable recommendations. The colonies, he thought, should enjoy greater autonomy and even independence under the scepter of a member of the Spanish royal house. Free trade would enrich them without damaging the political relationship—the 'family compact' Malaspina proposed as the future of Spanish America.

There was a moment when the Spanish New World might have been saved from the bloody revolutions that threatened. But Malaspina's vision was unfulfilled. When he got back to Spain in 1794, he found that the effects of the French Revolution had transformed everything. The court was paralysed by fear of political change. A reactionary ministry had replaced Malaspina's friends in government. The good intentions with which the expedition had set sail four years before were now regarded as incendiary and treasonable. Malaspina was jailed. The reports and collections he brought back were confided to lock and key with a strict prohibition against their publication. Malaspina became 'more famous for his misfortunes than for his discoveries.'[33] The expedition was conceived with the aim of equaling or surpassing the scientific researches of its English and French predecessors, and there is no doubt that the aim had been achieved. But history intervened and the voyages of Cook, La Pérouse, and Bougainville continue to dominate historical scholarship and the historical imagination.

The Return to the Northwest Passage

In the 1790s, attention became focused on the extremities of the diagonal Cook had explored, in Australia and, especially, Alaska, where British merchants' ambitions drove the world toward crisis. The establishment of a British trading station at Friendly Cove on Nootka Sound in 1788 linked two routes: one operated by fur traders across the Pacific, via Hawai'i, to link up with oceanic routes to European markets; the other a projected route, envisaged by John Meares, an English naval officer who had many connections in the China trade and who practiced 'man-on-the-spotism,' linking Canton with Pacific North America.

A race to the extremities and unpenetrated wastes of North America was on. Empires stretched feeble fingertips to meet at the limits of their reach. Spanish agents raised their flag on the upper Missouri; in the fledgling United States, Thomas Jefferson began to imagine the incorporation, for science and empire, of barely envisaged expanses of desert and mountain beyond that river; British expeditions from Canada probed the edges of the Arctic Ocean in the far northwest; Russians hoped to preempt rivals on patches of the Pacific coast as yet unsecured by Spain. The Spanish authorities were already alarmed at the establishment of Russian trading stations on the coast and the frequency of whalers' visits to harbours in the far south of the South American cone, and were sending out patrols to turn foreign shipping away or impound recalcitrant vessels. In July 1789, the Spaniards turned the British merchants out of Nootka

Sound and appropriated the labor of their Chinese colliers to build a Spanish base. The British government decided to enforce its own subjects' right to trade at Nootka but not to attempt to interfere with peaceful Spanish trade.[34] The parties prepared for war and rattled sabers, but came to a peaceful accommodation: the British got their establishment back and the right to touch uninhabited portions of the Pacific American coast in the far north and south for watering and refuge. In return, they promised to stay well away from Spanish colonies.

This was a great encouragement to explorers in the north. The British moved at once to take advantage of the concessions made by Spain by reestablishing a Nootka base

with a view to the opening a commercial intercourse with the natives, as for establishing a line of communication across the continent of north America, and thereby to prevent any future intrusion, by securing to this country the possession of those parts which lie at the back of Canada and Hudson's Bay, as well as the navigation by such lakes as are already known or may hereafter be discovered.[35]

Completion of the crossing of North America

The mission was entrusted to George Vancouver, who as a young midshipman had shown his zeal for exploration on Cook's second voyage, perching on the *Resolution*'s bowsprit as she began her turn to the northward at the southernmost point of the voyage, and crying, 'Ne Plus Ultra!' Cook was his hero and his work a continuation of Cook's, making charts of the accuracy for which the master was renowned but which, on his North American excursion, he had no time to make.

Vancouver's instructions were to scour the coast from 30 to 60 degrees north. Originally, they included a line to the effect that 'the discoveries of Captain Cook and of the later navigators seem to prove that any actual Communication by sea, such as has commonly been understood by the name of a Northwest Passage, cannot be looked for with any probability of success.' In the final version, these words were crossed out and others substituted to call for 'accurate information with respect to the nature and extent of any water-communication which may tend, in any considerable degree, to facilitate intercourse, for the purposes of commerce, between the north-west coast, and the country upon the opposite side of the continent.'[36]

On balance, it seems that Vancouver was supposed to look for a series of freshwater links. In practice, he had no means of doing so, though he did manage to send boats up the Columbia River 100 miles upstream. They turned back, divided about how far away the source was, but believing that the river 'might communicate with some of the lakes on the other side of the ocean.'[37] For his part, however, Vancouver seems never to have believed in the existence of a passage and ended convinced of its impossibility. In 1792 he spent three months charting the coast and confirming the nonexistence of a passage. He was aware of 'the barrier of lofty mountains which, covered with eternal frost and snow, extend nearly in a connected chain, along the western border of the continent I believe, to its utmost Northern limits.'[38] 'I trust,' he concluded,

> the precision with which the survey of the coast of North America has been carried into effect, will remove every doubt, and set aside every opinion, of the existence of a north-west passage, or any water communication navigable for shipping, existing between the North Pacific, and the interior of the American continent, within the limits of our researches.[39]

> No navigable communication whatever exists between the North Pacific and North Atlantic Oceans, from the 30th to the 56th degree of north latitude, nor between the waters of the Pacific, nor any of the lakes or rivers in the innermost part of the continent of North America.[40]

Hope, however, continued to triumph over experience. Russian expeditions dispatched to investigate rumors excited by Cook's appearance in those waters produced admirable maps of the Alaskan coast, which remained unknown in western Europe, and which mapped features—especially native settlements—otherwise unrecorded. In 1816 Otto von Kotzebue entered one of the earlier discoveries, Kotzebue Bay, mistaking it at first for the longed-for passage. In 1820 M. N. Vasiliev and G. S. Shishmarev reached beyond 71 degrees north, keeping a wary eye for a Northwest Passage while concentrated on prospecting for hunting grounds for sea otter pelts. In 1824 Russia dispatched an overland expedition to preempt the English in the region, and, in particular, to find the coordinates of the mouth of the Mackenzie and the northernmost reach of the Rockies. 'They could,' according to the explorers' brief, 'be accepted as a natural frontier between the possessions of our American Company and that of England.'[41]

Meanwhile, wars convulsed Europe—unleashed by the French Revolution and sustained by the ambitions and enemies of Napoleon. In a sense, they stimulated science, because Napoleon attached high value to scientific prestige. But they also interrupted expeditions. The greatest scientific traveler of the age, Alexander von Humboldt, kept finding his plans frustrated: in 1798 he intended to study hydrography on the Nile, but a French invasion stopped him. In 1812 he planned to investigate magnetism in Siberia, but Napoleon launched his ill-starred invasion at the most inopportune moment. Moreover, war absorbed money, ships, and naval personnel who might otherwise have been available for exploration. By 1815, however, the wars were over, liberating plenty of vessels and nautical expertise.

The British government, at first, and then British private patrons renewed the quest. But they did so in a new spirit. Patriotic pride exempts explorers from sanity. The search for the Northwest Passage became a pathological quest, an irrational obsession, which men pursued as if blinded by the snow and maddened by the ice. Vowing they would ne'er return, they returned lovelessly, under a fascination they begrudged and an impulse they resented. Everyone who took part was aware that—in the words of William Scoresby, a scientist with much whaling experience who was widely regarded as the best authority on boreal seas—'as affording a navigation to the Pacific Ocean, the discovery of a northwest passage would be of no service.'[42] It was evidently going to be too long and laborious a business to be profitable. Scoresby believed that 'if such a passage does exist, it will be found only at intervals of some years: this I deduce from attentive observation of the nature, drift and general outline of the polar ice.'[43] Events would prove him right. No ship could cross the American Arctic in a single sailing season; and years might elapse without a summer warm enough to melt sufficient ice for a ship to get through. But despite the poor prospects and elusive rewards, patriotic fervor, scientific curiosity, and a new desire to defy previously indomitable environments were enough to keep the effort going.

Renewed attempts via the west coast of Greenland and to either side of Baffin Bay led only to the perilous ice that threatened to crush William Parry's ship in Viscount Melville Sound in 1820 during the first winter he spent immured in it. Parry was a career navy man, with long and—to most minds dreary—experience as a commander of whaling escort vessels. But he loved ice. Parry used canned food to keep his men alive and amateur theatricals to buoy their spirits. The expedition's survival proved a snare to successors. Parry knew in his heart that his quest was impossible: there was simply too much ice to get through; but he had staked his reputation on success and was obliged to go on militating for more expeditions, and more sacrifices.

Meanwhile, John Franklin, a modest naval lieutenant of no prior reputation, notable for his lumbering gait and almost dim-witted determination, under-

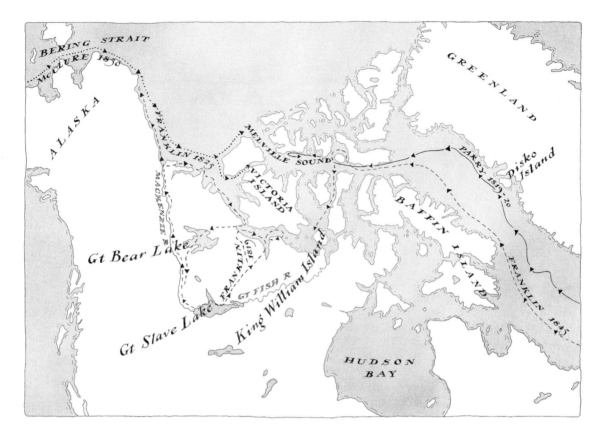

Seekers of the Northwest Passage, 1819–1850

took a coastal survey by land and inshore canoe, intended to complement the seaborne efforts. By the end he was eating spare shoes, grubs plucked from old deerskins, and lichen scraped from the rocks. One of his men went mad and slaughtered three or four companions for cannibalism. On his last survey, commissioned in 1826, he reformed his methods entirely. He hired a fishing expert to help feed his crew and took light boats that could be broken up for portage, 'packed like a large umbrella'[44] and easily reassembled in twenty minutes. He and his men explored 5,000 miles of coastline and mapped much of it. The result confirmed that there was no navigable route along the coast.

Private enterprise evoked the sneers of the naval establishment. There were plenty of ice-struck naval personnel, demobilized or on half-pay, for them to recruit. Among the most determined and most drawn to the ice was John Ross. In 1829–30, when Ross was 53 years old and had spent forty-three of them in naval service, a private philanthropist funded him on an expedition that spent two winters in the ice, 'in a miserable kind of ship . . . for some purpose or other' in the dismissive language of an Admiralty official.[45] Really, it was a creditable venture, based on Ross's argument that the best chance of finding a

James Clark Ross's Arctic expedition in search of Franklin, 1848–9

Northwest Passage was in a shallow, engine-powered craft, close to shore. Ross spoke for many:

> amid all its brilliancy, this land, the land of ice and snow, has ever been, and will ever be a dull, dreary, heart-sinking monotonous waste, under the influence of which the mind is paralyzed, ceasing to care or to think, as it ceases to feel what might—did it occur but once, or last but one day— stimulate us by its novelty; for it is but the view of uniformity and the silence of death.[46]

In 1837, after generations of inertia, the Hudson's Bay Company sponsored an expedition to chart the coasts Franklin had left incomplete. George Simpson, the indefatigable Company administrator, appointed his nephew Thomas to the expedition. Thomas effectively took it over and wrote a rather egotistical *Narrative of Discoveries on the North Coast of America* (1845), in which he declared that 'I and I alone have the well-earned honour of uniting the Arctic to the great Western Ocean.'[47]

Franklin, meanwhile, pressed for a chance to make another attempt to find the way through the ice by sea, but it took nearly eighteen years before the Admiralty agreed. By that time he was nearly 60. The chances of success seemed good. The whole of the Arctic coast of America had been mapped. Ice-worthy ships were available. Canned food enabled them to stock with three years' provisions. But Franklin's two ships and 134 men sailed from Disko

Island off Greenland on 13 July 1845, and were never seen again. 'Only the eskimo,' sang the balladeers, 'in his skin canoe knows the fate of Lord Franklin and his gallant crew.'

Records discovered later under grisly cairns told a grim story. In September 1846 the ships were beset by ice northwest of King William Island, lured into a cul-de-sac by a season of uncharacteristically good weather. There they remained through two winters and two thaws. Franklin and thirty-four men perished of mysterious maladies—perhaps poisoning from imperfectly sealed cans. The survivors abandoned ship in April 1848 and headed south across the ice, perhaps hoping to find the Great Fish River, where there was a Hudson's Bay Company trading post. They all died on the way—some of scurvy, some of starvation, some of lead poisoning from the solder used on their food cans. Meanwhile, in England, Franklin's widow became a popular heroine—personification of a Victorian ideal of womanhood: first, the patient wife waiting for her husband's homecoming; then the stoical widow sacrificing her fortune to search for his body.

The relief parties she lobbied for came too late. In 1853, however, one of them found the passage Franklin had sought. On 25 October, Robert McClure, approaching from the west, reached the point in Melville Sound at which Parry had turned back thirty years before. The Northwest Passage existed: McClure could see it. But, clogged with ice, it still eluded navigation. McClure bent to the task with fanatical devotion, forgetting Franklin in his frenzy to complete the passage. He wintered beyond the range of his rations. He cut his men down to one meal a day and halved their lemon juice allowance. He stinted the use of coal and oil even in record-breakingly low temperatures. When rescuers arrived, he tried to turn them away, even though his men were dying or going mad around him. All he could do was to walk across the last ice that barred the passage. The Northwest Passage was useless to commercial shipping: an unreliable labyrinth through waters which, when not choked by ice, were infested with icebergs.

Antarctica

A parallel struggle with extreme cold was going on around the edges of Antarctica. Cook had found the South Sandwich Islands on his last voyage, in latitudes where krill fills the sea, attracting innumerable seals and whales. A midshipman described the seals' favored haunts, 'where the surf breaks with great violence. . . . Every spot of sand . . . is literally covered with them,' wallowing, mired in the feces of penguins.[48] In the late eighteenth and early nineteenth centuries, sealing became so intense in the region that colonies of the creatures were exterminated in successive locations, and the hunters could never relent in the search for new grounds. Sealers had an incentive to find the remotest, coldest lands. On their way, they muddled the map, reporting spurious islands, and possible mainlands, raising in scientists' minds back home problems of the relationship of ice and land that required verification on the spot. Perhaps Terra Australis did not exist at all. Perhaps sea stretched to the Pole. The sealers' discoveries demanded official attention. They were important not only for the European powers with existing competitive interests in the area but also for the new South American republics of Chile and Argentina, as they emerged in the early nineteenth century from the bloody wars that ended in the separation of the Latin American states from the Spanish monarchy.

In 1819 Faddei Bellingshausen was chosen to resume Russia's search for a Pacific empire. He was a veteran of a round-the-world voyage of 1803–6, which had discovered a previously uncharted island in the Hawai'ian archipelago and mapped much of the west coast of Japan during an unsuccessful attempt to open trade with that country. Now his task was to find new harbors to make Russian navigation between oceans independent of other powers. He failed. But he had a personal objective, too: to reconstruct the route of his hero, Cook. Having surveyed the South Sandwich Islands en route, he probed the ice pack to their south. After spending the winter in Australia and New Zealand, he returned to discover Ostrov Petra and Alexandra Island, which he mistook for a continental shore, and numerous other islands. On 27 January at 60 degrees 23 south, as one of his crew recorded, 'we encountered an ice sheet of extreme height.' The snow closed in, obscuring a momentarily glimpsed 'wonderful view.' They pressed southward, but 'we kept encountering the ice continent each time we approached.' Bellingshausen put this 'continent of ice behind small floes and islands' at 69 degrees 7 minutes 37 seconds south and longitude 16 degrees 15 east. It had 'edges broken perpendicularly and stretched beyond the limit of our vision, sloping up towards the south like a shore.'[49]

One of the sealers—an exceptionally learned and communicative member of a generally single-minded and secretive profession—was William Smith. He discovered land to the south of Cape Horn in 1819, while hiring out his vessel on a commercial venture from Buenos Aires to Valparaiso with a cargo including tobacco, pianos, and eau de cologne. He pressed south to above 60 degrees, in the hope of avoiding the westerly winds. He sighted land again intermittently in the same vicinity on the return voyage, concluding that he was off a long coastline, which he estimated at 250 miles. He was ridiculed—not altogether unjustly. He had discovered the South Shetlands.

He returned at the beginning of the following year under the command of Edward Bransfield, master of a naval vessel that was on patrol off the Chilean coast, to safeguard British interests during the independence struggle that was then in progress on shore. They picked their way along the southern shores of the islands. On 30 January the fog cleared. They saw a vast shore, 'half encompassed with islands,' with a 'high rude range running in a NE and SW direction.' They had no doubt that it was a mainland, though they stood off as soon as the fog closed in again and made them afraid for their safety. They named it Trinity Land after the building in London that housed the office of the Admiralty. 'That New South Britain,' thought the young midshipman who accompanied the voyage, 'may add another Fishery to the crown of Great Britain remains only to be proved by the arrival of a few ships on her shores whose expedition in filling will at once decide how profitable a harvest may be reaped—and this will be found to consist of whale oil, sea elephant oil and seal skins.'[50]

The seas off Antarctica were getting busy. Smith met Nathaniel Palmer, of Stonington, Connecticut, who was looking for new sealing grounds. In 1821 he joined a vessel commanded by George Powell, who discovered Coronation Island in the South Orkneys and made the first detailed charts. It was typical of the sealers' intense exploration of the region that within a few days James Weddell arrived to make a cull. On his return voyage in 1823 Weddell had explicit instructions to 'prosecute a search beyond the track of former navigators.' He sailed south, between 30 and 40 degrees west further than anyone previously, to beyond 74 degrees 30 without finding land or even much ice. The location and extent of the continent were now major puzzles. Weddell himself believed there might be sea all the way to the Pole.[51] The myth of an Antarctic Ocean was eroding Terra Australis into oblivion.

Expeditions with scientific teams, including hydrographers and geologists, flocked to the rocks of Antarctica. By the mid-1830s competing expeditions converged from far and wide. From France came Jules-Sébastien-César Dumont d'Urville, a polymath more famous as the connoisseur who purchased the Venus de Milo for France. He added Terre Adélie to the map during his voyage of 1837–40. The United States was bound to take an interest. The traders of New England relied on the westerlies of the southern oceans to communicate with the world. The whalers and sealers of the region were implicated in the southward drive for new hunting grounds. The United States, meanwhile, was chasing manifest destiny across North America. The acquisition of the republic of California gave the States a window onto the Pacific, which the beginnings of settlement in Oregon in the 1840s would soon widen. Americans' reluctance to involve government in overseas adventures matched the US government's reluctance to be involved. But it was practically impossible for Americans to sit back and let competitors preempt them in a region of untold commercial potential. In 1836 Congress voted for an expedition 'to the South Seas.' Charles Wilkes, who led it, proved to be a poor observer (and a disastrous commander of men, whose expedition ended in bitterly exchanged recriminations with his officers and a series of embarrassing courts martial). Dumont beat him to the portion of coast he claimed to discover. Wilkes, however, registered a meritorious achievement: hugging the Antarctic coast for 1,500 miles, he demonstrated that there was a continuous land mass there, not a mere mass of islands.[52]

James Clark Ross outdid him for Britain—or at least, so he claimed. Wilkes injudiciously sent him a rough map of his route, which Ross used to denigrate his rival, pointing out errors, hinting that Wilkes was a liar or a fool. Ross had plenty of experience of ice worlds. He had accompanied his uncle John Ross in his quests for the Northwest Passage. In 1829 he had taken part in a voyage north from Spitzbergen in search of the North Pole, abandoned at 82 degrees 48½ north—a record unbroken for another fifty years.[53] He had determined the location of magnetic North on the Boothia peninsula in Canada in 1831. Now, he was on a mission to locate its antipoint, dreaming of being the man 'to plant the flag of our country on both the magnetic poles of our globe.'

His expedition left England in 1839 in mortar-bearing vessels, chosen for the strength of construction that enabled them to withstand the kick of the mortars. In the course of the voyage he identified much of the coast of Antarctica. His account is brilliant with the glare of ice flows. His style juxtaposes exalted language and many poetic and pious invocations of God with charming details of daily life—a glass of cherry brandy to toast success in penetrating the ice pack, a penguin butchered or a petrel shot, hydrocyanic acid to kill penguins.

On New Year's Day 1841 he crossed the Antarctic Circle. A few days later his ships nosed into the ice. They made little headway at first. On 9 January, as the fog rose, they were in a clear sea. 'At noon we had a most cheering and extensive view: not a particle of ice was to be seen from the masthead.' On 11 January 1841 they came upon what they called Victoria Land. On the same day, they passed Cook's furthest south. On the 23rd, they broke Weddell's record when they passed 74 degrees 15 south. They sailed on to Franklin Island, and sighted the volcanoes they named Mount Erebus and Mount Terror. The mountains that covered the site of the southern magnetic pole were within sight. Every indentation was filled with ice. Ross's frustration and pride are both apparent in his letter to Prince Albert.

It is some satisfaction to have approached the pole more nearly by some hundreds of miles than any of our predecessors, and from the multitude of observations that have been made in both ships . . . its position may be determined with nearly as much accuracy as if we had actually reached the desired spot.[54]

He lost his smile and even his love of the ice, declaring 'he would not conduct another expedition to the south pole for any money or pension to boot.'[55]

Australia

The story of Australian exploration is inseparable from that of the adjoining Pacific and Antarctic regions. Like Antarctica, Australia was a magnet of myth, luring seekers of the 'great southern continent,' and a secret environment, challenging to circumnavigate and defiantly hard to penetrate. In the 1790s, Matthew Flinders and George Bass established that a strait separated Tasmania from what came to be called Australia, raising a presumption that more straits might cleave Australia into islands, or into accessible portions. Between 1801 and 1803 French and English expeditions between them completed the circuit of Australia's coasts: Flinders actually met Nicolas Thomas Baudin in Encounter Bay on 8 April 1802. Little doubt remained of the continuous nature of the Australian land mass. But what mysteries did it enclose?

In the second decade of the new century the English colony around Sydney—still the only toehold on the mainland—began for the first time to seek routes inland in search of new pasture. The leading figure was Gregory Blaxland, a true pioneer who had migrated to Australia, without any domestic unpleasantness to evade, purely in the belief that the new frontier represented new opportunities. In May 1813, after many attempts, Blaxland found a way across the Great Dividing Range, linking the valleys of the Hunter and Namoi. There he saw 'forest and grass land sufficient to feed the stock of the colony for the next thirty years.' Beyond the mountains vast fields and 'verdant plains' emerged along the Murray–Darling river system, but it took a long time for the rivers to be traced. The Macquarie marshes formed a barrier uncrossed until 1828, when Charles Sturt, the governor's secretary, followed the Murray to the point where it joined the Darling. Though Tasmania in the same period was crossed and recrossed in every direction, in continental Australia beyond the river line all was obscure, except in the vicinity of the coastal settlements founded in the 1820s and 1830s in Queensland, Victoria, and Western and South Australia.

When the Geographical Society of London was founded in 1830, its president envisaged Australia as one of its priorities.

> Hitherto a country as large as Europe has been presented on our maps as a blank. Today, as this extensive territory will, in all probability, in process of time, support a numerous population, the progeny of Britons, and may be the means of spreading the English language, laws and institutions over a great part of the Eastern Archipelago, it is presumed that every accession to our knowledge of its geographical features will be acceptable to the Society.[56]

The big problems for exploration to address arose from new myths of an Australian Amazon—some great river that might lead deep into the continent —or of inland seas like the Great Lakes.

By the 1840s few Australians had much hope that these myths might be true; but Charles Sturt was among them. In particular, he was convinced that beyond the Murray and Darling lay a great basin, somewhat like that of the North American West, where rivers drained from the rim toward an Australian counterpart of North America's Great Salt Lake—one of the newly discovered geographical curiosities of the day. In 1844 Sturt was down on his luck, out of a job, in debt, and, by his own admission, 'in despair.'[57] He proposed to undertake a glorious adventure, if the government would undertake the expense: to cross Australia from south to north and from east to west. It seemed a pointless escapade, but it offered the prospect of elucidating a matter of genuine interest: 'whether,' as Sturt's instructions from the government put it, 'in the country lying on the right banks of the Darling, there is a chain of hills trending from NE to SW . . . so as to form a great natural division of the continent, and of examining what rivers rise in this supposed chain of hills, and what appears to be the course of these rivers.'[58] The expedition set out from the recently founded southern coastal town of Adelaide in August 1844, with 7 tons of provisions and equipment on bullock carts, 200 head of sheep for a supply of fresh meat, and a whaling boat to launch on the sea he hoped to find.

Sturt was so fixated on reaching the midmost point of Australia, and finding a great lake, that between Floods Creek and Evelyn Creek, four months into his journey, he passed through a gap in the hills he was ordered to seek without noticing them. By January, he was stranded beside an oasis in the middle of a desert, without being able to move for want of other water sources within 250 miles. He had no choice but to wait for rain. When it came, in July, making the country glitter with false hopes, fresh food had run out and scurvy was rife in the camp. Yet instead of returning to Adelaide, Sturt pressed on, convinced by the salty terrain and low altitude that he was approaching a coast. From his base camp at Fort Grey, near the modern junction of Queensland, New South

Crossing Australia

Wales, and South Australia, he made sorties in every direction, encountering only deserts that even he dared not attempt to cross. By November, the water holes they would need to rely on for the return journey were drying up. Sturt himself was paralysed with scurvy, and had to be dragged back toward Adelaide.

America

Access to the Pacific remained the goal of explorers who struggled westward across North America. Revelations about the size of the continent did not entirely subvert the search for a quick route across the continent to Asia; the possibility remained that there might be another lake system west of the Great Lakes that would connect with the Pacific, as the St Lawrence joined the Atlantic. The riches and potential of America never seemed to satisfy its conquerors until the second half of the nineteenth century, when industrialization opened up new ways of exploiting the interior.

French efforts focused at first on the search for a great inland sea—presumably compounded of native reports of various lakes—that would link with rivers and enable them to speed across the continent. In 1736 the soldier turned fur trader Pierre Gaultier de Varenne de La Vérendrye reached Lake Winnipeg; this was encouraging, but the rate of flow of the Saskatchewan River was not. So La Vérendrye turned south. Late in 1738 he met the Mandans on the upper Missouri. He switched back to the north to attempt the navigation of the Saskatchewan, while his sons pressed on southward through endless prairies. Other expeditions swept the region west of St Louis, the French outpost on the middle Mississippi, from where the Mallet brothers reached Santa Fe in 1739. No sign of a lake system appeared.

The Hudson's Bay Company—the commercial consortium that effectively handled the exploitation of Canada north of the St Lawrence valley for the British crown—was forced to respond. The Company ordered northward

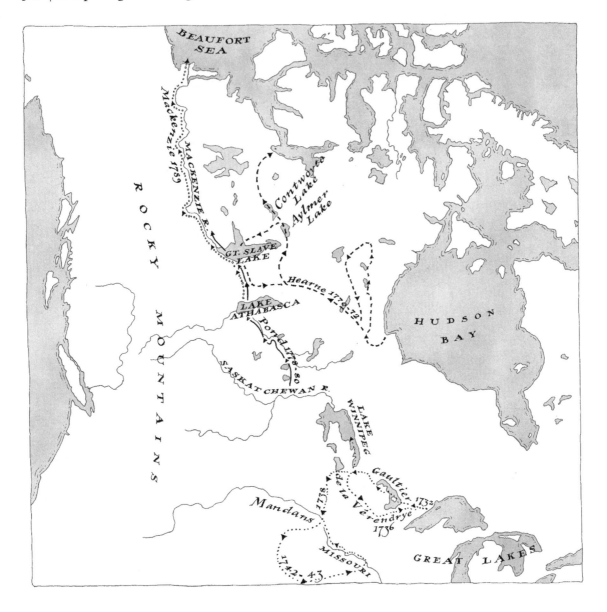

From Hudson's Bay and the Great Lakes to the Rockies and the Arctic

probes to find new trades to rival those of the French, to locate the sources of the copper used by some of the Inuit to the northwest of Hudson Bay, and to establish the northward extent of the continent, which in turn would help to show the practicability of a Northwest Passage. The further north the Arctic shore lay, the less likely it was that the sea beyond it would be navigable. In 1763 the Company's task got easier. The Treaty of Versailles handed French Canada over to Britain. In 1770–2, with Chipewyan guides, Samuel Hearne crossed

Aylmer and Contwoyto Lakes and struck overland to the Coppermine River. Canoeing down it, he reached the coast, placing it hopelessly far north—nearly 72 degrees, he thought. This was an overestimate by about 4 degrees, but it was dispiriting news for investors. The Company then concentrated on founding new trading ventures deep inland: at Cumberland House on the Saskatchewan in 1774, and Lake Athabasca in 1778. From there the Company's representative, Peter Pond, recommended a further search for a route to the Pacific via Great Slave Lake. In 1789 Alexander Mackenzie tried, down the river now named after him. But the Mackenzie led only to the Arctic. In 1793 he made another attempt, reaching the Pacific by a tortuous route.

Mountains seemed everywhere to be in the way. Spaniards had found them equally intrusive in all their attempts to find transcontinental routes to the Pacific. In the 1770s, extended Spanish navigation along the Californian coast, the discovery of wonderful harbors at San Francisco and Monterey, and the opening of a series of coastal missions whetted appetites for routes to connect northern California with settlements in New Mexico and missions in Arizona. In 1776 Spanish friars cut a stairway into sheer rock to cross the Sierra Nevada in a failed attempt to open a direct route from New Mexico to California. The range of their journeys exceeded local knowledge; so instead of on Indians, they relied on oracles to guide them, 'having implored the intercession of our most holy patrons in order that God might direct us in the way that might be most conducive to his service.'[59] Silvestre Vélez de Escalante chronicled the explorations which took them as far north as Lake Utah and back across the Colorado, at what has since been known as the Crossing of the Fathers. Misunderstanding what the Yuta Indians told them, they thought Lake Utah was part of Salt Lake: in consequence, maps of the depths of the Great Basin were long filled with a distortedly large inland sea.

One of the most enterprising missionaries, Francisco Garcés, made the attempt to trace a route across the mountains in the reverse direction; but although he was famous for his winning ways with Indians—conversing patiently in their fashion, eating and praising their food, which fellow Spaniards generally condemned as unpalatable—Hopi hostility eventually forced him to turn back near Oraibi. Spanish communications across the mountains therefore remained unsatisfactory; the Sierra Nevada continued to divide the Spanish dominions, and missions north of San Gabriel remained dependent on sea-borne links. For a moment, however, it seemed to the Spaniards that 'the door will be opened to a new empire' in the hinterland of California,[60] and missions were established accordingly on the Yuma River; but Indians wiped them out in 1781 and the effort was not renewed.

America's spine of mountains had been revealed. Their extent was baffling.

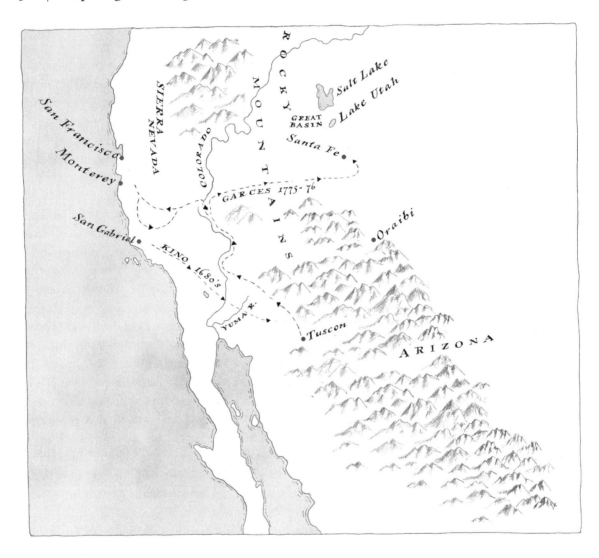

But how impenetrable were they? Where were there passes accessible to trade? Had the French and British explorers missed a lake-and-river route to the Pacific that might bypass or cleave the mountains? Attempts to answer those questions were renewed in 1804.

Spanish exploration in North America in the late seventeenth and eighteenth centuries

For the checkered history of the Louisiana territory had changed the game. In 1763 France, despairing of ever effectively colonizing the region, had off-loaded to the Spanish crown this vast and ill-defined land, comprising the Mississippi valley and much of that of the Missouri, with a disputed stretch of prairie beyond. In 1800, in a moment of imperial overenthusiasm, Napoleon claimed the territory back. In 1802, however, he recoiled from further empire building in America when rebellion in Saint-Domingue proved impossible to suppress. The following year he sold the Louisiana territory to the United States for $15 million. For Thomas Jefferson, it was the fulfillment of a hope long nourished. He speculated that 'a single day's portage might carry an expedition from the uppermost Missouri to the Columbia River and a swift descent to the sea.' He entrusted the effort to Meriwether Lewis, who had won the president's confidence as a member of his staff. Lewis in turn recruited William Clark to be his co-commander. The two leaders were perfectly matched by temperament and perfectly linked by friendship. 'I assure you, wrote Lewis to Clark, inviting him to join the expedition, 'that no man lives with whom I would prefer to undertake the difficulties of such a trip than yourself.' Lewis was urbane and reliable, Clark rash and unreflective.

Their primary objective was 'to explore the Missouri River, and such principal stream of it, as by its course and communication with the waters of the Pacific Ocean offer the most direct and practicable water communication across the continent, for the purposes of commerce.' Political objectives were paramount. The Spanish government knew what the United States wanted: a route under its own control—a 'way by which the Americans may some day extend their population and their influence up to the coasts of the South Seas.' Lewis swaggered through native American lands, claiming suzerainty, demanding redress for banditry, confirming chiefs, and at least once—among the Mandan—nominating one chief to be paramount. These political interventions were marked by bestowals of gifts. They did not mean much to the recipients, except occasions of largesse. The Mandans were always being mistaken for willing, self-inscribed subjects of 'great white fathers.'

Lewis and Clark wintered among the Mandans, acquiring the services of a precious guide. Sacajawea was the 16-year-old wife of a French trader. Her people, the Shoshone, lived athwart the passes that Lewis and Clark needed to cross to get to the far side of the Rockies. After a long spell of captivity among the Mandans, and marriage to a French trader, she had the advantage of speaking a number of languages that qualified her to be the expedition's principal interpreter. She was reputed, moreover, to be of chiefly birth among her own people. The disadvantage was that she was in an advanced stage of pregnancy; but she proved invaluable to the expedition and neither she nor her baby ever held the party up. As so often in the modern history of exploration, everyone involved, except a few great white chiefs and heroes, stays on the margins of the story, despite occupying a central place in events. Sacajawea's contribution is barely discernible in the records of the expedition, but it was obviously crucial.

As they set off up the Missouri on 7 April 1805, Lewis commended his 'little fleet' as 'not quite so respectable as those of Columbus or Captain Cook.'

> We were now about to penetrate a country at least two thousand miles in width, on which the foot of civilized man had never trodden; the good or evil it had in store for us was for experiment yet to determine, and these little vessels contained every article by which we were to expect to subsist or defend ourselves. However, as the state of mind in which we are generally gives the colouring to events, when the imagination is suffered to wander into futurity, the picture which now presented itself to me was a most pleasing one. Entertaining, as I do, the most confident hope of succeeding in a voyage which had formed a darling project in my mind for the last ten years, I could but esteem this moment of my departure as among the most happy in my life. The party are in excellent health and spirits, zealously attached to the enterprise, and anxious to proceed; not a whisper or murmur of discontent to be heard among them, but all act in unison, and with the most perfect harmony.[61]

They followed the Missouri until they could straddle it and reached the highest ridge of the mountains near the source of the Lehmi River, roughly where modern Idaho and Montana join. A short way downstream they came to salmon spawning grounds: proof that the river they were on flowed on, ultimately, to the Pacific. They were on a tributary of the Columbia river system. Many mountains lay ahead and the rivers were unnavigable, even in canoes, with heavy baggage. In October they descended the Snake River. Beyond the Cecilo Falls they found signs of the approach of their goal. Indians with European trade goods appeared—assurance that the ocean was not far away. They wintered near the mouth of the Columbia, where the constant roar of the ocean kept Lewis awake on the coast of that ill-named sea: 'and I have not seen one pacific day since my arrival in the vicinity, and its waters are foaming and perpetually break with the immense waves on the sands and rocky coasts, tempestuous and horrible.' The return journey was arduous and dispiriting. They had to barter for horses and hunt for food or scrounge both from the Indians. They mismanaged their trade goods and ran out of truck on the homeward voyage. Despite many excursions in search of a commercially exploitable route through the mountains, they could not find one. Though they cut a dashing swathe through difficult country, the expedition was a heroic failure.

The expeditions which followed demonstrated the difficulties. Much of the west seemed unworthy of exploration: it led nowhere and was effectively uninhabitable. When the French vacated Louisiana, Spanish military scouts reconnoitered routes of communication to link the Mississippi and Rio

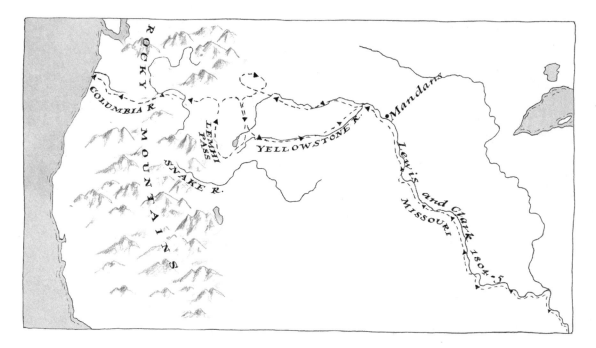

The expedition of Lewis and Clark

Grande, eventually establishing a direct trail from Santa Fe to St Louis. But these remained tenuous links between military outposts, not causeways of commerce or highways for settlement. Even after wide-ranging explorations of the rivers and plains of the west by the military, the prairie seemed a desert. Stephen Long, who commanded the operations between 1816 and 1824, and crossed the prairie along the line of the Platte River, denounced it as 'almost wholly unfit for cultivation, and of course uninhabitable by a people depending upon agriculture for their subsistence.'[62] In the novel he set on the prairie in 1827, James Fenimore Cooper agreed. Even while describing the slow invasion of white squatters, which would eventually contribute to a new look for the plains as a land of rich farms and cities, he could see there only 'a vast country, incapable of sustaining a vast population.' At the time, he was quite right. The technology that transformed the plains—the steel ploughs to bite the soil, the machined nails that built the towns, the railways that carried wood in and wheat out—had not yet arrived. The prairie, like the mountains, was an obstacle, not an opportunity, on the way west.

At first, therefore, settlement had to bypass or cross the prairie. The rich Pacific coastal territories in Oregon and California—especially from the 1830s, when California became first an independent republic, then a remote state of the union—were the target of the great pioneer drive to the west. Cheap land was the lure. In the 1820s, Jed Smith linked the Spanish trails into a continuous

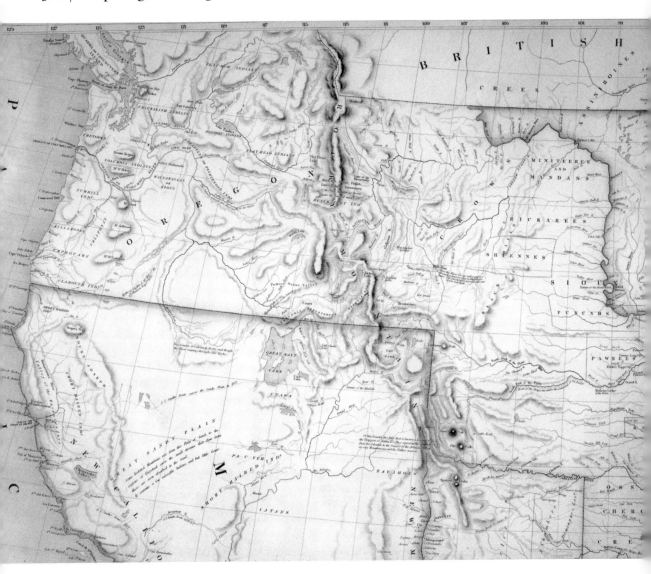

route across the Sierra. He was a trader with an oddly pantheistic religious vocation, who claimed to explore 'that I may be able to help those who stand in need.'[63] Between the lines, his copious journals disclose another motive: he could not bear his own ignorance of the country that surrounded him or accept reports he had not verified. His maps of the central Rockies and the Great Basin fed into the later, more self-consciously scientific cartography produced by federal expeditions and railway surveyors from the 1840s.

On the way to Oregon, meanwhile, propagandists advertised 'a level open trail . . . better for carriages than any turnpike in the United States.' Shrewd utopians such as the American Society for Encouraging the Settlement of the

The routes of the explorer and fur trader Jed Smith across the central Rockies and the Great Basin, 1820s. Smith's original map no longer exists; this map was made from accounts of Smith's travels by David Burr and published in 1839

Oregon Territory bought up land to sell to settlers with the promise of a 'city of Perfection' in the west. Misleading maps were available, which suggested that there was an easy river passage from Great Salt Lake along nonexistent waterways. In 1813 the *Missouri Gazette* declared that 'a journey across the continent might be performed with a wagon, there being no obstruction in the whole route that any person would dare to call a mountain.' In the year of this overoptimistic pronouncement, a party of fur traders stumbled on a pass through the Rockies that would became the vital link for the Oregon Trail. South Pass, a fairly flat plain about 32 kilometers wide around the Wind River range in Wyoming, remained unpublicized until 1824, when Jed Smith saw it on a deerskin map made by Crow Indians.

The first trading wagons crossed South Pass as early as 1824; fur traders traveled from Independence across the mountains and into Oregon in 1832. but without iron axles the wagons were too fragile for unbroken trails of this kind. In an arid climate, where, in the words of a missionary's wife in 1836, 'the Heavens over us were of brass and the earth of iron under our feet,' dried-out spokes sprang out of place and iron rims slipped from shrunken wheels.

One solution to the problem of shrinking wheels was to remove the iron rims and enlarge the wheels by nailing on extra pieces of wood—or tying them on, with rawhide cords, when the nails ran out. The iron rims were heated as much as possible, eased into place, and then shrunk by dousing with cold water. Wagons had to be manhandled up steep climbs and then lowered down cliff faces with ropes—a feat which might take eighty men to one wagon. Ravines had to be filled with rubble.

The first settler wagons to make it across set out in 1840. The party of missionaries who pioneered the venture hired a trapper, Robert 'Doc' Newell, to lead them and their two wagons from Green River, on the eastern edge of the Rockies, over the mountains to Fort Vancouver on the Williamette River. The party left Green River on 27 September and traveled as far as they could on their wagons, clearing a road as they went. When they could go no further, they shifted their goods to packhorses and stripped the wagons to their chassis. Eventually, they broke one up to provide spares for the other. When they reached Fort Walla Walla in what is now Washington State, Newell built a barge and hauled the remaining wagon along the Columbia River to the mouth of the Williamette. Newell was jubilant, if wrong, when he wrote on 19 April 1841 'that I, Robert Newell, was the first who brought wagons across the Rocky Mountains.'

The Route to Romanticism

Within North America, the routes opened up in the eighteenth and early nineteenth centuries were not primarily routes of commerce or even—except toward the end of the period, in Oregon—of colonization. But they did lead to emotionally inspiring landscapes and intellectually stimulating cultural contacts between European incomers and Native peoples. In the broadest context, the most important discovery the French made in North America was not of any of the majestic geographical features Hennepin enumerated, but of the peoples who fed the growth of the notion of the noble savage. The original 'noble savage,' explicitly so called, was a Micmac Indian of the Canadian woodland, described by Marc Lescarbot, who spent a couple of years in Nouvelle France in the early seventeenth century. He regarded the Micmac as 'truly noble' in the strictest sense of the word, because their menfolk practiced the noble occupations of hunting and arms. But they also exhibited virtues that civilization corroded: generosity ('this mutual charity which we seem to have lost'), a natural sense of law ('so they have quarrels very seldom'), common life and property. Ambition and corruption were unknown among them. But this was an imperfect Eden, where violence was often vindictive and austerity unknown in meat and drink. Nor did Lescarbot's admiration for Micmac morality make him less inclined to justify conquering them and depriving them of their sovereignty and their land.

The idea of the noble savage really became rooted in Western tradition when it transferred to the Huron, who lived southwest of the Micmac on the northeastern banks of the Great Lakes. Unlike other Iroquoian-speaking peoples, the Huron welcomed the French, because they needed allies in their perpetual wars against their neighbors. Although hard to wean from some of their pagan rituals—such as the human sacrifices in which they slowly tortured prisoners to death in ways designed to maximize pain over periods of several days—they proved remarkably hospitable to Christianity. Franciscans and Jesuits alike praised them as embodiments of natural wisdom, crediting them with skills in artisanship, building, canoe-craft, and farming and with moral superiority: kindness to strangers and to each other, and a bias toward peace with outsiders and equality among themselves. They were even credited with possession of a proto-writing system: symbols—used to scratch tree trunks with records of victories and messages about the whereabouts of game.

They became the most prolific and influential source of ideas about the nobility of savagery. The notion formulated with reference to the Micmac, who lived in the forests to the northeast, rapidly got transferred to the Huron.

Missionaries were candid in their criticisms of the defects of the savage way of life. But the secular philosophers who read the missionaries' accounts tended to accentuate the positive and eliminate the negative. Cautionary tales were filtered out of the missionary relations and only an idealized Huron remained. This transformation of tradition into legend became easier as real Huron literally disappeared—first decimated, then virtually destroyed, by the diseases to which European contagion exposed them and the wars they fought with French help against neighboring peoples.

The great secularizer of Huronophilia was Louis-Armand de Lom de L'Arce, who called himself by the title his family had sold for cash, Sieur de Lahontan. Like many refugees from a hostile acceptance world at home, he went to Canada in the 1680s and set himself up as an expert on its curiosities. The mouthpiece for his freethinking anticlericalism was an invented Huron interlocutor called Adario, with whom he walked in the woods, discussing the imperfections of biblical translations, the virtues of republicanism, and the merits of free love. His devastating satire on the Church, the monarchy, and the pretensions and pettiness of the French *haut monde* fed directly into Voltaire's tale of the 1760s of an 'ingenuous' Huron sage in Paris.

The socially inebriating potential of the Huron myth was distilled in a comedy based on Voltaire's work and performed in Paris in 1768. The Huron excels in all the virtues of noble savagery, as a huntsman, lover, and warrior against the English. He traverses the world with an intellectual's ambition: 'to see a little of how it is made.' When urged to adopt French dress, he denounces imitation as fashion 'among monkeys but not among men.' 'If he lacks enlightenment by great minds,' opines an observer, 'he has abundant sentiments, which I esteem more highly. And I fear that in becoming civilized he will be the poorer.' Victimized by a typical love triangle of the comedy of manners, the Huron exhorts the mob to breach the prison fortress of Paris, the Bastille, to rescue his imprisoned love. He is therefore arrested for sedition. 'His crime is manifest. It is an uprising.'

Meanwhile, extended exploration of the Pacific topped up the stock of images. Encounters multiplied that stretched the limits not only of peoples' knowledge of each other, but also their notions of themselves and their concepts of humankind as a whole. The specimens Pacific explorers brought home confirmed the nobility of the savage. Philibert de Commerson, the naturalist on the Bougainville expedition, praised 'the state of natural man, born essentially good, free from all preconceptions, and following, without suspicion and without remorse, the gentle impulse of an instinct that is always sure because it has not yet degenerated into reason.'[64] Bougainville brought Ahutoru home from Tahiti. The newcomer hobnobbed with scientists and aristos; the duchesse de Choiseul became his patroness. He frequented the Opera and the park, where—according to a sentimental poem by the Abbé Delille, advocate of contrivedly Romantic landscape—he clasped a tree 'he had known since his earliest days. . . . He bathes it with his tears, covers it with kisses.'[65]

Omai, a restless misfit in Polynesia, was similarly lionized in England in 1774–6. Duchesses praised his natural grace. Reynolds painted him as the embodiment of uncorrupted dignity. Lee Boo, from Palau in Micronesia, was even more adept in the assimilation of gentlemanly accomplishments; when he succumbed to smallpox in 1783, he was buried in Rotherhithe churchyard under the inscription

> Stop, reader, stop! Let Nature claim a Tear—
> A Prince of mine, *Lee Boo*, lies bury'd here.

Visitors to the Pacific found a voluptuaries' paradise, painted by William Hodges, who sailed with Captain Cook in 1772. His image of Tahiti is of a ravishing habitat for the nymphs in the foreground. One invitingly presents a tattooed behind. Another swims supine under a diaphanous film of water. The sexual hospitality of the island tried the discipline of Cook's men and broke that of Bligh's. In Diderot's influential and rather solemn satire *Supplément au voyage de Bougainville* of 1773, a French chaplain on Tahiti—'a monk in France, in Tahiti a savage'—cannot understand the attraction Tahitian girls seem to feel toward him, of which he takes full advantage. A native interlocutor explains simply that sexual desire is natural for good, natural reasons, and should not be resisted.[66] The Pacific, in short, had just the combination of liberty and license which ennobled the savage in eyes suitably disposed.

Alongside these potent cultural encounters, explorers opened up routes to a kind of self-discovery, as European intellectuals explored their own feelings, under the influence of the extended experience of the world that exploration revealed. Transmuted by the eighteenth-century cult of sensibility, the landscapes of the New World came to occupy a permanent place in the Romantic imagination. The tradition began with the beautiful and exciting drawings made by Jorge Juan and António de Ulloa.[67] Their representations of their observations always took the ostensible form of scientific diagrams but were always calculated to arouse the senses with awestruck reverence for untamed nature. Their drawings, for instance, of Cotopaxi erupting, with the phenomenon, depicted in the background, of arcs of light seen in the sky on mountain slopes at Panambarca, combines diagrammatic precision with rugged romance. The Andean settings they recorded remained the source of the most powerful Romantic images of the Americas. Cotopaxi became the favorite subject of American landscape painters. The high point of the tradition was marked by the illustrations from journeys in mountain regions, especially of the Andes, by Alexander von Humboldt in *Vues des Cordillères*, published between 1806 and 1814.

Born in the same year as Napoleon, Humboldt was a Napoleonic figure, with the same world-conquering ambitions in science as Napoleon had in war. He worked to classify natural phenomena at the highest possible level, where the whole cosmos could be arrayed in a single coherent scheme. Yet this detached scientist, whom Darwin called 'the greatest scientific traveller of all time,' was first inspired to travel by desire to see 'Nature in all her variety of grandeur and splendor.' His journeys in America were undertaken by accident, in substitution for frustrated plans to go to Egypt. At his own expense, with the goodwill of the Spanish crown, he made a hero's progress and a triumphant return.

Most of his endeavors unfolded within a framework already in place, thanks to the tremendous progress the Spanish and Portuguese authorities had made in tracing the river systems of their American empires, and establishing the borders between them in the depths of South America. Private entrepreneurs had taken a lead in these tasks in the early eighteenth century. In 1742, for instance, the prospector João de Sousa de Azevedo traced the Tapajos from its source in the Mato Grosso to the Amazon, while Manuel Felix de Lima pioneered a similar route via the Madeira. In the second half of the century, however, the initiative passed to official expeditions, chiefly because of the redrawing of the mutual limits of Spanish and Portuguese expansion in the Treaty of Madrid. In 1782 the engineer Francisco de Requena, charged with mapping the boundary, had completed the exploration of the Amazon system. When Humboldt sailed from the Orinoco to the Amazon in 1800, his voyage was hailed as a new venture; really, it was a tracing of routes well known to Indians and colonists, but not yet divulged in Europe.

Literally the highest point of Humboldt's endeavors was the ascent of Cotopaxi's twin peak, Mount Chimborazo, in the summer of 1802. It was then thought to be the highest mountain in the world, the untouched summit of creation. Humboldt's account of his climb, cleverly restrained, is a poignant litany of the cult of the unattainable so characteristic of Romanticism, so essential to its spirit. He climbed through clouds and edged along a 10-inch-wide ridge. 'To our left was a precipice of snow; to our right lay a terrifying abyss, 800 to 1000 feet deep, with huge crags of naked rock sticking out of it.' At 17,300 feet his worst discomfort was to his hands, cut on the rocks. After another hour, he was numb with cold and starting to feel nauseous and breathless. Sickened by the altitude, racked by the cold, bleeding copiously from nose and lips, he was forced to turn back just short of the top by a impassable crevasse 60 feet across and 400 feet deep. He paused only to collect a few fragments of rock 'as we foresaw that in Europe we should frequently be asked for a piece of Chimborazo. . . . All my life I have imagined that of all mortals I was the one who had risen highest in the world.' In his visual record of the mountain, he appears stooping in the foreground to pluck a botanical specimen.

Views like Humboldt's of the Andes defined a Romantic image of America for subsequent painters. Thomas Cole, the founder of the Hudson River School, started a vogue for South American settings as scenes of cosmic high drama. He painted his vision of Eden with the expulsion of Adam and Eve in 1828 after a long sketching tour in the West Indies. 'Preserved untouched since the creation,' America's mountains were 'hallowed to my soul,' he wrote, in a continent where 'all Nature is new to art.'

Africa: 'White' Men's Graves

While the Americas and the Pacific gradually became part of Europeans' 'known world,' Africa remained a 'dark continent' of the imagination and a white space on the map. The obstacles to long-range route finding, which had restrained activity in previous centuries, remained in place. The technology of the time still had no adequate solutions to the problems of malaria, of terrain, of transport, of kit, or of clothing for Europeans attempting to penetrate Africa. And though native, Arab, and Zanzibari slavers continued to develop trails, as they penetrated ever further in search of their grisly wares, their routes remained trade secrets, uncommunicated to the world.

Parts of southern Africa, however, were exceptional, where the climate was relatively temperate and the terrain accessible to bullock carts. South Africa was well mapped as far as the Orange River by the end of the eighteenth century. Between 1819 and 1854, in a prodigious series of journeys to establish and maintain Methodist missions among the Tswana and the Ndebele, Robert Moffat crossed the Kalahari. He was a former gardener whose missionary vocation had led him from a subordinate position on an aristocratic estate in England to a powerful paladin, who had converted at least one formerly troublesome African chief, known as Afrikaner, on the frontier of the Cape. In 1820 his more learned colleague John Campbell, working among the Tswana, became the first white man to reach Kureechane, the impressive chief town of the Marootze, and found the source of the Limpopo. The most spectacular trailblazers, however, were farmers of Dutch descent, trying to open up areas of settlement in the interior beyond the reach of British rule.

Penetration of the South African interior in the early nineteenth century

Trekking was already a way of life to frontier Boers whose homes were their wagons as they moved between watering holes. They had evolved the ideal vehicle with which to colonize the high veld, the plateaus of the South African interior: a tented wagon, up to 4 feet wide and 17 feet long, drawn by up to twenty oxen. They took huge droves of cattle and sheep with them—perhaps 200 head of cattle and up to 3,000 sheep per family. They crossed the fords of the middle Orange River on a front 100 miles broad. Those who then turned east to Natal had to cross the Draksenberg, which the Zulus called Quathlamba—'heaped-up and jagged.' The trekkers coaxed hundreds of their wagons up and down steep defiles. One of their most determined leaders, Louis Tregardt, sought a route to the sea that would keep the Boers independent of Britain. He reached Lourenço Marques but most of the trekkers there died of malaria.

The effort to incorporate East Africa in European awareness of the world revived when the adventure-hungry Scottish landowner James Bruce arrived in Ethiopia in 1768 to find—he said—at his own expense the source of the Nile. His claim to have made a discovery 'which had baffled the genius, industry, and inquiry of both ancients and moderns for the course of three thousand years' was wrong in almost every particular. The Blue Nile was a tributary of the Nile, not its source. The source of the Blue Nile in Lake Tana had been recorded by Pedro Páez more than a century and a half before.[68] It had been known to Ethiopians from time immemorial, and to find it Bruce had merely had to ask for the emperor to supply him with local guides. But he was a copious observer whose information about flora, fauna, and political events enormously enhanced the outside world's knowledge of Ethiopia. His return journey was a heroic escapade, crossing the Nubian desert north of Shendi before rejoining the Nile. In 1793–6 W. G. Browne sought to retrace Bruce's steps in an attempt to verify his claims; but he was refused permission to enter Ethiopia and decided instead to explore west of the Nile into Darfur, reaching El Fasher.

In one sense, the episode initiated by Bruce foreshadowed the future of exploration: his was a voyage without missionary, commercial, or imperial objectives, motivated only by Faustian yearnings for knowledge and fame. But for the time being, commerce and evangelization were the only activities likely to generate enough investment to open routes into the African interior. And Bruce and Browne had not told the merchants and missionaries what they really wanted to know about the Nile: was it connected with the Niger, the great artery of commerce of West Africa, where most European commercial interests lay?

The course of the Niger, between malarial forests and the barren Sahara, was one of the great mysteries that lured explorers. The efforts of Bruce and Browne did not dispel suspicions that the Niger might be identical with the Nile or flow into it. The assumption that the Niger flowed east left open the question of where else it might debouch: into the Atlantic on the underside of West Africa's bulge, or into the Congo, or into Lake Chad? Alternatively, it might flow west into the Atlantic or join the Gambia or Senegal: that was the information of Leo Africanus, the sixteenth-century writer who was still, at the time, reckoned to be the most authoritative source available.

As well as intriguing for its geography, the Niger was alluring for its rumored wealth. Along the river lay emporiums long associated with 'the golden trade of the Moors,' where salt was exchanged for gold.[69] The banks of the Niger, according to a speculative account of 1809, were 'as populous as those of any river in China.' The most renowned city was Timbuktu, where the ruler 'possessed an infinite quantity of pure gold' and dined off gold in a palace built with golden rivets.[70] In reality, the grandeur of Timbuktu was long past, but Europeans could not know that. None of them had yet seen it. It was not a 'forbidden city' in the same sense as Mecca or Lhasa, but the Muslim rulers would not let Christians in or, if they reached that far, let them out.

Efforts in the 1780s and 1790s to reach the river across the desert or along the Gambia or Senegal from the West African coast all came to grief. No white man, it seemed, had a constitution strong enough, or a spirit sufficiently foolhardy, to complete the journey. Then Mungo Park came along.

Park was the victim of a potentially fatal syndrome: poverty and ambition. As a newly qualified physician, only 23 years old, he developed a taste for far-flung adventure when his patron, Joseph Banks, obtained a job for him as a ship's surgeon on a sailing to Sumatra in 1793. Banks was the great manipulator at the ends of the strings of empire. He had accompanied Cook, promoted the colonization of Australia, and gathered the plants of the world at Kew Gardens. In 1788, with dining companions and fellow scientists, he formed an association for advancing 'the discovery of the interior parts of Africa,' ignorance of which was the 'reproach of the present age.' Other aims were less disinterested: as Park put it, the objectives confided to him were 'rendering the geography of Africa more familiar to my countrymen, and opening to their ambition and industry new sources of wealth and new channels of commerce.'

In 1794, after a series of would-be explorers had died on their way to the Niger, Banks was casting around for a suitably desperate character to resume the attempt. Park was admirably qualified: restless, vainglorious, irrepressible, penniless, easily biddable, insatiably curious, and indefeasibly tough. His account of his first journey in the Niger region, *Travels in the Interior Districts of Africa*, was a best-seller in 1799. The history of travel and exploration is full of stupefyingly impressive texts, but this was one of the most riveting ever. Five themes stand out: the horrors of the journey; the cheerfulness with which Park endured them; the wonder and contempt with which native peoples beheld the adventurer; the sheer impracticality of the entire endeavor; and Park's barely suppressed dissatisfaction with the range of his achievements and the scale of his rewards.

It has to be said that Park's publications, like all subsequent African explorers' narratives, were written—and therefore perhaps overwritten—for profit. They probably exaggerate hardships, embellish wonders; they certainly ladle sensationalism. Each traveler seemed determined to outdo his predecessors in improbable tales of valor, privation, and titillation. Sex is an enlivening and probably misleading presence in all the books. Pacific travelogues of the late eighteenth century had established descriptions of native sex lives and sexual hospitality as an almost inescapable source of entertainment for readers. Victorian prudery had not yet closed in. Park amused readers with an account of his 'ocular demonstration' of his uncircumcised state to prurient black women. Until the 1840s, at least, his successors included much similar material. Among those on whose accounts we must depend in the course of the rest of this chapter, Hugh Clapperton told an improbable tale of his lovelorn loss of a Fulani beauty; Richard Lander recited many instances of his bashful reticence in the face of proposals of marriage or dalliance with eager women and available girls; Dixon Denham interspersed self-praise for his moderation in the face of copiously proffered African damsels with stories of hair-raising escapes from battles with poisoned arrows bristling from his hat, and encounters with snakes, leopards, and crocodiles that would leave any reader of juvenile literature skeptical.

Park set off from England in May 1795, pausing for a few months on the Gambia to learn Mandingo and acquire a little troop of guides and servants. By the time he set off for the interior, he had also acquired malaria. How he survived the disease and endured recurring bouts of it are among the mysteries of his journey. He made good progress upriver as long as he was in country known to European slave traders. He could use their promissory notes to buy supplies, and could buy security from chiefs along the route by presenting gifts at established rates. His callow skill as a surgeon earned him extra goodwill, since bloodletting was something of a fashionable novelty along his route. In Fatteconda, the wives of the king of Bondu gigglingly got him to bleed them.

Beyond the reach of regular European traders, however, he could not count on being well received. To natives he was a freak, with an appearance monstrous because of his white skin and pinched nose, or, to Muslim communities, barbarous because uncircumcised. To rulers he was suspect as a spy; to merchants menacing as a potential rival; to Muslims contemptible as an infidel. No survival strategy was available to him, except to buy goodwill by handing over truck as he went. But as he had no means of denying the plunderers, despoilers, and extorters who waylaid him at every stage, his stock was soon depleted.

The turning point in his fortunes occurred in the land of Khaarta. Here some of the women and children took good-natured fright at his weird appearance, approaching in curiosity and scampering away in affected unease with comforting shudders. The king was affable, recognizing in Park a representative of potential trading partners. But he warned the traveler that war with neighboring peoples was imminent. The only wise course was to turn back. Park had heard such stuff often before: every community he visited was anxious to keep him from its neighbors for fear of losing a possible competitive advantage in trade with Europeans. Park treated all such warnings with insouciance. On this occasion, however, the king's advice was good, 'and perhaps I was to blame,' Park wrote, 'in not following it. But I reflected that the hot months were approaching, and I dreaded the thought of spending the rainy season in the interior of Africa. These considerations, and the aversion I felt at the idea of returning without having made a greater progress in discovery, made me determine to go forwards.'[71] Owing to the war, only one route remained open: a detour northward, toward the edge of the Sahara, into the Muslim kingdom of Ludamar.

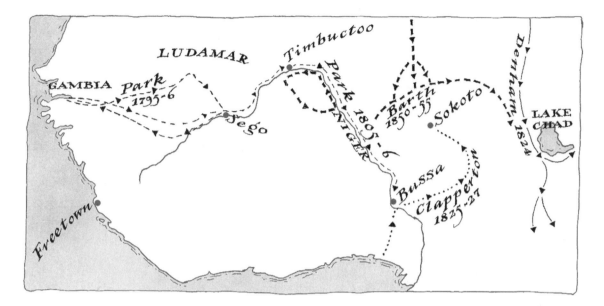

The Niger region 1795–1855

Here the king, finding that Park could not repair guns or make dyes, and even seemed incompetent as a barber, could see no use for him except as a captive in whom to display the inferiority of the infidel. He was, by his own account, penned with a hog, starved, menaced, and stripped of all his remaining possessions except his compass, which was perhaps mistaken for a demonic talisman. On 1 July, Park escaped alone and in rags, through terrible privations, without water or food, or any means of getting either, except during a chance rainstorm. After three days, he reached Fulani country, where enough people took pity on him to spare his life and even to feed him. With the last buttons off his tunic, he bought his passage to the Niger.

On 20 July, at Sego, 'I saw with infinite pleasure the great object of my mission—the long sought for majestic Niger, glittering to the morning sun, as broad as the Thames at Westminster, and flowing slowly *to the eastward*.' Park italicized the last three words, but the direction of the river no longer surprised him,

> for although I had left Europe in great hesitation on this subject, and rather believed that it ran in the contrary direction, I had made such frequent inquiries in the course of my progress, concerning this river, and received from Negroes, of different nations, such clear and decisive assurances that its general course was towards the rising sun, as scarce left any doubt on my mind.[72]

He was now among commercial communities who were aware of white men's potential profitability and prepared to deal with him on credit. Sego impressed him. 'The view of this extensive city; the numerous canoes upon the river; the crowded population, and the cultivated state of the surrounding country, formed altogether a prospect of civilisation and magnificence, which I little expected to find in the bosom of Africa.'[73]

His plan was to sail downriver to the mouth of the Niger, charting its course as he went, or at least to reach the fabled emporium of Timbuktu. He got as far as Silla. But he was destitute, 'half naked,' racked by fever, fearful of the 'merciless fanatics' whose territory he would have to cross, and apprehensive 'that I should sacrifice my life to no purpose, for my discoveries would perish with me.'[74] At the end of July 1796, he turned back. Floods and bandits almost finished him off. In Kamalia, however, he fell in with a slave dealer who, on the promise of future repayment, looked after him until he was well enough to travel again, then sent him to the coast with a slave caravan. The only available ship took him to Antigua, from where he returned to England in December 1797, where he found that everyone he knew assumed that he was dead.

Park's experiences should have been a deterrent to other explorers—and especially to himself. But his exceptionally robust constitution concealed the lethal nature of the climate, and the deadpan style of his narrative masked the evils of the journey. And he had registered an undeniable achievement. Despite being abandoned by his men and held captive by Muslim tribesmen, he confirmed what Herodotus and medieval Arab geographers had claimed: that the Niger flowed from west to east. As Park acknowledged, this only confirmed a logical inference from what was already known. But it seemed a solid enough conclusion to justify further efforts and sharpened appetites for a sight of Timbuktu and a study of navigation along the Niger.

The difficulties were reemphasized in 1800, when Friedrich Hornemann set out from Murzuk with a trading caravan south toward Bornu, where he turned west through the kingdoms of Hausaland; but he died before reaching the great river. So, in the spring of 1805, Park returned to trace the river from the interior to its mouth. He had forgotten nothing and learned nothing. He supposed that his previous error had been weakness: he needed force to protect his truck. He therefore mounted a huge expedition, protected by thirty-five soldiers supplied by the British government. This was the wrong strategy: he had survived on his first expedition only because he traveled light and seemed unthreatening. The more companions he acquired, the more victims there would be to the insalubrious country, in default of his uniquely resilient metabolism. He made an error from which his existing knowledge of the country might have spared him, relying on asses instead of native porters. These unmanageable beasts could not cope with the terrain, and had to be laboriously unloaded and reladen every day. Each ass carried twice a man's load, but required a driver; so the manpower advantage vanished. Sickness so enfeebled the soldiers that they could not defend their treasures against thievery and extortion.

The expedition was a catalog of disasters. Park's surviving notes list men abandoned or perished through sickness, and miseries inflicted by the rains, the fever, the intractability of the asses, and the depredations of enemies. All but four of the band died before Park even reached the Niger in November 1805. 'Lonely and friendless amidst the wilds of Africa,' the survivors built a boat. 'If I could not succeed in my mission,' Park wrote just before setting sail, 'I would at least die on the Niger.'[75] One of the slaves in the expedition later made his escape to Freetown on the Atlantic coast. He reported how the party had been ambushed by local inhabitants in the Bussa rapids, about 800 kilometers upriver. Park perished trying to swim for the bank.

Park was the only European known to have survived the Niger for over 300 years. The river continued to claim victims. They came, for the most part, because they had to, as servants of their states or seekers of their fortunes. The suppression of the slave trade increased the motives for exploration. Diplomacy needed to reach inland rulers whose influence could be harnessed for the cause. Trade needed new products. As soon as the Napoleonic Wars were over, the Royal Navy sent James Kingston Tuckey to sail up the Congo and verify whether the Niger joined that river. Two hundred miles upstream, faced with the Yellalla cataracts, he had to disembark and begin to struggle overland. Yellow fever struck. Within a couple of months, he and almost all his men were dead. In view of his and Park's experiences of the deadliness of approaching the Niger through the tropics, a descent from the north, across the Sahara, began to seem more practical.

An opportunity arose in 1822, when Hugh Clapperton and Dixon Denham left for Sokoto, descending from the Sahara, in order to try to open diplomatic relations with the Fulani empire as escorts to the prospective British consul in that kingdom. They hated each other. Clapperton regarded himself as contributing 'what is civil and scientific' to the expedition, and resented Denham's attempts to impose military discipline.

Denham's account of the Sahara crossing seems calculated to torture the reader with its evocations of the bone-strewn desert, scattered with eerily mangled corpses of men and camels where slave coffles had perished. He proved a dedicated explorer and managed to trace most of the shores of Lake Chad. He discovered the Shari, but was unable to pursue its course. And he made no map, pleading the impossibility of making sketches or undertaking surveys without exciting suspicions of espionage. Clapperton, meanwhile, undertook traveling up the Yobe or Yeau to Kano, through lands which had 'never been trod by European foot.' Although the consul died on the way, Clapperton continued and, on arrival in Sokoto, took upon himself the role of Britain's diplomatic representative, returning with letters proposing an alliance in 1825. At least he disposed of one myth, that the Yobe was the Niger. But his enquiries at Sokoto convinced him that the natives wanted to keep the course of the river secret, in order to deter European imperialism. The information he brought home, according to an article the *Quarterly Review* published at the time, 'entangled the question more than before.'[76]

Almost immediately Clapperton resumed the effort to trace the course of the Niger. On his return he took a different route via the Bight of Benin, crossing the Niger at Boussa, the remotest point known to Park. He carried diplomatic gifts for the Fulani ruler, including firearms, pictures of the royal family, and a copy of Euclid's *Geometry* in Arabic. His first task was to return to Sokoto. It was also his last, for there he succumbed to fever.

His servant, who, because of his superior intelligence, soon became more of a companion, Richard Lander, got back to England by retracing his steps, but resolved to return to 'settle once and for all the problem of the Niger,' opining, with the humility of a victim of snobbery, that if he died in the attempt, 'the gap we may make in society will be hardly noticed at all.'[77] In 1830 he navigated from Yauri to the river mouth and reported that the Niger could provide 'a water-communication with so extensive a part of Africa that a considerable trade will be opened.' But when he returned in 1832 with a project to set up a steamship trade, he was ambushed and fatally wounded at Angiama, apparently by agents of the king of Brass, who wanted to maintain his position as a middleman for Europeans' inland trade. It took twenty years of painstaking effort to produce perfect charts of the stretch of river he had explored.[78]

Meanwhile, Alexander Gordon Laing attempted to resume the effort to chart the Niger by approaching the headwaters from the west coast. He was a garrison officer at Freetown, whose conceit and pedantry made him unwelcome among his brother officers. The governor dispatched him inland to seek trading opportunities in order to get rid of him. Laing took the opportunity to exceed his orders, seek the source of the Niger, and fill in the uncharted reaches of the river. On his first attempt, he managed to explore the entire length of the Rokelle River but could not get much further. The notoriety his account of his travels earned him led to a new commission from the government to try to find the way to Timbuktu overland across the Sahara. He made it by what was for a long time to be the only safe stratagem: disguise in the role of a Muslim pilgrim. But almost at the outset of his homeward journey, his subterfuge was rumbled, his life forfeit, and his papers destroyed.

Meanwhile, the Société Géographique de Paris offered a reward of 10,000 francs to any Westerner who could reach Timbuktu. René Caillié was in the tradition of the romantically inspired readers of chivalric literature who had sought adventure in the African Atlantic and the New World in the fifteenth and sixteenth centuries.[79] He claimed to have been distracted from trade by stories of voyages and 'inflamed' by reading Robinson Crusoe. He created an elaborate alias, pretending to be an Egyptian called Abdallahi, who, kidnapped in childhood by the French, was now returning to his family and faith. He learned Arabic and with his savings bought £100 worth of trade goods and an umbrella. He set out from Kakondy, north of Sierra Leone, on 19 April 1827. Traveling among people who had never heard of Egypt, he was obliged to change his story, becoming 'a real sherif of Mecca'—a descendant of the prophet. Disguise was the key to success. British travelers had disdained it, 'determined,' as Denham said 'to travel in our real character as Britons and Christians,' not only out of pride of race but also to avoid the worst consequences of a detected imposture.[80]

Caillié passed from caravan to caravan and guide to guide, but in August he fell ill with foot sores and scurvy. He took almost a year to reach the Niger, where a local chief arranged transport by boat to Timbuktu in exchange for the Frenchman's umbrella. The barge, made of planks bound together with vegetable fiber, caulked with straw and clay and covered with mats, needed constant bailing with empty gourds. It carried a cargo of rice, honey, textiles, and nearly fifty slaves.

On 20 April 1828, Caillié arrived. He went through a rapid succession of emotions—suppressing, for fear of detection, his

> indescribable satisfaction . . . . How many grateful thanksgivings did I pour forth for the protection which God had vouchsafed to me, amidst obstacles and dangers which appeared insurmountable. This duty being ended, I looked around and found that the sight before me did not answer my expectations. I had formed a totally different idea of the grandeur and wealth of Timbuctoo.

At first sight Timbuktu seemed no more than a smattering of earth houses surrounded by dreary, barren plains. Yet 'there was something imposing in the aspect of a great city, raised in the midst of sands, and the difficulties surmounted by its founders cannot fail to excite admiration.'[81]

Caillié's return journey took him across the Sahara to Tangier. 'I have left a wide field of discovery for those who would come after me.'[82] He was a virtual captive of his traveling companions, who taunted him with suspicions as to his real identity, and kept him on short rations in order to extort bribes. But on arrival at Tafilet, the captain of his caravan purchased, as Caillié supposed, 'the silence of his conscience at a cheap price' by allowing him to go free with a few shillings in his possession.[83]

The Niger was no longer a 'mystery' but none of the explorers who had elucidated the problems of its course had found a way of forging a route of European commerce into the Sahel through which the river flowed. On a youthful tour of the Turkish empire, Heinrich Barth met a Hausa slave who said to him, 'Please God you shall go and visit Kano.' These words, Barth later avowed, 'were constantly ringing in my ears.' Could this story be true? Perhaps: for Barth was generally a colorless exponent, not easily given, like so many of his predecessors, to self-romanticization. He was a Prussian prodigy, somewhat in the mould of Humboldt: a polymath of immense energy and ill-disciplined ambitions. He got his chance to try for Kano in 1849, accompanying a British evangelical mission across the Sahara as a scientific expert, with the job of conducting independent researches once they got to Lake Chad. Though he traversed 10,000 miles, his efforts to pick a network of communications among the river systems of the region were dispiriting. The Benue, it turned out, did not flow from Lake Chad. There were few connections between rivers, and most were not easily navigable. 'By and by, I am sure,' he reported, 'a southern road will be opened into the heart of Central Africa, but the time has not yet come.'[84] Thereafter, the focus switched to East Africa. In the second half of the century, the Nile would reabsorb explorers' attentions.

Paths Ahead

Until the mid-nineteenth century, extreme environments remained a deterrent to explorers. But the means to overcome them were multiplying fast. Antiscorbutics, longitude-finding mechanisms, and rifled guns were among the first potentially transforming discoveries. Specialist tropical and arctic clothing followed. In Africa, antimalarial remedies were to prove as important as antiscorbutics at sea. Again, the traditional knowledge of Native American medicine men is generally accepted as the source of change: the marqués de Chinchón, viceroy of Peru, despaired of his wife's life until physicians brought him tree bark on the recommendation of the Indians; gradually, in the course of the early nineteenth century, methods of administering the drug improved in efficiency. In the second half of the century, it was grown on plantations and manufactured into pills by industrial processes. Industrialization generally was to prove deeply transforming. Steam-driven, iron-clad ships did not altogether liberate explorers from the tyranny of winds and currents, but they helped. Ironclads and engines were to prove particularly valuable in ice-infested seas. Railways, meanwhile, demanded new routes as they wrenched commerce in new directions. Railway prospecting was to be a major focus of explorers' endeavors from the 1840s.

The explorations of the early nineteenth century were the last of a pre-industrial age, when the transforming power of new technology could be glimpsed but not applied. It was too rudimentary, too unreliable. Tuckey, for instance, was originally scheduled to explore the Congo in a steamship, but it proved unseaworthy and was converted to sail before the expedition set off. The steamships Lander took to West Africa ended up rotting on the shore. In sub-Saharan Africa, most explorers of the era died. Only individuals of exceptional strength of body—such as Park, Laing, and Clapperton—could survive the climate with their health intact, and they usually ended up as victims of violence. In 1841 the ratio of deaths among Europeans serving in British stations on the coast of Africa was 58.4 per cent: three times as many as in the West Indies.[85]

Nor was the technology of the early industrial revolution yet equal to Arctic conditions. Franklin's men seem to have been poisoned by their own canned food. No expedition of the period survived more than two winters in the ice without terrible sacrifices of life and health. On his privately financed search for the Northwest Passage, John Ross trumpeted the virtues of steam, but when he reached the Arctic, he stripped out and discarded his engines as useless. The icebreakers with which James Ross cleft his way through to Antarctica in 1841, ramming and pounding their way through the pack, were fortified by entirely traditional means, with oak stretchers on the inside of the hull and copper sheathing outside.

Macgregor Laird, one of the dreamers who put steamboats into the mouth of the Niger in the 1830s, sketched his vision:

> British influence and enterprise would thereby penetrate into the remotest recesses of the country, one hundred millions of people would be brought into direct contact with the civilised world; new and boundless markets would be opened to our manufacturers; a continent teeming with inexhaustible fertility would yield her riches to our traders; not merely a nation, but hundreds of nations, would be awakened from the lethargy of centuries, and become useful and active members of the great commonwealth of mankind; and every British station would become a centre from whence religion and commerce would radiate their influence into the surrounding country. Who can calculate the effect that would be produced if such a plan were followed

out, and Africa, freed from her chains moral and physical, allowed to develop her energies in peace and security?

Watt was Laird's hero.

> By his invention every river is laid open to us, time and distance are short-ened. If his spirit is allowed to witness the success of his invention here on earth, I can conceive no application of it that would meet his approbation more than seeing the mighty streams of the Mississippi and the Amazon, the Niger and the Nile, the Indus and the Ganges, stemmed by hundreds of steam vessels, carrying the glad tidings of 'peace and good will towards men' into the dark places of the earth which are now filled with cruelty.'[86]

The moral expectations were unduly optimistic, but the potential effects of the application of industrial power in opening up unexplored and ill-explored regions were, if anything, understated.

Retrospect and Prospect: The Opportunities and Constraints of the Age

After the Napoleonic Wars, Britain leapt into preeminence in exploration, dominating the field as once Spain and Portugal had done. The late eighteenth century had been a period of rough equipollence, in which western Europe's three main Atlantic-side powers—Spain, France, and Britain—all took advantage of their privileged access to the oceans. From a less favored starting point Russia shared the honors. Between 1815 and the mid-century, Britain's near-monopoly was conspicuous and curious. Barth was a Prussian, but he traveled under the British flag, wrote English for preference, and called himself Henry rather than Heinrich. Giovanni Battista Belzoni was an Italian, a one-time circus strongman who made a reputation as a predatory archeologist, renowned for his talent in unearthing pharaonic tombs, who conceived an improbable ambition to explore the Niger. But he arrived in 1823 on a British ship—just before his death. Dumont d'Urville found his achievement rapidly eclipsed by James Ross. Caillié succeeded where his British predecessors had failed, but his was not an official expedition of the French state—only a cut-price adventure on his own initiative. Indeed, as reported by the *Quarterly Review*, he and his countrymen were rather proud of that: 'that which England has not been able to accomplish with the aid of a whole group of travellers and at an expense of more than twenty millions, a Frenchman has done with his scanty personal resources alone and without putting his country to any expense.'[87]

Why did Britain take this lead? It was evidently not a result of her supposed precocity in industrialization; on the contrary, her industries played little part except in supplying cheap truck for travelers, and even that often proved unreliable: the Landers were embarrassed on the Niger by the fact that the thousands of steel sewing needles they intended to distribute among the natives had no eyes. Nor was Britain's success merely a result of the way the wars had spared her soil, while ravaging that of her continental neighbors. Rather, two advantages outweighed all others. First, Britain emerged from the wars with a huge, underemployed navy and thousands of undemobilized officers desperate for glory on half-pay. Peace did not only make exploration possible: it made it essential.

Secondly, Britain's exploring agenda had a genius of demonic energy to preside over it. John Barrow was irascible, ungenerous, and usually wrong-headed. His own geographical opinions were wayward: he believed with dangerous passion in the navigability of a Northwest Passage, the accessibility of the Poles by sea, the connectedness of the Niger and the Congo. He was a poor judge of men, dismissing Caillié, for instance, as a charlatan, Richard Lander as an ignoramus, and Charles Sturt as incompetent. He thought the Congo would be good for Tuckey's health. From the comfort of the Admiralty he excoriated for cowardice failed explorers of the utmost intrepidity. But fo the thirty years he served the Admiralty as one of its chief administrator exploration was, thanks to his determination, one of the British navy's highe priorities; and in the 1830s, when official enthusiasm flagged, he used tl newly founded Geographical (later, Royal Geographical) Society of London, which he was the first president, to galvanize government, inspire patro harness explorers, and enthuse the public.

Explorers now frequented uninhabited regions of the far north and south the globe. Franklin took Indians and French trappers as guides on his expedition but found them clueless in the genuinely unexplored environm he had to map. He dispensed with their services thereafter. Inuit made n in sand, making mountains out of piles of sand and islands out of peb sticks for villages. His colleague, Beechey, mapped 600 miles of coast in apparently without native help. Normally, however, where existing popula lived, route finding remained dependent on indigenous expertise; the 'v man' was decisive in threading previously known routes together, repo them, mapping them, and extending them along pathways chosen as su for commerce or colonization. Cook learned from Tupaia. Lewis and needed Sacajawea. In boreal and tropical regions alike, explorers need draw on local knowledge. In 1829, when John Ross showed Inuit his gap map of the Arctic, they filled in missing features for him. Ahmad Bello

of Kano, drew a map of the Niger in the sand for Hugh Clapperton, though the Englishman could make no sense of it. Without the help of his converted native chief it is doubtful whether Robert Moffat would ever had reached the Kalahari, let alone found the way across it.

The nature of exploration was changing. The fanaticism of the search for the Northwest Passage demonstrated that. Route finding was no longer inspired solely or even primarily by the needs of commerce, war, and migration. Ways through previously untraversable environments were sought for their own sake. Between the lines explorers scored on the map of the world, the search for resources and for disinterested knowledge impelled enquirers to fill in the gaps. Late eighteenth- and early nineteenth-century explorers of Arabia and map-makers in India—to whose legacy we shall turn in the next chapter—were engaged in work of this sort.

Eighteenth-century exploration presaged these changes: Cook's fancy to get further than anyone had ever been showed the power of impractical ambitions, but it was, perhaps, in the Romantic, chivalric tradition that Western explorers had so long embodied. His and his contemporaries' desire to crisscross the Pacific, between the wind corridors and the established seaways, demonstrated the desire for completeness of knowledge—but, in part, imperial competition for the control of routes and resources also drove it. In the early nineteenth century, the desire to master nature, to conquer every environment, began to invade and infest explorers' minds. But they lacked the technology to accomplish the ambition. In the second half of the century, the means and motives, as we shall see, could coincide.

9 Globalizing
The Narrowing Horizon, c.1850–c.2000

Tho' much is taken, much abides; and tho'
We are not now that strength which in the old days
Moved earth and heaven; that which we are, we are;
One equal-temper of heroic hearts,
Made weak by time and fate, but strong in will
To strive, to seek, to find, and not to yield.

Tennyson, 'Ulysses'

Adventure is really a soft option. . . . It requires far less courage to be an explorer than to be a chartered accountant.

Peter Fleming, *Brazilian Adventure*

EXPLORERS of exploration—such as the readers and writer of this book—can easily get lost. Detours abound in the last century and a half or so of the history of the subject. As the work of tracing the routes of access between cultures neared completion, explorers diversified. 'The unknown' was almost over and the relatively less well-known checklist of geography absorbed their attention. They turned first to the perfection and improvement of routes already familiar: to meticulous mapping, to the identification of mountains men could tunnel, obstacles they could mine, spans they could bridge. Increasingly, they explored places where no one lives, the uninhabitable altitudes, the extremes of cold, the ocean depths, the soil and crust of the earth. They became surveyors and prospectors, delving or scanning for new resources, or identifying previously overlooked physical features of the earth, or scientists discovering new species or new aspects of the biosphere, rather than new peoples and new lands. Explorers became conquerors of hostile environments—just for the sake of it, not to blaze trails between regions hospitable to humankind. Scientific exploration—the craving to know the planet and everything in it—displaced route finding as their major objective. In central Asia, archeology was the spur; in the Malay world, it was botany and zoology. In the early twentieth century, anthropological fieldwork began to be a priority everywhere.

Or else the explorers abandoned the search for knowledge and returned to adventure—retracing routes already explored, but trying to do so faster than anyone else, or in worse conditions, or alone. In the late twentieth-century record breaking took over a rationally inexplicable amount of energy and investment. In some ways, this represented a reversion to type, for wanderlust, vainglory, and self-romanticization were always parts of explorers' psychic equipment. More prosaic motives—imperial, commercial, and scientific—had their moment of ascendancy before romance returned to the fore. At the same time, a new fashion arose for historical reconstruction of earlier explorations, or attempts to demonstrate how earlier feats might have been achieved: this was a form of experimental archeology, which, for instance, took scholars to Easter Island in balsawood rafts[1] or over the Atlantic in coracles,[2] or around the Arctic in an umiak,[3] or to Hawaii in a canoe,[4] or even, in 2005, to Flores in Indonesia in a dugout in an attempt to show that *Homo erectus* might have known the art of navigation.[5]

It is tempting to follow them. But this book has a bigger objective in view and one we can accomplish, if we stick to it: to trace the laying of the infrastructure of the history of the world—the routes that put sundered peoples back in touch with each other after their long history of divergence and enabled them to exchange objects, ideas, and personnel. So this chapter concentrates on the explorers' activities that advanced that cause: the penetration of regions and routes, in Africa, southeast Asia, Australia, New Guinea, Arabia, and Tibet, still unintegrated in the spreading web of worldwide exchange; the reconnoitering of the new routes that steam-powered transport and telegraphic communication demanded or facilitated; the reconnaissance of the previously unvisited recesses of the world in the Arctic and Antarctic, where, ultimately, air and submarine communications would follow the explorers; and the restoration of contact with the earth's remaining 'lost' regions and isolated or—as explorers' jargon said—'uncontacted' peoples. As the pace of exploration gathered, the fronts multiplied; it is hard to keep up with them. The scenes of this chapter shift like a whirligig and flash like a zoetrope.

Africa: The Battle of the Books

The late nineteenth century was the age of the last renaissance. Classical learning marked every educated Westerner. Greek and Latin were essential ingredients in the formation of imperial master classes. The transmission of the classical legacy to the wider world was a conscious obligation of colonial elites. Western interest in Africa bore the weight of ancient learning. Ancient geography tinted every reader's spectacles. Speculation and exploration wrote footnotes to Ptolemy and Herodotus. To vindicate or vilify classical geographers became the object of every participant in debate about what the African interior was really like.

In the mid-1850s, scientific curiosity centered on the problem of finding the source of the Nile in the lakelands and mountains of inland East Africa. The influential president of Britain's Royal Geographical Society W. D. Cooley, who founded the Hakluyt Society, was convinced that exploration would prove the ancients were right: the Nile would be found to rise below the equator in what Aristotle called the Mountains of Silver and other authorities called the Mountains of the Moon. These would be well to the east of the course of the known portion of the river, to allow for Herodotus' claim that the Nile flowed westward from its source. The image of twin lakes, below the mountains, feeding the river, was familiar from almost every map: it seems to have originated in a fourth- or fifth-century interpolation in Ptolemy.[6] A 'battle of the books' was joined: was geography science or scholarship? Would the texts be vindicated, or would observation explode their errors? The learned world of geography was divided between humanists in their armchairs and doctrinaire empiricists who itched for the field.

So when, in 1855, German missionaries glimpsed 'snow on the equator'—white-capped peaks in the depths of Kenya, the result was sensational. The revelation evoked disbelief, as did the reports they brought back of a vast lake. But snows and lakes suggested river sources and encouraged the classicists in confidence in Herodotus.

Under the auspices of the Royal Geographical Society, Richard Burton—an explorer of outstanding scholarly credentials and energy too abundant to be restrained or directed—set off from Zanzibar in June 1857 'to ascertain the limits of the inland sea.' Like other Europeans venturing into the African interior, he followed routes that slaving caravans had opened. It is impossible to exaggerate the importance of slavers as explorers. But in the second half of the nineteenth century, as the British empire waged its extraordinary, unremitting, and self-sacrificial war on the slave trade, slavery became an impediment.

Slavers did all they could to obstruct the passage of white men whose reports might be fatal to their trade.

The career of the biggest slaver of them all was just beginning at the time of Burton's expedition. Tippu Tip, a small, ever-smiling fixer with 'eyes full of fire,' claimed that his name derived from the sound of rifle fire. In the opinion of one of his collaborators in the Congo in the 1880s, 'from his immense plantations, cultivated by thousands of slaves, all blindly devoted to their master, and from his ivory trade, of which he has a monopoly, he has in his duplex character of conqueror and trader, succeeded in creating for himself in the heart of Africa a veritable empire.'[7] During the height of his wealth and power in that decade, Europeans depended on him for services as a factotum from Zanzibar to the middle Zaire.

Meanwhile, imperial emulation exacerbated the difficulties Burton faced. Said Barghash, the new sultan of Zanzibar, who came to the throne with youthful ambitions in 1856, was out to construct an empire of his own in the East African interior and did not want white explorers intruding on Western powers' behalf. The real curse of the expedition, however, was Burton's clash of temperament with his fellow explorer John Speke. Their relationship veered between love and hate and became poisoned by rivalry. In 1858 Speke, reconnoitering ahead of his companion, came upon the nyanza he dubbed Lake Victoria. Burton's famous summary of what happened foreshadows the controversy that was to follow:

> At length my companion had been successful, his 'flying trip' had led him to the northern water, and he had found its dimensions surpassing our most sanguine expectations. We had scarcely, however, breakfasted, before he announced to me the startling fact that he had discovered the sources of the Nile. It was an inspiration perhaps: the moment he sighted the Nyanza he felt at once no doubt but that the 'lake at his feet gave birth to that interesting river which has been subject of so much speculation and the object of so many explorers.' The fortunate discoverer's conviction was strong; his reasons were weak.[8]

Speke insisted that he had found the source of the Nile, though there seemed no convincing evidence: he had seen only the southern shore of the lake and had not established how big it was or even whether it was a single body of water. Returning the following year, he became embroiled in the politics of the highland kingdom of Buganda, which controlled access to the northern shore of the lake. Eventually, however, in 1862, he saw what he called the Rippon Falls pour lake water into what he supposed was the Nile—rightly, as it turned out, but with no proof of the fact to hand.

The inevitable disputes over Speke's findings deepened when he died of a self-inflicted gun wound in September 1864, just before a scheduled public debate with Burton. It was almost certainly an accident, but the theory of suicide was irresistible to those who thought him wrong. The Royal Geographical Society needed someone to supply the verification—or, as many hoped, the rebuttal—of Speke's claims. They chose David Livingstone.

Livingstone was already famous as the author of what he called 'missionary explorations.' It is not clear how far missionizing and exploring are congruent or even compatible activities. Missionary work is patient and painstaking. It demands compromises with alien cultures and collaboration with distasteful regimes. Livingstone was unsuited to the work. He displayed the convulsions of mood of a manic depressive.[9] Wanderlust or phrenesis always urged him on. He declared frequently that rest was the worst thing for sickness: only when his last illness struck was he 'glad of resting.'[10] He had a strong sense of his own election as a 'channel of Divine Power,' but how much of a missionary vocation he ever really had is doubtful. Notoriously, he is supposed only ever to have made one convert, who soon reverted to paganism. Exploration was his priority, or, as he put it, 'I view the end of the geographical feat as the beginning of the missionary enterprise.'[11] He did not see the gospel as a plant that needed tending in unfamiliar environments. He planted it and moved on, leaving barely evangelized natives to nurture or neglect it.

He was more concerned with removing political and geographical obstacles to exploration than with getting on with the propagation of the gospel. He tackled slavers and Boers and intractable native chiefs with gusto. His esteem derived in part, at least, from the way his objectives coincided with those of empire and trade. He believed in extending Britain's writ, because it would frustrate the slavers and promote the gospel. He believed in nurturing legitimate commerce, because it would displace slavery and promote security. 'We ought to encourage the Africans,' he wrote in his first book, 'to cultivate for our markets, as the most effectual means, next to the Gospel, of their elevation.'[12] He was a trailblazer for British interests.

As a geographer, he was an autodidact, whose zeal was unrestrained by knowledge. His first focus was on the upper Zambezi around Linyanti. But Portuguese explorers and extenders of empire were already active in the region, so he headed downriver, discovering Victoria Falls in 1855. This was enough to ensure a massive reputation and copious sales of his books. His follow-up expedition, from 1858 to 1863, was a joint venture of the government and the Universities Mission Society. 'The thousands invested,' *The Times* reported, 'have been productive only of the most fatal results.'[13] The

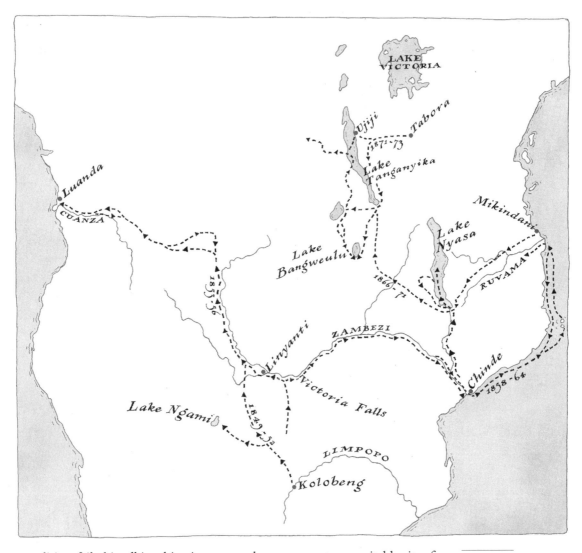

Livingstone's travels

expedition failed in all its objectives: no trade, no converts, no suitable sites for British colonization, no new geographical discoveries resulted.

When Livingstone turned his attention to the question of the Nile, almost all his suggestions and speculations proved false. Forced into distasteful collaboration with slave traders, he scoured the wrong region, looking for the source which Speke had already found. In 1871 he returned to the shores of Lake Nyasa, at Ujiji, too discouraged to continue, too disappointed to go home. Livingstone was not 'lost': everyone in the region knew his whereabouts, but his meanderings took him nowhere useful.

Meanwhile, press and public, anxious for news of him, grew panicky as the years lengthened. He was a celebrity and a potential scoop. 'Draw a thousand pounds now,' the proprietor of the *New York Herald* told his crack reporter Henry Morton Stanley, 'and when you have gone through that draw another thousand, and when that is spent draw another thousand . . . and so on; but FIND LIVINGSTONE.'

Where Livingstone used the Bible, Stanley used a bludgeon. He spent his patron's wealth and his men's lives with equal profligacy. He powered through the jungle with 157 porters bearing his personal tent with its enamel bath and Persian carpet. His motto, like Marshal Blücher's and applied with equally little discrimination, was 'Forward.' Later in his career, as Stanley fought his way up the Zaire, his men nicknamed him Bula Matari—Breaker of Rocks. An army of slavers blocked his route to Ujiji and forced him into a long detour. His diary became feverish as malaria took hold. 'No living man shall stop me . . . But death? Not even this. . . . I shall find him—and write it larger—FIND HIM! FIND HIM!'[14]

By 6 November 1871, Stanley despaired of reaching Livingstone 'without being beggared' by the extortions of local chiefs. Buying up as much food as he could carry, he bribed an expert local guide to lead his party away in small groups westward, off the beaten track, under cover of darkness. Four days later they emerged within sight of Ujiji. Stanley broke out the champagne and silver goblets he had stowed for the occasion. The words in which he recorded his meeting with the missionary are among the most quoted in the history of exploration, but are too good to resist repetition:

> I pushed back the crowds and . . . walked down a living avenue of people . . . As I advanced slowly towards him I noticed he was pale, looked wearied, had a grey beard, wore a bluish cap with a faded gold band on it, had on a red-sleeved waistcoat and a pair of grey tweed trousers. I would have run to him, only I was a coward in the presence of such a mob—would have embraced him, only, he being an Englishman, I did not know how he would receive me; so I did what cowardice and false pride suggested was the best thing—walked deliberately to him, took off my hat and said, 'Dr Livingstone, I presume.'

After an exchange of raised caps, 'I thank God, Doctor,' Stanley continued, 'that I have been permitted to see you.' The other replied, 'I feel thankful that I am here to welcome you.'[15]

Livingstone reacted politely but clearly resented the 'rescue.' After his death the following year, Stanley settled the question of the Nile in his characteristically direct fashion. In 1874–6 he headed straight for Lake Victoria, sailing it extensively, and confirming the significance of the falls Speke had found. Over the next fifteen years, using the power of steam and the persuasion of guns, he sorted out another of Africa's 'mysteries': the extent of the Congo system and its relationship to the lakes.

He did not mop up all the prizes. Between 1879 and 1884 the Royal Geographical Society sponsored successful expeditions to find direct routes from the coast to the lakes—from Dar es Salaam to Lake Nyasa and on to the Congo river system via the Lualaba and from Mombasa to Lake Victoria. Joseph Thomson, who led both missions, was an engaging eccentric in the old mould, quelling the Masai with pretensions to magic powers by brandishing his false tooth and making fruit salts fizz. But such methods were not good enough to open permanent routes. The lakes region seemed a promising environment, with highlands that rose above the malarial forest; but it continued to be hard to get at—screened by grueling terrain and unwelcoming inhabitants, penetrated by unnavigable or barely navigable rivers.

Meanwhile, in any case, the initiative in exploration had passed from the intrepid enthusiasts—missionaries, scientists, and independent adventurers—to the big bucks and big battalions. In African exploration, the era of the amateur was over. Stanley worked for millionaires or governments. The other big successes in exploring transcontinental routes in the 1870s were government-inspired and publicly funded: Pierre Savorgnan de Brazza penetrated the Congo basin for France, establishing the Ogowe River as a viable route, while Portuguese explorers reached the lakes and, ultimately, the Indian Ocean from Angola. This was the result of a conscious national effort, paid for by a government anxious for other European governments to acknowledge its prior but long-neglected claims to supremacy inland from its colonies in Angola and Mozambique.

In the 1880s European powers scrambled for territory. Boundary fixing became crucial. Surveyors crawled, clambered, and sidled their way across mountains and through swamps and forests in attempt to fix the limits of the jurisdictions claimed by royal powers. Trees had to be felled to expose enough sky for astronomical readings. Until the twentieth century, guesswork predominated. The 30-degree meridian east, for instance, was selected as the basis for a number of frontiers, but no one could agree where it lay. Only the introduction of time checks by radio (not invented until 1901) prevented disputes. Even so, the continent emerged scored by irrational frontiers, dissecting traditional polities and communities and forcing enemies to share political space.

Southeast Asia: Slow Boats to China

In southeast Asia, too, geography became a public responsibility for European governments as Britain, France, and the Netherlands effectively partitioned most of the region between them. Here, as in Africa, imperial objectives were beginning to dominate explorers' priorities by the 1860s. If global history is properly conceived as the history of cultural exchange, southeast Asia, of all parts of the world, probably least needed integration with the rest. Because it lies athwart the monsoons, between China and India, maritime southeast Asia is one of the great corridors of long-range trade. But inland communications were another matter.

The region had always proved hard to reach overland from China, Tibet, and India: the long rivers—the Salween, which flows through Burma, and the Mekong, which winds through the region to the South China Sea—fall abruptly from the Himalayas. No other causeways cleave the dense forests. The big new opportunity for route finding—so the colonial authorities opined—lay along the Mekong River, which, on the map, at least, looked like a short cut to China from British-held Burma or French-controlled Indochina. An Indian army officer, T. E. McLeod, had seen the upper Mekong while reconnoitering the traditional trade route from Burma to China in 1837. But the main benefit, if a new route could be found, would accrue to the French.

In 1866 the French authorities in Saigon sent an expedition up the Mekong with orders to reach China. The Mekong River Expedition was therefore an imperial venture. The French government paid for it. Its leader was a government official: Ernest-Marc-Louis de Gonzague Doudart de Lagrée was a diplomat who had induced the Khmer king to accept a French protectorate. The most active propagandist was François Garnier, a naval officer in his twenties, who spun from a tissue of fables what the salons of Saigon called the 'great idea' of 'unknown riches enfolded in the valleys and mountains that enclose these rivers. 'If one believes the travellers' tales,' Garnier wrote, 'these valleys contain active and industrious peoples who trade with the celestial empire. What is certain is that the Chinese province of Yunnan each year sends many workers to the mines of amber, serpentine, zinc, gold and silver that lie along the upper course of the Mekong.'[16] Along their way the explorers stopped periodically to look for the fabled mines without finding them.

A few days into their journey, rapids defeated them, 'where the water boiled and the·current was thunderous.'[17] Garnier insisted that a powerful steamer could conquer the Sambor rapids. But when they were six weeks upriver from Phnom Penh, the river bottom was too shallow—or at least the deep channels were too shifting and elusive—for anything but a canoe. Consigned by fever to eighteen days of delirium, Garnier must have realized that his dream was impossible. By the time they reached the Khone Falls on 17 August, more than two months out from Phnom Penh, the expedition was no longer nourishing hope: it was thriving on illusion. At Christmas in Bassac, cut off from the capital by rebellion along the river, Garnier continued to cling to the claim that all the difficulties of which he had proved the existence would somehow evaporate. In reality, the narrows, rapids, and extended longueurs of portage that lay ahead were even more daunting than those already encountered. On 18 October 1867, they crossed the Chinese frontier. So they could claim to have reached the terminus of their journey, even though they had explored a practically useless route and found no way of making the river navigable. They had run out of money with which to pay porters and guides and bribe officials. Local rebellions prevented them from progressing. In January 1868, Lagrée died, tortured by fever and dysentery. The surviving members of the expedition exchanged recriminations for the rest of their lives.

Australia: The Road to Mount Hopeless

The Mekong expedition en route through a ravine near Sop Yong

Official sponsorship and public finance did not exempt explorers from amateurish behavior. No endeavor demonstrates this truth better than the Trans-Australia Expedition of 1860. Crossing Australia had no particular point or merit. No one by then really expected a land route to be useful. The way the expedition unfolded demonstrated that this was a project unrestrained by common sense. It was a grand gesture, to demonstrate the wealth and enterprise of the city that served as the explorers' point of departure.

Melbourne was the capital of the colony of Victoria, the glory of Australia, and the envy of the British empire. An observer in 1858 recorded progress 'utterly surpassing all human experience' and growth 'unparalleled in the history of the world.'[18] From a small town of 23,000 people in 1850 it leapt to metropolitan status with 126,000 inhabitants by the time the expedition set off. Sheep and gold were the bases of the city's wealth. When the expedition came to be organized, no expense was spared. Twenty-three explorers took part, under Robert O'Hara Burke, an impetuous, 40-year-old, failed gold prospector turned inspector of mounted police. Twenty-five Indian camels were among the train, amply supported with other livestock. Ox carts bore 21 tons of provisions. By the time it left in August 1860, the expedition had already cost £12,000—more than five times as much as any previous expedition. Public subscriptions accounted for half the sum; the government of Victoria paid for the rest. 'No previous expedition has ever departed under more favourable circumstances,' declared the leader. Yet by the time they reached first base at Menindee in western New South Wales, dissension and diffidence divided the camp and resignations had depleted the expedition's higher ranks. William Wills, a 27-year-old surveyor, became the new second-in-command.

Burke pressed ahead to establish a base camp at Cooper's Creek. The rearguard should have joined him there promptly, but misunderstandings and incompetence delayed them. By December, Burke lost patience. He made a 'dash to Carpentaria' with Wills and two others. They took no experienced guides and only three months' provisions. They reached the gulf in a couple of months. Or rather, they tasted salt water in the mouth of the Flinders River but were unable to hack a way through the mangrove swamps to the sea. They turned back with just one month's rations left for a journey of two months. During March 1861, they ate or lost most of their camels and their only horse. Discarding everything except firearms, the survivors mounted their last two camels and rode for Cooper's Creek. When they arrived on 21 April, they found it deserted. Only a few hours earlier, the men of the garrison had left for Menindee. Their own despair had driven them away—with no news either of the dashers or of the rearguard, which was still 75 miles south.

Even so, ample provisions remained at the camp and Burke could have followed the trail to Menindee or awaited rescue. Instead, he tried to trace a new route to the police station at Mount Hopeless in South Australia. But the group lost their way and then fell sick, perhaps because of experimenting with seeds from the nardoo fern, which the Aborigines gather and process into a kind of flour. Unless prepared properly, the seeds poison, weaken, and kill. By the beginning of July, both Burke and Wills were dead. The only survivor was the camel expert John King.

Aborigines rescued him. When Edwin Welch found him on 15 September 1861, the cameleer wore nothing but scarecrow rags. 'Who in the name of wonder are you?' asked Welch—or perhaps, as he later confessed, he used another expression, which he thought unfit to print.

'I am King, sir . . . the last man of the exploring expedition.'

'What! Burke's? Where is he—and Wills?'

'Dead! Both dead long ago!' cried the scarecrow and collapsed in a faint.[19]

The most important legacy of the trans-Australian expeditions were the vibrant paintings by Ludwig Becker. They exposed the naked glow of the barren deserts and pitiless skies.

Meanwhile, John McDougall Stuart, a surveyor who had worked with Sturt,[20] had launched a series of more modest attempts to cross the continent from Adelaide. His efforts were self-financed until he obtained a grant of £2,500 from the government of South Australia, Victoria's rival colony—younger and poorer—and neighbor to the east. More prudent than Burke, Stuart turned back whenever supplies threatened to run out or impassable country barred the way. As a result his life was spared—but only just. In October 1861, with Burke's fate uncertain, Stuart made his last attempt. It took him over seven months to reach the northern coast just east of the Adelaide River. He still had to get back. From August 1862, his journal was a chronicle of scurvy, 'terrible, gnawing pain,' incipient blindness, dry waterholes, abandoned horses, and harassment from hostile Aboriginals. By October he was enduring 'the greatest agony that it is possible for a man to suffer.' He was so far gone in scurvy that he felt 'in the grasp of death.'[21] He managed to get back to settled territory toward the end of November, to report that the country he had traversed from the Roper northward was 'well adapted to the settlement of an European population, the climate being in every respect suitable, and the surrounding country of excellent quality.'[22] The history of exploration might be a brief tale, but for the extraordinary property of human memory, which filters out suffering and casts a retrospective glow over disaster.

Thereafter, explorers took another decade and a half to convince themselves that there were no great lakes or exploitable lands in midmost Australia. This was a discovery that could equally have well been made by taking the Aboriginals' word for it. There were, however, useful results: transcontinental routes for telegraph lines, which began to cross Australia in the 1870s. Books about 'undiscovered' Australia 'where the map does not count' were still appearing in the 1920s, and indeed the vastness of the interior included some bleak, blank spots until aerial mapping perfected knowledge of them; but the framework of Australia-wide communications was in place.[23]

New Guinea: exploration of the interior

New Guinea: 'A Country Really New'

The spirit of Burke lived on in New Guinea, which acquired a not undeserved reputation as the world's last lingering frontier of the unknown. It was 'a relief,' said a missionary who arrived in 1871, 'to visit a country really new, about which little is known, a country of bona fide cannibals and genuine savages, where the missionary and explorer truly carries his life in his hand.'[24]

Otto von Ehlers was typical of the new breed of adventurer, fueled by vanity and financed by the profits of his own best-selling travelogs. Novelty sold, and no one had yet made a crossing of New Guinea's central mountain ranges. When Ehlers decided to cross them in 1895, he admitted candidly, as a German colonial official reported, 'that he did not want to perform a scientific deed. He said his only intention was to make a breakthrough.'[25]

In some ways, the route Ehlers proposed was a modest one, traversing the island at a relatively narrow point, where it was only 105 miles across, following the Francisco River upstream and using the Lakekamu to reach the south coast.

But the scale of the interior mountains was unknown. Ehlers reckoned the whole trip would take twenty-eight days. It was a guess. It was wrong. A further miscalculation followed. He thought he would need to carry only 600 kilograms of rice to keep his party of forty-three men fed. A police officer delegated to accompany him commented, 'What use are fame and money to me when I am dead? I have no faith in this enterprise. It will fail for sure.'[26]

By the time they crested the mountains, they had been without food for eight days. Twelve men were already dead. The survivors had lost or broken their compasses. They had no other direction-finding gear. The rainy season deluged them incessantly. Red maggots infested the wounds that blood-sucking leeches opened all over their bodies. They were about seven weeks into the journey when some of the native bearers mutinied, shot the Germans, and bolted for survival.

The feat that eluded Ehlers was accomplished in 1906 by the fast-shooting, hard-pounding British magistrate Christopher Monckton, who judged it 'the biggest thing yet done in New Guinea.'[27] As for the even more daunting mountains in the heart of the island at its broadest point, where the Fly River rises, no one managed to find a way through until 1927, when British and German rivalries finally stung the authorities in Port Moresby into authorizing a private expedition. Charles Karius, an assistant magistrate, and the locally born policeman Ivan Champion crossed what the bearers called 'devil country'—an almost perpendicular limestone barrier 9,000 feet high.

Arabia: Frustrations of the Forbidden

By then Arabia was the only arena that remained open to real innovation by amateur explorers. Mecca lay under a sacred prohibition that was rarely relaxed. The peninsula was closed to official European expeditions under suspicion of harboring imperial designs. But Muslim geographers had always neglected the region; only the seventeenth-century compiler of travelers' data Evliya Çelebi had described any part of it in detail. And although the haj made routes to Mecca the best-known avenues in Islam, the pilgrims stuck to well-worn approaches and avoided the ill-documented dangers of south and central Arabia.

In the late eighteenth century the Dane Carsten Niebuhr made a start at detailed scale mapping of the peninsula in the fertile and prosperous Hadramut. In the early nineteenth century, his greatest successor, the Swiss Jakob Burchardt, won Muslim confidence. He was even welcomed in Mecca, where

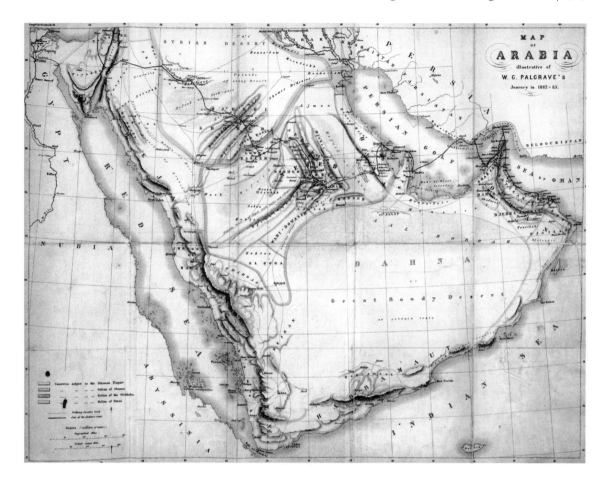

Arabia mapped by W. G. Palgrave, while the Suez Canal project was being aired in the 1860s, with vast, indistinctly recorded regions

Christians were normally excluded on pain of death. The studies he completed before his death in 1817 made Syria, Jordan, and northern Arabia vividly knowable in the West. For the rest of the first half of the century, exploration—such as it was—followed the front of invading Egyptian forces. In the 1840s French technicians accompanying Egyptian troops—the botanist E.-F. Jomard, the hydrographer J.-P. Chedufau, the outstanding archeologist P.-E. Botta—made maps of the southwestern peninsula and collected botanical, geological, and antiquarian specimens. But Egyptian attempts at creating an Arabian empire all failed. Richard Burton, meanwhile, sought rumored, nonexistent gold mines in western Arabia before turning his attention to the Nile.

In the 1860s the Suez Canal project made Arabia strategically important for Europeans. Napoleon III sponsored intelligence-gathering missions that penetrated the Nafud and the Nejd. In the mid-1870s, Charles Doughty, a more responsible and reliable explorer than Burton, set to work. Animated by romantic enthusiasm for the Bedouin way of life, he collected and critically sifted information on regions he was unable to reconnoiter in person. In 1895 Renato Manzoni, a grandson of the novelist, published a meticulous account of routes to Mecca. A decade later, D. G. Hogarth, an Oxford tutor who liked to think of himself as a 'wandering scholar,' summed up the results of the previous 100 years or so of effort. The peninsula was unknown 'in a relative sense': available data made clear what was there and how to get around it; mapping, however, was still rudimentary. And in the central zone of the south

> lies a still virgin tract, obscure enough to give a geographer pause. . . . a dark space of 650 miles span from north to south, and 850 from west to east. . . . vast enough to hide many secrets of which the geographer has no inkling as yet; it does, in fact, hide certain half-secrets that he suspects but cannot unriddle. Until it be better explored, the problem of the course and destination of all the copious inland drainage of the southwestern part of the peninsula remains insoluble. There may be an important central lake, as Chedufau thought, or there may be more than one, or there may be a southern trans-Arabian channel above or below ground. . . . Resultant on such watercourses there may be unknown tracts of fertility and nomad or settled societies of which no rumour has reached us. Or there may be none of these things, but only sand and rock.[28]

It took a long time to verify that sand and rock predominated.

Hogarth realized that 'the great unseen,' as he called it, had two zones: in the northwest was steppe-like country relieved by oases; but the southwest was the 'Empty Quarter'—'a teasing mistress that beckons only to forbid.'[29] Plenty of explorers 'crazed with the spell of far Arabia' tackled Hogarth's program. The growing importance of oil in the world economy, as a result of industrialization and the rise of the petrol-driven engine, was a valuable incentive. But the Empty Quarter defied every attempt: the climate was too torrid, the Bedouin too hostile, the surrounding states too wary.

Aerial surveying was a solution widely canvassed as a way of eluding the difficulties. Bertram Thomas, however, objected. He was a British officer who served as liaison with Arab forces during the First World War and stayed on in the service of a series of regional chiefs. The fauna, the inhabitants, the geological structure of the Empty Quarter, he pointed out, could not be studied from the air. His real objections were romantic. 'There seems something indelicate,' he wrote, 'in the intrusion of Western machines into these virgin silences; a feeling not to be confused with the thrill of the unknown, bounded here by the rim of the inverted bowl of the heavens, or with the mental stimulus that comes from plans in the slow process of precarious accomplishment.'[30]

Thomas, in short, was a dogmatic primitivist who refused to exploit modern technology. But he had certain advantages over his unsuccessful predecessors. After the First World War he spent thirteen years in the service of various governments around the fringes of the peninsula; he knew more about local conditions than any rival and enjoyed the acquaintance of many of the region's most powerful men. He was thoroughly acclimatized. He had, by his own account, 'a peculiar knowledge of tribal dialects and of Arab ways.'[31] His private fortune gave him the means to mount his expeditions in secret, without having to seek official permission. Before attempting to cross the desert he got to know its extremities or, as he put it, on his 'first flirtation. . . . I cherished no illusions . . . of an immediate and final conquest.'[32] He did not start an attempted crossing until he knew the whereabouts of every waterhole and had established relations of confidence with guides who knew every clue furnished by a camel's track and the meaning of every shift of sand, for 'tracking in Arabia,' according to Thomas, 'is an exact science, beside which the finger-print methods of the West are limited in scope, for the sands are a perfect medium.'[33] In December 1930 he was ready at last. Even so, it was a grueling journey. During the final eighteen days' dash across the deadliest part of the desert, which began on 10 January 1931, Thomas subsisted largely on camel's milk. His instruments clogged with sand. The fluctuating temperatures tortured him between scorching day and near-freezing night. His report makes fascinating reading, cleverly intercalated with campfireside tales of Bedouin heroes, which shadow the log of his own endeavors. He was a copious and accurate observer. But he proved that the Empty Quarter really was empty. None of the speculations about the Arabian interior, which had accumulated since Carsten Niebuhr's late eighteenth-century explorations, and to which the geographer Hogarth had alluded, turned out to be true.

Tibet: The Horizon Mislaid

In its way, Arabia enclosed the profoundest mysteries of geography to remain concealed from explorers in the twentieth century, because it was so close to the longest-serving long-range trade routes of Europe and Asia, and because of its importance in the history, religions, and cultures of so much of the rest of the world. These circumstances made its secrets perplexing and intensely challenging. Tibet, by contrast, had a long history of isolation; but it, too, lay almost athwart major historic routes of cultural exchange—between China and India, east and central Asia. And like Arabia it was a standing provocation to outsiders' curiosity, with a reputation as a forbidden and forbidding land. In

Tibet, *1933, by the Russian painter and spiritual teacher Nicholas Roerich. His dramatic paintings, which seemed to invest landscape with life, nourished the romantic image of Tibet as a spiritually powerful land*

Tibet, too, as in Arabia, resistance to Western official missions was hard to overcome or circumvent, but here amateurs were no more successful than government agents, who succeeded in penetrating the country, at first in disguise and at last in arms.

Everyone has two images of Tibet. First, it is the 'icy country,' as Tibetans themselves call it, of killer mountains and wastes encrusted with soda and salt, where the 'abominable snowman' roams. It is the highest country in the world and one of the harshest. It is also home of the Lost Horizon—the place where dreams of Shangri-La can come true, where long life and lasting peace can flourish. But purity is always in danger. In Tibet, in the eighteenth and nineteenth centuries, the extremities of nature and the prudence of the rulers combined to keep out foreign pollutants.

Tibet's natural defenses are the most daunting in the world. From China, the approach is easier than from the north, west, and south, but until the mid-twentieth century it took eight months to get from Peking to Lhasa. On other fronts, the relief is precipitate, the passes few, high, and dangerous. Sven Hedin, a Swedish preincarnation of Indiana Jones who combined antiquarianism with adventure, found it 'one of the most difficult countries on earth to conquer for purposes of human research and knowledge.' He made his first forays into the country in the 1890s.

> I knew that the first requisite was a heart so strong that its fibres and valves would not crack and burst . . . and the functions of animal combustion must become acclimatised to one half of the quantity of oxygen to which

they have become accustomed. I knew that not a tree nor a shrub can be found on these heights and that pasturage in the valleys is insufficient for the domesticated pack animals and that the resistance of both men and beasts is put to the severest tests by the everlasting storms, the bitter cold and the beating summer rains that soften the sterile ground in which the animals are mired.[34]

On Hedin's climb toward Lhasa, along passes over 17,000 feet high, his best camel died, frozen inextricably in mud, and 'men fled us but the ground held us fast.'[35] Difficulties like these make every success surprising.

In the late eighteenth and early nineteenth centuries travel to Tibet was, if not commonplace, at least possible. Plant hunters and envoys from British India made the visit. So did Armenian merchants and Jesuit missionaries. So, in large numbers, did Chinese officials and Buddhist pilgrims from China, India, and Mongolia. In 1811 an English physician, Thomas Manning, made the journey through Bhutan as an independent tourist. But Chinese jealousy of the remote dependency intervened.

A Lazarist priest, Évariste Huc, arrived in Tibet in 1846 to resume the missionary work that had faltered in the previous century when the Jesuits were disbanded. The authorities seemed unafraid. 'If the doctrine these men hold is false, Tibetans will not embrace it. If it is true, what have we to fear?' But the Chinese were apprehensive of missionaries who, experience showed, were often harbingers of European imperialism. The Chinese Resident asked, 'Does not the introduction into the country of the religion of the Lord of Heaven lead directly to the destruction of the sanctuary of the Potala, and consequently to the downfall of the Lamaist hierarchy and the Tibetan government?'[36] The native Tibetan authorities were disinclined to accept this—suspecting, perhaps, that the Chinese were more concerned with the maintenance of their own control than with the authority of the Dalai Lama. But they were powerless to defy China. In 1846 the Chinese expelled French missionaries from Lhasa and banned all further penetration by Europeans.

A defiant environment, religious taboos, political hostility, and, in China, a remote and uncommitted hegemonic power combined to keep outsiders at bay. But Britain and Russia were deeply and increasingly interested parties—neighbors of Tibet by virtue of their interests in south and central Asia respectively. Though neither power wished to detach Tibet from Chinese influence or control, both wanted to open the country up to exploitation by way of trade. In the late nineteenth century Tibet was caught between the Great Survey of India and the Russian Survey of Central Asia. Between them, these projects illustrated the transformation of exploration—from tracing the routes to mapping the gaps between them. In the 1860s and 1870s, the British used

Indian 'pundits' to map the country. Sir Thomas Holdich summarized their virtues in 1906:

> Skilful, faithful, persistent and *cheap*, there is nowhere they will not venture, and no physical difficulty of mountain or desert that they will not face. . . . No European has assisted them excepting so far as the surveyors of the Himalayas have fixed for them by triangulation a number of the remoter peaks . . . which have been their guiding points in the field, and references by means of which the final record of their surveys has been pieced together. Various have been the artifices whereby these explorers have effected their purpose. Instruments have been concealed beneath the false bottoms of boxes containing merchandise and tea. Their daily records of distance and bearings have been written in verse, and recited as a Buddhist poem. Their clothes have been made useful by a dozen different devices, and in their hands these pious pilgrims have carried their Buddhist rosaries, counting their paces and dropping a bead as every one hundred or one thousand has been completed.[37]

They also concealed surveying instruments in prayer wheels and pilgrims' staves. A representative story is that of the pundit Kinthup, known as KP. (For intelligence reasons the British kept the explorers' real names secret.) Sent to Tibet in 1880, and twice enslaved, he escaped in 1881 and took refuge in a monastery. From there he resumed his explorations in the guise of a pilgrim. He found a direct route to Lhasa without following the river. He eventually got back to India four years after the start of his odyssey. As a result of his efforts and those of his colleagues the course of the Brahmaputra was mapped almost in its entirety from its source as far as India and the great bend southward.

Though pundits could slip in and out of Lhasa in disguise with some hope of eluding detection, this was not so easy for explorers of Western appearance. Lhasa became a cynosure, like Mecca or, in former times, Timbuktu, a must-have trophy, irresistible because unattainable. The Chinese kept the Russians out, though Nikolai Przhevalsky roamed the fringes of Tibet, accumulating scientific data and scorchingly good stories. Unfriendly officials turned him back on his attempts to reach Lhasa four times between 1870 and 1888. The scholarly American Walter Rockhill had no better luck. Others who sought Lhasa in the 1890s—French adventurers, a Dutch missionary—died in the attempt, darkening the mystery of the 'Forbidden City.' Less formidable but equally effective foes were officials who detected all attempts and turned the presumptuous away. Hedin made his attempt with shaved head 'anointed with fat and soot. . . . My appearance was terrible! But no ladies were present to invite coquetry and I did not have a single acquaintance on the road to Lhasa.'[38] Not even this sacrifice—considerable, for he was a vain man—availed.

In 1899, however, two subjects of the Russian empire made the break-through. Gombozhab Tsybikov was a student who inherited central Asian looks from at least one parent's side and convincingly played the role of a Buddhist pilgrim in a caravan from Mongolia. Meanwhile Agran Dorjiev, a Buryat who really was a Buddhist, became a close adviser to the Dalai Lama and used his influence to promote Russian interests. The British were alarmed, perhaps because long exclusion from Tibet had a titillating effect. Thomas Holdich summarized the situation in 1906:

> There are in the world of geography certain links between well known and much traversed systems of communication yet unopened, and even unexplored, which, in the course of time, as the commercial world develops and the necessities of international communication become too pressing to be longer set aside in favour of political inaction, will inevitably become links in the world's highways. One such certainly appears to exist at the present time in the Dihong, or Brahmaputra, valley, which links together two great commercial highways, i.e., the Tsanpo, or upper Brahmaputra, and Assam, or lower Brahmaputra.[39]

This was the stimulus that made the British at last lose patience and force their way through to Lhasa with bayonets fixed in 1904. Francis Younghusband's foolhardy winter march reminded participants 'more of the retreat from Moscow than the advance of a British army' as they clawed their way up the ice-filmed edge of what one of the footsloggers memorably called 'one of the fucking tableland's fucking table-legs.'[40] Over 4,000 yaks were lost in the crossing. Almost as much goodwill was wasted as money and blood. Tibet reverted to aloofness and the routes explorers had pioneered and armies forced continued to carry little but pilgrims. There was no 'Lost Horizon.' It had just been temporarily mislaid.

The Trails of Steam: Route Finding for an Industrial World

In the second half of the nineteenth century steam enveloped the world. Railways and shipping lines bound the globe ever more tightly together. Long-range exchange of goods in bulk broke all records. So did the scale of migration and the distances migrants traversed. Industrialization and imperialism combined to create a new kind of global economy, in which some regions specialized in primary goods and the supply of labor, others in manufactures. For explorers, the new demand was for routes that facilitated these changes.

First, good overland routes were needed, capable of bearing heavy traffic, for intracontinental migrants, especially in North America, where the biggest concentrations occurred. Then—above all—steam trails were demanded: routes suitable for railways and steam navigation. Increasingly, other new technologies created demands or opened possibilities. From the 1840s there were electric cable lines to be laid: by the 1860s they were being laid under oceans. By the early twentieth century submarine and aeronautical navigation and the internal combustion engine were beginning to have an impact.

In most of the world, surveyors of roads and railways did not have to pioneer new routes: it was more commonly a question of smoothing existing ways, making rough places planer and cutting banks and tunnels. In North America, however, the surveyors had to be trailblazers.

The railway surveyors' exemplar was John Charles Frémont, who preceded them in the 1840s, investigating the routes to the West for wagoners on behalf of Congress. Before that, Frémont himself had got his early experience as a topographical surveyor on the Charleston–Cincinnati Railway in 1836–7. The following year he was one of the first recruits to the army's new Corps of Topographical Engineers. The main historical importance of his work was that he perceived the agricultural potential of the prairie, which previous explorers had dismissed as a desert.[41] But his devotion to scientific observation also set a model for the surveyors who followed. His expeditions in what he named, for the first time, the 'Great Basin' headlined the importance of geological and botanical investigations. He was a brilliant technician, who extemporized an ersatz barometer cistern from a piece of powder horn.[42] 'Frequent interruptions from the Indians' disturbed his 'astronomical calculations' and mapping. His reports are austere—which makes one of his few attempts at humor (recorded on the Laramie River, near the junction with the Nebraska, in 1842) worth repeating:

> Occasionally a savage would stalk in with an invitation to a feast of honor—a dog feast—and deliberately sit down and wait until I was ready to accompany him. I went to one. . . . The dog was in a large pot over the fire, in the middle of the lodge, and immediately on our arrival was dished up in large wooden bowls. . . . The flesh appeared very glutinous, with something of the flavour and appearance of mutton. Feeling something move behind me, I looked round and found that I had taken my seat among a litter of fat young puppies. Had I been nice in such matters, the prejudices of civilization might have interfered with my tranquillity; but fortunately I am not of delicate nerves, and continued quietly to empty my platter.[43]

That is one of the more restrained of the passages in which Frémont disclosed his affectations. He was always striving to contrive the image of a rough-cut paladin who knows the pretensions of civilization and how to resist them. He really was a 'man of action' with a restless spirit, an impatient temperament, and a need of constant exertion. He was at his best a long way from higher authority.

He was, if not the prototype, the epitype of the American hero. His fame makes objective judgment hard. He was hardly an explorer at all. Most of the time, he was revisiting known routes in order to map them and make improvements: in particular, where best to build forts and staging posts. Below the surface of his reports lurk rumors of wars: part of his job was to reconnoiter routes for the movement of armies, should war break out with Britain over Oregon or—as indeed happened—with Mexico over Texas or California or with the native peoples of the West over the disposal of their lands. How much Frémont achieved by way of new information is hard to assess. His discovery of the Great Salt Lake on 6 September 1843, after climbing a butte, is in the tradition of exploration's great moments: the style, indeed, seems inspired by maritime explorers' conventional descriptions of first landfalls; the imagery recalls Chapman's Homer. But the scouts in his party had seen it before:

> and ascending to the summit, immediately at our feet beheld the object of our anxious search—the waters of the inland sea stretching in still and solitary grandeur far beyond the limit of our vision. It was one of the great points of the exploration; and as we looked eagerly over the lake in the first emotions of excited pleasure, I am doubtful if the followers of Balboa felt more enthusiasm when, from the heights of the Andes, they saw for the first time the great Western Ocean.[44]

He was not, of course, the first beholder—not even the first white or Yankee beholder—of the Great Basin. But he was its godfather, who named it and nurtured its fame:

> The whole idea of such a desert, and such a people, is a novelty in our country, and excites Asiatic, not American, ideas. Interior basins, with their own systems of lakes and rivers, and often sterile, are common enough in Asia; people still in the elementary state of families, living in deserts, with no other occupation than the mere animal search for food, may still be seen in that ancient quarter of the globe; but in America such things are new and strange, unknown and unsuspected, and discredited when related. But I flatter myself that what is discovered, though not enough to satisfy curiosity, is sufficient to excite it, and that subsequent explorations will complete what has been commenced.[45]

Though Frémont himself was among America's early railway builders, the railways barely pricked the interior of the continent when he first surveyed the West. Though a wagon route to Oregon existed,[46] there was not even a viable road for wagons to California when the 1849 gold rush sent scores of thousands of settlers hurtling across the plains and the Rockies to get there. Military expeditions against the Navajo sought a route as a sideline to their main missions over the following few years, but without success. Merchants, meanwhile, chafed at the frustrations of exploiting the gold-happy markets that gleamed on the Pacific coast. For American commerce, access to the Pacific and the 'East India' and China trades had long been both vital and laborious. Via the Pacific ports a transcontinental railway would cut prices and stimulate demand for Oriental products all over the country, as well as easing the means of importing cheap Indian and Chinese labor.

Political deadlock between promoters of rival routes hamstrung decision making. The possibilities were numerous. The route originally proposed by Asa Whitney in 1844 would have linked the shores of Lake Michigan to the Pacific at the mouth of the Columbia River. Other promoters canvassed for routes from Chicago via South Pass, or St Louis via the Cochetpa Pass, or Memphis or Fulton along the thirty-fifth parallel, from Vicksburg along the Gila River, and from Springfield (Illinois) via Albuquerque—to mention only the most widely supported options. Every departure point and terminus had its boosters. In 1848–9 a preemptive attempt by Frémont to find a route that would favor his financial backers in St Louis exacerbated the problem. He tackled the task with deceptive optimism. Ten of his men died in the snow. Frémont had to turn back, still asserting that 'neither the snow of winter nor the mountain ranges were obstacles.'[47] No other private ventures in the following years accomplished much more or satisfied their rivals. As so often in the history of capitalism, competitors stifled each other. Federal action was the only way forward.

In 1853 Congress decreed that the government would fund a series of expeditions—complete with botanical and zoological specialists and official artists—to find railway routes across the continent. Science would determine objectively a decision that sectional interests disputed. Route finding went hand in hand with scientific enquiry, as the surveyors had to check the elevation and gradient of every pass, and report on the climate, resources, and native peoples along the proposed routes. The model appeared in the instructions the surveyor I. I. Stevens wrote for himself when he was dispatched to explore Whitney's suggestions. He was

> to examine the passes of the several mountain ranges, the geography and meteorology of the whole intermediate region, the character, as avenues of trade and transportation, of the Missouri and Columbia Rivers, the rains and snows of the route, especially in the mountain passes, and, in short, to collect

every species of information bearing upon the question of railroad practicability.[48]

Congress's approach to the rival routes was selective: the route along the thirty-second parallel was exempted from the attentions of the surveyors—presumably because it was thought to be viable and because it was supported by strong sectional interests in the South, which, at the time, the federal government needed to appease. Fixation with the thirty-second parallel probably arose from an error in the calculation of latitude made by Mormon frontiersmen in Guadalupe Pass in 1845.[49] Yet really the thirty-second parallel was effectively impassable. Even today the railway has to dip south into Mexican territory to cross the United States at about that latitude.

The thirty-fifth parallel offered much better prospects, and a survey conducted in 1853 proved that fact, cleaving a pretty straight route from Fort Smith on the Arkansas River to Los Angeles; in reputed desert the party found plenty of fertile valleys suitable for settlement along a route they deemed 'eminently advantageous.' But the officer responsible, Lieutenant Amiel Whipple, grossly overestimated the construction costs with deterrent, depressant effects. The official artist described the end of the expedition's tolerable discomforts, as the party approached Los Angeles, with unmistakable relish:

> the wilderness had reduced most of the garments indicative of civilization to such a state of decay that they either hung in rags or had their deficiencies supplied by patches of leather blackened by the smoke of many a camp fire. The same useful material wrapped around the feet supplied the place of boots, a distinction of which few could boast even in the most attenuated form, and our round felt hats had assumed every conceivable fantastic shape, and seemed to adhere to the tangled hair, which in many cases hung down on the shoulders. But, though conscious that our costume and personal appearance might have admitted of some improvement, we were not without a certain feeling of pride in the evidence of our long and toilsome journey, afforded by the aspect of our brown and long-bearded company, and their meagre, tired cattle.[50]

The 'cattle' consisted entirely of mules: the sheep and cows had all been killed off for food—even the oxen that dragged the vehicles.

For the rest, the surveyors' reports were so voluminous, so opaque, so mutually contradictory, and so hard to compare that the facts were long obscured. All the proposals were impractical, as the explorers revealed, and the route of the Union Pacific Railroad, when it was finally built, was different from all of them.[51]

While America waited for railways, army engineers and, sometimes, private firms opened wagon roads across the continent: dirt tracks, enhanced by engineers who flattened awkward gradients, spanned gorges, and smoothed bumpy rides. These roads were monuments not so much to the patience of the topographers as to the impatience of the public. In May 1856, 75,000 Californians petitioned Congress for a wagon road from the frontier of Missouri.[52] North–south routes across the Great Basin were largely ignored until the army took the work in hand in the late 1860s. Meanwhile, a new breed of civilian scientists began to take over the work of promoting interest in the West.

The army had left one conspicuous area unknown except to its natives. Joseph Christmas Ives, charged with finding an invasion route from the south into Mormon country, had clambered painfully out of the Grand Canyon with little more than his life in January 1858. No one—perhaps not even Indians— had got further along the Colorado, unless the wild story James White told was true. Prospecting in the San Juan Mountains, he had leapt on a raft to elude a Ute war party and had washed up 500 miles further on, in September 1867, half mad with exhaustion and hunger. Could he have done it? Was it even possible? John Wesley Powell was already planning an expedition that would find out.

He was a war hero who had lost an arm at the Battle of Shiloh, fighting, as he rather naively saw it, against slavery. As the promoter and first director of the Illinois State Natural History Museum, he raised money privately for a canyon expedition: this was a decisive break with the tradition of exploration by state-paid soldiers. From now on, in the mapping of the United States, civilian geographers would preponderate. In May 1869, Powell's team, rather capriciously hand-picked and full of eager, greenhorn undergraduates, set out from Green River, Wyoming. By 13 August they were short of rations, heading into the canyon. 'We are now ready to start,' wrote Powell in a passage of his diary that has become famous:

> on our way down the Great Unknown. . . . We have but a month's rations remaining. . . . We are three quarters of a mile in the depths of the earth, and the great river shrinks into insignificance as it dashes its angry waves against the walls and cliffs that rise to the world above. . . . We have an unknown distance yet to run; an unknown river yet to explore. What falls there are, we know not; what rocks beset the channel, we know not; what walls rise over the river, we know not. Ah, well! We may conjecture many things. The men talk as cheerfully as ever; jests are bandied about freely this morning; but to me the cheer is sombre and the jests are ghastly.[53]

Another member of the expedition, the restless army sergeant George Bradley, contemplating the canyon with an unromantic eye, expressed frank distaste.

It was 'a loathsome little stream, so filthy and muddy that it fairly stinks. . . . It is no place for a man in my circumstances but it will let me out of the Army and for that I would almost agree to explore the river Styx.'[54] Indians killed two fainthearts who clambered out, but, more by luck than judgment, Powell emerged at the far end.

On his next expedition, Powell's men paddled up the Escalante, a previously unrecorded river. The 'arid regions' he devoted himself to mapping were a testbed of American freedom. Only cooperative methods and strict regulation could eke out the water fairly. Individualism had to yield. But all Powell's efforts failed, while homesteading continued. He withdrew to organize the Bureau of Ethnology, first as a government department, then at the Smithsonian, then as part of the Geological Survey: a permanent, government-funded unit, staffed by scientists, to survey the United States. He ended up deploring the rape of the wilderness and calling for a halt to the settlement of the West.

Eventually, the railways became realities. The first railroad from sea to shining sea—or strictly speaking from New York to Sacramento, where a steamer passage completed the trip to San Francisco—opened at last in 1869, just as Powell's party was gathering for the assault on the Grand Canyon. The Trans-Siberian Railway echoed the achievement, beginning in 1891. Pioneers dreamed of trans-African railways to match those of America: When Louis Binger crisscrossed the lands west of the Volta basin in 1887–9, he was looking for suitable ground on which to lay railway tracks. A 'Cape to Cairo' railway became an incantation to exempt British imperialists from realism. A trans-Saharan railway played a similar role in French imperial imaginations. Those dreams never came true, but Africa came to bristle with roads and railways, many of which were carved from defiant environments where barely a trail had existed before.

Meanwhile, steam was affecting maritime routes. The effects accumulated slowly. For a long time, operators of regular packet lines eschewed steam as unreliable. The first transatlantic steamer kept up steam for only eighty hours of the crossing: she was scrapped and sold as a sailing ship.[55] Gradually, however, technical improvements to propulsion and fuel consumption confirmed the steamers' future. Steam-powered vessels did not need new routes. Nor, on the whole, did they make use of them: most early steamships spent the greater part of any journey under sail and used their engines only for supplementary power or as a device to escape calms. Even ships that dispensed with sailing rig altogether still found the advantage of the assistance of winds and currents useful. In some respects, however, steam vessels could buck the wind. The effect was most noticeable in the North Atlantic, where the busiest westward routes, between northern European and North American ports, were extremely

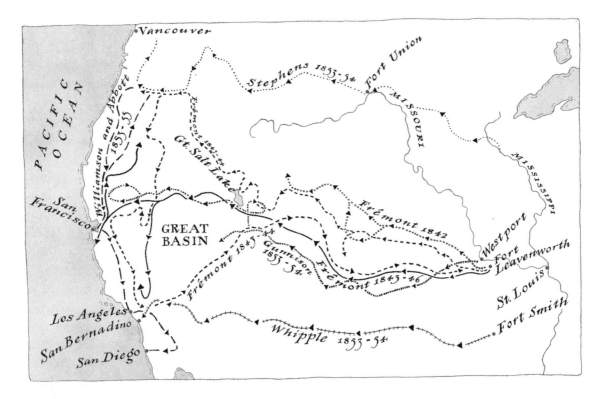

Exploring potential rail routes in the United States

laborious for sailing ships because of the detours imposed by the prevailing westerlies. The first transatlantic steam packet service opened in 1838. By the late 1840s a ten- or twelve-day crossing was normal.

Steamers could strike more directly across the ocean, taking the risk of sticking close to the limits of favorable conditions. They had to sail in all weathers, for regularity was as important as speed to the commercial appeal of the service. Paintings—there is a great collection in the Peabody Essex Museum in Salem, Massachusetts—bring the discomforts home. Vessels plunge and buck through stormy seas. Sometimes, in the propaganda spirit of the artists' commissions, they outperform sail. Sometimes the painters include symbolic hints of better times—a shaft of sunlight, a glimpse of blue skies. Sometimes they stick to the bland ease of summer. The best and most dramatic pictures share the 'staggering, heaving, wrestling, leaping, diving, jumping, throbbing, rolling and rocking' Charles Dickens described on his Atlantic crossing of 1842. His vision of the ship braving the headwinds 'with every pulse and artery of her huge body swollen and bursting' is recognizable in some of the canvases.

Intersecting rail and shipping lines were the scaffolding of the world, along which trade and travelers could clamber to every part of it. James Hill, the

Transatlantic steamship of the National Line, founded in Liverpool in 1863

railway millionaire and philanthropist who built the marble cathedral of St Paul, Minnesota, founded a steamship line that linked the fastest route across the Rockies with the Trans-Siberian Railway, which opened in 1900. The great food-producing and -consuming belt of the world, from Vladivostok to Vancouver, was linked by steam transport. By making cheap bulk haulage possible by land, steam made a startling difference: it really did wrench world trade in new directions, away from coasts, toward interiors and across continents. The world's great hinterlands, far from seas and ports and even navigable rivers, in the innermost parts of the continents, could be integrated into an increasingly global economy.

Steamships laid the next links in the interlocking system of worldwide communications: electric cables. The transatlantic cable broke repeatedly; nine years of unsuccessful efforts were necessary to build up the experience to get it right before the link became reliable in 1866. By 1924, as demonstrated in London, a telegraphic message could circle the world in 16 seconds. That was impressive: the original Puck took 40 minutes to put a girdle round the earth. In theory, cables could connect anywhere to anywhere else, but in practice, because ships had to lay them, they followed the shipping lanes' existing routes. In 1901, however, wireless telegraphy made route finders really redundant. With the help of tall masts in high places, radio waves could cover the world, unstaunched by climatic boundaries and geographical obstacles. The story of this book really was approaching its end.

The Extremes of Cold: Arctic and Antarctic Routes

However limited the new routes were that technologically inspired surveys opened up, the last great route-finding project in the world began in the nineteenth century and was accomplished in the twentieth: the creation of great-circle routes via the North and South Poles. Only aviation and submarine transport could exploit them, but the explorers who first traced them had no such means at their disposal.

The legend of an ice-free passage to the North Pole gained ground in the late eighteenth and early nineteenth centuries, thanks to whalers' stories of the iceless seas north of Spitzbergen. It would have been a huge commercial breakthrough to sail via the Pole from Europe to the Pacific, but every attempt found the way blocked. In 1827 the navy sent William Parry to try sledging over the Arctic ice from Spitzbergen to the North Pole. His reindeer refused to budge and his men had to haul sledges weighing over half a ton across shifting ice floes, only to find that, as they struggled to advance, the current drove them back at a rate of 4 knots a day. They got to 82 degrees 45 north.

The effort resumed in the second half of the nineteenth century, driven by a German publicist, August Petermann, who interested the *New York Herald* proprietor—the same James Gordon Bennett who was Stanley's patron—in his conviction that the Arctic was navigable. Expeditions probed from almost every possible point, always with the same result. The last attempt was the most tragic and the most fruitful. In 1881 the American George de Long died in the ice when his ship was crushed in the East Siberian Sea. But wreckage turned up in Greenland, suggesting that the current could be used as a means of getting around the Arctic Ocean. A new style of ice exploration vessel, the *Fram*, was built with sharply sloping, curving sides, so that she could slip between the floes and rise above the ice as the pressure built up on her hull. In 1893 Fridtjof Nansen deliberately stuck his ship in the ice north of the New Siberian Islands. Three years later the *Fram* emerged into the open sea off Franz Josef Land.

Evidently, there was no way northward through the ice. Only by sledging or walking could the Pole be reached. For men on sleds, the open water, for which earlier explorers longed, became the enemy. 'It was like crossing a river on a succession of giant shingle,' reported Robert Peary, while accumulating experience for an attempt at reaching the Pole.

> On the polar ice, we gladly hail the extreme cold, as higher temperatures and light snow always mean open water, danger and delay. Of course, such minor

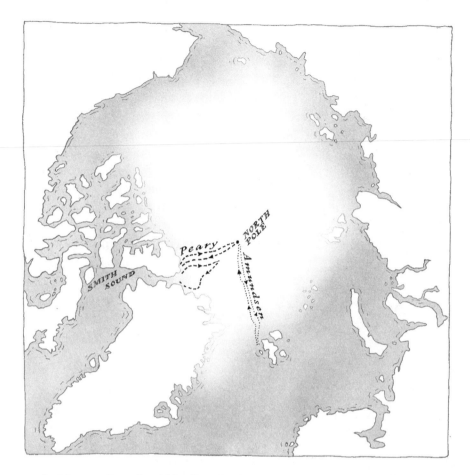

Explorers' routes to the North Pole

incidents as frosted and bleeding cheeks and noses we reckon as part of the great game. Frosted heels and toes are far more serious, because they lessen a man's ability to travel, and travelling is what we are there for.[56]

During twenty years of preparation, Peary spent nine winters in the north, befriending the local Inuit. They taught him the secrets of Arctic survival, including how to hunt, how to build a snowhouse, how to handle huskies. He hired Inuit sledders at Cape Sheridan at the extremity of Smith Sound and set off as winter lifted in 1909, carrying 30,000 pounds of pemmican. The advanced party trudged on snowshoes, with sleds in support carrying the supplies. They built snowhouses as they went to provide shelter on their return. Early in April temperatures had risen to minus 8 degrees. They were still 14 degrees short of the Pole. Peary decreed a dash with one unsupported sled and a crew of six: himself, his trusted black servant Matthew Henson, and four Inuit. Three days later, on 6 April, they reached what they thought was the Pole. Peary himself seemed hardly able to believe it. 'The prize of three centuries, my goal for twenty years! I cannot bring myself to realise it. It seems all so simple.'[57]

The achievement was much disputed—at first, by a rival explorer who claimed to have been there first. 'I'll be Peary,' sang the music-hall entertainers, 'you be Dr Cook. If you don't believe me, come and have a look.' Cook was an obvious fraudster. But Peary's honest claims were also unverifiable, and whether he correctly identified the location of the Pole remains a matter of doubt. Disputes over priority are among the most tiresome distractions in the history of exploration. The same sequence recurs all too often: first, critics deny a discovery, then they dispute its priority, then they question the accuracy with which it was reported. They usually end by dismissing its significance.

Meanwhile, Roald Amundsen demonstrated the paradox of the North-west Passage. The American Arctic was navigable between the Pacific and Atlantic—but uselessly so. Amundsen used a small vessel and hugged the coast. But the brief sailing seasons between impenetrable ice confined him and it took four years, from 1903 to 1906, to finish the job.

By then Antarctic exploration had also resumed, after a long interruption since the mid-1840s.[58] The voluminous data compiled by Dumont d'Urville and James Ross had seemed to demonstrate the uselessness of further work: no exploitable Terra Australis existed; there was no marine short cut via the South Pole. Dumont's twenty-nine volumes seemed to choke the scientific community and staunch the flow of imperial salivation. Whalers, instead of naval commanders, became the pioneers of the south, for industrialization and militarization created huge new demands for fats and lipids to grease weapons and machinery and to feed armies and cities. In the 1860s numerous expedients coincided: palm oil planting in West Africa, drilling for fossil oil in North America, the invention of margarine, and the perfection of the industrial whaler—steam-powered and mounted with deadly harpoons. Bigger whales and farther seas than ever now came within the whalers' scope.

Whaling and exploration, however, could be a frustrating combination. When the whaler *Dundee* headed south in 1892–3, the Royal Geographical Society installed a naturalist and an artist on board. 'We are in an unknown world,' cried the latter, 'and we stop for—blubber.'[59] In the late 1880s, Henryk Johan Bull, a Norwegian businessman, proposed to pay for exploration with the profits of sealing and whaling. His expenses, at first, proved higher and his yields lower than he had hoped, but in 1895 various strands united. Bull made the first recorded landing on the Antarctic continent. Meanwhile, the results of an expedition of more than twenty years before were at last published in their entirety: the voyage of the *Challenger* was the first attempt by the Royal Navy to produce a global geological map of the ocean floor. It did not sail far south by the standards of earlier explorers—only to just below 66 degrees south. But it gathered matter displaced by Antarctic glaciers, demonstrated the vastness of the continent, and revived interest in the possibilities of prospecting for mineral wealth in and around Antarctica. In 1893, moreover, Sir Clements Markham, a tireless advocate of Antarctic exploration, became president of the Royal Geographical Society. He was a stopgap, elected to fill a vacancy caused by a crisis in the society, which had split over the question of whether to admit women as fellows.[60] But his election reinvigorated exploration at a time when the Society had been shifting its work towards educational objectives; and it guaranteed that the Antarctic would now be the focus of the Society's endeavors.

In 1895 the Sixth International Geographical Congress expressed the new mood, declaring officially,

> with reference to the exploration of the Antarctic Regions . . . that this is the greatest piece of geographical exploration still to be undertaken; and in view of the additions to knowledge in almost every branch of science, which would result from such a scientific exploration, the Congress recommends that the various scientific societies throughout the world should urge, in whatever way seems most effective, that this work should be undertaken before the close of this century.[61]

That timetable was a little too optimistic, but sixteen expeditions from nine countries were launched before the First World War. In 1898 a Belgian expedition wintered in the Antarctic ice. In 1899 the grandiloquent Dane Carsten Borchgrevink, who had sailed as a seaman with Bull and disputed the claim to have first set foot in Antarctica, spent a winter on the mainland, demonstrating the usefulness of dogs. In 1904, on a government-sponsored British expedition, Captain Robert Scott faced scurvy, snow blindness, dying dogs, depleted food stocks, and dissension among his men in getting to beyond 82 degrees south. In 1903–5, and in a further expedition in 1908–10, Jean-Baptiste Charcot of France found his 'soul uplifted' in Nature's 'sanctuary of sanctuaries' while plotting nearly 2,000 miles of coastline. In 1908 Scott's unruly sidekick Ernest Shackleton reconnoitered a promising route toward the Pole, as far as beyond 88 degrees south. And all the time the desire mounted, as Scott said, 'to get inside that white space.'[62]

Scott was an irresponsible commander. On his 1904 expedition, he persisted despite the loss of navigational tackle, without which he could not accurately record his route. He jeopardized his men by refusing to recognize the obvious symptoms of scurvy. In confronting the task of reaching the South Pole, his biggest single error was, perhaps, to undervalue the usefulness of dogs. 'In my mind,' Scott wrote, 'no journey ever made with dogs can approach the height of that fine conception which is realised when a party of men go forth to face hardships, dangers, and difficulties with their own unaided efforts.' It was a prejudice Scott shared with—even, perhaps, in part owed to—Markham. Dragging sleds, according to Markham, bonded men as a team—like a rowing eight or a soccer eleven—and developed and celebrated the 'manliness' over-estimated by the products of Victorian boyhood. 'Surely in this case,' Scott averred, 'the conquest is more nobly and more splendidly won.'[63] A British form of sentimentality perverted his judgment. He could not bear to see dogs suffer, could not bear to shoot them, could not bear to eat them. His great rival Roald Amundsen, by contrast, regarded dogs as 'living souls.' By espousing a higher estimation of dogs' value, he could make them partners in his enterprise; by valuing them without sentiment, he could exploit them without pity.

Not that Scott was a doctrinaire opponent of the use of dogs: he envisaged getting to the Pole by a combination of human, equine, and canine muscle power. But in the event, his failure to appreciate dogs' vital importance proved fatal to his hopes. He thought they would be unable to haul sleds up the steep inclines the explorers faced; so he was sanguine about leaving them behind. In consequence, Scott encumbered his expedition with steppeland ponies. So his sleds had to carry a lot of humanly indigestible food. Unlike the dogs, horses could not eat their own fallen colleagues. When they got stuck in crevasses, they were hard to retrieve. When sheltering from the snow, they could not make their own shields and hollows.

Notoriously, his expedition ended as one of the heroic failures the British love to celebrate. Its most famous episode occurred when Captain Oates relieved his companions of the burden of his presence by walking to his death in the snow, uttering the classic English understatement 'I am just going outside and may be some time.' Scott's final message with its pathos and patriotism, its historic nostalgia and its unspecific religion, was perfectly calculated to appeal to British sensibilities and match the common notions the British share of themselves:

> . . . I do not regret this journey, which has shown that Englishmen can endure hardships, help one another, and meet death with as great a fortitude as ever in the past. We took risks, we knew we took them; things have come out against us, and therefore we have no cause for complaint, but bow to the will of Providence, determined still to do our best to the last. . . . Had we lived, I should have had a tale to tell of the hardihood, endurance, and courage of my companions which would have stirred the heart of every Englishman. These rough notes and our dead bodies must tell the tale.[64]

The race to the South Pole

It was not a wholly disingenuous message. Scott had always sought occasions of moral improvement. He had never tried—as Amundsen did—to make the tasks easier or more practicable. He embraced danger as a constituent of moral fiber—a kind of cement which bonded men in comradeship. But despite the fine words, they had died demoralized, unwilling or unable to go on, though they were only 11 miles from a food dump and only a little more than 100 miles from their base camp. The suspicion abides that they were virtual suicides, who preferred to die dramatically rather than live in obscurity.

Scott's excuse for failure was bad luck—especially with the unusually bad weather that truly shadowed his steps. The dogs made a decisive difference. But the reasons why Amundsen outpaced him to the Pole are more complex. Amundsen was fleeing from defeat in a previous race. He had originally planned a voyage to the North Pole and raised money with that end in view. But Peary beat him to it, and what Amundsen wanted was the glory of being first. Without telling his backers—who, ironically, included the Royal

Geographical Society, Scott's principal patrons—or most of his companions, he secretly decided on a change of destination.

When his ship reached Madeira he summoned his men.

> He said he had deceived us and also the Norwegian nation. But that could not be helped. . . . Anyone on board who didn't want to go to the South Pole was at liberty to leave the ship right away . . . Now he wanted to ask us all if we were ready to go with him to the South Pole.

Amundsen described the meeting from his own perspective:

> Now and then I had to glance at their faces. At first, as might be expected, they showed the most unmistakable signs of surprise, but this expression swiftly changed, and before I had finished they were all bright with smiles. I was now sure of the answer I should get.

The revelries on board that night were such 'that one would have thought the work was successfully accomplished instead of being hardly begun.'[65] Amundsen was candid about conceiving the expedition as a race and postponing work of scientific importance, while Scott claimed to consider such a compromise improper. Amundsen devised a route of his own, starting from the Bay of Whales, whereas Scott, guided by Shackleton, had rejected that option because of the instability of the ice. But it was 60 miles closer to the Pole than Scott's base, and it abounded in seals for food. The outcome of Amundsen's combination of advantages was inevitable. On 14 December 1911, Amundsen and his men smoked cigars at the South Pole.[66]

The major effects of polar exploration were long-delayed, but worldtransforming. First, in the Arctic, a new, world-spanning route was opened up. The Arctic has become the world's last great long-range ocean of commerce and cultural exchange. The forging of an Indian Ocean space produced an Islamic lake in the Middle Ages. From the crossing and recrossing of the Atlantic, modern Western civilization emerged. In a shadowy way, we can see how the development of the Pacific has begun to bring a new community of peoples into prominence around that ocean: a potential Pacific civilization. The Arctic will dominate the last phase of the oceanic history of the world, as planes and submarines zoom under and over the North Pole, cutting distances dramatically. Now there are cities beyond the Arctic Circle. Noril'sk, with nearly 200,000 inhabitants, has houses built on stilts above the permafrost and heated for 288 days a year, constant snowplowing, and 'street lamps four times brighter than those in southerly Russian cities.'[67] To a lesser extent, airborne routes via the South Pole will have increasing importance in the world's communications networks. If globalization fulfills its ultimate promise, and a genuinely global civilization comes into being, historians will eventually come to describe how it took shape around great-circle routes, as its predecessors did around their home oceans. The Arctic may come to be seen as the home ocean of the world.

The New Encounters

As the world got 'smaller', travelers' tales grew taller. Imaginations followed unexplored frontiers into ever remoter corners of the biosphere. In the late nineteenth and early twentieth centuries, writers of fiction sought lost worlds in which to cast unlimited adventures. Jules Verne's heroes found the under-sea ruins of Atlantis. Conan Doyle located an underevolved world of dinosaurs in the Guiana highlands and a monster-haunted world in the upper atmosphere, just beyond the reach of early aviators. James Hilton placed a wonderland of eternal youth in the recesses of the Himalayas. H. P. Lovecraft imagined a vanished civilization that throve in ice in Antarctica.

Real-life Munchausens abounded. The commercial travel writers were to blame for feeding the appetites of a credulous, craving public. The genre had always been popular: now it could make writers celebrities and millionaires. In 1875, to take an extreme instance, a writer who called himself Captain J. A. Lawson published a work apparently calculated to strain readers' credulity. In *Wanderings in the Interior of New Guinea* he described giant apes and daisies, spiders as big as dinner plates, deer with long silky manes, a tree measuring 84 feet around the trunk, a giant crimson lily whose perfume clung to his hands for hours, and a mountain taller than Everest, rising in abrupt isolation. He claimed to have climbed it to a height of 25,314 feet. And all this—remarked a skeptical reviewer—while showing 'so much philological knowledge as to be able to converse freely with savage chiefs ready to cut his throat.'[68]

In a sense, there really were lost worlds to be discovered. First, there were 'lost cities.' The nineteenth century became accustomed to the rediscovery of ancient civilizations. The ruins of Borobudur—the stupendous temple where ship reliefs attest to the prowess of Javanese explorers of the Sailendra period[69]—were unreported until 1814. In the 1840s, J. L. Stephens kept stumbling over Maya cities poking through the forest. The mendacious showman who called himself the Great Farini reported ruins in the Kalahari—perhaps honestly mistaken rocks. In the 1860s, the first citizens of Phoenix, Arizona, so named their city because they felt inspired by the ruins of the Anasazi and Hohokam civilizations. Previously unknown or uncertainly suspected ancient cities yielded to the researches of Heinrich Schliemann, Arthur Evans, Aurel Stein, and a score of less famous archeologists. The lure of the 'lost city' never altogether abated. Hiram Bingham stumbled on Machu Picchu in 1925, while seeking another genuinely lost city, Vilcabamba (actually located in nearby lowlands). In the same year, the obsessive sportsman Colonel Percy 'Jack' Fawcett, who does seem to have been mentally unhinged, disappeared in the jungles of the upper Xingu seeking a mythical city in nonexistent mountains.

More significantly for our purpose in this book, there were also lost peoples: isolated communities, sometimes unknown even to near neighbors, uncontacted by most of the rest of the world, unthreaded into the web of global communications. Exploration kept up the supply of ethnographical curiosities to enlighten or amaze Western readers. Frémont, for instance, occasionally had the sensation that the Indians he met were 'first contacts,' who had never seen 'white men' before. Railway and road surveyors in the North American southwest encountered previously unreported peoples: the Mojave in their grass skirts, the Paiute locust eaters.

The growing demand, however, was for physically unusual specimens of humankind. Scientific racism slavered for examples of bestial craniums. Criminology sought evidence that inferior folk had 'faces of degeneracy.' Imperialism looked for a scientific justification of a world sliced and stacked in order of race. Paleoanthropology began, in the 1840s, to turn up proofs of the existence of hominid species in the past. From 1859 the theory of evolution excited expectation of the discovery of a 'missing link' between apes and humans. Just as the Middle Ages craved wild men and *similitudines hominis*, or the Enlightenment longed for wolf children and noble savages, so the modern West sought odd anthropoids of its own.

Pygmies seemed the most promising objects of the quest. They had been familiar to European visitors in the Philippines and the Andaman Islands since the sixteenth century. Their existence in central Africa was known from ancient reports. Homer imagined pygmies doing battle with storks. They were among the prodigies Sebastian Cabot drew on his world map in 1544, where he showed them conversing with mannered, Renaissance gestures, and handling walking sticks: this was an attempt to reassure beholders that these people, though small, were fully human, endowed with reason, and not to be classified among the monsters widely anticipated in newly explored lands.

Stanley was responsible for the first reported contacts with pygmy societies of central Africa. He was in the 'wild Eden' of the neighborhood of the Ituri forest in 1887–8, effecting another of his 'rescues' of reluctant victims: this time, it was Emin Pasha, governor of the Egyptian province of 'Equatoria' in the great lakes region, which revolt in the Sudan had cut off from the normal route of communications along the Nile. Stanley got to know the pygmy peoples of the region and to describe their singularities with some accuracy: their diversity in appearance, pigmentation, culture, and languages, and the extraordinary degree of isolation which kept them from contact with all but their closest neighbors. The first pygmies he saw were women, captured by an Arab slaver, near the confluence of the Ituri and the Lenda. His initial impressions were clouded with exoticist clichés, as he beheld 'a perfectly formed young woman' 33 inches in height,

> of about seventeen, of a glistening and smooth sleekness of body. Her figure was that of a miniature coloured lady, not wanting in a certain grace, and her face was very prepossessing. Her complexion was that of a quadroon, or of the colour of yellow ivory. Her eyes were magnificent, but absurdly large as that of a young gazelle; full, protruding, and extremely lustrous. Absolutely nude, the little demoiselle was quite possessed, as though she were accustomed to be admired, and really enjoyed inspection.

A 'pygmy queen' encountered as an Arab's slave a few months later was also 'a very pleasing little creature.'[70]

A fully grown male specimen, however, eluded Stanley. He found, at first, only deserted villages and camps, then captured a few women and children. Despite the 'monkey eyes' and prognathous jaws Stanley detected in some specimens, the impression they made on him continued favorable. At last, on 28 October 1888, Stanley met his first adult male pygmy:

> Not one London editor could guess the feelings with which I regarded this mannikin from the solitudes of the vast central African forest. To me he was far more venerable than the Memnonium of Thebes. That little body of his represented the oldest types of primeval man, descended from the outcasts of the earliest ages, the Ishmaels of the primitive race, for ever shunning the haunts of the workers . . . eternally exiled by their vice, to live the life of human beasts in morass and fen and jungle wild. Think of it![71]

While relegating them to the nether links of the chain of being, Stanley did at least acknowledge pygmies' humanity. 'Though their souls were secreted under abnormally thick folds of animalism, and the finer feelings inert and torpid through disuse, they were there for all that.'[72]

The second front of the search for pygmies was in New Guinea. Here pygmies met British ornithologists who were researching New Guinea's Nassau Mountains in 1910. A Dutch team sponsored by a scientific committee found the 'potato-bellied' Tomorini pygmies in 1921, while mountaineering at the western end of the same range. Yet when Matthew Stirling led an airborne expedition to find more such peoples in 1926, the Nogullo pygmies still took him by surprise, which they returned—the women by biting their middle fingers and fanning their breasts, the men by clicking with their fingernails the phalli that sheathed their private parts.[73]

The pygmies were by no means the most surprising new people—new, that is, to the outside world—to be found in New Guinea. In a sense, there could be no real surprises, since expectations of the island, and of the novelties its unknown depths might enclose, were so extravagant. New Guinea was uniquely mysterious—appearing to one early explorer as 'a vague vast wonderland where . . . the adventures of the Arthurian age might be eclipsed' and to another as like 'some of the enchanted regions of the Arabian Nights, so dim an atmosphere of obscurity rests at present on the wonders it conceals.'[74] In the very year 'Captain Lawson's' spoof appeared, a French sailor, wrecked among cannibals on the north coast of New Guinea, started the last legend of El Dorado. Louis Trégance's adventures capped even Lawson's. He claimed to have fled inland, where he stumbled on a gold-rich empire of city dwellers and mounted aristocrats whom he called Orangwoks. It was not, on the face of it, an implausible tale. His readers knew nothing about the mountains he described, except that they existed. No traveler was known to have been there before. The fantasy turned out to be false. New Guinea had no horses—indeed, no quadrupeds larger than pigs and pygmy kangaroos. Nor was there any metallurgy, for the inhabitants of the interior spurned the gold that trickled in the rivers, in favor of rare shells from the distant sea. Instead of a great empire the interior enclosed hundreds, perhaps thousands, of tiny, mutually warring polities.

These were real-life 'lost worlds.' The reality was almost stranger than Trégance's fiction. Undisturbed and uninfluenced by the outside world, a dense population throve for millennia, unknown to anyone beyond the island's shores.

In June 1930, the gold prospector Michael Leahy turned the map of New Guinea 'all cockeyed,' as a British official averred, by crossing the island from the Markham and Ramu Rivers to the Purari by a previously unknown network of waterways.[75] When he first saw the grasslands above the Bismarck Range in June 1930, he assumed that the land had been cleared by forest fires. But in the night he spotted in terror the flickerings of a thousand camp fires. He had found an intensely inhabited world where no one expected one. He and his men stood to arms all night.[76]

Yet the natives, though constantly at war with each other, proved remarkably hospitable to new arrivals. 'A white man could go anywhere,' Leahy reported, 'with no better weapon than a walking stick.'[77] The explorers could frighten warriors into submission by clattering a set of dentures and wash gold out of rivers without arousing cupidity. They could buy women and pigs for handfuls of shells or steel blades.

The new encounters multiplied. In 1933 Leahy spotted another promising valley, the Goroka, from a point 7,000 feet high near Bena Bena. He returned by plane to examine it and saw from the air the Chimbuy valley,

> possibly twenty miles wide and no telling how many miles long, between two high mountain ranges, with a very winding river meandering through it. Below us were evidences of a very fertile soil and a teeming population—a continuous patchwork of gardens laid off in neat squares like chessboards, with oblong grass houses in groups of four or five dotted thickly over the landscape. Except for the grass houses, the view below us resembled the patchwork fields of Belgium as seen from the air. Certainly the 50,000 or 60,000 new people we had found on the upper Purari were as nothing compared to the population that must live in this valley.[78]

In fact the figures suggested by early beholders of these valleys were all grossly underestimated. The myth of uninhabited mountains filling central New Guinea was no longer tenable. The Goroka valley had over 100,000 people, the Chimbuy half as many again. In all, there were well over half a million people living in highland areas unknown before the 1930s.

No contacts remained to be made on this scale anywhere in the world. The great work of explorers, rethreading the links between separated human communities, was nearing its close. But deep forests still kept some small groups separated and out of touch with the world beyond their immediate neighbors. The world—the part of the world self-proclaimed as civilized—supposed that these were failed communities, which had missed out on progress. Really, they should be considered the most successful societies in history: they had achieved a conservative nirvana, preserving their culture against change, resisting the convulsive lurches of 'modernity.' Of course, relatively few of them had managed to stay entirely aloof from the frenzied global exchanges of culture of the last 500 years or so. Most of them relished such products of the industrial world as came their way, especially cutting metals and indestructible trinkets, and got them by war or barter from neighbors who were in touch with the edges of the global marketplace.

The problems of defining an isolated or uncontacted community became obvious in 1971, when Manuel Elizalde, a Filipino politician and philanthropist with strong connections to the ruling dictator, announced the discovery of a group of twenty-six or twenty-seven cave dwellers in the rainforest of South Cotobato, only a few hours' journey on foot from the nearest modern settlement. The Tasaday, as they called themselves, wore leaves, used tools of stone and bamboo, and ate wild, gathered foods. They seemed to fit every primitivist stereotype, with a supposedly pacific nature, a language that lacked words connected with warfare, and an attitude of reverence for Elizalde, whom they dubbed a god. They did not even kill to eat and, according to early reports, had no knowledge of how to hunt. The government virtually sealed them in a protected habitat, but when a journalist hiked into the area some twelve years later, perplexing inconsistencies came to light. The Tasaday, it turned out, used cultivated bamboo for their tools, and did not seem to use stone tools at all except for display. They appeared to have access to cultivated rice and other products from outside the forest; their language, though distinctive in some ways, was close to—perhaps derived from—those of neighboring communities. Some Tasaday supported claims that their existence as a tribe was a hoax perpetrated by their 'discoverer.'

The truth remains obscure, but, on currently available evidence, the Tasaday seem to have been a self-created group of dropouts from nearby communities, and were never as isolated or as innocent of hunting or agriculture or conflict as romantic primitivism painted them.[79] Their story is cautionary at two levels: on the one hand, it demonstrates the dangers of perceptions distorted by a romantic mindset; it also shows that even highly traditional communities, hostile to change, are not changeless, but split and come to life or even revert to isolation after sampling contact. In the modern world, isolation is a relative term.

Nonetheless, throughout the twentieth century, it is fair to say that a great laboratory of new encounters has existed in Amazonia. At the start of the century, surviving forest peoples seemed numerous but doomed. According to most supposedly expert opinions, evolution would condemn them to extinction, or 'order and progress'—the ideals embroidered on the Brazilian flag—would demand their suppression. Because 'no serious or sustained labour can be expected' from them, argued Hermann von Ihering, scientific director of the São Paulo Museum in 1908, 'we have no alternative but to exterminate them.'[80] Railway construction littered the forest with dead Indians and priests who tried to protect them.

On the other hand, there were always Brazilians who regarded the natives as national treasures, and progress as a process bound to redeem them, in time, of their 'savage' characteristics. This was a form of reculturation or reconfiguration of culture as effective as any genocide. In 1912, for instance, the recently formed Indian Protection Service made contact with its first 'new' people, the Kaingang. The naked arrivals in the camp 'were immediately dressed.' The government proudly announced their 'pacification': railway men 'may now penetrate with impunity into their remotest dominions.'[81] New diseases killed contacted people; their birth rate dwindled.

Railways and roads spread contact and sped death. Soon after the Second World War the Brazilian government decide to open a road through the forest from the Araguaia to the Xingu and Tapajós and clear airstrips along the way. The brothers Orlando and Cláudio Vilas Boas, who got interested in Amazonian exploration in a spirit of adventure in their youth, became, with experience, the heroic vanguard of the Indian Protection Service. They contacted undocumented groups ahead of the loggers and lawyers, miners and missionaries, with the aim of making Indians' introduction to modernity as painless as possible. At first, ox and mule trains supplied them as they went. Later, in the 1960s, air drops took over. In 1953 the brothers had their first great success. They tracked down the Mentukitre—Indians known previously only from their fierce reputation with other tribes. 'Men beat their chests and said they were our brothers. Women hastily hid behind trees or buried themselves in the forest; boys and girls ran about. Infants cried.'[82] In 1960 they found the Suyá—a people unheard of since 1884, when Karl von der Steinen initiated a new method of exploration in the Brazilian interior: instead of sticking to rivers as highways, which is relatively easy, he approached the upper Xingu River overland, across the northern Mato Grosso, before heading downriver, making the first recorded crossing of the Von Martius rapids. The Suyá illustrated one of the great problems of 'Indian protection': violence was part of their way of life, enmity toward outsiders part of their cosmology. They could not be 'pacified' without a sacrifice of identity.

One of the follow-up expeditions cut a route along the unmapped upper reaches of the Iriri River into the Cachimbo Hills in 1961, where no previously uncontacted people were known to live. The leader, Richard Mason, a young English idealist, was found dead on the trail, ahead of his companions, bristling with arrows and with his head bashed in. This was the first anyone knew of the Panará, who finally made contact with representatives of the Brazilian government in 1971. They were shunted back and forth between their homeland and new settlement areas, making way for commercial development, before at last achieving peace on a suitable reservation in 1996. John Hemming, who was just behind Mason when he died, took part in four other encounters over the next few years. 'One tribe was hostile, with the men constantly holding their bows and arrows; two groups were in a state of shock; and a fourth treated us strangers like gods, trying to give us all their few possessions.'[83]

In 1967–8 the opening of a road to Porto Velho on the Madeira led to more contacts, more disease, more colonization. Five distinct groups emerged from the hills north of the road, including the Cinta Larga and the Surui. Their

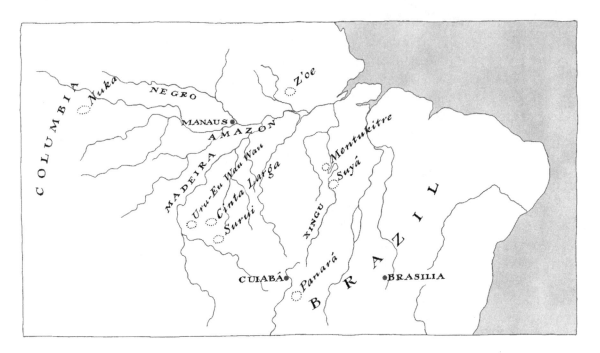

decline into a familiar cycle of depression, dependency, and deracination began, as commercial exploiters moved into their territory for ranching, logging, and mining. António Cotrim, hero of a series of encounters with Indians whose trust he won, resigned from government service in 1972, disillusioned with the morbid and often mortal consequences of contact, which he had come to see as 'forcing a community to take the first step on a road that will lead them to hunger, sickness, disintegration, quite often to slavery, the loss of their traditions, and in the end death in complete misery that will come all too soon.'[84] In the same year, a Brazilian government inquiry exposed 'sordid complicity in greed, cruelty and murder' by staff of the Indian Protection Service.[85]

Myths and misunderstandings made contact hazardous. Before contact, the Panará were believed to be giants, because a boy captured in infancy by a nearby tribe grew (freakishly, as it turned out) to be over 6 feet tall. When the Panará tried to make peaceful overtures, the air force flew in paratroopers with machine guns. The conflict of perceptions of the Indians in Brazilian society was still as strong at the time as in the early years of the century. When Robin Hanbury-Tenison, one of the founders of Survival, toured Brazil to compile a report on the needs and prospects for international aid for the Indians in 1970, his discussions with government officials, who saw rapid integration as the only future for the Indians, contrasted with the words of Cláudio Vilas Boas, who realized that

The location of native peoples in Brazil during the 'contacts' of the twentieth century

Brazilian Indian of the Surui people

it is stupid to try and integrate the Indian, for the Indian is better than we are, knows how to live much better than we do, and has more to teach us than we could ever teach him. . . . Trace any process of integration which has taken place and watch the destruction of the people concerned.[86]

Missionaries were similarly divided, between those from evangelical and fundamentalist churches, who saw it as their duty to uproot indigenous culture, and their competitors, mostly post-Vatican II Catholics, who saw it as their duty to work with and within the Indians' own cultural traditions. By 1987 the business lobby was accusing the Church of a conspiracy 'to make the Brazilian state accept restricted sovereignty over indigenous territories' and stop exploitation of the riches of Amazonia.[87]

New contacts seemed inexhaustible. In 1981 the Uru-Eu-Wau-Wau at last responded to feelers government agents had been putting out for years on the Jarami River south of Porto Velho. But their counsels were divided and bands of hostiles continued to resist for years. Indians began building their villages under the forest canopy to conceal them from airborne reconnaissance, making them harder than ever to locate. In May 1989 a contact episode took place under television cameras: the existence of the Zo'e—133 people in four villages—was known by report from the early 1970s; aviators had spotted their villages in 1982.[88] The presence of an isolated tribe less than 200 miles from the city of Santarem seemed sensational, as television viewers saw the Ż'oe offer broken arrows to signify their peaceful intentions. It happened on the upper Cuminapanema River, which joins the Curua, where Protestant missionaries were the pioneers. New contacts continued in the 1990s, when the Nukak emerged: people who really did live a preagrarian way of life as hunters and gatherers. At the beginning of the twenty-first century, there were still reckoned to be over forty uncontacted Indian communities in Brazil.[89]

Awfully Big Adventures

The story of exploration in the late nineteenth and twentieth centuries is paradoxical: individual failure and cumulative achievement. Almost all the tasks were accomplished, almost all the stories concluded. Except for those remaining Brazilian communities, everyone in the world was in touch with everyone else by the end of the period. The history of cultural divergence had been reversed. The resumed work of convergence was well advanced. Yet almost all the explorers who have featured in this chapter were failures in their way, hampered by characteristic vices: amateurism, naivety, profligacy, credulousness, distractedness, quarrelsomeness, bombast, mendacity, romantic myopia, sheer incompetence.

Some of the problems that defeated them were structural—derived from the nature of exploring as a business and, in particular, from the way it was financed. Much exploration was in the nature of a speculative venture. The railway surveys, for instance, were expected to store up prospects of profit; though they usually relied on government initiatives, a good deal of private finance went into many of the efforts. Stanley's swathe through the forests of the Congo was intended to lay the infrastructure for exploitation—and pretty ruthless exploitation it turned out to be. Gold miners and coal seekers were largely responsible for opening routes into the secret places of New Guinea. Most of the Antarctic expeditions relied on independent finance, from philanthropists and businessmen or from public subscription. The biggest subscriber to Scott's work was a paint manufacturer who had no obvious commercial interest in the undertaking. The German and Japanese governments all financed entire expeditions. The British government matched Scott's first foray fifty-fifty and made grants toward other efforts. France, Mexico, Brazil, Chile, Argentina, New Zealand, Australia, all made supplementary contributions to privately sponsored efforts.

The press was vital. Newspapers, publishers, and—by the time of Scott's fatal expedition—cinema companies paid for explorers' stories. The American press baron was Henry Stanley's great patron. *Le Matin* raised money for Charcot from its readers. It was not just the explorers who needed money: the institutions that organized their efforts were usually missionary groups or learned geographical societies, who were also competing for public subscriptions. So without good copy, there would have been no money for the explorers.[90] Without great stories and glorious heroes, public support and interest would have withered. Hyperbole and hypocrisy were among the consequences, and a great waste of ink and blood.

The means of finance dragged exploration away from scientific goals. Adventure kept obtruding. The last phase of so many expeditions became a 'dash.' Explorers like Amundsen, who admitted that they put sensation above science, were rare. Evasions were more usual, like those of Douglas Mawson, who pretended that science and adventure were indivisible. The leadership of Britain's Royal Geographical Society—still the world's most zealous promoter of exploration in the age of Scott—was unwavering in its explicit insistence that no exploration was justified except by the value of the scientific results; and Scott seems genuinely to have shared that view, until the glare of the ice got in his eyes and the scent of the quest in his nostrils. Then he forgot his 'plain duty . . . to achieve the greatest possible scientific harvest which the circumstances permit'[91] and went all out to race for the Pole. Although the Royal Geographical Society retained scientific priorities, there can be no doubt that the Society's own need for funds tugged at its heartstrings: the Society needed explorers with éclat and *succès d'estime*—or, in English terms, 'pluck' and 'grit.' Whenever public sentiment needed galvanizing, patriotic competition seemed to take over from other objectives. Amundsen rhapsodized about the sight of his young country's 'dear flag' flying over the South Pole. He addressed the last lines of his account of the episode to the flag—a rhetorical device breathtakingly crude and alarmingly effective. Explorers became adrenalin addicts. 'A day without a new emotional experience,' Garnier found, 'is a disappointment.'[92]

Shackleton's attempted transantarctic expedition, which followed Scott's failure in an attempt to redeem it, was pointless from a scientific point of view. It was justifiable only on grounds of unalloyed adventure. It became another heroic failure. The expedition came to grief as soon as it began; but the leader's fantastic voyage to South Georgia in an open boat to get help and his return to rescue his stranded crew made it all seem glorious. Douglas Mawson, a companion of Shackleton's earlier expedition, expressed the confusion that deluded so many explorers into madcap adventures: 'Science and exploration have never been at variance; rather, the desire for the pure elements of natural revelation lay at the source of that unquenchable power—the "love of adventure".'[93] He led his own expedition in 1911–14, with the aim of mapping the section of Antarctica that lies opposite Australia and staking, in effect, an Australian claim to a share of the potential spoils. On his attempt to establish the easternmost limits of the region, he ran out of food, buried his men, ate his dogs, and struggled back to camp starving and gangrenous.

Garnier on the middle Mekong was another explorer who exhibited breathtaking temerity, forcing his native oarsmen at gunpoint to paddle him through the Preatapang rapids, which roar and plunge and buck for 30 miles along the west bank of the river. His excuse was to verify his guides' claim that the rapids were too dangerous to navigate downstream and too powerful to navigate upstream. He could have accepted the local knowledge but as he confessed on another occasion, 'I was accustomed to having the natives predict difficulties and then never encountering them. I thus did not take any objection seriously.'[94] Instead, he survived by a hair's breadth before accepting that his informants were right.

For some explorers, the best career move was death. Their endeavors were astonishingly profligate of each other's lives. The models to follow were nearly all of men who had 'given their lives': Cook, La Pérouse, Park, Laing, Livingstone projected shadows onto every explorer's tombstone. Garnier and his companions derived inspiration from the example of Henri Mouhot, a lone French naturalist who had died in the depths of Laos in 1861. Scott and his companions made a cult of 'risk.' Their deaths masked their failures and became a perverse kind of success. Facing death in central New Guinea in 1910, the young Donald Mackay[95] wrote, 'I guess, if I have to swing over the Edge, I won't have such a rough spin when I put out on the last Great Adventure. Strange that, at last, every man has to explore the Unknown.' This was a Boys' Own shibboleth, ingrained in readers of juvenile literature of the time. For Peter Pan, who never grew up, death could seem 'an awfully big adventure.'

Clearly, in some respects, technology transformed exploration, redirecting route finding toward industrially determined ends, multiplying explorers' reach and range, blasting Stanley's rocks, carving tunnels, laying hills low, making rough places plain, and at last rendering every climate and depth and altitude on earth accessible. But perhaps because of the prevalence of the spirit of adventure and the trappings of romance, some technical innovations took slow effect. Speke discovered the source of the Nile in three-piece tweeds, eschewing tropical kit. Bertram Thomas wanted to explore Arabia in the old-fashioned spirit, without technology to spoil the fun. Even in the 1960s, John Hemming and his companions in Brazil used techniques of astronomical observation and triangulation unchanged since the eighteenth century, with instruments not much different from those of the former era.

Of course, the growing technology gap helped to impress, cow, bribe, or zap locals, who might otherwise have impeded exploration. But it was often the minor miracles of modernity that proved most useful. Thomson affected magical powers by flashing false teeth. So did Lieutenant Tidball among the Mojave on Whipple's railway survey in the North American southwest.[96] The New Guinea gold hunter Michael Leahy was the last explorer to rely on the magical resonances of the click of dentures. Hedin found his pocket watch useful for impressing Tibetan guards. 'They could not understand its perpetual motion. . . . I explained that there was a little god inside.'[97] Garnier and his companions showed off their surveying equipment so effectively that they left the Laotian governor at Khong convinced 'that very surely Buddha must have been born in France.'[98]

Still, as technology improved and the gaps in the map grew narrower, white explorers relied less on native guides—or, at least, they showed them less respect. The 'pundits' who gathered information about Tibet for the surveyors of India were treated as unschooled handymen. François Garnier, shooting the rapids of Preatapang, evinced typical contempt: when the current was racing at 6 or 7 miles an hour and 'it was too late to turn back,' the 'comic anguish of my oarsmen would have made me laugh had I not been fully engaged in the study of the section of the river that was before my eyes.'[99] Frémont made much use of Indian guides, but more of white trappers and prospectors who knew the trails but not how to map them. When Sven Hedin's Taghlik guides tried to steal from him, he found they were 'no more skillful as guides than as thieves.'[100] Whipple's surveyors set out with no guide except a 'little Mexican boy, who knew nothing of the route.'[101] Beyond the Little Colorado in New Mexico, they relied on trappers. But they still relied on natives' help in other ways. Without sustenance from the Mojave as they approached the Colorado ' 'tis impossible,' wrote Sherburne, 'to tell how we could get along.'[102]

It is hard, too, to tell how explorers got along with locals, especially in the regions of most intense new contacts, in Brazil and New Guinea, where the huge differences of language made the speech of neighboring peoples mutually unintelligible: this was in itself a measure of the long prevalence of cultural divergence. No doubt implicit misunderstandings were commonplace; as we have seen, incommensurable gestures kept some Brazilian natives from contact. The Vilas Boas brothers used an expansive repertoire of actions to communicate their peaceful intentions—waving gifts, bestowing hugs—and generally succeeded in making themselves understood. The power of sign language should not be underestimated, especially where a sort of lingua franca of signs was in place. Stanley's conversation with the pygmy guide whose services he enjoyed briefly in 1888 suggests its scope:

> 'How far is it to the next village where we can procure food?' He placed his right hand across the left wrist. (More than two days' march.)
>
> 'In what direction?' He pointed east.
>
> 'How far is it to the Ihuru?'
>
> 'Oh!' He brought his right hand across his elbow joint—that is double the distance, four days.

'Is there any food north?' He shook his head.

'Is there any west or north-west?' He shook his head and made a motion with hand as though he were brushing a heap of sand away.

'Why?'

He made a motion with his two hands as though he were holding a gun, and said 'Dooo!' . . .

'Are there any "Dooo" in the neighbourhood?' He looked up and smiled with a gush as artful as a London coquette, as if to say, 'You know best! Oh! naughty man, why do you chaff me?'

'Will you show us the road to the village where we can get food?'

He nodded his head rapidly, patted his full-moon belly, which meant, 'Yes, for there I shall get a full meal; for here'—he smiled disdainfully as he pressed his thumb nail on the first joint of his index finger—'are plantains only so big, but there they are as big as this, and he clasped the calf of his leg with two hands.'

'Oh, Paradise!' cried the men, 'bananas as big as a man's leg!'[103]

'Captain Lawson' was a comprehensive liar—but his claim to be able to converse with natives in New Guinea were less incredible than *The Times* declared.

What Remains?

John Hemming often heard this question, when he was Director of the Royal Geographical Society, 'from educated, intelligent and well-meaning people.' He was amazed. 'Someone who penetrates beyond the world known to his own society, discovers what lies there, and returns to describe it to his own people,' in Hemming's definition, will always have work to do, because even within this planet unknown worlds are always multiplying and reconfiguring. Evolution never stops. Species emerge and die out; cultures change unrecognizably. Climate change never ceases. Ecosystems are continually self-reformed. Geomorphology never stops changing the lie of the land, the course of the waters. Technology renders environments useful and products exploitable, or provides new ways of seeing things—closer up, or from new angles. The twentieth century, in Hemming's experience, was a 'golden age' of discovery.[104] The world's highest mountains—the giants over 8,000 meters tall—remained unscaled by climbers who survived to tell the tale, until the 1950s. No one, as far as we know, navigated the entire length of the Blue and White Niles until 2004.

The deep ocean, the earth below its crust, the rainforest canopy, the upper atmosphere—exploration here is still in its infancy. We have mapped the surface of the globe but have hardly scratched the biosphere. Most species are still undescribed and uncataloged.

Yet the main historic work of pathfinding and mapping is over and as long ago as the mid-nineteenth century was manifestly drawing to a close. The world-linking, world-girdling routes are all in place. Now globalization is turning once sundered communities into one world. This chapter has been a chapter of endings. Horizons have shrunk, frontiers closed. Adventure has become elusive. Even the genuinely unknown is predictable: staked out by cameras and radio telescopes ahead of the spacemen or divers. Earlier explorers really did not know what was round the next hill or wave, with no radar or robotics to alert them. By comparison, astronauts seem drearily cosseted. Technology stifles romance. This effect has long been predictable. As early as 1933, Peter Fleming—then still a rookie journalist before becoming a famous travel writer—realized that

> adventure in the grand old manner is obsolete, having been either exalted to the specialist's job or degraded to a stunt. . . . Of course, there is still plenty of adventure of a sort to be had. You can even make it pay, with a little care; for it is easy to attract public attention to any exploit which is at once highly improbable and absolutely useless. You can lay the foundations of a brief but glorious career on the Music Halls by being the First Girl Mother To Swim Twice Round the Isle of Man; and anyone who successfully undertakes to drive a well-known make of car along the Great Wall of China in reverse will hardly fail of his reward. Here you can make some show of keeping within the best traditions, and set out to take the Illustrious Dead down a peg by repeating their exploits with a difference. Rivers which they ascended in small boats you can ascend in smaller; if they took five months to cross a desert, go and see if you can do it in four.[105]

Perhaps we should not repine at the resumption of adventure in place of exploration, or the degeneration of what was once science into showmanship. An inescapable lesson of this book is that exploration has been a march of folly, in which almost every step forward has been the failed outcome of an attempted leap ahead. Explorers have often been oddballs or eccentrics or visionaries or romancers or social climbers or social outcasts, or escapees from the restrictive and the routine, with enough distortion of vision to be able to reimagine reality. The least and most useful of their common vices has been overambition. The splash, the scoop, and the sensation have nearly always been up there among the objectives, alongside knowledge and the enrichment of culture. Even the current gigantic folly of wasting billions of cash on space exploration—when there are so many more deserving projects close to home, and while we still know so little of our own biosphere—seems consistent with the past traced in the course of this book. If space exploration ever puts humankind in touch with nonhuman cultures in other galaxies, I suppose I shall have to add another chapter, and admit that the pathfinders who have peopled these pages did not complete the work of laying down all the gangways of cultural convergence. Indeed, that was Monty Python's justification for continuing the work of exploration beyond the earth. Let us hope, with Eric Idle, the ensemble's leading voice and lyricist, that intelligent life exists out there, because 'there's bugger all down here' on dear old Earth.

Notes

CHAPTER 1

1. When this book was already in the press, David Northrup proposed a new way of periodizing global history, according to a similar scheme, but with a different chronology ('Globalisation and the Great Convergence,' *Journal of World History*, 16 (2005), 249–67).
2. J. Goodall, *The Chimpanzees of Gombe: Patterns of Behavior* (Cambridge, Mass., 1986); F. de Waal, *Chimpanzee Politics: Power and Sex among Apes* (Baltimore, 1998), 19, 153, 210–13. For a summary of differences between chimpanzee and human culture, see M. Tomasello, 'The Question of Chimpanzee Culture', in R. Wrangham *et al.* (eds.), *Chimpanzee Cultures* (Chicago, 1994), 301–17.
3. F. de Waal, *The Ape and the Sushi-Master* (New York, 2001), 199–212.
4. B. Sykes, *The Seven Daughters of Eve* (New York, 2001), 49–62, 196–286. On the problems of dating, see L. M. Vigilant *et al.*, 'African Populations and the Evolution of Human Mitochondrial DNA,' *Science*, 258 (1991), 1503–7.
5. R. P. Clark, *The Global Imperative: An Interpretative History of the Spread of Humankind* (Boulder, Colo., 1997), 24–8.
6. B. Fagan, *The Journey from Eden: The Peopling of Our World* (London, 1990), 104–38; L. and F. Cavalli-Sforza, *The Great Human Diasporas: The History of Diversity and Evolution* (Reading, Mass., 1995), 120–3.
7. C. Gamble, *Timewalkers: The Prehistory of Global Colonization* (Cambridge, Mass., 1994), 110.
8. These variables are the subjects of useful maps in L. Cavalli-Sforza, P. Menotti, and A. Piazza, *The History and Geography of Human Genes* (Princeton, 1994). See L. and F. Cavalli-Sforza, *The Great Human Diasporas*, for a conspectus.
9. See below, pp. 210–12.
10. E. Morgan, *The Aquatic Ape Hypothesis* (London, 1997).
11. S. Oppenheimer, *The Real Eve: Modern Man's Journey out of Africa* (New York, 2003), 220–41; fig. 5.5, p. 221; fig. 5.7, p. 233; fig. 5.9, p. 241.
12. Ibid., fig. 3.1, pp. 130–8.
13. T. Taylor, *The Prehistory of Sex* (New York, 1997).
14. A. H. Brodrick, *The Abbé Breuil, Prehistorian* (London, 1963), 11. Cf. S. R. James, 'Hominid Use of Fire in the Middle and Lower Pleistocene,' *Current Anthropology*, 30 (1989), 1–26, who points out that the evidence is inconclusive.
15. R. Wrangham, 'The Raw and the Stolen,' *Current Anthropology*, 40 (1999), 567–94.
16. J. Goudsblom, *Fire and Civilisation* (Harmondsworth, 1994), 21–5.
17. K. Lorenz, *On Aggression* (New York, 1996); R. Ardrey, *The Territorial Imperative* (New York, 1997).
18. M. Mead, 'War Is an Invention, Not a Biological Necessity,' *Asia*, 40 (1940), 402–5.
19. L. H. Keeley, *War before Civilization* (New York, 1996), 37.

20. R. Wrangham and D. Peterson, *Demonic Males: Apes and the Origins of Human Violence* (London, 1997), 83–199.

21. B. de Vries and J. Goudsblom (eds.), *Mappae Mundi* (Amsterdam, 2002), 57.

22. J. Adovasio, *The First Americans* (New York, 2002), 146–88.

23. T. Dillehay, *Monte Verde: A Late Pleistocene Settlement in Chile*, 2 vols. (Washington, DC, 1997, 2002), ii. 1–24.

24. M. W. Helms, *Ulysses' Sail* (Princeton, 1988); *Craft and the Kingly Ideal* (Austin, Tex., 1993).

25. J. Mellaart, *Çatal Hüyük: A Neolithic Town in Anatolia* (New York, 1967), 131–78.

26. J. Haas *et al.* (eds.), *The Origins and Development of the Andean State* (Cambridge, 1987), 44–5.

27. D. R. Harris (ed.), *The Origins and Spread of Agriculture and Pastoralism in Eurasia* (Washington, DC, 1996).

28. S. Mithen, *After the Ice* (Cambridge, Mass., 2004), 407–13.

29. J. Diamond, *Guns, Germs and Steel* (New York, 1999).

30. J. B. Harley and D. Woodward (eds.), *The History of Cartography*, ii/iii (Chicago, 1987–), 26.

31. Ibid. 27.

32. Ibid. ii/i. 307; E. Neumeyer, *Prehistoric Indian Rock-paintings* (Delhi, 1983), p. 68, fig. 26e.

33. Harley and Woodward (eds.), *History of Cartography*, ii/ii. 132.

34. T. Save-Sondebergh, *Ägypten und Nubien* (Lund, 1941), 11–30.

35. J. Tyldesley, *Hatshepsut: The Female Pharaoh* (London, 1996), 144–53, 170–4.

36. H. Goedicke (ed.), *The Report of Wenamun* (Baltimore, 1975), 58–87.

37. Hesiod, *Works and Days*, 392–420, 450–75, 613–705; trans. A. W. Mair (Oxford, 1908), 11, 15–17, 23–5.

38. M. R. Bierling (ed. and trans.), *The Phoenicians in Spain: An Archaeological Review of the Eighth—Sixth Centuries B.C.E.* (Winona Lake, Ind., 2002).

39. Herodotus, *Histories*, I. 163, IV. 152.

40. Cunliffe, *The Extraordinary Voyage of Pytheas the Greek* (London, 2002).

41. Herodotus, *Histories*, IV. 42–3.

42. L. Casson, *Ships and Seamanship in the Ancient World* (Baltimore, 1995).

43. Harley and Woodward (eds.), *History of Cartography*, i. 177–200.

44. Strabo, *Geography*, I. 1. 8–10.

45. Horace, *Odes*, 3. 29. 27.

46. J. Needham, *Science and Civilisation in China*, i (Cambridge, 1956), 173–96.

47. R. and S. Whitfield and N. Agnew, *Cave Temples of Mogao* (Los Angeles, 2002), 19–20.

48. Needham, *Science and Civilisation in China*, i. 196–206.

49. L. Casson (ed.), *The Periplus Maris Erythraei* (Princeton, 1989), 61–91.

50. D. T. Potts, *The Arabian Gulf in Antiquity*, 2 vols. (Oxford, 1990), ii. 23–264; M. Rice, *The Archaeology of the Arabian Gulf* (London, 1994), 121–6.

51. E. B. Cowell (ed.), *The Jatakas; or, Stories of the Buddha's Former Birth*, 7 vols. (Cambridge, 1895–1913), i. 10, 19–20; ii. 89–91; iv. 10–12, 86–90.

52. Harley and Woodward (eds.), *History of Cartography*, ii/ii. 72.

CHAPTER 2

1. P. V. L. Kirch, *On the Road of the Winds: An Archaeological History of the Pacific Islands before European Contact* (Berkeley, 2000), 215–19.

2. Ibid. 230.

3. T. Heyerdahl, *The Voyage of the Kon-Tiki* (London, 1952); *American Indians in the Pacific: The Theory behind the Kon-Tiki Expedition* (London, 1952); *La navegación marítima en el antiguo Peru* (Lima, 1996).

4. P. Bellwood, *The Polynesians: The History of an Island People* (London, 1978), 39–44; *Man's Conquest of the Pacific: The Prehistory of Southeast Asia and Oceania* (Auckland, 1979), 296–303; G. Irwin, *The Prehistoric Exploration and Colonisation of the Pacific* (Cambridge, 1992), 7–9, 43–63.

5. D. L. Oliver, *Oceania: The Native Cultures of Australia and the Pacific Islands*, 2 vols. (Honolulu, 1989), i. 361–422.

6. P. H. Buck (Te Rangi Hiroa), *Vikings of the Sunrise* (New York, 1938), 268–9.

7. Above, p. 28.

8. A. Fienup-Riordan, *Boundaries and Passages: Rule and Ritual in Yup'ik Eskimo Oral Tradition* (Norman, Okla., 1994), 266–98.

9. J. Bockstoce, *Arctic Passages* (New York, 1991), 18–19, 32.

10. Ibid. 41–8.

11. G. Jones, *A History of the Vikings* (Oxford, 1968), 270.

12. *Navigatio Sancti Brandani Abbatis*, ed. C. Selmer (Dublin, 1989), 12.

13. T. Severin, *The Brendan Voyage* (London, 1978).

14. *Navigatio Brandani*, 80–1.

15. V. I. J. Flint, *The Imaginative Landscape of Christopher Columbus* (New Haven, 1992), 87, 91–7, 162–7.

16. F. Fernández-Armesto, 'The Indian Ocean in World History,' in A. Disney and E. Booth (eds.), *Vasco da Gama and the Linking of Europe and Asia* (Delhi, 2000), 11–29, at 14.

17. I. Glover and P. Bellwood, *Southeast Asia from History to Prehistory* (London, 2004), 238.

18. J. Miksic, *Borobudur: Golden Tales of the Buddha* (Hong Kong, 1990), 17, 67–93.

19. Al-Masudi, *Les Prairies d'or*, ed. C. Barbier de Meynard and A. Pavet de Courteille, 9 vols. (Paris, 1861–1914), iii. 6; F. Fernández-Armesto, *Millennium* (London, 1999), 23.

20. G. R. Tibbetts, *Arab Navigation in the Indian Ocean before the Coming of the Portuguese* (London, 1971), 2.

21. Buzurg ibn Shahriyar, *The Book of the Wonders of India*, ed. G. S. P. Freeman-Grenville (London, 1981), 41 ff.

22. K. N. Chaudhuri, *Trade and Civilisation in the Indian Ocean* (Cambridge, 1985), 19; *Asia before Europe* (Cambridge, 1990).

23. Tibbetts, *Arab Navigation*, 189.

24. Ibid. 12.

25. D. Keene, *Anthology of Japanese Literature* (New York, 1960), 82–91; T. J. Harper, 'Bilingualism as Bisexualism,' in W. J. Boot (ed.), *Literatuur en Teetaligheid* (Leiden, 1990), 247–62.

CHAPTER 3

1. I. C. Glover, 'The Southern Silk Road: Archaeological Evidence for Early Trade between India and Southeast Asia,' in N. Chuttiwongs *et al.* (eds.), *Ancient Trades and Cultural Contacts in Southeast Asia* (Bangkok, 1996), 57–85, at 81; V. M. Di Crocco, 'References and Artifacts Connecting the Myanmar Area with Western and Central Asia and China Proper,' ibid. 161–80.

2. *The Literary Works of Ou-yang Hsiu*, ed. R. C. Egan (Cambridge, 1984), 113.

3. R. von Glahn, *The Country of Streams and Grottoes* (Cambridge, Mass., 1987), 12, 36, 85–90.

4. R. and S. Whitfield, *Cave Temples of Mogao* (Los Angeles, 2002), 5–20.

5. O. Lattimore, *The Desert Road to Turkestan* (Boston, 1929), 183.

6. Si-yu-ki, *Buddhist Records of the Western World: Chinese Accounts of India*, i (Calcutta, 1957), 11–12.

7. *The Travels of Marco Polo*, ed. R. Latham (Harmondsworth, 1972), 85.

8. M. Ipsiroglu, *Painting and Culture of the Mongols*, trans. E. D. Phillips (London, 1967), 70–81, 102–4.

9. Lattimore, *Desert Road to Turkestan*, 274.

10. J. Mirsky, *The Great Chinese Travellers* (London, 1964), 29–118; Si-yu-ki, *Buddhist Records*, i. 7–9, 74–81.

11. Above, pp. 35, 56–7, 60–1.

12. Mirsky, *Great Chinese Travellers*, 124–71.

13. Ibid. 34–82.

14. *Travels of Marco Polo*, 39.

15. M. Rossabi, *Voyager from Xanadu* (Tokyo, 1992).

16. Ibid. 186.

17. Mirsky, *Great Chinese Travellers*, 185.

18. H. Yule, *Cathay and the Way Thither*, 4 vols. (1913–16), iii. 146–52.

19. Above, p. 31.

20. Yule, *Cathay and the Way Thither*, iii. 146–52.

21. I. de Rachewiltz, *Papal Envoys to the Great Khans* (Stanford, 1971), 109.

22. G. G. Guzman, 'Reports of Mongol Cannibalism,' in S. D. Westrem (ed.), *Discovering New Worlds* (New York, 1991), 31–68.

23. *The Travels of Friar William of Rubruck*, ed. P. Jackson (Cambridge, 1981), 72–101.

24. H. Cortazzi, *Isles of Gold: Antique Maps of Japan* (New York, 1983), 4.

25. Above, p. 22.

26. J. Veillard, *Le Guide du pèlerin* (Macon, 1938), 50, 26, 28.

27. Adam of Bremen, *History of the Archbishops of Hamburg-Bremen*, ed. F. J. Tschan (New York, 1959), 186.

28. Ibid. 202.

29. E. Christiansen, *The Northern Crusades* (Harmondsworth, 1997), 18.

30. Adam of Bremen, *History of the Archbishops*, 134.

31. Ibid. 194–7.

32. Ibid. 189.

33. Ibid. 204.

34. P. M. Watts, *Nicolaus Cusanus: A Fifteenth-Century Vision of Man* (Leiden, 1982), 26.

35. Ibid. 212.

36. Ibid. 214.

37. A. S. Cook (ed.), 'Ibn Fadlan's Account of Scandinavian Merchants on the Volga in 922,' *Journal of English and Germanic Philology*, 22 (1923), 54–63.

38. N. Levtzion and J. F. K. Hopkins (eds.), *Corpus of Early Arabic Sources for West African History* (Cambridge, 1981), 13.

39. Ibid. 25.

40. Ibid. 270–1.

41. Ibid. 130–1, 190–1, 272–3.

42. D. Drew, *The Lost Chronicles of the Maya Kings* (London, 1999); D. Stuart, 'The Arrival of Strangers,' in D. Carrasco, L. Jones, and S. Sessions (eds.), *Mesoamerica's Classical Heritage* (Boulder, Colo., 2000), 465–513; S. Martin and D. Grube, *Chronicles of the Maya Kings and Queens* (London, 2000), 28–9.

43. R. T. Zuidema, *El sistema de ceques del Cuzco* (Lima, 1995).

CHAPTER 4

1. S.-S. H. Tsai, *Perpetual Happiness: The Ming Emperor Yongle* (Seattle, 2001), 178–208.

2. J. Duyvendak, 'The True Dates of the Chinese Maritime Expeditions in the Early Fifteenth Century,' *T'oung Pao*, 34 (1938), 399–412.

3. Ibid. 399–406.

4. L. Levathes, *When China Ruled the Seas* (New York, 1994).

5. R. Finlay, 'The Treasure Ships of Zheng He: Chinese Maritime Imperialism in the Age of Discovery,' *Terrae Incognitae*, 23 (1991), 1–12.

6. Duyvendak, 'True Dates of the Chinese Maritime Expeditions,' 410.

7. Ma Huan, *The Overall Survey of the Ocean's Shores*, ed. J. R. V. Mills (Cambridge, 1970), 69, 70, 179.

8. E. L. Dreyer, *Early Ming China* (Stanford, 1982), 120.

9. Kuei-Sheng Chang, 'The Ming Maritime Enterprise and China's Knowledge of Africa Prior to the Age of Great Discoveries,' *Terra Incognita*, 3 (1971), 33–44.

10. V. Rau, *Estudos sobre a història do sal portugues* (Lisbon, 1984).

11. Above, pp. 34–7, 63–5.

12. A. V. Berkis, *The Reign of Duke James in Courland* (Lincoln, 1960).

13. Petrarch, *De Vita Solitaria*, ed. A. Altamura (Naples, 1943), 125–6.

14. F. Sevillano Colom, 'Los viajes medievales desde Mallorca a Canarias,' *Anuarioi de estudios atlánticos*, 23 (1978), 27–57.

15. A. Rumeu de Armas, *El obispado de Telde* (Madrid, 1960).

16. F. Fernández-Armesto, *Before Columbus* (Philadelphia, 1987), 143.

17. Cf. above.

18. *Monumenta Henricina* (Coimbra, 1960–), i. 201–6.

19. E. Serra Ráfols and M. G. Martínez, 'Sermón de Clemente VI Papa acerca de la otorgación del Reino de Canarias a Luis de España, 1344,' *Revista de Historia Canaria*, 19 (1963–4), 99–104.

20. C. Rosell (ed.), *Crónicas de los reyes de Castilla*, 3 vols. (Madrid, 1875–8), ii. 274.

21. J. Pérez Vidal, *Endechas populares* (La Laguna, 1952), 52, 38.

22. A. J. Russell-Wood, *The Black Man in Slavery and Freedom in Colonial Brazil* (London, 1982), 20.
23. P. E. Russell, *Prince Henry 'the Navigator': A Life* (New Haven, 2000), 73–4.
24. Ibid. 136.
25. *Monumenta Henricina*, v. 91.
26. Fernández-Armesto, *Before Columbus*, 188–91; Russell, *Prince Henry*, 14–18.
27. *Crónica dos feitos notáveis que se passaram na conquista de Guiné*, ed. T. Sousa Soares, 2 vols. (Lisbon, 1978–81), i. 45.
28. G. Beaujouan, 'Fernand Colomb et le traité d'astrologie d'Henri le Navigateur,' *Romania*, 82 (1961), 96–105.
29. *Monumenta Henricina*, v. 256.
30. Cf. below, p. 146.
31. *Monumenta Henricina*, ii. 235–7.
32. C. de la Roncière, *La Découverte de l'Afrique au moyen-age*, 3 vols. (Paris, 1924–7), ii. 162–3, iii. 1–11.
33. P. E. Russell, *O Infante Dom Henrique e as Ilhas Canárias* (Lisbon, 1979), 38–52.
34. Fernández-Armesto, *Before Columbus*, 192.
35. C. Verlinden, 'Un précurseur de Colomb: Le Flamand Fernand van Olmen,' *Reivista portuguesa de història*, 10 (1962), 453–9.
36. F. Fernández-Armesto (ed.), *Questa e una opera necessaria a tutti li navig[an]ti* (New York, 1992).
37. P. E. Russell, 'White Kings on Black Kings,' in I. Michael and R. A. Cardwell (eds.), *Medieval and Renaissance Studies in Honour of Robert Brian Tate* (Oxford, 1986), 151–63.
38. Fernández-Armesto, *Before Columbus*, 188–91; Russell, *Prince Henry*, 14–18.
39. Above, pp. 109–14.
40. F. Fernández-Armesto, 'Naval Warfare after the Viking Age,' in M. Keen (ed.), *Medieval Warfare* (Oxford, 1999), 230–52.
41. A. Hess, 'The Evolution of the Ottoman Empire in the Age of Oceanic Discoveries,' in F. Fernández-Armesto (ed.), *The Global Opportunity* (Aldershot, 1999), 199.
42. R. Cormack and D. Glaser (eds.), *The Art of Holy Russia* (London, 1998), 180.
43. G. Vicente, *Obras completas*, ed. A. J. da Costa Pimpão (Lisbon, 1956), 55.
44. G. Diez de Games, *El vitorial*, ed. J. de Mata Carriazo (Madrid, 1940), 40–7, 86–96, 201, 256–61, 300; J. R. Goodman, *Chivalry and Exploration, 1298–1630* (Woodbridge, 1998), 170.
45. W. D. and C. R. Phillips, *The Worlds of Christopher Columbus* (Cambridge, 1992), 97–8.
46. F. Fernández-Armesto, 'Inglaterra y el Atlantico en la baja edad media,' in A. Bethencourt *et al., Canarias e Inglaterra a través de la historia* (Las Palmas, 1995), 11–28.
47. J. Canas (ed.), *Libro de Alixandre* (Madrid, 1988), 182.
48. C. Varela (ed.), *Cristobal Colón: Cartas y documentos completos* (Madrid, 1984), 205.
49. C. Picard, *L'Océan Atlantique mussulman au moyen-age* (Paris, 1997), 31–2.
50. M. Tymowski, 'Le Niger: Voie de communication des grands états du Soudan jusqu'à la fin du XVIe siècle,' *African Bulletin*, 6 (1967), 73–98.

CHAPTER 5

1. T. McGovern, 'The Economics of Extinction in Norse Greenland,' in T. M. L. Wigley, M. J. Ingram, and G. Farmer (eds.), *Climate and History: Studies in Past Climates and Their Impact on Man* (Cambridge, 1980), 404–34; cf. K. A. Seaver, *The Frozen Echo: Greenland and the Exploration of North America, ca. AD 1000–1500* (Stanford, Calif., 1996).
2. R. Laguarda Trias, *El enigma de las latitudes de Colon* (Valladolid, 1974).
3. F. Fernández-Armesto, 'Cartography and Exploration,' in D. Woodward (ed.), *History of Cartography*, iii (Chicago, forthcoming).
4. F. Fernández-Armesto, 'The Origins of the European Atlantic,' *Itinerario*, 24/1 (2000), 111–28.
5. F. Fernández-Armesto, 'La financiación de la conquista de Canarias durante el reinado de los Reyes Católicos,' *Anuario de estudios atlánticos*, 28 (1981), 343–78.
6. A. Szasdy-Nagy, *Un mundo que descubrió Colón: Las rutas del comercio prehispánico de los metales* (Valladolid, 1984).
7. Above, pp. 57, 106, 156.
8. J. A. Williamson, *The Cabot Voyages and Bristol Discovery under Henry VII* (Cambridge, 1962), 197–203.
9. Ibid. 26–8.
10. Above, p. 137.
11. J. de Barros, *Ásia*, Decade I, bk. IV, ch. 1 (Lisbon, 1778), i. 270.
12. S. Subrahmanyam, *The Career and Legend of Vasco da Gama* (Cambridge, 1997), 64–7, 224–79, 320.
13. Barros, *Ásia*, Decade I, bk. IV, ch. 1, i. 271–6.
14. Subrahmanyam, *Vasco da Gama*, 144.
15. J. C. van Leur, *Indonesian Trade and Society: Essays in Asian Social and Economic History* (The Hague, 1955), 122, 268–89; A. Disney (ed.), *Historiography of Europeans in Africa and Asia, 1450–1800* (Aldershot, 1981), 95.
16. G. Winius, 'The Settlement of Goa in the Bay of Bengal,' *Itinerario*, 7 (1983), 83–101; S. Subrahmanyam, *Improvising Empire: Portuguese Trade and Settlement in the Bay of Bengal, 1500–1700* (Delhi, 1990), 90.
17. P. Marshall, 'Retrospect on J. C. van Leur's Essay on the XVIIIth Century as a Category in Asian History,' *Itinerario*, 17 (1993), 45–58.
18. M. N. Pearson, *The Indian Ocean* (London, 2003), 113–89.
19. M. Rossabi, 'The Decline of the Central Asian Caravan Trade,' in J. Tracy (ed.), *The Rise of Merchant Empires: Long-Range Trade in the Early Modern World, 1350–1750* (Cambridge, 1990), 351–70.
20. F. Fernández-Armesto (ed.), *Columbus on Himself* (London, 1992), 162.
21. Subrahmanyam, *Vasco da Gama*, 111.

CHAPTER 6

1. Above, pp. 46–7, 49.
2. M. Fernández de Navarrete, *Obras*, ed. C. Seco Serrano, 3 vols. (Madrid, 1954–5), i. 358.

3. C. Varela (ed.), *Cristobal Colón: textos y documentos completos*, 2 vols. (Madrid, 1984), 170–6.

4. A. Rumeu de Armas (ed.), *El Tratado de Tordesillas y su proyección* (Madrid, 1992), 207–9; J. Cortesão, 'João II y el tratado de Tordesillas,' ibid. 93–101.

5. R. Ezquerra, 'Las Juntas de Toro y Burgos,' in Rumeu de Armas (ed.), *El Tratado de Tordesillas*, i. 155; 'La idea del antimeridiano,' in A. Teixeira da Mota (ed.), *A viagem de Fernão de Magalhães e a questão das Molucas: Actas do II Coloquio Luso-espanhol de Historia Ultramarina* (Lisbon, 1975), 12–13; Navarrete, *Obras*, ii. 89; U. Lamb, 'The Spanish Cosmographical Juntas of the Sixteenth Century,' *Terrae Incognitae*, 6 (1974), 53.

6. Navarrete, *Obras*, ii. 87.

7. A. Laguarda, *El predescubrimiento del Río de la Plata por la expedición portuguesa de 1511–12* (Lisbon, 1973), 62.

8. M. L. Díaz-Trechuelo, 'Filipinas y el Tratado de Tordesillas,' in Rumeu de Armas (ed.), *El Tratado de Tordesillas*, i. 229–40; D. Goodman, *Power and Penury: Government, Technology and Science in Philip II's Spain* (Cambridge, 1988), 59–61.

9. R. A. Laguarda Trías, 'Las longitudes geográficas de la membranza de Magallanes y del primer viaje de circunnavegación,' in Teixeira da Mota (ed.), *A viagem de Magalhães*, 151–73.

10. Navarrete, *Obras*, ii. 612; cf. Colón, 'Declaración del derecho que . . . Castilla tiene,' in *Colección de documentos inéditos para la historia de España*, xvi (Madrid, 1850), 382–420.

11. Díaz-Trechuelo, 'Filipinas y el Tratado,' 235.

12. Lamb, 'Spanish Cosmographical Juntas'; Díaz-Trechuelo, 'Filipinas y el Tratado,' 236.

13. Goodman, *Power and Penury*, 59.

14. Ibid. 56.

15. *Colección de documentos inéditos para la historia de ultramar*, ii (Madrid, 1886), 109.

16. Ibid., 2nd ser., ii (Madrid, 1887), 261.

17. C. Jack-Hinton, *The Search for the Islands of Solomon, 1567–1838* (Oxford, 1969), 1–27; *The Discovery of the Solomon Islands by Alvaro de Mendaña in 1568*, ed. Lord Amherst of Hackney and B. Thomson, 2 vols. (London, 1901), vol. ii, p. iv.

18. *The Voyages of Pedro Fernández de Quirós, 1595–1606*, ed. C. Markham, 2 vols. (London, 1904), i. 137.

19. Ibid. i. 33.

20. Jack-Hinton, *Search for the Islands of Solomon*, 132.

21. *Voyages of Quirós*, i. 105.

22. *Sucesos de las Islas Filipinas by Antonio de Morga*, ed. J. S. Cummins (Cambridge, 1971), 104.

23. *La Australia del Espíritu Santo: The Journal of Fray Martin de Manilla, OFM, and Other Documents Relating to the Voyage of Pedro Fernández de Quiros to the South Seas (1605–6) and the Franciscan Missionary Plan (1617–27)*, ed. C. Kelly, 2 vols. (Cambridge, 1966), i. 216.

24. Ibid. ii. 286.

25. Ibid. ii. 223.

26. B. de Las Casas, *Historia de las Indias*, ed. A. Millares Carló, 3 vols. (Mexico City, 1951), i. 189; *Voyages of Quirós*, i. 33.

27. H. Tracey, *Antonio Fernandes, descobridor do Monomotapa* (Lourenço Marques, 1940).

28. G. W. B. Huntingford, *The Historical Geography of Ethiopia from the First Century AD to 1704* (Cambridge, 1989).

29. Above, p. 176.

30. C. F. Beckingham and G. W. B. Huntingford (eds.), *Some Records of Ethiopia, 1593–1646, being Extracts from the History of High Ethiopia or Abassia, by Manoel de Almeida, together with Bahrey's History of the Galla* (London, 1954), 154.

31. Above, pp. 169–71.

32. F. Fernández-Armesto (ed.), *Columbus on Himself* (London, 1992), 148, 171.

33. W. P. Cumming (ed.), *The Discovery of North America*, 2 vols. (London, 1972), i. 80–4; S. E. Morison, *The European Discovery of America: The Northern Voyages* (Oxford, 1971), 191–2.

34. Above, pp. 171–4.

35. F. Fernández-Armesto, 'Inglaterra y el atlántico en la baja edad media,' in A. Bethencourt Massieu *et al.*, *Canarias e Inglaterra a través de la historia* (Las Palmas, 1995), 16.

36. P. French, *John Dee: The World of an Elizabethan Magus* (London, 1972), 184.

37. Fernández-Armesto, 'Inglaterra,' 14–15.

38. C. R. Markham (ed.), *The Voyages of William Baffin* (London, 1881), 221.

39. W. Strachey, *The Historie of Travell into Virginia Britannica* (1612), ed. L. B. Wright and V. Freund (London, 1953), 59–61.

40. *Relación y documentos de Pascual de Andagoya*, ed. A. Blázquez (Madrid, 1986), 13, 111–13.

41. A. R. Pagden (ed.), *Hernán Cortes: Letters from Mexico* (New York, 1971), 327.

42. Ibid. 52, 55.

43. J. Hemming, *The Search for El Dorado* (London, 1978), 97–109.

44. W. Brandon, *Quivirá* (Athens, Ohio, 1990), 27.

45. Ibid. 31.

46. *The Journal of Coronado*, ed. G. Parker Winship (Golden, Colo., 1990), 117.

47. Ibid. 129.

48. Ibid. 119.

49. Brandon, *Quivirá*, 36.

50. A. Nuñez Cabeza de Vaca, *Naufragios y comentarios*, ed. R. Ferrando (Madrid, 1985), 72, 101.

51. L. A. Clayton, V. J. Knight, and E. C. Moore (eds.), *The De Soto Chronicles: The Expedition of Hernando de Soto to North America in 1539–1543*, 2 vols. (Tuscaloosa, Ala., 1993), i. 84.

52. G. P. Hammond and A. G. Rey, *Don Juan de Oñate, Colonizer of New Mexico, 1595–1628*, 2 vols. (Albuquerque, N. Mex., 1953), ii. 94–118.

53. G. Pérez de Villagrá, *Historia de la Nueva México, 1610*, ed. M. Encinias, A. Rodríguez, and J. P. Sánchez (Albuquerque, 1992), 210.

54. Hammond and Rey, *Don Juan de Oñate*, ii. 1007.

55. G. de Carvajal, P. Almesto, and A. de Rojas, *La Aventura de Amazonas*, ed. R. Díaz (Madrid, 1986), 47–67.

56. F. Fernández-Armesto, *The Americas* (London, 2003), 75.

57. Nuñez Cabeza de Vaca, *Naufragios y comentarios*, 200–68.

58. R. Cook (ed.), *The Voyages of Jacques Cartier* (Toronto, 1993), 117.

59. Ibid. 10.

60. A. Szaszdi Nagy, *Los guías de Guanahaní y la llegada de Pinzón a Puerto Rico* (Valladolid, 1995), 7–8.

61. Ibid. 14; Las Casas, *Historia de Indias*, bk. 1, ch. 74.

62. A. Szaszdi Nagy, *Un mundo de descubrió Colón* (Valladolid, 1984), 105–6.

63. F. Fernández-Armesto, 'Maps and Exploration,' in D. L. Woodward (ed.), *History of Cartography*, iii (Chicago, forthcoming).

CHAPTER 7

1. P. de Medina, *Arte de navegar* (Valladolid, 1545), preface, quoted in D. Goodman, *Power and Penury: Government, Technology and Science in Philip II's Spain* (Cambridge, 1988), 72.

2. C. Varela (ed.), *Cristoval Colón: Textos y documentos completos* (Madrid, 1984), 325.

3. W. Bourne, *A Regiment for the Sea and Other Writings on Navigation*, ed. E. G. R. Taylor (Cambridge, 1963), 294.

4. F. Fernández-Armesto (ed.), *Questa e una opera necessaria a tutti li navig[an]ti* (New York, 1992), 7–9.

5. C. Koeman, *Miscellanea Cartographica: Contributions to the History of Cartography* (Utrecht, 1988), 59; F. Lestringant, *Mapping the Renaissance World: The Geographical Imagination in the Age of Discovery* (Berkeley, 1994), 106.

6. J. Davis, *Seamans Secrets* (London, 1643), pt. 1, sig. G2.

7. M. Destombes, 'Les Plus Anciens Sondages portes sur les cartes nautiques,' *Bulletin de l'Institut Océanographique*, Monaco, special issue, 2 (1968), 199–222; Koeman, *Miscellanea Cartographica*, 53.

8. J. P. Snyder, *Flattening the Earth: Two Thousand Years of Map Projections* (Chicago, 1993), 43–9.

9. D. B. Quinn, *English New England Voyages* (London, 1983).

10. W. P. Cumming, R. A. Skelton, and D. B. Quinn, *The Exploration of North America* (London, 1971), 208–11.

11. Above, p. 222; Cumming *et al.*, *Exploration of North America*, 236–7.

12. Above, p. 221.

13. Above, p. 239; C. E. Heidenreich, *Explorations and Mapping of Samuel de Champlain* (Toronto, 1976).

14. Above, p. 214.

15. R. A. Skelton, *Explorers' Maps* (London, 1960), 275–8.

16. P. van Mil and M. Scharloo (eds.), *De VOC in de Kaart Gekeken* (The Hague, 1988).

17. C. R. Boxer, 'Portuguese Commercial Voyages to Japan Three Hundred Years Ago,' *Transactions and Proceedings of the Japan Society of London*, 33 (1936), 13–64.

18. F. C. Wieder (ed.), *Mon Cart* (The Hague, 1925).

19. T. Blundeville, *M. Blundevile his Exercises* (London, 1613), 649.

20. A. Fontoura da Costa, *A marinharia dos descobrimentos* (Lisbon, 1960), 147–57.

21. Above, p. 147.

22. O. H. K. Spate, *The Spanish Lake* (London, 1979), 106–9.

23. J. B. Leighly, *California as an Island* (San Francisco, 1972).

24. Skelton, *Explorers' Maps*, 119; R. Hakluyt, *A Discourse of Western Planting*, ed. D. B. and A. M. Quinn (London, 1993), 84–7.

25. B. Bailyn, *New England Merchants in the Seventeenth Century* (Cambridge, Mass., 1955), 41, 98.

26. Above, p. 239.

27. Above, pp. 235–6.

28. Above, p. 233.

29. G. de Carvajal, P. Almesto, and A. Rojas, *La aventura del amazonas*, ed. R. Diaz (Madrid, 1986), 237.

30. O. H. K. Spate, *Monopolists and Freebooters* (Minneapolis, 1983), 44.

31. Above, p. 212.

32. Spate, *Monopolists and Freebooters*, 50.

33. W. Dampier, *A New Voyage Round the World*, ed. M. M. Penzer (London, 1927), 313.

34. Spate, *Monopolists and Freebooters*, 51.

35. Dampier, *A New Voyage Round the World*, 311.

36. J. Roggeveen, *Journal*, ed. A. Sharpe (Oxford, 1970).

37. R. H. Fisher, *The Voyage of Semen Dezhnev 1648* (London, 1981), 139.

38. Ibid. 137.

39. Ibid. 51.

40. Ibid. 45.

41. Ibid. 170.

42. A. Wood, 'Avvakum's Siberian Exile, 1653–64,' in A. Wood and R. A. French (eds.), *The Development of Siberia: People and Resources* (Basingstoke, 1989), 11–35.

43. E. Bobrick, *East of the Sun* (London, 1992), 150.

44. O. W. Frost, *Bering: The Russian Discovery of America* (New Haven, 2003), 34; B. Dmytryshyn, T. Vaughan, and E. A. Crownhart-Vaughan (eds.), *Russia's Penetration of the North Pacific Ocean* (Portland, Oreg., 1988), 69.

45. T. Armstrong, *Yermak's Campaigns in Siberia* (London, 1975), 88.

46. Frost, *Bering*, 43.

47. Ibid. 44.

48. Ibid. 68.

49. Ibid. 88.

50. Ibid. 73.

51. Ibid. 137.

52. Below, pp. 284–5.

53. R. Law, *The Slave Commerce of West Africa* (Oxford, 1998), 45–52.

54. P. E. H. Hair and R. Law (eds.), *Barbot on Guinea: The Writings of Jean Barbot on West Africa, 1678–1712*, 2 vols. (London, 1992), vol. i, p. xliii.

55. Ibid. ii. 454.

56. Above, p. 213.

57. M. G. da Costa and C. F. Beckingham (eds.), *The Itinerario of Jeronimo Lobo* (London, 1984), 51.

58. C. F. Beckingham and G. W. Huntingford (eds.), *Some Records of Ethiopia* (London, 1957), 192–3.

59. M. de Aguiano, *Misiones Capuchinas en África* (Madrid, 1950), 67.

60. P.-L. M. de Maupertuis, *The Figure of the Earth, Determined from Observations Made by Order of the French King, at the Polar Circle* (London, 1738), 34, 38–40.

CHAPTER 8

1. Above, p. 284.

2. P.-L. M. de Maupertuis, 'Lettre sur le progrès des sciences,' in *Oeuvres*, 4 vols. (Lyons, 1768), i. 384–6.

3. Quoted in T. Ran, 'Le Président des Terres Australes: Charles de Brosses and the French Enlightenment,' *Journal of Pacific History*, 37 (2002), 170.

4. W. Barr and G. Williams (eds.), *Voyages to Hudson Bay in Search of a Northwest Passage*, 2 vols. (London, 1993–4), i. 2.

5. Ibid. ii. 352.

6. Above, p. 25.

7. Above, p. 292.

8. Barr and Williams (eds.), *Voyages to Hudson Bay*, ii. 171.

9. G. Williams, *The Prize of All the Oceans* (London, 2000), 45–6.

10. Quoted in F. López-Rios Fernández, *Medicina naval española en la época de los descubrimientos* (Barcelona, 1993), 85–163.

11. M. E. Hoare, *The Resolution Journal of Johann Reinhold Forster*, 4 vols. (London, 1981–2), iii. 454.

12. P. LeRoy, *A Narrative of the Singular Adventures of Four Russian Sailors Who Were Cast Away on the Desert Island of East Spitzbergen* (London, 1774), 69–72.

13. *The Journal of Jean-François Galaup de La Pérouse*, ed. J. Dunmore, 2 vols. (London, 1994), ii. 317, 431–2.

14. M. Palau (ed.), *Malaspina '94* (Cadiz, 1994), 74.

15. G. Vancouver, *A Voyage of Discovery to the North Pacific Ocean and Around the World*, ed. W. K. Lamb, 4 vols. (London, 1984), iv. 1471–2.

16. G. Robertson, quoted in G. Williams, 'Seamen and Philosophers in the South Seas in the Age of Captain Cook,' *Mariner's Mirror*, 65 (1979), 7.

17. *The Pacific Journal of Louis-Antoine de Bougainville*, ed. J. Dunmore (London, 2002), p. xx.

18. Above, pp. 205–7.

19. Above, pp. 204–6.

20. J. Beaglehole, *The Life of Captain James Cook* (London, 1974), 366.

21. A. David (ed.), *The Charts and Coastal Views of Captain Cook's Voyages*, 3 vols. (London, 1988–97).

22. *The Journals of Captain Cook on His Voyages of Discovery: The Voyage of the Endeavour*, ed. J. C. Beaglehole, 3 vols. (Cambridge, 1955–67), i. 117.

23. Ibid. 366.

24. Quoted in *Journal of La Pérouse*, ed. Dunmore, p. xix.

25. *Journals of Captain Cook*, ed. Beaglehole, ii. 239.

26. Ibid. ii. 643.

27. Ibid. i. 243.

28. J. King, *A Voyage to the Pacific Ocean* (London, 1785), iii. 185, quoted in R. Langdon, *The Lost Caravel* (Sydney, 1975), 273.

29. *Journals of Captain Cook*, ed. Beaglehole, i. 335.

30. *Journal of La Pérouse*, ed. Dunmore, vol. i, p. cxi.

31. Ibid. i. 148.

32. J. Pimentel, *La física de la monarquía: Ciencia y política en el pensamiento colonial de Alejandro Malaspina (1754–1810)* (Madrid, 1988).

33. A. Humboldt, *Ensayo político sobre el reino de la Nueva España* (1822), quoted in I. Engstrand, 'Of Fish and Men: Spanish Marine Science During the Late XVIIIth Century,' *Pacific Historical Review*, 69 (2000), 4.

34. A. Frost, *The Global Reach of Empire* (London, 2003), 219.

35. Ibid. 242.

36. G. Vancouver, *A Voyage of Discovery to the North Pacific Ocean and Round the World, 1791–1795*, ed. W. K. Lamb, 4 vols. (London, 1984), i. 41.

37. Ibid. i. 112.

38. Ibid. i. 182.

39. Ibid. iv. 1390.

40. Ibid. iv. 1552.

41. A. V. Postnikov, 'The Search for a Sea-Passage from the Atlantic Ocean to the Pacific via North America's Coast,' *Terrae Incognitae*, 32 (2000), 31–54.

42. Quoted in E. S. Dodge, *The Polar Rosses* (London, 1973), 35.

43. Quoted in F. Fleming, *Barrow's Boys* (London, 1998), 33.

44. Quoted ibid. 171.

45. Ibid. 306.

46. J. Ross, *Narrative of a Second Voyage in Search of a Northwest Passage* (London, 1835), 191.

47. P. Berton, *The Arctic Grail* (Toronto, 1988), 134.

48. *The Discovery of the South Shetland Islands: The Voyages of the Brig Williams, 1819–1820*, ed. R. J. Campbell (London, 2000), 161.

49. Ibid. 73.

50. Ibid. 73, 160.

51. J. Weddell, *A Voyage Towards the South Pole* (London, 1827).

52. N. Philbrick, *Sea of Glory* (New York, 2003).

53. M. J. Ross, *Ross in the Antarctic* (London, 1982), 8.

54. Ibid. 99.

55. Ibid. 203.

56. Fleming, *Barrow's Boys*, 276.

57. R. C. Davis (ed.), *The Central Australian Expedition* (London, 2002), p. xliii.

58. Ibid. 329.

59. L. R. R. Hafen and A. W. Hafen, *The Old Spanish Trail: Santa Fé to Los Angeles* (Glendale, Calif., 1954), 68.

60. Bernardo Miera y Pacheco, quoted in G. G. Cline, *Exploring the Great Basin* (Norman, Okla., 1963), 53.

61. *The Journals of Lewis and Clark*, ed. B. DeVoto (Boston, 1953), 92 (7 Apr. 1805).

62. R. L. Nichols and P. L. Halley, *Stephen Long and American Frontier Exploration* (Newark, NJ, 1980), 167.

63. Hafen and Hafen, *Old Spanish Trail*, 108.
64. *Journal of La Pérouse*, ed. Dunmore, p. lvi.
65. Quoted ibid., p. lix.
66. A. R. Pagden, *European Encounters with the New World from Renaissance to Romanticism* (New Haven, 1992), 142.
67. Above, p. 214.
68. Above, pp. 99–102.
69. Above, p. 101.
70. J. G. Jackson, *An Accurate and Interesting Account of Tahiti* (London, 1814), 296.
71. *Mungo Park's Travels in Africa*, ed. R. Miller (London, 1954), 72.
72. Ibid. 149.
73. Ibid. 150.
74. Ibid. 162.
75. Ibid. 364–5.
76. Fleming, *Barrow's Boys*, 198.
77. Ibid. 254.
78. C. Lloyd, *The Search for the Niger* (London, 1973), 139.
79. Above, pp. 130–1, 145–8.
80. D. Denham, H. Clapperton, and W. Oudeney, *A Narrative of Travels and Discoveries in North and Central Africa*, 2 vols. (London, 1828), i. 14.
81. R. Caillié, *Travels Through Central Africa to Timbuctoo*, 2 vols. (London, 1968), ii. 49.
82. Ibid. 84.
83. Ibid. 173.
84. Lloyd, *Search for the Niger*, 173.
85. Ibid. 159; cf. P. Curtin, *The World and the West* (Cambridge, 2000), 43.
86. Lloyd, *Search for the Niger*, 144–5.
87. Fleming, *Barrow's Boys*, 212.

CHAPTER 9

1. See above, p. 47.
2. Above, pp. 54–7.
3. Above, p. 51.
4. Above, p. 47.
5. Above, pp. 5–6.
6. F. Relaño, *The Shaping of Africa* (Aldershot, 2002), 198.
7. N. R. Bennett, *Arab versus European: Diplomacy and War in Nineteenth-Century East Central Africa* (New York, 1986), 47.
8. R. Burton, *The Lake Regions of Equatorial Africa* (London, 1860), 401.
9. O. Ransford, *David Livingstone: The Dark Interior* (London, 1978).
10. *The Last Journals of David Livingstone in Central Africa*, ed. H. Waller, ii (London, 1874), 296.
11. D. Livingstone, *Missionary Travels and Researches in South Africa* (London, 1857), 673.
12. Ibid. 675.
13. Quoted in A. Ross, *David Livingstone: Mission and Empire* (London, 2005), 187.
14. H. M. Stanley, *How I Found Livingstone* (London, 1872), pp. xviii, 309.

15. Ibid. 411–12.
16. Quoted in M. Osborne, *River Road to China* (London, 1975), 32.
17. F. Garnier, *Voyage d'exploration en Indochine*, ed. J.-P. Gomane (Paris, 1985), 43.
18. A. Briggs, *Victorian Cities* (Harmondsworth, 1968), 278–302.
19. A. Moorehead, *Cooper's Creek* (London, 1963), 139.
20. Above, pp. 317–19.
21. *Explorations in Australia: The Journals of John McDougall Stuart*, ed. W. Hardman (London, 1964), 453, 460, 466.
22. Ibid. 482.
23. G. H. Wilkins, *Undiscovered Australia* (London, 1928).
24. G. Souter, *New Guinea: The Last Unknown* (London, 1964), 4.
25. Ibid. 80.
26. Ibid.
27. Ibid. 85.
28. D. G. Hogarth, *The Penetration of Arabia* (London, 1904), 325–6.
29. B. Thomas, *Alarms and Excursions in Arabia* (London, 1931), 257.
30. B. Thomas, *Arabia Felix* (London, 1932), p. xxvii.
31. Ibid., p. xxv.
32. Thomas, *Alarms and Excursions*, 257.
33. Thomas, *Arabia Felix*, 251.
34. S. Hedin, *A Conquest of Tibet* (London, 1935), 71–2.
35. Ibid. 104–5.
36. J. Bedier (ed.), *High Road in Tartary* (New York, 1948), 208.
37. T. Holdich, *Tibet, the Mysterious* (London, 1906), 225–6.
38. Ibid. 113.
39. Ibid. 214.
40. P. Fleming, *Bayonets to Lhasa* (London, 1961), 232–3, 240.
41. Above, p. 325.
42. Fleming, *Bayonets to Lhasa*, 166.
43. J. C. Frémont, *Narratives of Exploration and Adventure*, ed. A. Nevins (New York, 1958), 136.
44. Ibid. 243.
45. Ibid. 424.
46. Above, p. 327.
47. W. H. Goetzmann, *Exploration and Empire: The Explorer and the Scientist in the Winning of the American West* (New York, 1966), 270.
48. Ibid. 279.
49. Ibid. 257.
50. H. B. Möllhausen, *Diary of a Journey from Mississippi to the Coasts of the Pacific*, 2 vols. (New York, 1969), ii. 335–6; J. P. Sherburne, *Through Indian Country to California: John P. Sherburne's Diary of the Whipple Expedition, 1853–4*, ed. M. McDougall Gordon (Stanford, Calif., 1988), 212.
51. W. H. Goetzmann, *Army Explorations in the American West 1803–63* (New Haven, 1959), 263–6.
52. Ibid. 343.
53. J. W. Powell, *The Exploration of the Colorado River and Its Canyons* (New York, 1997),

247, quoted in Goetzmann, *Exploration and Empire*, 549; D. Worster, *A River Running West: The Life of John Wesley Powell* (New York, 2001), 184–5.

54. Worster, *River Running West*, 183.

55. G. R. Taylor, *The Transportation Revolution* (New York, 1951), 113–14.

56. R. E. Peary, *Nearest the Pole* (New York, 1907), 125.

57. J. E. Weems, *Peary: The Explorer and the Man* (Boston, 1967), 270.

58. Above, pp. 316–17.

59. W. G. Burns Murdoch, quoted in M. H. Rosove, *Let Heroes Speak* (Annapolis, Md., 2000), 57.

60. M. Jones, *The Last Great Quest* (Oxford, 2003), 51.

61. Rosove, *Let Heroes Speak*, 67.

62. R. F. Scott, *The Voyage of the Discovery* (London, 1905), ii. 32.

63. Ibid. i. 467–8.

64. R. F. Scott, *Scott's Last Expedition*, ed. L. Huxley (London, 1913), i. 605–7.

65. Rosove, *Let Heroes Speak*, 181.

66. Ibid. 192.

67. R. Vaughan, *The Arctic: A History* (Dover, NH, 1994), 240.

68. J. A. Lawson, *Wanderings in the Interior of New Guinea* (London, 1875), 13.

69. Above, pp. 36, 60–1.

70. H. E. M. Stanley, *In Darkest Africa*, 2 vols. (London, 1890), i. 198, 353.

71. Ibid. ii. 40–1.

72. Ibid. ii. 44.

73. Souter, *New Guinea*, 154.

74. B. Connolly and R. Andersen, *First Contact* (New York, 1987), 9.

75. Ibid. 180.

76. Ibid. 24.

77. Ibid. 29.

78. Ibid. 181–2.

79. R. Hemley, *Invented Eden: The Elusive, Disputed History of the Tasaday* (New York, 2003).

80. J. Hemming, *Die If You Must: Brazilian Indians in the Twentieth Century* (London, 2003), 17.

81. Ibid. 30.

82. Ibid. 149.

83. J. Hemming, *The Golden Age of Discovery* (London, 1998), 19.

84. Hemming, *Die If You Must*, 286–7.

85. E. Brooks *et al., Tribes of the American Basin in Brazil in 1972: Report for the Aborigines Protection Society* (London, 1973), 1.

86. R. Hanbury-Tenison, *A Question of Survival for the Indians of Brazil* (New York, 1973), 45–76.

87. Hemming, *Die If You Must*, 348.

88. Ibid. 404.

89. Ibid. 635.

90. B. Riffenburgh, *The Myth of the Explorer: The Press, Sensationalism and Geographical Discovery* (Cambridge, 1994).

91. Jones, *Last Great Quest*, 75.

92. Osborne, *River Road to China*, 87.
93. Quoted in Rosove, *Let Heroes Speak*, 242–3.
94. Osborne, *River Road to China*, 75.
95. Souter, *New Guinea*, 103.
96. Sherburne, *Through Indian Country*, 198.
97. Hedin, *Conquest of Tibet*, 156.
98. Garnier, *Voyage d'exploration*, sig. G54.
99. Ibid. 43–4.
100. Hedin, *Conquest of Tibet*, 27.
101. Sherburne, *Through Indian Country*, 61.
102. Ibid. 184.
103. Stanley, *In Darkest Africa*, i. 42–3.
104. Hemming, *Golden Age of Discovery*, 8.
105. P. Fleming, *Brazilian Adventure* (London, 1933), 28–30.

Picture Acknowledgements

akg-images: **188**; Herbert Kraft/akg-images: **20**; © Fundació Amattler. Arxiu Mas: **160**; Bibliothèque de l'Assemblée nationale de France (MS 1248.ED,19): **198**; Bibliothèque nationale de France (cliché RC-B-18155): **124**; Palazzo Ducale, Venice/Alinari/The Bridgeman Art Library: **plate V**; The British Museum, London/The Bridgeman Art Library: **plate I**; John Carter Brown Library, Brown University, RI, USA/The Bridgeman Art Library: **200**; Private collection/The Stapleton Collection/The Bridgeman Art Library: **plate IV**, **312**; Royal Geographical Society, London/The Bridgeman Art Library: **plate VI**; The Worshipful Company of Clockmakers' Collection, UK/The Bridgeman Art Library: **295**; The British Library: (OIOC15406.a.74/1) **22**, (MS Add.11696, ff.39v–40) **152** (detail), **185**, (G.7033) **207**, (48.h.18) **219**, (MS Harley 3450, f.10) **228**, (MS Royal 17.A.XLVIII, f.9v) **250**, (AC.6172/108) **262**, (maps C21.e.1.(2.)) **273**, (36.g.8, vol V) **298**, (W7140, vol III) **248** (detail), **301**, (145.e.8) **326**, (V10222) **348**, **358**, (10077.dd.21, vol 1) **363**; © Philadelphia Museum of Art/Corbis: **111**; © Albrecht G. Schaefer/Corbis: **xviii** (detail), **36**; © Swim Ink 2, LLC/Corbis: **377**; © Paulo Whitaker/Reuters/Corbis: **393**; The Master and Fellows of Corpus Christi College, Cambridge (MS 66A, f.67r): **86**; With permission of the Dunhuang Academy, China/photo courtesy of the International Dunhuang Project: **70** (detail), **75**; Courtesy of the Hispanic Society of America, New York: **192** (detail), **217**; Leiden University Library, Special Collections (MS Or.3101, pp. 4–5): **plate II**; Museu Marítim de Barcelona: **plate III**; Jonathan Wright/National Geographic Image Collection: **40** (detail), **52**; Ninnaji, Japan: **88**; Novosti: **140**; From the collection at Parham Park, West Sussex, UK: **303**; Photo12.com/Oronoz: **247**; Nicholas Roerich Museum, New York: **366**; © Collection Roger-Viollet: **244** (detail), **280**; John Pickard/St. Mary Redcliffe, Bristol: **172**; The British Library/HIP/TopFoto.co.uk: **plate VII**; Derrick Witty/TopFoto.co.uk: **plate VIII**; © The Viking Ship Museum, Denmark/photo Werner Karrasch: **54**; From Mao Yüan-I, *Wu-pei-chih*, Records of Military Preparations, 1621: **108** (detail), **112**.

Index

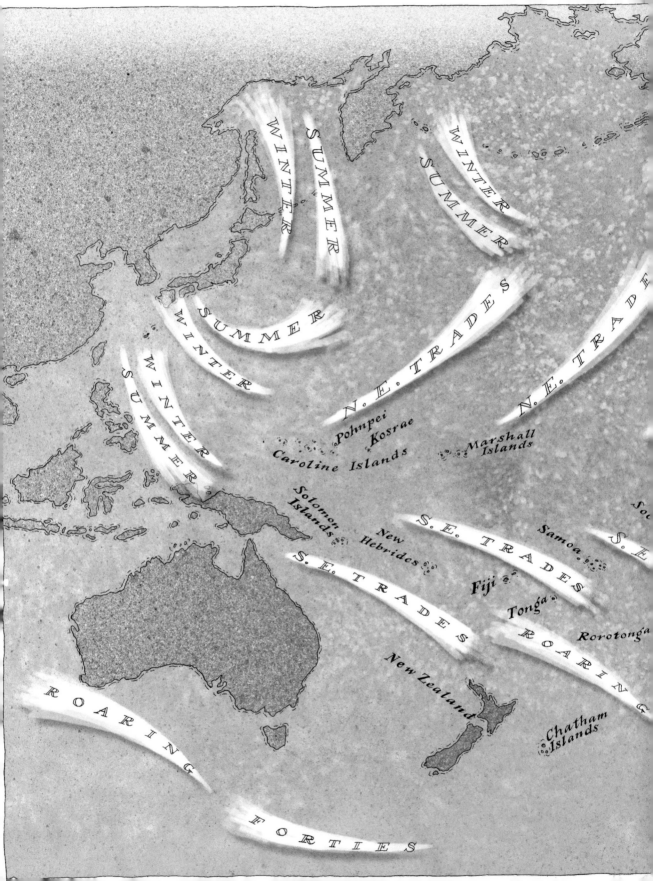